W9-CUZ-269

WITHDRAWN

338.973
P75

134665

DATE DUE			

The
Politics
of
Industrial
Policy

The
Politics
of
Industrial
Policy

Claude E. Barfield and William A. Schambra, editors

CARL A. RUDISILL LIBRARY
LENOIR RHYNE COLLEGE

A conference sponsored by the
American Enterprise Institute for Public Policy Research
Washington, D.C.

338.973
P75
134665
ajn. 1986

The publication of this volume was supported by a grant from the U.S. Department of Commerce.

The editors gratefully acknowledge the assistance of Robert Benko, who made substantial contributions to the editorial content of the volume.

Library of Congress Cataloging-in-Publication Data
Main entry under title:

The Politics of industrial policy.

"Competing in a changing world economy project."
1. Industry and state—United States—Congresses.
2. Industry and state — Congresses. I. Barfield, Claude E.
II. Schambra, William A. III. American Enterprise
Institute for Public Policy Research.
HD3616.U47P63   1986   338.973   86-1085

ISBN 0-8447-2261-8 (pbk.: alk. paper)
        0-8447-2262-6 (cloth: alk. paper)

1 3 5 7 9 10 8 6 4 2

AEI Symposia 86A

©1986 by the American Enterprise Institute for Public Policy Research, Washington, D.C. All rights reserved. No part of this publication may be used or reproduced in any manner whatsoever without permission in writing from the American Enterprise Institute except in the case of brief quotations embodied in news articles, critical articles, or reviews. The views expressed in the publications of the American Enterprise Institute are those of the authors and do not necessarily reflect the views of the staff, advisory panels, officers, or trustees of AEI.

"American Enterprise Institute" and (AEI) are registered service marks of the American Enterprise Institute for Public Policy Research.

Printed in the United States of America

Contents

Contributors

Claude E. Barfield, Jr.
Resident Fellow in Science and Technology Policy
American Enterprise Institute

Bruce Bartlett
Vice-President
Polyconomics, Inc.

Sidney Blumenthal
National Political Correspondent
The New Republic

Stephen S. Cohen
Professor of City and Regional Planning
University of California, Berkeley

I. M. Destler
Senior Fellow
Institute for International Economics

Stuart E. Eizenstat
Partner
Powell, Goldstein, Frazer, and Murphy

Marvin L. Esch
Director of Seminars and Programs
American Enterprise Institute

James Fallows
Washington Editor
The Atlantic

Serge Halimi
University of California, Berkeley

Edwin L. Harper
Executive Vice-President
Overhead Door Corporation

Gary Hart
U.S. Senator
Colorado

Jeffrey A. Hart
Professor of Political Science
Indiana University

Ellis W. Hawley
Professor of History
University of Iowa

Hugh Heclo
Professor of Government
Harvard University

Chalmers Johnson
Walter and Elise Haas Professor of Asian Studies
University of California, Berkeley

Jack F. Kemp
U.S. Congressman
New York

William Lilley III
Senior Vice-President for Corporate Affairs
CBS

Thomas K. McCraw
Professor of Business Administration
Harvard University

Mancur Olson
Distinguished Professor of Economics
University of Maryland

Norman J. Ornstein
Visiting Scholar
American Enterprise Institute

Robert Pastor
Faculty Research Associate
School of Public Affairs, University of Maryland

James T. Patterson
Professor of History
Brown University

Robert W. Russell
Adjunct Professor of International Business Diplomacy
Georgetown University

William A. Schambra
Resident Fellow
American Enterprise Institute

Mario Schimberni
President
Montedison, Inc. (Italy)

William Schneider
Resident Fellow
American Enterprise Institute

Herbert Stein
Senior Fellow
American Enterprise Institute

Howard J. Wiarda
Resident Scholar
American Enterprise Institute

Aaron Wildavsky
Professor of Political Science and Public Policy
Survey Research Center
University of California, Berkeley

Timothy E. Wirth
U.S. Congressman
Colorado

John Zysman
Professor of Political Science
University of California, Berkeley

This conference was held at the
American Enterprise Institute for Public Policy Research
in Washington, D.C., on October 1, 1984

The American Enterprise Institute for Public Policy Research, established in 1943, is a nonpartisan, nonprofit research and educational organization supported by foundations, corporations, and the public at large. Its purpose is to assist policy makers, scholars, business men and women, the press, and the public by providing objective analysis of national and international issues. Views expressed in the institute's publications are those of the authors and do not necessarily reflect the views of the staff, advisory panels, officers, or trustees of AEI.

Council of Academic Advisers

Paul W. McCracken, *Chairman, Edmund Ezra Day University Professor of Business Administration, University of Michigan*

Donald C. Hellmann, *Professor of Political Science and International Studies, University of Washington*

D. Gale Johnson, *Eliakim Hastings Moore Distinguished Service Professor of Economics and Chairman, Department of Economics, University of Chicago*

Robert A. Nisbet, *Adjunct Scholar, American Enterprise Institute*

Herbert Stein, *A. Willis Robertson Professor of Economics Emeritus, University of Virginia*

Murray L. Weidenbaum, *Mallinckrodt Distinguished University Professor and Director, Center for the Study of American Business, Washington University*

James Q. Wilson, *Henry Lee Shattuck Professor of Government, Harvard University*

Executive Committee

Richard B. Madden, *Chairman of the Board*
William J. Baroody, Jr., *President*
Willard C. Butcher

John J. Creedon
Richard M. Morrow
Paul F. Oreffice
Richard D. Wood

Robert J. Pranger,
Vice President, External Affairs
Tait Trussell,
Vice President, Administration

Edward Styles, *Director of Publications*

Program Directors

Denis P. Doyle, *Education Policy Studies*
Marvin Esch, *Seminars and Programs*
Thomas F. Johnson, *Economic Policy Studies*
Marvin H. Kosters,
Government Regulation Studies
John H. Makin, *Fiscal Policy Studies*

Jack A. Meyer, *Health Policy Studies*
Michael Novak,
Religion, Philosophy, and Public Policy
Howard R. Penniman/Austin Ranney,
Political and Social Processes
Robert J. Pranger, *International Programs*
William A. Schambra, *Social Policy Studies*

Periodicals

AEI Economist, Herbert Stein, *Ed.*

AEI Foreign Policy and Defense Review,
Evron M. Kirkpatrick, Robert J.
Pranger, and Harold H. Saunders, *Eds.*

Public Opinion, Seymour Martin
Lipset and Ben J. Wattenberg, *Co-Eds.*,
Everett Carll Ladd, *Sr. Ed.*,
Karlyn H. Keene, *Mng. Ed.*

Regulation: AEI Journal on Government and Society, Anne Brunsdale, *Mng. Ed.*

Foreword

After many years of enjoying great economic success, brought about in large part by its leading position in the international markets, the United States now faces serious challenges abroad. Changing dynamics in the international marketplace as well as deliberate actions by some governments in restraint of free trade have combined to diminish the competitiveness of many American goods and services.

This challenge to America's competitive standing in the international economy has stimulated a reevaluation of U.S. policies on several fronts. Indeed, it has prompted a reevaluation of basic questions concerning the role of the public sector itself in fostering economic growth, technological advance, and sectoral and regional development.

The industrial policy debate that has emerged over the past several years has received considerable attention in the press, in academic circles, and in the political arena. The debate has focused, however, on the economic questions raised by various industrial policy proposals while other aspects—historical, political, cultural, and institutional questions—have largely been ignored. The American Enterprise Institute's conference "The Politics of Industrial Policy" was designed to redress that imbalance.

The conference was divided into four sessions covering the following broadly defined subject areas:
- American cultural and historical perspectives on industrial policy
- International experiences with industrial policy
- Special interest groups and industrial policy
- U.S. political institutions and industrial policy

Leading academics in these fields submitted papers that served as focal points for discussion in each session. Finally, panels of experts representing academia, the government, and the private sector commented on the individual papers. The conference also featured a lively and informative debate between two leading political figures in the industrial policy controversy: Senator Gary Hart and Representative Jack Kemp.

This volume contains the essays presented at the "Politics of Industrial Policy" conference and summaries of the panel discussions and the debates that followed their presentation. It also includes an edited version of the Hart-Kemp debate.

As record U.S. trade deficits elevate the issues of trade and American industrial competitiveness to the top of the public policy agenda in Congress, the White House, and the public at large, the industrial policy debate only grows in significance. By reviewing some of the neglected aspects of the industrial policy controversy, this volume enhances our understanding of the full dimensions of this continuing debate.

The "Politics of Industrial Policy" conference is just one of a series of conferences, seminars, publications, and special events developed under AEI's multiyear research project "Competing in a Changing World Economy." The "Competing" project is designed to examine the basic structural changes in the world economy and to explore strategies for dealing with new economic, political, and strategic realities facing the United States.

WILLIAM J. BAROODY, JR.
President
American Enterprise Institute

Part One
Cultural and Historical Perspectives on Industrial Policy

Introduction

The purpose of the first part of the conference is to examine current industrial policy proposals as they relate to enduring characteristics of the American political culture and to the historical experience of particular periods in the nation's history. Political scientist Aaron Wildavsky of the University of California, Berkeley, presents a model of the political cultures in American life and examines current industrial policy proposals through the prism of this model. Then historians Ellis Hawley of the University of Iowa and Thomas McCraw of the Harvard Business School present more detailed historical perspectives, McCraw drawing lessons from the nineteenth and early twentieth centuries and Hawley analyzing historical antecedents—or the lack thereof—from the 1920s and 1930s.

Aaron Wildavsky

Though Wildavsky identifies nine potential models of political culture, his paper deals only with the three "primary" cultures that he argues have been central to the American political experience: the competititve or market model, the hierarchical model, and the sectarian or egalitarian model. In Wildavsky's view, the shifting alliances among these three groups—not the traditional combat between the Left and the Right in American politics—explain the American political experience in general and the past and current debates over industrial policy in particular.

Hierarchies are characterized by strong group boundaries and numerous prescriptions to enforce a sacrificial ethic that is based on the ideal that the collectivized whole is greater than the sum of the parts. In Wildavsky's words, "Hierarchy is institutionalized authority. It justifies inequality on grounds that specialization and division of labor enable people to live together with greater harmony and effectiveness than do alternative arrangements."*

At the opposite end of the political spectrum, market competition is defined by weak group boundaries and a few prescriptions: "The social ideal of market cultures is self-regulation. . . . Adherents of a market culture wish to

---

*Quotations are taken from the presentations at the conference and therefore may not match exactly the revised papers in this volume.

regulate their lives by bidding and bargaining[;] they support equality of opportunity."

Between the market and hierarchical groups are the sectarians or egalitarians, who like the hierarchies exhibit strong group boundaries and collective decisions but who also believe in minimal prescriptions: "Committed to a life of purely voluntary association, sectarian cultures reject authority. They can live without coercion or authority only by complete equality of condition. . . . Every act is scrutinized to see that it does not lead to inequality of resources."

Wildavsky examines, through extension, the attitudes of the three groups toward certain social and economic goals—fairness or equity and growth. For the market adherents, fairness is simply the opportunity to compete in an unfettered manner; in hierarchies, "Fairness follows function"—that is, fairness is defined by one's station in life and by predictable rules regarding that station; in the egalitarian society, fairness means equality of resources or results.

It follows, asserts Wildavsky, that sectarians have no interest in economic growth; their concern focuses on equal distribution. Hierarchies want growth but hold (with sectarians) that limited resources dictate the necessity for collective allocation through bureaucratic means. The concept of limited resources, however, is an anathema to the marketeers, for it strikes directly at their belief that the free exchange of goods and services will lead to ever-expanding wealth for everyone over time.

Turning to historical record, Wildavsky notes first a paradox; that for much of the eighteenth and nineteenth centuries, certainly through the struggles in the early republic and the Jacksonian period, the political Left opposed powerful central government and business regulation, while the Right supported large-scale government intervention to produce national power and economic growth. In tracing the debate over the funding of the national debt, a new national bank, and protective tariffs, Wildavsky argues that the anti-Federalists were the sectarians in opposing debt assumption by the federal government, the creation of a national bank, and the imposition of high tariffs. Jefferson argued that assumption of the debt would produce in Congress "a machine of corruption" fostering patronage, large bureaucracies, and increasing inequality of wealth.

With the Jacksonian period came a full-blown alliance between the sects and the marketeers, based upon what Wildavsky holds was a truly exceptional belief, "something incredible that has not been believed, as far as I can tell, any place else. . . namely, that equality of opportunity rigorously and punctiliously pursued would actually lead to equality of condition; in cultural terms, that a market way of life would actually lead to a sectarian result." Left to their own devices, individuals, through individual competition, would produce a rough equality. Government in all of its activities introduced artificial inequalities through the creation of monopolies and the handing out of charters, franchises, and other subsidies to a privileged class. The struggles over the rechartering of the Second National Bank and later over Henry Clay's Whig doctrine of the American system of tariffs, internal improvements, and central banking operations pitted hierarchical Whigs against egalitarian pro-market Jacksonians.

The 1980s Industrial Policy Debate. Current industrial policy proposals revolve around two policies, states Wildavsky: sanctions and subsidies. And the political results stem from the atttitudes of the three main cultures about these policy alternatives and a shifting alliance among them in attempts to enact sanctions and subsidies. Coalition politics also necessitates compromise from the pure principles espoused by all three cultures. The market culture, left alone, would choose neither sanctions nor subsidies; forced to choose, it opts for subsidies as a means of getting back from the state resources exacted from them. Sectarians prefer the opposite: sanctions without subsidies. In addition, they make a large distinction between small and big business, with bigness constituting for them a major threat to egalitarian outcomes. Thus sectarians will seek either to break up bigness or to make it subject to worker or state control—in one case allied with market culture, in the other with the hierarchy.

The hierarchical culture opts for both sanctions and subsidies. It would control industry through sanctions for the collective good, but it is also willing to offer various inducements to bring industry along.

In our time, Wildavsky writes, the most common alliance has been between hierarchy and markets, based upon their common belief in economic growth. Over the past two decades, however, hierarchies have weakened, and sectarian elements in the political culture have grown stronger. This has meant more sanctions upon industry and more proposals to prevent plant closings, to increase worker control of industry, and to choose the general direction the economy will go. At the same time, subsidies for all elements of society—business and labor, middle-class, farmers, the poor—have increased. Why? The increase is the outcome, concludes Wildavsky, of a standoff in which all three cultures have been able to get some of their agendas enacted, continued, or increased: "All three primary cultures have a share in governing the political economy."

Thomas K. McCraw

Among the points made by Thomas K. McCraw in his extraordinarily rich and suggestive paper are (1) that the fundamental issues raised by the industrial policy debate are "as old as the nation state" and that these issues were debated from the beginning of the American republic; (2) that the most successful industrial policy in the United States emerged from the unintended and unforeseen consequences of antitrust or competition policy; and (3) the experience of Bismarkian Germany, the United States before the 1930s, and post–World War II Japan illustrate that, despite the conventional wisdom from economic theory, cartelization and a protected home market "promoted (economic) efficiency in ways that are very complex and that we are only beginning to understand."

In McCraw's view, industrial policy in the United States and in other nations constitutes a form of mercantilism, though it may not always exhibit all of the elements of that economic doctrine (particularly the priority of precious metal accumulation and the link to an aggressive military policy). But in the emphasis on promotion of selected industries, subsidization for exports, limitation of imports, and maintenance of an overall favorable balance of trade, industrial policy parallels the major doctrines of an economic theory dominant in the European political economy from the fifteenth century to the eighteenth century. The American Revolution is often portrayed as a triumph of the principles of the Enlightenment, including the emerging doctrines of free enterprise and open markets associated with Adam Smith and others. But, McCraw notes, the revolution was provoked more by specific British revenue measures than by overall policies associated with mercantilism. Indeed, the first great debates of the new republic pitted the essentially mercantilist principles of Alexander Hamilton against the agrarian, free trade ideals of Thomas Jefferson.

Hamilton's *Report on Manufactures* (1791) stands as one of the "most eloquent and persuasive briefs in favor of an American industrial policy ever written." Combined with his later works *On Public Credit* and *On the Bank of the United States,* Hamilton's *Report* encompassed many of the elements associated with both mercantilist and industrial policy principles, including strong central direction through a national bank; tariffs to protect a home market; and subsidies for selected, key industries.

Hamilton's comprehensive plan for America was rejected overwhelmingly by his fellow citizens, as were later similar large-scale schemes such as Henry Clay's American System. The lesson McCraw draws from these historical experiences is that, although elements of industrial policy—high tariffs, internal improvements, a central bank—have been adopted at times, "*coordinated* industrial policy has always been a hard sell in the United States. . . . The American political economy has never lent itself to coherent state direction except in time of war." Industrial policy, he stated at the conference, was at most a "tentative and reluctant tradition."

In the most strikingly original section of his paper, subtitled "Antitrust as an Inadvertent but Successful Industrial Policy," McCraw traces the unintended but highly salubrious results of the American tradition of vigorous, though selective, antitrust enforcement. He notes, at the outset, that antitrust policy has been fingered as a major villain in the drama of the attempt of U.S.

companies to survive in the fiercely competitive international marketplace of the 1970s and 1980s. These charges in the 1970s and 1980s present an interesting and puzzling historical problem, for they raise a further question as to why trust enforcement did not injure American enterprise in earlier periods. How was it, for example, that the first forty years of the Sherman Act enforcement coincided with great national prosperity and unprecedented economic growth? Total factor productivity increased at a rate six times faster between 1890 and 1930 than it had during the nineteenth century.

McCraw finds the answers to these questions stemming from the overall world economic conditions in the late nineteenth and early twentieth centuries and the unexpected impact U.S. trust laws had on corporate organization. The trust movement, he contends, arose not as a result of tariff protection, as some politicians argue, nor as a result primarily of entrepreneurs' seeking monopoly profits, as some economic theorists would hold. Rather, combinations arose from a problem faced by business in all industrialized nations: that is, a chronic overcapacity in an increasing number of manufacturing sectors.

In Europe the response of major industrial sectors was to move toward loose cartelization to fix prices and limit production and discourage new entrants into the field. Often these combinations were given official sanction and support by the national governments.

In the United States the situation was far different. Here an antimonopoly tradition had deep roots in English common law and in the national psyche. In 1890 the Sherman Antitrust Act brought the national government into play; and, beginning with the administration of Theodore Roosevelt, numerous suits were brought against the so-called trusts. Between 1905 and 1930 more than 300 suits were instituted, 80 percent of them successfully. This campaign set in motion a chain of events in relation to corporate organization that, argues McCraw, greatly benefited the American economy and enabled the United States to compete in world markets.

Initially the typical pattern for combination among companies had been a loose, horizontal alliance in which a few firms or several hundred firms agreed to maintain certain price levels for a group of products. Each firm retained individual ownership, identity, and management.

As it turned out, six out of seven of the 300-odd cases brought by the government between 1890 and 1932 were against small companies or their loose associations. This selective enforcement drove American business executives into a second form of combination, the tight horizontal combination, in which a group of companies merged into one company. The first wave of mergers between 1897 and 1901 was largely composed of such tight combinations, and it had partly been set in motion by federal antitrust policy.

Once a tight combination occurred, rationalization of the new company's resources inevitably followed: inefficient plants were shut down, and production was concentrated in the most efficient. This development produced a burst

7

of overall efficiency that reduced prices and, at the same time, maintained or even increased the quality of the product.

Rationalization in turn was soon followed by a third form of combination —vertical integration—in which companies moved forward into transportation and marketing and backward toward control of raw materials. In the case of Standard Oil, which McCraw cites, thirty-two of fifty-three refineries were shut down in the first few years of the combination, and the price of refining oil was cut by two-thirds. The vertical integration that followed pushed Standard Oil backward into pipeline control and crude oil production and forward into both wholesale and retail marketing.

Tying this common experience to industrial policy, McCraw argues that the evolution of larger, more efficient, and more integrated companies came more quickly in the United States than in other countries partly because of antitrust policy. Further, the results were quite the opposite of those intended by anti-big business reformers: antitrust policy actually promoted bigness.

In the final section of the paper, McCraw compares the experience of Japan and Germany with that of the United States. He finds common elements in the experience and tactics adopted in the United States from 1880 to 1940, in Bismarkian Germany of the late nineteenth and early twentieth centuries, and in Japan in the post–Second World War period. These common elements were a protected home market and cartelization (which took different forms in each of the three countries). Taking direct aim at prevailing economic theory, McCraw concludes that the historical record shows that in these cases protectionism and cartelization "promoted efficiency in ways that are very complex and that we are only beginning to be able to understand." Not surprisingly, this conclusion was sharply challenged by economist Herbert Stein in his commentary on McCraw's paper.

Ellis W. Hawley

Ellis W. Hawley anchors his paper and analysis upon an explicit definition of industrial policy. In his terms, it means a "national policy aimed at developing or retrenching selected industries so as to achieve national economic goals. . . . To have an 'industrial policy,' a nation must not only be intervening at the microeconomic level but also have a planning and coordinating mechanism through which the intervention is rationally related to national goals, a general pattern of microeconomic targets is decided upon, and particular industrial programs are worked out and implemented."

With this baseline definition established, Hawley examines the experience of the 1920s and 1930s with fragments of industrial policy. He concludes that throughout this period the United States was "not so innocent of industrial policy as is commonly assumed" but that the record also demonstrates that "America's political culture has had great difficulty in finding a place for such a policy." Thus any historical "lessons" are ambiguous, and both sides on the current debate will invoke portions of them in attempts to make their cases.

Though the 1920s is normally thought of as a period of retrenchment and a "return to laissez faire," Hawley points out that throughout the decade two strands of thought competed for control in government and society. Along with a group of policies that did stress laissez-faire and deregulation, there emerged—also from the wartime and progressive movement experiences—a second strand that envisioned the use of new management and planning capacities to control and mitigate economic instability and disorder. A loose coalition, led by former war administrators, engineering leaders, and scientific management experts, developed. Though committed to a capitalist, free enterprise economy, these people were "confident . . . that demobilization, deregulation, and privatization could go hand in hand with the building of new managerial capacities and stabilizing mechanisms." They found havens in various government and university departments, but symbolically they were centered in the Commerce Department under the leadership of Herbert Hoover.

Hawley notes the parallels to current industrial policy proposals in the attempts by Hoover and others to establish a philosophy of "cooperative competition," to create stronger public-private bonds and to develop industry-specific programs for "problem" industries or for sectoral "market failures." In pursuit of his goals, Hoover enlisted the aid of an interacting network of "industrial statesmen," volunteer specialists who formed the cadre for a parallel structure of industry and sectoral committees. Established through the auspices of the Commerce Department, this network produced a commingling of public and private agencies and functions not unlike elements of the current mode of operations of the Japanese Ministry of International Trade and Industry.

The system, however, lacked many of the elements characteristic of industrial policy in other nations. There was, for instance, nothing like an overall plan or document against which progress could be measured; and the Commerce Department, despite its energy and entrepreneurship during the period, never became a central planning agency. Nor did Hoover or his allies have at their disposal any of the political tools through which foreign bureaucracies advanced their goals, such as direct subsidies, tax breaks, antitrust exemptions, and government loans or guarantees. What the effort relied upon, writes Hawley, was "moral leadership, selective technical assistance, appeals to 'science,' personal and departmental imprimaturs, and networks for mobilizing and bringing to bear private power and social pressures."

Despite these drawbacks, during the 1920s Hoover and the Commerce Department did develop a number of industry-specific mechanisms and programs to assist "problem" industries where sectoral "market failures" produced an opportunity for the testing of more enlightened economic manage-

9

ment. Hawley chronicles these efforts in several industries, including lumber, housing, energy (petroleum, coal, electric power), railroads and shipping, and agriculture. There were some successes, but there was also a great deal of frustration and failure. The experience of the 1920s, Hawley concludes, demonstrated that the new ideas of scientific and economic management had opened greater opportunity for the implementation of certain industrial proposals; but it also demonstrated that "America's culture and polity still contained elements that were strongly resistant or downright hostile to their establishment and operation." These elements include a long history of revolt against central economic management that goes back to the Revolution itself, a distrust of autonomous bureaucratic power, a legal code that places individual over group rights, and a preference for seeking the public good through adversarial proceedings and no-holds-barred bargaining. Hawley notes, finally, the experience of the 1920s:

> The difficulties encountered in attempts to build and legitimate cooperative mechanisms said much about the continuing strength of individualistic, entrepreneurial, and adversarial traditions and ideals. And the relationships of the apparatus with Congress, with the courts, with other parts of the executive branch, and with fragmented or refractory industrial groups, particularly at times when those in charge of it reach for powers that depended on affirmative action by these other institutions, all indicated that the American situation was a long way from the kind of institutional deference characteristic of such relationships in the Japanese and French models.

The New Deal ushered in a wholly new set of circumstances, with new leaders and new attitudes toward public and private roles in the U.S. economy. The depth and magnitude of the economic crisis itself produced opportunities for economic experimentation; and, unlike the Hooverites, the New Dealers believed the state and the bureaucracy could effectively implement far-reaching economic change. Yet, in Hawley's view, the New Deal also spawned counterforces that ultimately proved even more hostile to rational top-down planning by apolitical elites and economically sound sectoral or industry-specific public intervention. Hence, "it should come as no surprise that the New Deal state, as it took shape in the years from 1933 to 1939, never developed much in the way of an American 'industrial policy' as the term is now used."

In the early days, New Dealers flirted with the idea of more central planning and authorizing the government to pick certain industries for special attention and assistance, through the use of financial and development guarantees or the creation of government-backed financial institutions. In addition, the National Recovery Administration (NRA) was the prototype of a sectoral-specific-implementing federal agency. Modeled on the War Industries Board, it exhibited some industrial policy characteristics, including a melding of public and private roles in both personnel and institutions, industry-specific plans for stabilization, and promotion within industries of cooperation and self-governing regulation.

What ultimately emerged, however, represents a lesson in interest group politics rather than an illustration of an attempt at rational planning for a more efficient industrial structure for the United States. The seeds of this evolution were to be found in the substantive goals, the predominant political philosophy, and the state of the government's technical and legal capabilities. Thus the individual NRA codes were not conceived as part of a rational, coordinated plan of industrial expansion and contraction but merely as a means of setting wages and prices and curbing the "excesses of competition." The bureaucratic machinery relied on both the technical and administrative resources of the private sector, and public officials had neither positive inducements (loans, subsidies, guarantees) nor punitive regulatory tools to enforce rational restructuring—even had they known how this could be accomplished. In the end, the NRA intensified intraindustry divisions, increased government-business conflict, and faced opposition by many political interests, including entrepreneurs, laborers, consumers, and service intellectuals. Hawley contends:

> The NRA experience . . . illustrates . . . the failure of either the economic crisis or the continuing organizational and managerial revolution to overcome those elements in the culture and polity that were hostile to national planning bureaucracies of any sort. An older set of populist, republican, and entrepreneurial symbols proved to be potent weapons in the political wars that swirled around the creation and operation of the code system. And while the NRA did stimulate a good deal of organizational activity, this tended to produce conflict-oriented organizations fighting to advance particular interests and secure proper shares in a pluralistic order rather than organizations that could become working parts of a planning system devising and implementing national plans.

The New Deal experience, Hawley concludes, added up to a "new allocation mechanism . . . one that subordinated managerial and planning impulses to a new political activism by interest groups and mass organization and thus gives us what various scholars have called the broker or compensatory state rather than a planning or a managerial or developmental one." Regarding the current debate, he states:

> What the historical experience that I studied would seem to suggest, then, is that the United States has not been untouched by managerial impulses and designs resembling those from which national industrial policies have sprung. . . . But the experience also suggests that the United States is not a place in which establishment of such an

11

apparatus would be an easy task and that attempting to do so may well have unintended and perverse consequences and bring forms of group behavior that would result in reduced economic welfare and retreats from the democratic ideal rather than the reverse.

Commentaries

James Fallows. In his comments on the three papers, James Fallows takes note of (1) the degree to which in all eras industrial policy proposals have been a "craving that dare not speak its name because it is so much at odds with other traditions in the American political tradition"; (2) the constant tension between twin diagnoses of the problem—one being that it stemmed from overcapacity and the other stressing the need to increase productivity; and (3) the "mild hypocrisy" of opponents of industrial policy who ignore persistent subsidies given to "even the most buccaneer of free marketeers" in the American economy.

Fallows, however, sees major differences from past eras. The major conflict in our own time is between those who want to encourage and those who want to oppose change. Opponents' concern stems from several sources. First there is a geographic element, described by Fallows as simply a "geographic distaste for the rise of the Sun Belt and decline of the Upper Midwest." Concomitantly, and more profoundly, there is the fear of a decline in the social cohesiveness that has characterized many of our manufacturing communities in the East and Midwest since the mid-nineteenth century. Finally, states Fallows, there are important political concerns, specifically "deep and unspoken fear" among Democrats that the political consensus of the Upper Midwest and East that formed the backbone of the old New Deal coalition is breaking up and cannot be retrieved.

Herbert Stein. Both the Wildavsky and McCraw papers, Herbert Stein states, adopt so loose and sweeping a definition of industrial policy that it becomes virtually synonymous with overall economic policy. Hawley, he maintains, is the only one of the authors whose view of industrial policy is akin to his own—encompassing a "notion of a comprehensive plan, a certain aura of science about it, [and] a certain devotion to a big picture of the future welfare of the economy."

Stein further takes issue with what he considers McCraw's model of achieving efficiency and growth through "protecting domestic industry and dumping the product on the rest of the world." Stein very much doubts that government will be able to choose the right industries to protect and foster because the political system will force interventions in other directions. He argues, further, that the important questions for political scientists to address are "what determines the speed of government expansion and what limits the speed of government expansion and is this limit different here from elsewhere." In Stein's view the U.S. economy is moving closer to the "competitive model," impelled by many forces, including overall technology advance, the information revolution, labor force mobility, and the opening of international markets: "It seems to me that the net of those forces has been and continues to be to increase the competitiveness and the freedom of the market."

Stein concludes by supporting Hawley's contention that "there is something [in the American political tradition] which resists [industrial policy] even if it is rather receptive to lots of particular interventions. There's something that resists this rather explicit comprehensive planning."

James Patterson. Picking up on Stein's concluding comment, James Patterson states that he sees great continuity in the papers, particularly those of McCraw and Hawley. He, like Stein, strongly associates himself with the skepticism expressed by both authors concerning the applicability and workability of industrial policy proposals in the American political climate and culture. "I am struck," he says, "by the continuity rather than the break that will continue to operate to inhibit the political realization of industrial policy in the comprehensive planning mode." McCraw's description of a "tentative and reluctant tradition of industrial policy" in the United States strikes him as particularly apt.

Probing more deeply, Patterson identifies "two important strands of twentieth-century popular American political culture that will inhibit the implementation of industrial policy proposals." The first is the enduring strength from the Left of a reform tradition dating back to Jackson but continuing through the Populist, Progressive, and New Deal movements that has as a central characteristic a deeply felt distrust of and hostility to special interests and special privilege in whatever corporate or social form it takes. From such hostility has stemmed the antimonopoly and antitrust movements that still exert a powerful influence in the American political tradition.

Linked to this first strand—a distrust of large-scale business enterprise— is a concomitant hostility toward the state and more particularly toward the federal government and its "faceless" bureaucracies. Industrial policy proposals, which often seem to envision a marriage of government and corporations, run directly counter to these beliefs and thus raise deep suspicions of a "conspiracy between government and big business."

Patterson concludes:

I speak as someone who has written books largely responsive to and sympathetic with the progressive tradition in American history. I would in some ideal world like to see us able to develop a compre-

13

hensive national industrial policy, but I do not think that the record of American history in the twentieth century suggests that there is much support in the political culture, in the popular mind for this kind of development, and I therefore don't expect to live to see it.

Industrial Policies in
American Political Cultures

Aaron Wildavsky

Industrial policy is economic policy; its purpose is prosperity. It is more than that, however, for economic relationships vitally affect the distribution of political power. Broadly viewed, therefore, every country has an industrial policy roughly equivalent to its political economy. The price system is the industrial policy of capitalism, state planning of socialism, and some of each of the mixed economy. Not having an industrial policy is not possible. The absence of state direction merely means reliance on markets. Both the pattern of regulation and its absence constitute industrial policy. End of discussion.

What is left? Only the details. These particulars are important because they reveal more variety than can be accommodated in the capitalism-socialism, bureaucracy-markets distinctions. Omitted are the rising cultural stars of the Western world, the egalitarian sectarians whose interaction with the established hierarchical and market cultures produces sufficient diversity to generate all current and proposed industrial policies. Nevertheless, the details are details; industrial policy remains the economic reflection of the major ways of life (the shared values and beliefs justifying desired social relations) we call culture.

What sort of people, organized into which ways of life, would support different industrial policies to strengthen their own culture and weaken opposing lifestyles? I shall try to answer this question in the context of the many other changes taking place in the diverse values, beliefs, and practices that make up American political cultures.

The first section outlines the objectives, and the instruments proposed to achieve them, of a spectrum of existing and proposed industrial policies. The second section discusses the political cultures found in American life. The preferences of the people organized into each culture, I claim, lead to choices of different and opposed industrial policies. The policies the people prefer depend on how they see their way of life affected by opposing cultures. Cultural context is controlling. To show how context alters policy positions, I analyze in the third section selected industrial policies from the early American republic. The fourth section relates industrial policies to contemporary cultural change in the United States. The fifth and final section reconsiders, on the basis of the checkered history of industrial policies, concepts of political change.

Instruments and Objectives of Industrial Policy

Since industrial policy reflects the political economy of the nation, the instruments used to effectuate its purposes are virtually as broad as government itself—credit, taxes, appropriations, and statutes regulating the economic and political behavior of business. Two aspects of these instruments of policy are worthy of note. One is the preponderant weight given to indirect expenditures that do not show up in the budget. Most of the resources are to come from loans, loan guarantees, tax preferences, and regulations imposing costs on private business, such as delays in closing plants or payments that have to be made to workers and local governments. Though these resources contribute to the deficit by reducing revenue, they do not, except for defaults on loans, show in formal accounting. This play with appearances may explain why programs to expand governmental influence without appearing to increase its expenses are attractive.[1]

The other noteworthy feature of instruments for implementing industrial policy is their contradictory character. For every instrument that climbs up the hill there is another designed to climb down. If some legislation is antitrust and antimerger, other legislation legalizes industrial cooperation, that is, to favor trusts and mergers. Regulation is countered by deregulation. Tariffs, quotas, and local-content legislation are met by proposals for freer trade and export subsidies. The various industrial banks that would establish priorities for building up certain industries would, by denying to some what they give to others (that is the meaning of priorities), drive other industries down.

Sometimes that these instruments of policy would work at cross-purposes is not apparent, but they would. Tax breaks, for example, are frequently proposed to increase employment and to subsidize capital intensive industry. The latter, however, has the tendency to reduce the former. Both sanctions (disciplining labor and capital) and rewards (subsidies galore) have been proposed to effectuate diverse industrial policies.

Objectives of industrial policy are polar opposites. There is agreement on the desirability of reducing unemployment, though not, of course, on how to achieve it without making other things, like inflation or the ability to adapt to foreign competition, worse. Securing higher wages via capital intensiveness and tariff barriers is opposed to achieving international competitiveness via reducing tariffs and unions' monopoly power so as to lower "excessive" wages. The goal of encouraging people to increase investment does not sit well with taxing away their "excess" profits. Adapting to new policies while preventing plant closures or providing subsidies to cushion economic decline will not be easy. Different voices urge subsidies for exports while inhibiting imports, raising up and tearing down defense industry. Even the objective of economic growth, once sacrosanct, has been challenged by a variety of measures to redistribute power (industrial democracy or worker control) and profits (curbs on runaway shops, adjustment assistance to workers).

Our task is to understand these rival objectives by relating them to different conceptions of the good life. According to which set of values and practices do the rival conceptions of industrial policy make sense to their adherents? And how, by contrast, did Americans, similarly divided in the past, rationalize their policy positions on related issues?

Political Cultures, or
You Can't Tell the Players without a Scorecard

Survey research documents large distances between Democratic and Republican activists on issues running from the size of government to its functions to its very legitimacy. Between those who see American political institutions as a source of evil, hence not worth defending, and those who see them as a source of good, hence deserving to be defended to the death, is a vast, perhaps impassible, gulf. Yet these political predispositions are explained as products of a unitary American culture, just as, presumably, the democratic and dictatorial dispositions of the Germanies are explained by German culture.

This explanation won't do. There cannot be just one culture, one set of shared values and practices, one way of life. More than one culture must exist in one country at a time, even if for a time one is dominant. The array of viable cultures is the same for all periods of history, but the cultures differ in the proportions in which they are combined.

My argument is that when individuals make important decisions, these choices are simultaneously choices of political culture. When choices are not completely controlled by conditions, people discover their preferences by deciding whether they will reaffirm, modify, or abandon their way of life. Put plainly, people decide for or against existing authority. They construct their culture in the process of decision making. Just as (but on a more cosmic scale) party identification enables individuals to cut their information costs, the continuing reinforcement, modification, and rejection of existing authority relations teaches them what to prefer.

Policy preferences emerge from social interaction in defending or opposing different ways of life. People choose their preferences as part of the process of constructing—building, modifying, rejecting—their institutions. The values people prefer and their beliefs about the world are woven together through their cultures.

17

The dimensions of cultural theory are based on answers to the two great questions of human life: "Who am I?" and "How should I behave?" The question of identity may be answered by saying that individuals belong to a strong group, a collective, that makes decisions binding on all members or that individuals' ties to others are weak in that their choices bind only themselves. The question of action is answered by responding that the individual is subject to few or many prescriptions, a free spirit or one that is tightly constrained. The strength or weakness of group boundaries and the numerous or few prescriptions binding or freeing individuals are the social components of their political cultures.

Strong groups with numerous prescriptions combine to form a culture of hierarchical collectivism. Strong group boundaries with few prescriptions form a political culture of egalitarian sectarianism, a life of voluntary consent, without coercion or inequality. Market competition joins few prescriptions with weak group boundaries, thereby encouraging endless new combinations. When boundaries are weak and prescriptions strong, so that decisions are made by people outside the group, the controlled culture is fatalistic (see figure 1).

FIGURE 1
MODELS OF CULTURES

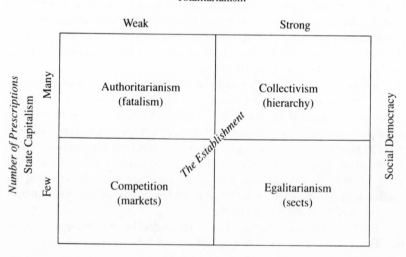

Group Strength
Totalitarianism

American individualism
(equality of opportunity leads
to equality of results)

No one of these ways of life is viable on its own, however. Markets need something—the laws of contract—to be above negotiating; hierarchies need something—a controlled "lowerarchy"—to sit on top of; sects need something —an inegalitarian market and an inequitable hierarchy—to criticize. It takes two poles to make a magnet, and it takes (at least) two parts to make a whole political regime.

The combination of hierarchy and sectarianism I call social democracy, after the European nations that add a strong egalitarian element to the sacrificial ethic of hierarchy, in which the individual parts are expected to aid the collective whole. When sects and markets combine, so that equality of opportunity is believed to lead to equality of results, as in the Jacksonian era of American political history, I call the mixture "American individualism." Extreme individualism in concert with the dominion of authoritarianism brings forth state capitalism. Authoritarianism together with hierarchy breeds totalitarianism. The alliance of hierarchies and markets can go by its colloquial name, the establishment. In this chapter I will omit discussion of state capitalism and totalitarianism as outside the historical range of American political cultures.

The social ideal of market cultures is self-regulation. They favor bidding and bargaining to reduce the need for authority. Hierarchy is institutionalized authority. It justifies inequality on grounds that specialization and division of labor enable people to live together with greater harmony and effectiveness than do alternative arrangements. Belief that hierarchy creates a caring collective, therefore, with rulers responsive to the ruled, is essential to its survival. Hence hierarchies are justified by a sacrificial ethic: the parts are supposed to sacrifice for the whole. Committed to a life of purely voluntary association, sectarian cultures reject authority. They can live without coercion or authority only by complete equality of condition. The best indicator of sectarian practices, therefore, is their attempt to reduce differences—between races, income levels, or sexes or between parents and children, teachers and students, authorities and citizens. Whether policies are designed to diminish, maintain, or increase differences among people is a tell-tale sign of which political culture is preferred.

Because sectarians believe in as few prescriptions as possible, so as to avoid coercion, every act is scrutinized to see that it does not lead to inequality of resources. Because members of hierarchies believe in solving the problem of social order through a graded division of labor, they espouse equality before the law. Who has the right to act is as important to them as what is done. And because adherents of a market culture wish to regulate their lives by bidding and bargaining, they support equality of opportunity. Among equality of result so people can have the same, equality of opportunity so they can be different, and equality before the law so they can maintain existing inequalities, there are profound differences.

19

Sectarianism advocates equality of results, collectivism is concerned with legal equality, and individualism advocates equality of opportunity; that is why, though all people (except fatalists) speak approvingly of equality, they all mean something different.

For those who have no control over the prescriptions that govern their lives, fairness is fate. Life is fair for adherents of markets when they have opportunity to enter and to benefit from competition. Failure is fair too, providing that the markets they enter are unfettered and that they have a chance to cumulate resources to try again. In a hierarchical collective, fairness follows function; being fairly treated does not mean being treated like everyone else but according to predictable rules affecting one's own station in life. In the egalitarian collectives I call sectarian, fair is equal. No one is to have more of anything, especially power, than anyone else.

Sectarians are not interested in economic growth, for abundance increases the temptation to differentiation, which interferes with equality. Far better for sectarians to concentrate on equal distribution, which keeps their people together, than on unequal development, which pulls them apart. The idea of resource scarcity is useful to collectivists who can then proceed to allocate physical quantities by direct (that is, bureaucratic) means. The idea of resource depletion is useful for sectarians who can blame the system for exploiting nature as it exploits people, and who can then try to get the authorities to change their inegalitarian lifestyle. The idea that resources are limited, however, is anathema to a market culture because it implies that exchange makes people worse off (and therefore has to be curtailed) and because it attacks the central promise of expanding wealth that will eventually make everyone better off.

Wealth creation belongs to the established cultures, but in different ways. The promise of hierarchies is that collective sacrifice will lead to group gain. Thus the collective culture plans to reduce consumption to create capital to invest for future benefits. Should its solidarity be threatened, the collective will adopt a limited redistributive ethic, buying off discontent, limiting exchange to limit losers. Not so our market men. They seek new combinations to create additional wealth so that they can keep more of it.

In discussing America, one must particularly observe the crucial distinction between markets and sects. Both share a desire to live with as few rules prescribing their behavior as possible. Market cultures, however, maintain equality of opportunity to enhance differences, and sectarians choose equality of result to reduce differences. The two cultures offer fundamentally different challenges to authority. Sectarians reject all authority. Members of markets will join with anyone (including hierarchical authority), provided their ability to bid and bargain is respected. Markets prefer minimal authority, sectarians none at all.

Let us suppose that something goes wrong: Who is to blame? Sectarian regimes blame the system, the established authority that introduced unnatural inequality into society. Hierarchies blame deviants who harm the collective by failing to follow its rules. Market regimes fault the individual for failing to be productive or for restricting transactions (not allowing the best bargains to be made).

Suppose a new development occurs. Without knowing much about the development, those who identify with each particular way of life can guess whether its effect is to increase or decrease social distinctions—guesses made more definitive by observing what like-minded individuals say. Members of a market or a sectarian culture do not need much evidence to decide whether they oppose or approve of a bail-out for business or a ban on plant closings; and a member of a hierarchical regime does not need much to surmise that a new reconstruction finance corporation is a way of disciplining labor and management for the collective good.

The policy preferences of people in political cultures follow from the desire to reinforce their way of life and to destabilize their opponents'. Their intentions—supporting, opposing, or minimizing authority; increasing, decreasing, or maintaining economic differences—remain constant; but their ideas about what will be efficacious vary according to the conditions of the times.

Industrial Policy in the Early American Republic

Imagine that today's left-wing liberals were opposed to the growth of government and to its regulation of business and that today's right-wing conservatives supported a larger government's actively intervening in the economy. That supposition would provide a much better guide to the struggles over the structure of the political economy from the founding of the republic to the Civil War. Reading back current attitudes to the object of industrial policy turns early industrial policy on its head. For the antifederalists, the Jeffersonians, and the Jacksonians believed that central government was the source of artificial inequality that threatened republican government. Once that idea is engraved on our consciousness—the political forces that we would now call progressive, left, or anti-establishment then identified government with inequality—we are in a position to understand the conflicts over Hamilton's funding of the debt, Jackson's opposition to the Bank of the United States, and Henry Clay's American system organized around internal improvements.

The objects of industrial policy are not only the forces of industry but also the bastions of government. The opposition to central funding of the debt, to a national bank, and to the tariff was not opposition to business or to private markets per se. On the contrary, most families were engaged in farming, and most farmers thought of themselves as engaged in business, buying and selling land as well as produce. Market competition was in high repute, provided only

21

that it was truly competitive, that is, uncontaminated by artificial restraints imposed by the central government. Nor was government itself the object of vilification: state governments were encouraged to do the very thing denied to the central government. Why this enmity to central government?

Jeffersonian Attitudes. "This measure," Jefferson wrote in "The Anas," referring to federal assumption of state debts, "produced the most bitter and angry contest ever known in Congress before or since the Union of the States."[2] This was so, Jefferson argued, because the debt acted "as a machine for the corruption of the legislature." Now by "corruption" Jefferson and his supporters did not mean financial dishonesty; he knew Hamilton to be personally honest. Rather, drawing on their fears of the reestablishment of monarchy in America, they meant the perversion of judgment caused by giving men with a financial stake in the debt a special interest in and an enhanced capacity for undermining the independent judgment of Congress. This political corruption, this fear of the decay of the foundations of disinterestedness required by republican government, is traced in Lance Banning's reconstruction of the contemporary struggles between the party of the King and the party of the country in England.

> Ministers could . . . call upon additional inducements in the form of governmental offices or pensions for their parliamentary supporters. Patronage and governmental influence in elections, . . . made it possible for ministries to exercise a certain measure of executive control of Parliament. . . . Court money was employed in parliamentary elections, purchasing the representatives and debasing the electors: "the little beggarly boroughs" were "pools of corruption."[3]

The source of this power, according to Bolingbroke's description of his quarrel with Walpole was, in Banning's words, that

> growing revenues and higher taxes make it possible for ministers to create a horde of officers, who fill the Parliament and exercise a rising influence in elections. The civil list provides vast funds for the corruption of Parliament, and the practice of anticipating revenues creates supplies. In fact, the means available to ministers have grown to such a great extent in recent years that the crown has now, through influence, powers just as great as it once had by perogative. The fate of English liberty depends on a union of good men against the progress of corruption.[4]

This, just this, is what Jefferson meant when he charged that "Hamilton was not only a monarchist, but for a monarchy bottomed on corruption."[5]

Commerce and agriculture and artisanship, yes, but large-scale industry, no. James Savage sums up Jefferson's position:

> Jefferson's great fear was that a central government burdened by deficits and debts would undermine its republican and constitutional

foundations while promoting widespread social and economic inequality. This inequality would emerge through two simultaneously occurring events. First, speculators, bankers, and the moneyed aristocracy could gain the financial leverage and profits derived from financing the national debt. Second, the government itself would spend its added revenues by promoting an industrialized economy through Hamiltonian policies resembling those of mercantilist and corrupted England. Once again, England served as the model to be avoided, for just as its government was corrupted in no small way due to its enormous debt, English society and its moral values were also corrupted by a system of manufacturing and industry that created vast social and economic divisions.[6]

All this was to be undone by keeping the central government small, by paying off its debts, and by preventing the Hamiltonian machine from being driven by the engine of a national bank.

Republican thought, memorialized in the antifederalist papers,[7] considered substantial inequality of resources and a large-scale government to be incompatible with personal liberty. Their sectarian views called for small agricultural communities in which an educated electorate, not far from one another in economic status and geographic distance, would handle their affairs on a face-to-face basis.

Jacksonian Attitudes. By President Andrew Jackson's time, commerce had developed, the industrial revolution had begun, and banking was considerably more important than it heretofore had been. Jacksonians faced certain choices: If they controlled markets, thereby preventing inequality from growing, they risked losing personal liberty and gaining unwanted governmental growth; if they tried to remove impediments to markets, thus allowing more people to compete, the result might be enduring inequality with its pernicious consequences for democratic life. In the end, they denied any conflict between economic competition and political equality.

The widespread belief among those who theorized about Jacksonian democracy in Jackson's times, a belief apparently shared by the citizenry as well, was that equality of opportunity, meticulously followed, would lead to an approximation of equality of result. The operation of economic markets, unimpeded by the federal government, would eventually approximate real equality of condition—as closely as innate differences in human ability permitted. At the very least, central government would not add artificial to natural inequality; thereby representative government would be preserved. This belief—not in undefined equality or in just one kind of equality but in the *mutual reinforcement of opportunity and result*—made America truly exceptional.

Individuals would be allowed, indeed encouraged, to keep all gain that

23

resulted from the unfettered use of their own talents. Everything artificial and unnatural, everything government imposed on man in his free state—such as charters, franchises, banks, and other monopolies—became an anathema. If every man could not be his own government, he could (and many Jacksonians advocated he should) become his own banker. "All government is evil," cried *The Democratic Review*, a Jacksonian organ, including the democratic kind; and, beyond the administration of justice, government should leave the rest of society "to the voluntary principle."[8] As William M. Gouge argued in discussing money and banking, "A man has . . . a natural right to . . . profits," but the distribution of wealth depends on a nation's institutions. Once government's granting of "peculiar commercial privileges" lays the "foundation of the artificial inequality of fortune," therefore, "all the subsequent operations of society tend to increase the difference in the condition of different classes in the community."[9] "Every corporate grant," as Theodore Sidgwick, Jr., wrote, "is directly in the teeth of the doctrine of equal rights, for it gives to one set of men the exercise of privileges which the main body can never enjoy."[10] The remedy was clear: Abolish the "monster."

If you believe, along with Jacksonian William Gouge, that banks "lay the foundation of an artificial inequality of wealth; and whenever this is done, the wealth of the few goes on increasing in the ratio of compound interest, while the reflex operations of the very causes to which they owe their wealth, keep the rest of the community in poverty,"[11] you would also agree with Jackson's attorney general, Roger Taney, that the Bank of the United States should not be rechartered because of "its corrupting influence . . . its patronage greater than that of the Government—its power to embarrass the operations of the Government—and to influence elections."[12] You would also understand why Jackson pledged that if he became president he would pay off the national debt "to prevent a monied aristocracy from growing up around our administration that must bend it to its views, and ultimately destroy the liberty of our country."[13] No wonder Jackson celebrated, in his own words, his "glorious triumph" when he "put to death, that mamouth *[sic]* of corruption and power, the Bank of the United States."[14]

Once inequality was laid at the door of central government, competitive markets could be reconciled with egalitarian sectarianism, equality of opportunity with equality of result, by claiming that an attack on authority (that is, central government) could increase equality of opportunity, which would then, once artificial fetters were removed, naturally lead to equality of result. That, in hearing about American equality, the citizen cannot tell whether the word refers to opportunity or result, and that, in regard to American "individualism," the citizen remains unaware of whether the regime referred to is market or sectarian is the idea.

The Whig program of federally funded internal improvements was closely connected to the debt and the tariff. Besides encouraging the growth of industry, the tariff provided the surplus revenues to expand roads, canals, and other facilities that today go under the general rubric of infrastructure. The debt also increased money in circulation, thus aiding industry as well as tying its holders to the central government. Put another way, all these devices gave the federal government and those who controlled it a role to play.

The rationale for internal improvements was to bind the nation together. The parts were to sacrifice for the whole by paying taxes to help the nation grow. Just as the authors of *The Federalist Papers* ingeniously countered the argument that there could not be a large-scale republic by identifying localism with parochial self-interest, citizen participation with reason-destroying passion, so the Whigs used a version of the public goods argument in behalf of a national whole greater than the sum of its parts. As Henry Clay said,

> In regard to internal improvements, it does not follow, that they will always be constructed whenever they will afford a competent dividend upon the capital invested. . . . But, in a new country, the condition of society may be ripe for public works long before there is, in the hands of individuals, the necessary capital to effect them . . . the aggregate benefit resulting to the whole society, from a public improvement, may be such as to justify the investment of capital in its execution.[15]

One can almost hear modern proponents of industrial policy saying that its social benefits exceed its economic costs.

What stopped this drive for a national program of internal improvements? Jacksonians believed that payment of interest on the national debt was reverse redistribution of income from poor to rich people. This was true, they believed, because the debt and interest upon it depleted the limited capital fund from which wages were drawn. If such capital were transferred from government into private hands, productivity would increase, and wages would also go up. To Jackson's supporters, voting down internal improvements meant helping the ordinary citizen.

Allied with a protective tariff that brought in ever-larger sums, President Polk believed that "the operation and necessary effect of the whole system [of internal improvements] would encourage large and extravagant expenditures, and thereby to increase the public patronage, and maintain a rich and splendid government at the expense of a taxed and impoverished people."[16] Favoring the common man to Jacksonian individualists meant promoting individual or state, not central governmental, enterprise.[17]

The struggle over industrial policy in the early American republic raised the same question it does today: How should Americans govern themselves? The answers in the form of preferred political cultures are the same, only the policy prescriptions are different. Then, as now, all believed in self-government; but, given their disagreement over social organization, they located leadership and virtue in different institutional arrangements. Based in different combinations of cultures, the rival forces proposed opposing policies. For the Jacksonian individualists, an alliance of sects and markets, virtue lay in participation by public-spirited citizens within local communities in which they were continuously active. Free government lay within the breast of the common man, so long as he possessed sufficient resources to compete and central government did not corrupt him through special privilege. Building up local initiative meant restraining central hierarchy; maintaining equality among individuals meant restricting economic agglomerations of power. Thus the individualist regime opposed funding the debt, national banks, and internal improvements. The establishment regime of Federalists and Whigs (an alliance of hierarchy and markets) located virtue within national elites who would act out of a desire to excel and who would both restrain themselves and the passions of those less qualified to rule. To the establishment, cementing the union meant creating a nexus of interests among elites promoted by internal improvements, debt and debt holders, and central banks.

Consider in this context the moral loading the rival political cultures gave to funding the Revolutionary War.[18] Everyone agreed that a moral obligation existed. But to whom? To men with a market mentality, those who bought the debt at a discount from the original holders were entitled to their profits, either because they were lucky or smart. Distinguishing among classes of debtors would weaken the guarantee behind the credit and therefore lead to less economic growth. They chose the highest economic product and the most unequal distribution. Supporters of hierarchy favored funding by nationalizing the debt to secure the legitimacy and the effectiveness of the central authority. If that action meant perpetuating inequality, why, such inequality was in the natural order of things. Sectarians would have either cut off secondary purchasers or given them less. For one thing, these speculators did not deserve to profit from the distress of the original holders. For another, their profits would create a cumulative inequality, first by enriching secondary holders at the expense of taxpayers and second by enabling these speculators to corrupt elections and officeholders.

The moral of this story is that the major participants knew what their disagreements were about. True, they were concerned with economic-cum-industrial policy; but they were more deeply concerned with the significance for political society of these alternative industrial policies. An so, nowadays, should we be.

Something for Everybody:
Industrial Policies in the 1980s

Viewed as a product of diverse political cultures, the wide array of proposed and actual industrial policies makes sense. Traced to their antecedents in competing visions of the good life, industrial policies tell us about ourselves.

Industrial policies offer a menu of subsidies and sanctions. How much of each depends on the relative power of the three primary cultures. Politics is coalition. What each political culture would do alone, were this possible, is not what it would agree to do to secure a broader base of support. Left to their own devices, members of a market culture would choose neither subsidy nor sanction; they would let the market decide. But this path is not possible. Enterprises exist to reward their owners through serving consumers. Subsidies mean they make more, at least in the short run. Those who would prefer to do without understand that competitors will seek such advantages, leaving purists in a poorer position. The necessity of alliances, moreover, means that markets must live within a web of taxes and regulations. Subsidies, in their eyes, are a means of getting their own back. Thus adherents of a market culture seek subsidies without sanctions, getting as much as possible of the benefits while paying as little as possible of the costs.

Members of a sectarian culture prefer the opposite—sanctions without subsidies. They distinguish between small and big business. Bigness they regard as a curse and a threat, a curse because it exemplifies the combination of inegalitarian outcomes and coercive hierarchy of corporate capitalism, a threat because great disparities in economic power translate themselves into cumulative inequalities of political power. Besides, sects cannot themselves be big, for large size militates against the equality of power and the face-to-face relations required to ensure individual consent on each issue that matters. Hence sectarians seek either to break up bigness or to subject it to worker or state control. Which route they take, as we shall see, depends on whether they are allied primarily with hierarchies or with market cultures, that is, whether they constitute a regime of social democracy or of American individualism.

Members of hierarchies choose both to impose sanctions and to offer subsidies. They wish to control industry to make it serve their notion of collective interests. Therefore, they wish to use a wide variety of policy instruments, from compelling labor to lower wage demands and forcing capital to reduce prices to subsidies encouraging industry to do the right things, such as investing in projects in poorer regions and establishing child care centers. Because they consider themselves responsible for the whole society, hierarchies, if they are competitive, as they are in democracies, wish to do something for each of their parts. How much for whom depends, again, on the alliances they establish.

The most common alliance is between hierarchy and markets, one bringing stability, the other change. They agree on the desirability of economic growth (hierarchies to make good intergenerational promises, thereby demonstrating that they bring the better life; markets to increase total product so the capable or fortunate can have more), but not necessarily on its distribution. The stronger the hierarchical partner in this marriage of conve-

27

nience, the more sacrifices are imposed on industry; the stronger the market forces, the fewer the sanctions and the greater the subsidies. Yet the participation of the sectarian culture has to be taken into account.

Because sectarian cultures reject authority, they are loathe to ally themselves with hierarchies. Because they desire equality of condition, alliance with market forces that generate inequality are troublesome. Hence sectarians are happiest in opposition, taking on their coloration from what they are against—the coerciveness and inequalities of hierarchies and markets. Unless they are to be destroyed, however (a frequent historical experience—one thinks of the Jansenists or the Social Revolutionaries), or impotent, crying out against injustice on the fringes of society, they must choose.

Sectarians whose opposition to inequality is dominant ally themselves with hierarchy to use governmental authority to redistribute resources. They give up overt opposition to authority in the form of big government to gain its help in beating down big business. They support tariffs, anti-plant-closing legislation, higher minimum wages, and excess profits taxes. Sectarians whose opposition to hierarchical coercion is dominant take the line made famous in Schumaker's "small is beautiful." Since they believe in perfect competition among small entities, they favor antitrust, worker control, and noncentralization. The difference between a social democratic regime (an alliance between hierarchy and sectarianism) and American individualism (an alliance of sectarian and market cultures) revolves around the size of central government, the extent of regulation of business, and the extent of subsidy. A social democratic regime desires large government, uniform regulations, and sizable subsidies so that inequality may be diminished (sects) and order may be maintained (hierarchy). A regime of American individualism advocates small central government (both sect and market cultures), equality among state and local communities (sects), and a reduction of subsidies to big business (markets).

The United States lacks a hereditary hierarchy; it has historically had weak hierarchies. A coalition composed of a strong market and a weak hierarchical culture ordinarily produces large subsidies but small sanctions. The talk of sanctions against business or labor has not usually been followed up by effective action. The past twenty years, however, have witnessed the increase in adherents to a sectarian culture, the further weakening of hierarchy, and the progressive reduction in power of the once-dominant market culture. One consequence has been the imposition of sanctions on industry in the form of regulations of all kinds. The sectarian influence has stiffened the resolve and increased the ability of central governmental hierarchies to control business behavior. Whereas in countries with dominant hierarchies, such as Britain and Japan, pluralism means that business interests are part of the whole and have to be accommodated, where sectarianism is strong, pluralism signifies a struggle to see who can control government to coerce the losers.[19]

Another consequence has been the serious consideration given to proposals, not yet enacted at the national level, to make plant closings more difficult, to regulate work practices and wages (for example, comparable worth), and to choose directions for the development of industry. At the same time, however, subsidies to all concerned—business; labor; agriculture; poor, middle income, and high income people—have increased. Why?

The answer lies in the standoff between the three primary cultures, all of which are able to get their proposals on the agenda and, to a degree, enacted. Hence there is, as we say, something for everybody. Expenditures, entitlements, loan guarantees, tax preferences are extraordinarily widely shared. Most of the benefits, the truth is, go to most of the people. (Were this not so, the efforts to alter the existing revenue system to a low-rate, broad-based tax would not meet with opposition from interests not usually thought of as inordinately privileged—homeowners, state and local governments, labor unions, universities, charities.) The same is true of who pays the costs. The spectacle not only of proposed policies but of existing programs running in opposite directions is due to pluralism with a vengeance: all three primary cultures have a share in governing the political economy.

One instrument of policy, however, has no counter. I refer to education for literacy, job training, and research. If anything survives the debate over industrial policy, therefore, education heads the list. Why so? Each of the three primary political cultures places a premium on education. Hierarchies want the people to learn the norms of the system and to develop expertise for its division of labor. Market cultures view education as a path to growth, and sects see education as a requisite of political participation. The United States is not only a land in which people grant their favors to diverse political cultures, it is also the home of the educated because that—education for different ways of life—is one thing we have always agreed about.

Change is Political, Not Psychological

The study of political economy, masquerading under the rubric of industrial policy, reveals that proclivity toward change depends on the gap between desired and actual power relationships, not, as is commonly believed, on innate psychological predispositions. The further the distance between the real and the ideal, the greater the desire for rapid and radical change. If this proposition is correct, it should follow that "left" or "progressive" forces, when they consider existing power relationships more desirable than proposals for change, should cling to the status quo with as much passion as any reactionary who prefers life in the last century to that in the present. Wandering in the void between the Articles of Confederation, interpreted as minimal central authority, and the Constitutional Convention, which, by comparison, elevated central power, the antifederalists, for example, preferred the past to

29

the future. Worrying about the return of monarchy or, just as bad, monarchical principles, however quaint that worry appears today when only one president has been able to succeed himself for more than two decades, the individualist Jacksonians, to choose another example, fought a rear-guard action against commercial capitalism. Similarly, the Federalist party, a hierarchy coalescing with market forces to form an establishment, fought to maintain the relative centralization of the Constitution—a radical change from the immediate past. If today the Democrats are perceived as the party of change and the Republicans the conservative party, why is the "changeful" party dead-set against the proposed balanced budget–spending limit amendment and the "changeless" party for it? This, too, is industrial policy, limiting, as it would, subsidy and spending both for capital and for labor.

Conservatives are conservative when there are hierarchical relationships they deem worth conserving, not otherwise. Thus they oppose industrial policies restricting the right of business to close down or to move, thereby diminishing differences between labor and management, or granting judges or administrators the right to determine salaries in the once-private sector, that is, comparable worth. The division of the political universe into liberals and conservatives, when based on innate tendencies toward change, is bound to be misleading as historical context alters whatever the various political cultures wish to preserve.

The usual questions in surveys of opinion do not consider the historical context that conditions the behavior of people who adhere to the different political cultures. Given the current context in which most proposals for government action involve redistribution of income or regulation of business, it is not surprising that people who are opposed have learned to dislike change. So, when asked, they say most change is for the worse. And people who prefer these programs respond that they like change. Were the tables turned, so that most legislation was in favor of maintaining social and economic differences, say anti-abortion and across-the-board tax cuts, contemporary liberals would learn that most change is bad and their conservative opponents that change is by-and-large good.

Dichotomizing attitudes toward political objects is unsatisfactory. It takes two to tango but at least three primary cultures, as well as the alliances among them, to adequately capture the diversity of industrial policy or the variety of political life.

Attitudes toward authority and equality, the basic dimensions of political life, are three-dimensional. Hierarchies support authority; sects reject it. So far so good. But this dichotomy does not include those who desire self-regulating market relationships to avoid reliance on authority. Thus the dichotomy cannot explain why, in some political systems, hierarchies compete for power and sects support strong central government. To explain that one must introduce the alliance between hierarchies and markets (the establishment) or between sects and hierarchies (social democracy), for their alliance with forces favoring markets has legitimated competition among hierarchies. When sectarians support nationalization of industry, they are allied with a strong hierarchy in a social democracy; when they seek decentralization of government, they combine with markets to form a regime of American individualism.

Sectarians advocate equality of condition, and market cultures advocate inequality of condition. This difference explains their disagreement over the distribution of income. Hierarchies also, however, favor modest redistribution to keep their people together. Thus the conventional dichotomy cannot explain why sects sometimes accept a modicum of inequality in political power when they ally with hierarchy to form social democracy or why market cultures accept a modicum of equality when they join the establishment by combining with hierarchy. Were hierarchies, sects, and markets not involved in shifting alliances, the historical changes in American industrial policy would be inexplicable.

Notes

1. See Aaron Wildavsky, "Squaring the Political Circle: Industrial Policies and the American Dream," in Chalmers Johnson, ed., *The Industrial Policy Debate* (San Francisco, Institute for Contemporary Studies, 1984), pp. 27–44, for a classification of industrial policy according to the mode of financing.

2. Adrienne Koch and William Peder, *The Life and Selected Writings of Thomas Jefferson* (New York: Modern Library, 1944), p. 123.

3. Lance Banning, *The Jefferson Persuasion* (Ithaca, N.Y.: Cornell University Press, 1978), pp. 43, 56.

4. Ibid., p. 59.

5. Koch and Peder, p. 126.

6. James Savage, "Balanced Budgets and American Politics," dissertation in progress, University of California, Berkeley, 1984.

7. Herbert J. Storing, *What the Anti-Federalists Were For* (Chicago: University of Chicago Press, 1981).

8. Joseph L. Blau, ed., *Social Theories of Jacksonian Democracy* (New York: Bobbs-Merrill, 1954), pp. 25–28.

9. Ibid.

10. Ibid., p. 227.

11. Ibid., p. 196.

12. Robert Remini, *Andrew Jackson and the Bank War* (New York: W. W. Norton, 1967), p. 44.

13. Robert Remini, *Andrew Jackson and the Course of American Freedom, 1822–1832*, vol. 2 (New York: Harper & Row, 1981), p. 34.

14. Remini, *Andrew Jackson and the Bank War*, p. 166.

15. William Letwin, ed., *A Documentary History of American Economic Policy since 1789* (New York: W.W. Norton, 1972), p. 63.

16. Lewis H. Kimmel, *Federal Budget and Fiscal Policy 1789–1958* (Washington, D.C.: Brookings Institution, 1959), pp. 31–32.

17. Ibid., p. 19; and Leonard D. White, *The Jeffersonians: A Study in Administrative History 1801–1829* (New York: Macmillan, 1951), p. 483.

18. See George Rogers Taylor, ed., *Hamilton and the National Debt* (Boston: D.C. Heath, 1950).

19. David Vogel, *National Styles of Regulation: Environmental Policy in Great Britain and the United States* (Ithaca, N.Y.: Cornell University Press, forthcoming).

Mercantilism and the Market: Antecedents of American Industrial Policy

Thomas K. McCraw

"Industrial policy," one of its leading advocates recently wrote, "is one of those rare ideas that has moved swiftly from obscurity to meaninglessness without any intervening period of coherence."[1] Yet what strikes the historian is not the rapid emergence or swift movement of the idea but rather its age and stability. The fundamental issues involved are at least as old as the nation-state. The term *industrial policy* itself, while not common in earlier times, was used more than a century ago in just the way we use it now. In 1876, for example, a book appeared bearing the title *The Industrial Policies of Great Britain and the United States*.[2] The author, a lobbyist for the American Iron and Steel Association, correctly characterized industrial policy as an inherently controversial topic because it necessitated helping some industries but not others. The book anticipated with uncanny accuracy the terms of today's debate: promotion of selected domestic industries, subsidies to exports, discouragement of imports, overall coordination of policy. The only difference is in the two major players and their roles. In 1876 the protectionist upstart United States threatened the supremacy of free trade Britain. Today protectionist Japan threatens free trade America.

The central question of this chapter is a historical one: What was the American attitude toward industrial policy from the late eighteenth century to the early twentieth? From the historical record, several conclusions seem obvious. If one were to set up four broad degrees of state intervention in capitalist economies—those four being substantial laissez faire, thorough but uncoordinated intervention, concerted state-led action, and systematized state management—the American experience would hover around the second category. It would move about within this category from one decade to the next but would never stray far. As a nation, we have spent no time in either the first or the fourth category, and only during the two world wars did we take up temporary residence in the third.

Another set of conclusions is not quite so apparent, and in this chapter I want to focus on those conclusions. The first is that wherever industrial policy has been instituted during the past two hundred years, it has materialized as a form of mercantilism. The second is that in America, despite a lack of coordination in policy making, the overall economic outcome—at least until the 1970s—did not differ appreciably from what it might have been under a coherent set of industrial policies. This ironic result derived in large part from the practical imperatives of populating and developing a rich continent. It also derived, as I shall argue with respect to antitrust policy, from the familiar phenomenon in which unanticipated results follow in the wake of economic regulation.

The Mercantilist Persuasion

Historically, mercantilism evolved as a cluster of principles dominant in European political economy from about the fifteenth century to the eighteenth.[3] The most important of these held that all economic policy should be designed to promote the interests of the nation-state as opposed to the individuals or groups within it or the welfare of other nations outside it. High priority was given to the accumulation of gold and silver, both as a measure of national success and as a storehouse of wealth for the fighting of future wars. Emphasis fell on maintaining a favorable balance of trade, as a means of accumulating precious metals. Mercantilism therefore required a series of policies designed to maximize exports (particularly manufactured goods of high labor content) while minimizing imports of all items not essential to the promotion of manufacturing. Policies to achieve these ends included tariff protection from imports, subsidization of exports, and tight control over foreign exchange.

In substantially this form, mercantilism as an idea represented the conventional wisdom in Britain and continental Europe well into the nineteenth century. In practice, no nation followed the policy completely, either during the high tide of mercantilist thought or later on in the twentieth century. If for no other reason, the difficulty of enforcing the cumbersome regulations required to implement it defeated any complete mercantilist system. Yet the broad outlines of the policy remained the lodestar of economic statecraft in the years before the Enlightenment; and vestiges of it persist down to the present.

By the middle of the nineteenth century, a good deal less was heard in praise of the theory than was observable in mercantilist practice. Looking back now, one would be comforted to think that advances in economic thought accounted for the intellectual retreat of mercantilism. Indeed, the doctrinal revolution embodied in the work of Adam Smith and David Ricardo provided the most powerful antimercantilist arguments. Some of the most effective charges against mercantilism, however, derived not from economic premises but from moral ones. Critics argued that mercantilism, through its emphasis on nationalistic goals, seemed to encourage preparation for war and to postulate victory in war as the highest achievement of the nation-state. Thus mercantilism amounted to the economic equivalent of an arms race. Since all countries obviously could not win either in war or in a contest for the fixed amount of wealth the world was thought to offer, mercantilism violated Enlightenment ideals about the brotherhood of man.[4]

Because Enlightenment principles so thoroughly undergirded the political philosophy of the American Revolution, mercantilism might seem to have been doomed in the new republic. We should recall, however, that for more than a century before 1775 the American colonists had supported the elaborate system of trade regulations that governed the British Empire. Our Revolution in fact was directed much less against British mercantilism than against the specific new revenue acts of the 1760s and 1770s. It was primarily against Britain's changing of her own rules that the colonists rebelled, as their emphasis on their own "rights of Englishmen" suggests.[5]

Thus no essential discontinuity existed between the principles of the Revolution and the modified mercantilism set forth in Alexander Hamilton's brilliant *Report on Manufactures* of 1791. This powerful document remains one of the most eloquent and persuasive briefs in favor of an American industrial policy ever written. Hamilton set forth a comprehensive plan for American economic growth. In particular, he analyzed methods available to promote "useful manufactures," focusing on "duties" (tariffs) and "bounties" (subsidies to certain industries). As he had done earlier in the *Federalist* papers, Hamilton carefully considered opposition arguments before proceeding to refute them. He quoted Adam Smith, for example, then amended Smith's principles of individualism and free trade to fit his own conception of reality.[6]

Here is Hamilton on the subject of alleged inequities and favoritism that might arise under his plan:

> There is a degree of prejudice against bounties, from an appearance of giving away the public money without an immediate consideration, and from a supposition that they serve to enrich particular classes, at the expense of the community.
>
> But neither of these sources of dislike will bear a serious examination. There is no purpose to which public money can be more beneficially applied, than to the acquisition of a new and useful branch of industry; no consideration more valuable, than a permanent addition to the general stock of productive labor.
>
> As to the second source of objection, it equally lies against other modes of encouragement, which are admitted to be eligible. As often as a duty upon a foreign article makes an addition to its price, it causes an extra expense to the community, for the benefit of the

35

domestic manufacturer. A bounty does no more. But it is the interest of the society, in each case, to submit to the temporary expense— which is more than compensated by an increase of industry and wealth; by an augmentation of resources and independence; and by the circumstance of eventual cheapness.[7]

Despite Hamilton's eloquence, he failed to move his target audience, which was the U.S. Congress. The lawmakers declined to enact his proposed system of bounties, and they waffled on most of his other suggestions. In fact, because Hamilton's *Report on Manufactures* was the only one of his three great reports not enacted (the other two being *On Public Credit* and *On the Bank of the United States*), its fate provides an unusually precise measure of the status of mercantilism and the desirability of an explicit industrial policy at this early date in American history. Full-blown mercantilism was not in the cards, and Hamilton's milder version of industrial policy represented a road considered but not taken.[8]

Even so, events over the next generation did promote the growth of home manufactures. Such episodes as the Napoleonic Wars, the American Embargo and Non-Intercourse Acts, and the War of 1812 accelerated the development of domestic manufactures by limiting America's access to imports. The events of these turbulent years also forced American policy makers into a sustained debate over the wisdom of protection, promotion, and other aspects of industrial policy. In the course of the debate, the Jeffersonians were driven by force of circumstance to retreat a bit from their preference for agriculture. Once in power, they were required to act more like their political opponents.

As is so often the case with industrial policy, the arguments of this period exhibit a distinctly modern ring, this time with Britain, which was then still mercantilist, playing the part today assigned to Japan. For example, Albert Gallatin, one of Hamilton's successors as secretary of the Treasury, commented in 1810 on the problems faced by Americans in export markets: "The only powerful obstacle against which American manufacturers have to struggle, arises from the vastly superior capital of Great Britain which enables her merchants to give very long term credits, to sell on small profits, and to make occasional sacrifices." Today, nearly two centuries later, one frequently hears the same kind of comment about Japan's advantages over the United States in international trade.[9]

The Tariff. Although public policy in America never adopted full-fledged mercantilism, it did tend strongly toward protection of the home market. This was true throughout our history, right up to World War II. Mostly favored device for implementing protection was the tariff. During the nineteenth century, no other issue in American public life proved more durable than the tariff, nor, with the exception of slavery, more divisive. Debates over free trade versus protectionism constituted *the* staple of American politics and even of academic political economy. (In the 1880s, the University of Pennsylvania required that its economists not support free trade, while Cornell University met the dilemma by appointing two lecturers, one on each side of the issue.) The free traders won the academic debates, but the protectionists usually triumphed in Congress.[10]

In our own time, we have become so accustomed to thinking of the United States as a bastion of liberal economic policy that we forget that our traditional position was protectionist. Table 1 illustrates how dramatically the post–World War II situation of free trade differs from what went before.

As is clear from the table, the tariff history of the United States is inseparable from the nation's larger history. In fact, a reasonably complete analysis of the nineteenth-century American economy could be organized around the single theme of the tariff. Certainly no issue produced more rhetoric, and most of the important politicians of the period delivered themselves of powerful protectionist sentiments at one time or other. It will be apparent how closely this rhetoric parallels twentieth-century debates over industrial policy:

> *James Madison.* The meaning of the phrase, "to regulate trade," must be sought in the general use of it; in other words, in the objects to which the power was generally understood to be applicable, when the phrase was inserted in the Constitution. The power has been understood and used by all commercial and manufacturing nations, as embracing the object of encouraging manufactures. It is believed that not a single exception can be named.

> *John Quincy Adams.* Protection is the price of allegiance. Protection is the object for which all government is instituted. When a government ceases to protect it must cease to claim obedience or submission.

> *Henry Clay.* Great Britain protects most her industry, and the wealth of Great Britain is consequently the greatest. France is next in the degree of protection, and France is next in the order of wealth. Spain most neglects the duty of protecting the industry of her subjects, and Spain is one of the poorest of European nations.

> *Horace Greeley.* Enlightened protection is emphatically the hope and stay of toiling millions over the whole face of the earth. . . . Let labor, therefore, with one mighty voice demand adequate, stable protection, and a wider, deeper prosperity will soon irradiate the land.

> *Abraham Lincoln.* I do not know much about the tariff, but I know this much, when we buy manufactured goods abroad we get the goods and the foreigner gets the money. When we buy the manufactured goods at home we get both the goods and the money.

> *William McKinley.* We lead all nations in agriculture; we lead

TABLE 1
Selected Events and Tariff Changes since 1789

Year	Event	Percentage of Duty Paid on Imports for Consumption[a]	
		All imports	Dutiable imports
1789	First tariff passed (average duty 9%)		
1812	Doubling of duties for war of 1812		
1816	Protection of cotton goods, iron, paper, glass	43[b]	45[b]
1832	Nullification Crisis in South Carolina	39	43
1846	Walker Tariff, moderate and simplified	29	34
1854	Elgin-Marcy Treaty, Canadian reciprocity	24	26
1861–1865	Wartime increases (South absent from Congress)	28	34
1890	McKinley Tariff, extension of protection	30	45
1909	Payne-Aldrich Tariff confirms Republican orthodoxy	23	41
1913	Underwood reductions, pushed by Woodrow Wilson	18	40
1930	Hawley-Smoot Tariff (1000 economists protest)	15	45
1934	Reciprocal Trade Agreements (White House control)	18	47
	1939–1945 World War II		
1947	General Agreement on Tariffs and Trade (GATT)	8	19
1955–1958	Stronger "escape" and "national security" clauses	6	11
1964–1967	Kennedy Round talks, with voluntary restraints	7	12
1971	First U.S. trade deficit since 1893; temporary 10% import surcharge imposed by President Nixon	6	9
1974	Trade Act, 60% reductions by White House allowed	4	8
1973–1979	Tokyo Round: all major industrial countries agree to reduce weighted average tariff rate on manufactured goods from 7% to 4.67% between 1980 and 1987; informal "new protectionism" on rise: orderly marketing agreements, voluntary export restraints, countertrade		
1981	Constant dollar volume of world trade, which grew at 0.5% per year from 1913–1948 and at 7% per year from 1948–1973, turns downward		

a. Years ending September 30, 1821–1842; June 30, 1843–1915; calendar years thereafter.

b. These percentages, and those throughout the table, are not across the board for all items but are total duties paid as percentages of total imports (left-hand column) and of dutiable imports (right-hand column). Tariff rates for individual items might range from a few percentage points to more than 100%.

Source: Adapted from J. J. Pincus, "Tariffs," in Glenn Porter, ed., *Encyclopedia of American History* (New York: Scribner's, 1980), p. 440.

all nations in mining; we lead all nations in manufacturing. These are the trophies which we bring after twenty-nine years of a protective tariff.[11]

Of course, it would not be difficult to compile a list of equally powerful criticisms of protection, from a similarly distinguished gallery of voices. Some of the voices would be the same on both sides, speaking now for and now against, according to the need of the moment.

Rhetoric aside, protection clearly held sway as the nation's considered policy throughout the nineteenth century, with only minor exceptions. Regrettably for the scholar and the twentieth-century policy maker, the real effects of the tariff remain uncertain. The classic early studies by Frank Taussig argued that neither the iron and steel, cotton, nor woolen industries actually benefited from the protection so energetically won by their political spokesmen. Later on, however, Taussig shifted ground, admitting that a mass of contradictory evidence left him feeling that the tariff may indeed have stimulated the growth of these industries.[12] More recently, several historians have applied econometric tools to the same kinds of questions Taussig addressed. Often the evidence has proved contradictory and the results inconclusive.[13]

This is not to say that such academic efforts have gone for naught. We have learned a good deal, much of it confirming the intuitions of contemporaries about the effects of tariffs on their own interests. One scholar has argued that the chief overall effect of the antebellum tariff was to injure the interests of southern slaveholders. Another has advanced the thesis that tariff policy, along with management of the federal debt, helps to explain the otherwise mysterious rise in investment as a percentage of GNP during the two decades spanning the Civil War.[14] Still a third argues in favor of applying, retrospectively, the twentieth-century economic theory of "effective" tariffs, as distinct from formal and nominal rates. When this theory is applied, he says, the effective rate of protection for numerous items apparently becomes much larger than the nominal tariff rate. Most important for present-day discussions of industrial policy, the highly protected industries of the late nineteenth century were not those for which industrial growth proved most rapid. Instead, both the effective rate of protection and the political agitation for even higher rates proved much stronger for existing labor-intensive industries such as leather and textiles than for infant manufacturing industries such as machinery and refining. Students of politics might have deduced as much.[15]

Internal Improvements and the "American System." Both in content and in the way it was used as a slogan, Henry Clay's phrase, "American System," represented the nineteenth century's closest approximation of "industrial policy." The term derived from a celebrated speech made by Clay in 1824 in support of the tariff. The Kentucky senator had long envisioned a federally sponsored development of canals and turnpikes. These "internal improvements" were to be financed from the proceeds of the tariff. In his speech of 1824, Clay argued that his program would fulfill America's destiny; and again the language has a familiar modern ring:

> The greatest want of civilized society is the market for the exchange and sale of its surplus produce. This market may exist at home or abroad, but it must exist somewhere if society prospers. The home market is first in order and paramount in importance. . . . We must speedily adopt a genuine American policy. Still cherishing the foreign market, let us create also a home market, to give further scope to the consumption of the produce of American industry. Let us counteract the policy of foreigners, and withdraw the support which we now give to their industry, and stimulate that of our own country.[16]

Like industrial policy, the American System combined an economic strategy of import substitution with the political goal of national harmony. Under Clay's plan for a network of canals and turnpikes, the industrializing North-east and Middle Atlantic states would secure new markets for their products in the American South. The South itself would keep its vast export market for cotton but would now purchase American-made products rather than European imports. Clay's own West, meanwhile, would be opened for development by a transportation system designed to penetrate the Allegheny barrier. As for the tariff, it would not only protect American manufactures but would also provide revenues for this new network of internal improvements. Overall, the salient aspect of the American System was that it did in fact represent a system, not merely a convenient marriage of unrelated policies.

In practice, the American System never reached fulfillment as a coordinated program. It raised too many possibilities for pork barrel appropriations to favored congressional districts, and it smacked of far more directive a government than a majority of American voters were prepared to accept. Clay received some backing for his program during the administration of President John Quincy Adams; but Adams's successor, Andrew Jackson, called a halt to further development. Jackson's strongly worded veto of Clay's Maysville Turnpike bill defined for an entire generation the limits of federal support. Not until much later, through land grants to transcontinental railroads, did the national government act in decisive support of internal improvements. And even then the government insisted on a quid pro quo in the form of favorable shipping rates for federal cargo.[17]

In the meantime, an extensive network of roads and canals did material-ize, as American cities, towns, and especially states stepped into the breach. Through special charters, the states made ingenious use of the business corporation as a means of mobilizing private capital for public functions. During the first part of the nineteenth century, an era in which general laws of incorporation were unknown, the states gave charters to turnpike, bridge, canal, banking, and railroad companies.

Sometimes the states invested directly. In the 1820s, for example, the legislature of New York expended the unheard-of sum of $7 million on the Erie Canal. Over the next two decades other states, rushing to emulate the astonishing success of that famous project, emptied their coffers in support of canal and turnpike schemes. Pennsylvania, Georgia, Ohio, and Illinois were especially active, but no state entirely neglected the pressing need for transportation development. Several states, caught up in a frenzy of competitive boosterism, began to exhibit mercantilist tendencies of their own. Many public-works projects went forward despite only remote chances of success, and by the 1850s several states had been forced into the humiliating step of defaulting on their bonds. But the overall result of these efforts, together with the federal protective tariff and the evolution of the American railroads, largely fulfilled Clay's American System without concerted federal direction. As one scholar aptly stated, all of this activity, though uncoordinated, meant that King Laissez Faire was "not only dead; the hallowed report of his reign had all been a mistake." Again, the same sort of comment applies accurately to public policy in the twentieth century as in the nineteenth. States today vie furiously with each other in their attempts to attract investment. They offer all sorts of tax incentives for American and foreign corporations to locate factories within their borders. Often they engage in such unbridled competition that they give away too much. Like some of the canal promoters of nineteenth-century America, they become so obsessed with immediate goals that they lose sight of the ultimate objective of promoting overall economic growth.[18]

Antitrust as an Inadvertent but Successful Industrial Policy

In the late twentieth century, the observation has become commonplace that the results of a given policy often diverge from what its well-meaning architects intended. As in the example just mentioned, states give away their tax bases in efforts to attract investment. Within cities, rent control encourages housing shortages. On the national scene, the minimum wage increases unemployment, and the social security system diminishes the nation's capital stock. In the ongoing debate over industrial policy, one frequent target of critics has been antitrust enforcement. Antitrust, so the reasoning goes, has shackled U.S. companies in their battle for survival against foreign competition, thereby taking its place as still another self-defeating regulatory policy with unanticipated consequences.

However true this argument might be, it raises for the historian an interesting problem. If antitrust has hobbled American enterprise in the 1970s and 1980s, then why did it not work equal injury in earlier periods? Why were the first forty years under the Sherman Act (1890–1929) characterized by an unprecedented growth of productivity, a spurt in real GNP, and overwhelming national prosperity?

The answer to this question provides clues not only about the reasons for dramatic growth during that earlier period, it also suggests some points relevant to the current debate over industrial policy. For in its early phase antitrust had a therapeutic effect, an ironic and mostly unintended promotion of efficiency through rationalization and vertical integration. This same kind of effect, as it turned out, was achieved more deliberately in such countries as Germany and Japan, and these policies played a significant role in those nations' miracle growth.

The Sherman Antitrust Act of 1890 responded to a movement that had begun in the 1870s, with the formation of the first trusts. The trust movement developed during the period of high protective tariffs and after the major phase of internal improvements had been completed. A contemporary slogan of antitrust proponents announced that "the tariff is mother to the trusts," and indeed some connection would not seem out of the question: trusts, protected from foreign competition, could charge high prices without fear of losing market share. To this day, however, no clear relation between tariffs and trusts has been drawn by scholars. It appears likely that powerful interfirm competition within the vast American market reduced the opportunity for excessive prices.

Overall, the trust movement arose less in response to the tariff or to any other public policy than to a specific new problem of industrialization. This problem was a generalized industrial overcapacity, tied to the boom and bust business cycles typical of developed economies in the late nineteenth century. Just as worldwide overcapacity today lies behind the periodic "sickness" of such industries as steel, fibers, and footwear, so in the late nineteenth century industrial overcapacity plagued the economies of all developed nations. The basic reason was that the industrial revolution initially took the form of a revolution in production. Corresponding shifts in distribution and marketing lagged behind, and this created a temporary but serious gap between nations' capacity to produce and their ability to consume. The sequence, of course, was in some respects a natural one. The rise of the department store in the 1870s, for example, could hardly have preceded the invention of the sewing machine in 1844.

The industrial revolution substituted interchangeable parts for hand-tooled components, the energy of coal for that of wood and water, and machine mass production for human and animal labor. And the revolution was not confined to manufacturing. The simultaneous mechanization of agriculture proceeded so rapidly that it freed large numbers of workers for the burgeoning industrial system. One American farm worker produced sufficient food for 4.0 persons in 1830, 9.8 in 1930, and 47.1 in 1970. Given the thoroughgoing federal system of support for agriculture, this evolution represents still another dynamic of our history relevant to modern debates over industrial policy.[19]

Even as workers fled the farm for the factory, investment in machines was multiplying rapidly. In manufacturing, capital invested per worker grew from $700 in 1869 to $2,000 in 1899; and total capital invested in manufacturing grew from $2.7 billion in 1879 to $8.2 billion in 1899 and to $20.8 billion in 1914. Whereas 33 percent of value added in commodity production was in manufacturing and 53 percent in agriculture in 1869, these numbers were exactly reversed by 1899. The industrial revolution, then, was primarily a revolution in production.[20]

This exploding production was accompanied by sharply declining prices. The wholesale price index in America, which stood at 193 in 1864, dropped to 68 by 1896, even though real per capita GNP rose during the same period by about 30 percent. The single statistic most revealing about what was happening to the economy, however, is the remarkable growth of total factor productivity. The best estimates suggest that annual increases in productivity, which had held steady at about 0.3 percent for most of the nineteenth century, began to rise very rapidly as the twentieth century approached. So dramatic was the spurt that the figure for 1889–1919 reached nearly *six times* the rate that had prevailed for 1800–1889.[21] With rising productivity came overcapacity, not only in the United States but throughout the industrialized world, as reflected in the worldwide price declines of the period. Among business executives in every developed country, the initial response was to combine in agreements to limit the total output of their plants, maintain the price levels of their goods, and discourage the entry of new companies into their industries.

In Europe, this inclination to combine in self-defense against overcapacity had different results from those in the United States. Europeans generally accepted business combinations more readily than did Americans. Price and production cartels, set up in every country to meet the overcapacity problem, usually enjoyed the official sanction of the state. The law was actually on the side of cartels, and the police power could be used to enforce contractual articles of cartelization against rebellious price cutters desperate to service the high fixed costs typical of mechanized production. In Europe, where large public bureaucracies had long been in place, and where government had always taken a strong hand in business affairs, industrial overcapacity represented simply another new problem for a mature state to help manage. In fact, the official sanctioning of cartels was one convenient way for the state to keep peace both within troubled industries and among the major sectors of the economy. The rise and success of such combinations in manufacturing, transportation, wholesaling, and retailing tended to soften and stabilize the industrialization process in Europe by protecting the prior vested interests of individual firms. Direct harm to particular companies was minimized. In the European setting, antitrust represented an unfamiliar American ideology, hostile to the cartelizations that formed the bedrock European response to the overcapacity problem.[22]

In America, meanwhile, antitrust flourished. Though the Sherman Act did not become law until 1890, forms of antitrust sentiment had appeared as early as colonial times. Opposition to European-style royal monopolies awarded to court favorites such as the East India Company had helped to define the distinctive American approach to economic policy making. Later on, the antimonopoly political parties of the 1870s promoted such causes as currency inflation and tariff cuts. And the common law in America, even more than its English parent, looked askance at cartel-like business arrangements "in restraint of trade."[23]

True enough, the initial American response to overcapacity took more or less the same form it was taking in Europe. American business managers energetically combined with each other in loose cartels designed to limit production, maintain prices, and divide markets so that all could prosper. The difference was that they seldom succeeded. The common law and national culture were so deeply opposed to monopoly that American courts refused to enforce cartel arrangements against recalcitrant members who slashed prices. In 1890 the Sherman Antitrust Act formalized the common law's hostility to cartels, and, despite the indifference of the first attorneys general who dealt with it, the act was to have a significant and in part unanticipated impact.

Antitrust activity began slowly, with only 22 cases being entered by the Department of Justice during the period 1890–1905. Between 1905 and the 1930s, however, about 300 cases were brought. By the time of the New Deal, antitrust activity had become institutionalized on a large scale. Whereas only five lawyers had worked in the Antitrust Division during Theodore Roosevelt's administration, several hundred worked there after Franklin D. Roosevelt's. Both Republican and Democratic administrations pursued antitrust as a matter of routine. Moreover, the Justice Department not only instituted large numbers of cases; it also won a high proportion of them—more than 80 percent. This high percentage of victory is significant in understanding why certain cases and not others were chosen for prosecution and also what the department was trying to do in its overall antitrust program. It seems likely that the lawyers in the Antitrust Division most often chose candidates for prosecution not on the basis of a coherent economic philosophy but rather on the basis of what cases could be won. Like most lawyers, they did not like to lose, and they chose their cases accordingly.[24]

Given this general pattern of enforcement, together with the victory rate of more than 80 percent, the next question that occurs to the historian is, Who were the targets of antitrust enforcement? Which types of companies were prosecuted? Here the answer is very surprising; for, despite the prominence of early "big cases" against Standard Oil and American Tobacco, by far the majority of all Justice Department antitrust prosecutions, and an even larger percentage of Federal Trade Commission cases, were brought not against big businesses but against associations of small businesses. As best I can determine by a preliminary count, about 6 out of every 7 of the 300-odd antitrust cases instituted in the years before the New Deal were brought against small companies or their associations. Perennial targets of antitrust enforcers included companies located in such decentralized industries as lumber and wood, agricultural production, building materials, and retail trade.[25]

The implications of this surprising identity of antitrust targets will be explored later in this chapter. First, however, a brief comment about the problems of categorizing companies and industries is in order. Ever since I realized that antitrust prosecutions did indeed hit small firms harder than large ones, I have searched for a way of distinguishing between companies in a more precise manner than simply "large" versus "small." Here several academic disciplines can provide help. In history, easily the most important work has been that of Alfred D. Chandler, Jr., and I am deeply indebted to his pioneering efforts. Among many other contributions that Chandler has made, he has come close to propounding a historical theory of oligopoly, and his work has already influenced several disciplines besides history, just as he himself has drawn on those disciplines for his own benefit.[26] In economics, the large literature on perfect competition, oligopoly, and monopoly has been very useful both to Chandler and to me.[27] And in political science and sociology, several scholars have begun to classify types of business enterprise as a means of classifying labor markets.[28]

The most useful typology I have come across in disciplines other than history is the so-called dual economy. This approach relies on a distinction between "core" or "center" firms and industries on the one hand, and "peripheral" firms and industries on the other. The dual economy model has been used extensively by sociologists and political scientists, and a little less so by economists, who apparently remain suspicious of its incompatibility with the paradigm of perfect competition.[29]

Center firms and industries, on one hand, tended to have a set of common characteristics. All were capital intensive, requiring large outlays of investment. All were technologically advanced, with their production facilities dominated either by continuous process production (in such companies as American Sugar Refining, United States Steel, and Standard Oil) or by some combination of large-batch production with machine mass production (Quaker Oats, Pillsbury Flour, Singer Sewing Machine, American Tobacco, International Harvester). All center firms enjoyed some significant scale economy in the production or packaging process, and all were vertically integrated. Center firms also adopted a long-range perspective in planning for the future. Because of the enormous investments they required, long-term survival was a far more important goal for them than was short-term profit. Several center firms engaged in organized research for the development of new products. To manage their many internal functions, they developed complex managerial hierarchies.

Peripheral firms and industries, on the other hand, were small, labor intensive, managerially thin, and benefit of scale economies. Concerned primarily for short-run survival, they looked more to this year's profits than to five-year plans. Peripheral industries included furniture, leather goods, clothing, building materials, hotels, and food service. The distinction between center and peripheral is not perfect, but the two terms may be considered as the polar ends of a spectrum: pronounced differences are evident from one end of the spectrum to the other, but the differences become less dramatic toward the middle.

Common sense would suggest that antitrust prosecutions focused on center firms, but this is not what happened. To repeat, about six of every seven cases brought by the Department of Justice between 1890 and 1932 were directed against companies in industries best characterized as peripheral. Why was this so? And what is the relevance to industrial policy?

Why was convicting small companies easier than convicting large ones? Was it that large firms could afford to hire better lawyers? Perhaps so, but a more important reason was that the price-fixing and market-dividing activities of small businesses—their only avenues to protection from domestic competition—were easy to detect and, being per se violations of the antitrust laws, easy to use as the basis for prosecution. Conversely, the much more subtle and long-term activities of giant firms were harder to detect, and, once understood, were found not necessarily in violation of the law. To understand these differences fully, we must inquire into the reasons the two categories of companies themselves behaved in the way they did: why small companies in certain industries habitually engaged in illegal activities and why large companies, which materialized in distinctly different industries, often did not have to do so to show healthy profits.

The first thing to get straight is the different forms of combination and association that both types of companies tended to form and to specify what period we are discussing. I want to focus on the first two generations of the rise of center firms, which ran from approximately 1875 to 1920, and to explore three different types of combination.

The first type was horizontal combination of the loose variety, as when all shoe manufacturers around some shoe center such as Boston or St. Louis agreed not to sell their products below a certain minimum price. Scores of small companies were involved, and all retained their individual ownership, identity, and management. Price and production quotas were set by an industry committee, and information was freely exchanged. Those companies that broke the agreements could not be easily punished under this system, however, and that turned out to be its primary drawback.[30]

A second form of combination was also horizontal: in this case, a tight combination—so tight as to be called horizontal integration. This kind of association materialized when all of, say, the cigarette manufacturing companies in a certain state or region decided to merge into one large company. Each constituent firm gave up its independence in exchange for a share in the new giant company. This pattern was just the kind that developed with the American Tobacco Company under James B. Duke and with the Standard Oil Company under John D. Rockefeller—horizontal integration into a giant company that then dominated the industry.

The third type of combination was not horizontal—all the companies being in the same line of business—but was vertical. An oil refiner, for example, might integrate forward into transportation and marketing, and integrate backward into crude oil exploration and production. Even today, such firms as Exxon, Mobil, and Shell are called fully integrated oil companies because they do everything from exploration and production on one end to retail marketing through franchised service stations on the other.[31]

Since combinations of all three types became extremely common in the early years of industrialization in America, the following questions arise: Why did combination happen when it did? Why were companies so anxious to combine with each other? And why did some industries take one form of combination and other industries another? One answer is simply that all the companies wanted to make excess profits. The historical record suggests, however, that the initial motives behind horizontal combination were primarily defensive; they had more to do with simple survival than with the reaping of monopoly profits. Usually, in going into loose horizontal agreements with each other, the companies in a given industry were trying to escape the intractable problem of overcapacity.[32] If the producers in an industry could agree with each other to control prices, and perhaps restrict output, then they could all survive simply by dividing up the market. Certainly most of them would rather divide the market than actually merge into a giant horizontal integration. They preferred a loose combination because it would permit them to retain their firm's individual identity as a business and their own positions as owners and high-ranking executives.

If American law had encouraged loose combinations in the form of price and production cartels, that might have been practically the end of the story, at least in the short to medium term. American business history during this period might have been a story of loose associations involving large numbers of cigarette companies, oil companies, steel, aluminum, chemical, and perhaps even automobile companies. Instead, of course, each of these industries became dominated by only a few companies. One important reason for this was that in America, the law prevented the smooth working of loose price and production cartels, because the law prohibited price fixing, monopolization, and any other "restraint of trade." Even before passage of the Sherman Act in 1890, state legislation and the common law discouraged the smooth working of cartel agreements by preventing their effective enforcement. If a member of the cartel wanted to violate the agreement by cutting prices, then the law would not prevent his doing so, as it would in Europe.[33]

47

In America, many business managers, denied their preferred route to security through loose horizontal combination, next chose tight combination. They merged with each other, and hence the creation of all those familiar company names expressing the principle of combination in the very language of the title: so many "amalgamateds" and "consolidateds"; so many "Generals"—as in General Motors, General Foods, General Mills; so many words expressing a national organization—as in National Biscuit, United States Steel, United States Rubber, American Tobacco, American Can.

I want to emphasize here the extremely important fact that not all tight horizontal combinations worked well. Many, many such ambitious mergers failed. Who remembers National Cordage, for example? National Starch? American Cattle? American Wallpaper? United States Leather? Standard Rope and Twine? All of these were thought at the time of their creation to be viable big businesses, right along with American Tobacco, United States Steel, and Standard Oil. But all failed as tight horizontal mergers. Why?

I think the answer is that almost all of the failed giant mergers occurred in peripheral industries, just as nearly all the successful ones were in center industries. Thus reasons for success and failure along this one dimension had much to do with the inherent characteristics of the industries involved—their capital intensity, potential for scale economy, suitability for vertical integration—and practically nothing to do with the individual skills of business managers. Because the executives of that period lacked the conceptual apparatus developed later on, nothing except trial and error would show them why it was unwise to merge a series of peripheral firms into one giant company.

Later in this chapter I will return to this point about successes and failures under tight horizontal combination and relate those experiences to our earlier questions about antitrust enforcement. First, however, I want to say a bit about the third form of combination—vertical integration. Now, the successfully merged center firms, once they were in operation, felt powerful urges to take care of other aspects of their businesses. If, for example, the company specialized in oil refining, it now had such huge investments wrapped up in its refineries that it was at great risk if its crude oil suppliers decided to raise the price or if some transportation bottleneck into or out of the refineries occurred. Hence the new company of merged refiners might decide to invest heavily in both crude oil supply and in transportation facilities—might buy into the Texas oil fields, might build its own pipelines. Of course, my example is not a hypothetical one, for this is just what Standard Oil did, and just what Gulf, Texaco, and the others did a little later.

Overall, what is striking for the historian about the oil, steel, tobacco, and other center firms that underwent the two-stage integration process between about 1875 and 1920—that is, tight horizontal integration followed by systematic vertical integration in which they combined mass production with mass marketing—is how long they have survived and prospered. If we compare the identity of the largest 200 companies in America in 1917, and then the largest 200 in 1973, we discover some remarkable similarities. Many are the same companies, and the configuration of these companies within their industries also persists over the same period. The following list gives some further breakdown of these industries and companies—the largest 200 measured in assets:[35]

• In 1917, 22 of the largest 200 companies were in the petroleum business. In 1973, 22 of the largest 200 were still in petroleum. For the most part, they were the same 22.

• In 1917, 5 of the largest 200 companies were in the rubber business. In 1973, 5 of the largest 200 were still in rubber. Four of these five were the same (Goodyear, Goodrich, Firestone, and Uniroyal). The fifth, Fisk, merged with Uniroyal—then called United States Rubber—in 1939.

• In 1917, 20 of the largest 200 companies were in the machinery business. In 1973, 18 of the largest 200 were still in machinery. For the most part, they were the same companies.

• In 1917, 30 of the largest 200 companies were in the food products business. In 1973, 22 of the largest 200 were still in food products, and several other food companies remained in the top 200 as parts of conglomerates.

• In 1917, 26 of the largest 200 companies were in the transportation equipment business. In 1973, 20 were still in transportation equipment (down, partly as a result of mergers, from 26 in 1948).[34]

What, if anything, does all this have to do with antitrust and industrial policy? Over the very long term—75–100 years—perhaps little. I say that not because the companies described above have done so well for so long, but because a similar experience has been typical of industrial capitalism elsewhere. In most other market economies, whether it be Japan, Germany, France, Britain, Italy, Canada, or whatever, the large industrial enterprise—the center firm—has tended to arise in the same kinds of industries as was the case in the United States. The following data show this remarkable similarity, as to industry location, between the American and foreign experiences with very large companies. Here the category of company is a little different from that in the previous list. The largest companies here are identified as those with 20,000 or more employees each, and the two columns denote the number of companies headquartered inside and outside the United States. Approximately one-half of the total of 379 were American firms, and half were foreign.[35]

	U.S. (192 companies)	*Abroad* (187 companies)
Center Industries		
Transportation equipment	22	23
Electrical machinery	20	25

	U.S. (192 companies)	Abroad (187 companies)
Stone, clay, and glass	7	8
Tobacco	3	4
Chemicals	24	28
Rubber	5	5
Petroleum	14	12
Peripheral Industries		
Furniture	0	0
Printing	0	0

The striking similarities between industrial experience in the United States and in other market economies suggest strongly that the economic and technological characteristics of certain industries encourage them to assume either a center or peripheral configuration and to maintain that configuration over a long time. These characteristics seem much more important than differences in legal systems or national cultures; they appear almost to determine the relative size and organizational structure of firms within the industries represented. Although I am disinclined to accept such a historical determinism, these similarities are so dramatic that we should consider the possibility that one thing is causing the other. Surely these similarities are of surpassing importance to anyone interested in assessing the historical record of big business in the United States, a record that includes all attempts to regulate monopolistic trusts.

Am I saying here that antitrust did not matter in America, that because our own experience over the long run was so similar to that of other major market economies that our crusades for antitrust made no difference? Only in part. For the pace of change, and therefore the short-to medium-term advantage one country's companies enjoyed over another country's, was not the same here and abroad. In the short run, and probably over the long run as well, antitrust enforcement actually helped the American economy, in ways partly unintended by the original proponents of antitrust.

Here what I am suggesting is a bit speculative. The argument indeed may be empirically untestable, and I want to advance it only as a series of hypotheses:

First, because antitrust policy both before and especially after the Sherman Act prohibited price fixing as a per se violation of the law, loose horizontal combinations could not work in America the same way as in Europe. Thus business managers, if they wanted to protect themselves against overcapacity, had a much stronger incentive to take the next step; that is, to merge with each other and form very large companies.

Second, when they did form these large companies, their strategies then looked to "rationalize" their production processes by shutting down their least efficient plants. (Here, incidentally, the historical record is clear; a lot of evidence exists to show that they did in fact rationalize.)[36] When they did, their overall costs of production fell, and the prices of their products to consumers also declined. This is the first way in which antitrust benefited the consumer even though it promoted bigness.[37]

Third, companies that engaged in successful horizontal combination then usually took the next step and integrated vertically. They did this primarily to protect their large investments against an interruption in the supply of raw materials, a sudden transportation bottleneck, or some other problem. Their chief operating goal was to keep their most efficient plants running full and steady. The bigger the investment represented by the newly merged companies, the bigger the incentive to integrate vertically and protect that investment. Now, for consumer welfare the point is that vertical integration nearly always resulted in lower costs to the company because it meant that every part of the operation could be matched, organizationally, to every other part. The flow of production could then proceed smoothly, without interruption, around the clock if necessary; and what business executives later called the experience curve would then produce progressively lower costs.[38]

The pattern I have sketched, it should be emphasized, worked only in those industries that were core or center in their underlying character. It did not work for peripheral firms, even though large numbers of them tried it, as I mentioned earlier with respect to American Wallpaper, National Cordage, National Salt, and the rest. Where it did work, however, it worked marvelously well. It persisted over a long time, and it helped to give the American economy an early lead on its competitors in other countries. Those countries did not have antitrust laws, and to that extent they lacked the early incentive to push forward the kinds of organizational innovations I have sketched.

This story says little so far, of course, about the recent triumphs of Japanese enterprise compared with American, or how antitrust might have become a handicap once the rest of the world caught up with American industry. Here, then, I want to compare and contrast the American experience under antitrust with the German and Japanese experiments with deliberate and very specific types of cartelization. Before doing that, however, I want to make one final comment on the gravity of the overcapacity problem in the early years of industrialization. A measure of the intractable nature of the problem is that business executives in America were willing to endure an entire generation of political upheaval in order to secure their meliorating structures in the form of large horizontally and vertically integrated center firms. The antibigness rhetoric typical of the two decades spanning the turn of the twentieth century made the trust question easily the leading political issue of the day in America, as the populist movement and the careers of William

Jennings Bryan, Robert M. La Follette, Theodore Roosevelt, and Woodrow Wilson all remind us. By contrast, the most prominent European politicians of this period—Otto von Bismarck, Georges Clemenceau, David Lloyd George —had no reputation as trustbusters anxious to break up large business enterprises.

In countries where cartel behavior could be legally enforced, the general phenomenon of tight horizontal integration followed by rationalization and then by substantial vertical integration came either in a different form or much more slowly than it did in the United States. Thus, on the one hand, these countries never experienced quite the high degree of political disruption characteristic of the trust movement in the United States. On the other hand, the immense productive efficiencies available from rationalization and vertical integration did not materialize as generally or as early as they did in the United States. Very likely, these organizational factors help to explain the unparalleled success of American business, first in the United States and later in world markets.

The Industrial Experience of Germany and Japan

The experience of these two principal losers in World War II and two conspicuous champions of the postwar world economy would seem to cast doubt on the foregoing argument. As we know, both Germany and Japan have long encouraged industrial cartels of one sort or another, just as, unlike the United States, they have integrated their major banks into industrial planning. How, in the absence of an American-style antitrust tradition, did organizational efficiencies develop in Germany and Japan? How did price-and-production cartels play a role in their economic miracles, contrary to the teachings of neoclassical economic theory?

One part of the answer, oddly enough, is that they did it in much the same way as the Americans did: through large, horizontally and vertically integrated, extremely cost-efficient companies. In the case of Germany and to a lesser extent Japan, such companies first appeared in the late nineteenth century, in different forms from that of the U.S. center firms but at about the same time. The German and Japanese economic miracles of the post–World War II generation had roots far back in the business history of each country. And in both periods—the late nineteenth century and the post–World War II era, both Germany and Japan had a coherent, well-coordinated industrial policy.

The common elements of the two countries' industrial organization are somewhat obscured by a profusion of other important factors in their post–World War II economic miracles: the deep and advantageous currency devaluations in both countries, American aid in the Marshall Plan for Europe and the Korean War expenditures that benefited Japan, the emergence of the

52

European Economic Community and its powerful stimulus to German industry, and the often decisive role of the Japanese economic ministries in promoting dynamic industries while denying resources to old ones. The organizational commonalities between German and Japanese industry remain striking, however, and on close examination a few of these same characteristics apply also to the United States during the forty years spanning the turn of the twentieth century. In the remainder of this article I will focus on two of these organizational and strategic commonalities: vertical integration and the role of the home market in a strategy of import substitution and export promotion.

The United States, 1880–1920. At the time the organizational revolution was going forward, circumstances within the American market were working further advantages to the kinds of companies that followed a strategy of merger and subsequent vertical integration. In the first place, the American market had already become the largest in the world, which meant that a given scale economy might be more advantageous in the United States than anywhere else. Second, the American market was not only large but for the most part was highly protected. As noted earlier, the actual effects of this protection remain controversial, but the fact of protection is beyond dispute. Thus in significant measure the modern American industrial plant sprouted and grew to maturity behind high tariff walls. Although in economic theory high tariffs are supposed to discourage innovation and efficiency, these effects appear to have been minimized by the presence of competitive firms operating within the giant home market. Also, in still another case of unanticipated consequences, high tariffs stimulated additional vertical integration because they raised the price of industrial inputs. If a steelmaker located on the Atlantic Coast had to pay a protected market price for pig iron or coking coal from Western Pennsylvania, rather than importing it cheaply by ship from Canada, he would be more likely to integrate backward and acquire these inputs at their unprotected cost.

Germany, 1885–1915. Modern industrial cartels appeared in Germany in the 1870s, about the same time and for the same reason they appeared in the United States. Whereas the law struck them down in America, they persisted in Germany. Articles of cartelization were treated as legally enforceable contracts, and in this sense the state stood behind the practice. In many cartelized industries, the net result was industrial peace among competitors and persistent high prices to consumers. In others, however—those industries that in the United States produced such giant companies as United States Steel, General Electric, and Du Pont—the results varied from one industry to the next, and the overall effects are not easily summarized. In one important industry, steel, something like the following sequence occurred: (1) The

German government, like the American, erected high tariff barriers to protect the home market from foreign competition. (2) The cartels, protected under German law and sometimes promoted by powerful German banks, coordinated the activities of their member firms, often forming syndicates for the common purchase of raw materials and the joint marketing of products. (3) The system of cartels, combined with the protective tariff, created a situation in which German manufacturers could use protected prices in the home market as an umbrella under which they could service their large fixed costs, meanwhile selling aggressively abroad at or below unprotected world prices. That is, they could prosper at home, use the experience of constant operation of their plants to reduce production costs, and incorporate new technology as soon as it came on stream, while simultaneously dumping or selling at marginal costs abroad. In this way they could systematically increase their share of world markets, often at the expense of the free-trade-oriented British producers. Recent research has found that "in ten of the years between 1876 and 1896 the average cost *(Selbkosten)* of [steel] rails from the Krupp firm exceeded the average export price, the world price with which the British had to contend. The domestic price, on the other hand, always exceeded average cost by over ten marks per ton."[39]

In this peculiar way, then, the efficiency of the German steel industry seems to have been enhanced by the coordination of two policies, protection and cartelization, which are supposed to yield inefficiency. Much as in the American experience under antitrust, the actual results of the policies could not be deduced solely from the principles of economic theory but had to be observed empirically.

Japan since World War II. The dimensions of the Japanese economic miracle are well known. Here I will only emphasize that between 1952, when the American occupation ended, and 1971, when the first raw material supply shocks began, Japan's real gross national product grew at a compound annual rate of 10.2 percent, a record never matched before or since for such a large industrialized economy. Total real growth of GNP during this period was 469 percent for Japan, 193 percent for West Germany, 165 percent for France, 89 percent for the United States, and 73 percent for the United Kingdom.[40]

For the argument here, my central concern is the way in which the Japanese organized their business strategy to pursue miracle growth. Over the retrospective of almost thirty years, it is now clear that, despite important differences, a major part of the strategy resembled the earlier German system for steel. The Japanese strategy, however, went far beyond one industry and applied to a large part of the entire economy.[41]

The Japanese government thoroughly protected the home market through a complex mixture of tariffs and nontariff barriers, including quotas, deposit requirements, inspections, complex distribution channels, and extraordinary tight constraints on American and European multinationals operating in Japan. Being resource poor, Japan naturally was compelled to import large stores of raw materials; but Japanese companies then manufactured or processed a large proportion of these materials for reexport. As a matter of policy, Japanese business managers and government bureaucrats held the importation of manufactured goods for domestic consumption to a minimum seldom matched in the modern world.

Japan permitted and often encouraged the formation of industrial cartels, much as Germany had done in the earlier period. These cartels, guided by the government, by large Japanese banks, and by the industry groups themselves, protected Japanese firms from overcapacity and excessive price competition, facilitated their members' movement toward vertical integration, and insured participating firms against risk in the making of big, forward-looking investments.

Again in a manner strikingly reminiscent of the German steel experience during the late nineteenth century, Japan's combined strategy of closing the home market and encouraging cost-efficient cartels led to a situation in which Japanese companies, building on the organizational legacies of the pre-war *zaibatsu*, could use the large Japanese home market to service their fixed costs while they sold abroad at attractive prices. Like the German steel manufacturers earlier, Japanese managers in many different industries prospered at home, sold at marginal cost or dumped abroad, and used the experience gained through the constant employment of their factories to drive their cost curves perpetually downward.

What are the lessons of these speculations? Here the historian must become wary. Like most of my professional colleagues, I am reluctant to draw broad, present-day implications from the past. The only true lesson of history, someone once said, is that there are none. I do not believe it can be shown from historical evidence that tariffs, internal improvements, or antitrust laws are always either effective or ineffective in promoting economic growth. The result always depends on the context. What the historical record does show is that such policies are not necessarily inconsistent with high economic performance.

The other generalization suggested by the examples cited is that a successful industrial policy may require the presence, somewhere, of a large export market. In the case of the early German steel industry, a substantial part of that market was in Eastern Europe, with smaller parts in Latin America and free trade Britain, which imported low-priced German products to the eventual injury of the British iron and steel industry.

For American manufacturers, the most important free trade area was the enormous home market of the United States, defined by the Constitution as immune from internal customs duties. (The Founding Fathers took fourteen years, from 1775 to 1789, to abolish interstate tariffs. The architects of the

European Economic Community, who were trying to do the same thing, took about the same length of time.) For nineteenth-century America, the principal exports were agricultural or extractive, and the cost advantages were immense: cotton to British and French factories, grain to Europe and Latin America, petroleum products to the world.

Most recently, for post–World War II Japan, the crucial areas have been the protected home market in combination with exports to the United States and other wealthy countries. The American market in particular, as we know, has absorbed such colossal quantities of Japanese steel, automobiles, motorcycles, television sets, and recorders that American domestic manufacturers —however efficient or inefficient, the point is not at issue here—have suffered loss of market share and in that sense have suffered injury.

Meanwhile, in all three cases—Germany at the turn of the twentieth century, the United States before the 1930s, and Japan after World War II—the home markets remained closed to equal competition. In the earlier period, Germany imported practically no iron and steel from Britain and the United States, its major competitors. Similarly, postwar Japan imported very few manufactured goods from Europe or America, irrespective of price and quality. Japan freely imported only food, industrial raw materials, and technology.

Thus, in all three examples, the situation was one of a closed system exploiting open ones. In each case, the protected home market was employed to service the large fixed costs of capital-intensive industries, thereby making possible the charging of low prices in the export market. Assuming that the open market remained open and the closed one closed, it was a strategy that could not possibly fail, so long as comparative productivity remained high. Of the three examples, Japan has employed the strategy most deliberately, systematically, and successfully. Indeed, this very success, measured in the extraordinary growth of Japanese market share of world exports, represents the fundamental reason that free-trade advocates inside Japan together with outside negotiators from the United States are having such difficulty forcing a change in Japanese trade practices. No country wants to jettison a strategy that has served it so well for so long.

One final suggestion from our own history: Coordinated industrial policy has always been a hard sell in the United States. Each of the American policies discussed in this chapter—tariffs, internal improvements, the American System, antitrust—developed in a piecemeal manner. Each emerged as an ad hoc, catch-as-catch-can measure. None evolved in systematic, planned fashion. Given the underlying nature of the American political economy, the story could hardly have been otherwise. Except in time of war, our system has never lent itself to coherent state direction. Only palpable external threats have overcome the nation's powerful commitment to individual freedom of choice. For any economy, industrial policy tends to diminish such freedom and to increase coercion; and Americans have accepted extensive coercion only in the face of an enemy. Without such an enemy, without a scapegoat on which to blame the need for more coercion, no coordinated and thoroughgoing industrial policy is likely to materialize in the United States.

This is by no means a prediction that it cannot happen. One can easily imagine that given a sufficiently severe recession, that the United States could turn Japan into the required scapegoat. For one thing, the Japanese miracle has given us our most vivid example of a successful industrial policy. Other attempts, such as that of the French, have not been nearly so effective. The Japanese miracle remains the image that advocates of industrial policy habitually invoke, and the image has now reached mythological proportions. In addition, the Japanese are widely viewed as the chief threat to continued prosperity, including the maintenance of millions of jobs, in important American industries. It may not be too much to say that the conspicuous flooding of the American market by high-quality Japanese products underlies the entire industrial policy debate. If Japan did not exist, the debate would likely collapse.

Viewed against the broad background of history, the Japanese example emerges as a remarkably sophisticated variety of twentieth-century mercantilism. What the Japanese have done in the years since 1945 is not appreciably different from the orthodox mercantilist prescriptions of the seventeenth century. Only in the lessened emphasis on the accumulation of precious metals, in Japan's eschewing of military power, and in the abandonment of the underlying assumption of zero-sum wealth do the differences matter. In other respects, the parallel holds. That circumstance in turn suggests some troubling thoughts about the underlying nature of industrial policy: that it is inescapably a form of economic nationalism; that there are practical and ethical problems of country-to-country competition conducted under two sets of conflicting rules; and that the United States faces the terribly difficult dilemma of preserving the post-World War II regime of free trade while simultaneously looking after the interests of the American people.[42]

Notes

1. Robert B. Reich, "Small State, Big Lesson," *Boston Observer,* vol. 3 (July 1984), p. 32.

2. James M. Swank, *The Industrial Policies of Great Britain and the United States* (Philadelphia: American Iron and Steel Association, 1876).

3. The classic study of mercantilism remains Eli F. Heckscher, *Mercantilism,* rev. ed., 2 vols. (New York: Macmillan, 1955). An excellent summary of the history of the idea may be found in Jacob Viner, "Mercantilist Thought," *International Encyclopedia of the Social Sciences* (New York: Macmillan, 1968), pp. 435–43.

4. Viner, "Mercantilist Thought," pp. 441–42.

5. This point is strenuously argued in Oliver M. Dickerson, *The Navigation Acts and the American Revolution* (Philadelphia: University of Pennsylvania Press, 1951). For full analyses of the entire subject, see Bernard Bailyn, *Ideological Origins of the American Revolution* (Cambridge: Harvard University Press, 1967); and Gordon S. Wood, *Creation of the American Republic, 1776–1787* (Chapel Hill: University of North Carolina Press, 1969).

6. Hamilton's *Report* is excerpted in William Letwin, ed., *A Documentary History of American Economic Policy since 1789* (New York: Norton, 1972). pp. 5–26.

7. Ibid., pp. 18–19.

8. For an intriguing but ultimately unconvincing argument that American policy was indeed mercantilistic, see William Appleman Williams, "The Age of Mercantilism: An Interpretation of the American Political Economy, 1763 to 1828," *William and Mary Quarterly*, 1958.

9. Quoted in Jacob Viner, *Dumping: A Problem in International Trade* (Chicago: University of Chicago Press, 1923), p. 38.

10. One historian has recently commented that "In terms of passions aroused, revenue generated, and industries affected, the tariff was the most important economic policy of the nineteenth-century federal government"; see J. J. Pincus, "Tariffs," in Glenn Porter, ed., *Encyclopedia of American Economic History* (New York: Scribner's, 1980), p. 439. See also A. W. Coats, "Economic Thought," in ibid., p. 469. On the tariff generally, see F. W. Taussig, *The Tariff History of the United States*, eighth ed. (New York: Putnam's Sons, 1930); Edward Stanwood, *American Tariff Controversies of the Nineteenth Century* (Boston: Houghton Mifflin, 1903), two vols.; and Sidney Ratner, *The Tariff in American History* (New York: Van Nostrand, 1972).

11. The quotation from F. W. Taussig, ed., *State Papers and Speeches on the Tariff* (Cambridge: Harvard University Press, 1892), p. 275; the other quotations are from George B. Curtiss, *The Industrial Development of Nations and a History of the Tariff Policies of the United States, and of Great Britain, Germany, France, Russia and Other European Countries*, vols. 2 and 3 (Binghamton, N.Y.: Curtiss, 1912).

12. Ratner notes this shift in *The Tariff in American History*, p. 82.

13. Compare, for example, Paul A. David, *Technical Choice, Innovation and Economic Growth: Essays on American and British Experience in the Nineteenth Century* (Cambridge: Cambridge University Press, 1975), with Robert W. Fogel and Stanley L. Engerman, "A Model for the Explanation of Industrial Expansion during the Nineteenth Century: With an Application to the American Iron Industry," *Journal of Political Economy*, vol. 77 (1969).

14. John A. James, "The Welfare Effects of the Antebellum Tariff: A General Equilibrium Analysis," *Explorations in Economic History*, vol. 15 (1978); Jeffrey G. Williamson, "Watersheds and Turning Points: Conjectures on the Long-Term Impact of Civil-War Financing," *Journal of Economic History*, vol. 34 (1974).

15. G. R. Hawke, "The United States Tariff and Industrial Protection in the Late Nineteenth Century," *Economic History Review*, vol. 28 (1975). An excellent analysis of political pressures for export promotion (which came far more from troubled traditional industries than from new infant manufacturers) is William H. Becker, *The Dynamics of Business-Government Relations: Industry and Exports, 1893–1921* (Chicago: University of Chicago Press, 1982).

16. Quoted in Taussig, ed., *State Papers and Speeches on the Tariff*, pp. 258, 265.

17. See Robert S. Henry, "The Railroad Land Grant Legend in American History Texts," *Mississippi Valley Historical Review,* vol. 32 (1945); and the numerous rejoinders to this article in ibid., vol. 33 (1946).

18. The quoted historian is Robert A. Lively, "The American System: A Review Article," *Business History Review,* vol. 29 (1955), p. 32. See also James Willard Hurst, *Law and the Conditions of Freedom in the Nineteenth Century United States* (Madison: University of Wisconsin Press, 1956); Oscar and Mary F. Handlin, "Origins of the American Business Corporation," *Journal of Economic History,* vol. 5 (1945); Carter Goodrich, "Internal Improvements Reconsidered," *Journal of Economic History,* vol. 30 (1970); Louis Bernard Schmidt, "Internal Commerce and the Development of National Economy before 1860," *Journal of Political Economy,* vol. 47 (1939); Guy S. Callender, "The Early Transportation and Banking Enterprises of the States in Relation to the Growth of Corporations," *Quarterly Journal of Economics,* vol. 17 (1902); Ronald E. Shaw, *Erie Water West: A History of the Erie Canal, 1792–1854* (Lexington: University of Kentucky Press, 1966); Harry N. Scheiber, *Ohio Canal Era: A Case Study of Government and the Economy, 1820–1861* (Athens: Ohio University Press, 1969); Albert Fishlow, *American Railroads and the Transformation of the Ante-Bellum Economy* (Cambridge: Harvard University Press, 1965).

The contemporary battle for investments has produced some innovative measures. In addition to traditional state offices designed to attract domestic industries, nearly two dozen states employ representatives in Japan whose job it is to attract foreign direct investment. Many states have gone to elaborate lengths to give tax incentives for both domestic and foreign industries. For a recent analysis of such investments in five southern states, see Cedric L. Suzman, ed., *The Costs and Benefits of Foreign Investment from a State Perspective* (Washington, D.C.: Commerce Department, 1982).

19. *Historical Statistics of the United States from Colonial Times to the Present* (Washington: Government Printing Office, 1975), pp. 467, 468, 498; Wayne D. Rasmussen, "Agriculture," in Porter, ed., *Encyclopedia of American Economic History,* pp. 344–60.

20. Paul Uselding, "Manufacturing," in Porter, ed., *Encyclopedia of American Economic History,* pp. 409–11. Figures for capital per worker are in constant dollars, and for total capital invested in current dollars.

21. Ibid. See also *Historical Statistics of the United States,* pp. 200–201; and John W. Kendrick, "Productivity," in Porter, ed., *Encyclopedia of American Economic History,* pp. 157–66.

22. The overcapacity issue is ably treated throughout Naomi Raboy Lamoreaux, "Industrial Organization and Market Behavior: The Great Merger Movement in American Industry," unpublished Ph.D. dissertation (History), Johns Hopkins University, 1979. On the European experience, see the following essays, all in Norbert Horn and Jurgen Kocka, eds., *Law and the Formation of the Big Enterprises in the 19th and Early 20th Centuries* (Gottingen, West Germany: Vandenhoeck & Ruprecht, 1979): William R. Cornish, "Legal Control over Cartels and Monopolization 1880–1914. A Comparison," pp. 280–303; Leslie Hannah, "Mergers, Cartels, and Concentration: Legal Factors in the U.S. and European Experience," pp. 306–14; and Morton Keller, "Public Policy and Large Enterprise. Comparative Historical Perspectives," pp. 515–31.

23. Arthur P. Dudden, "Antimonopolism, 1865–1890," unpublished Ph.D. dissertation (History), University of Michigan, 1950; Hans B. Thorelli, *The Federal Antitrust Policy: Origination of an American Tradition* (Baltimore: Johns Hopkins Press, 1955); James Morison Russell, "Business and the Sherman Act, 1890–1914," unpublished Ph.D. dissertation (History), University of Iowa, 1966; Peter Hamilton Crawford, "Business Proposals for Government Regulation of Monopoly, 1887–1914," unpublished Ph.D. dissertation (Political Science), Columbia University, 1963.

24. Richard A. Posner, "A Statistical Study of Antitrust Enforcement," *Journal of Law and Economics,* vol. 13 (1970). For a commentary on motivations in case selection for later years, see Suzanne Weaver, *Decision to Prosecute: Organization and Public Policy in the Antitrust Division* (Cambridge: MIT Press, 1977).

25. These numbers are based on rough calculations of cases as described in the "Bluebook" of antitrust: *The Federal Antitrust Laws, with Summary of Cases Instituted by the United States, 1890–1951* (Chicago: Commerce Clearing House, 1952).

26. Chandler's two most important works are *Strategy and Structure: Chapters in the History of the Industrial Enterprise* (Cambridge: MIT Press, 1962), and *The Visible Hand: The Managerial Revolution in American Business* (Cambridge: Harvard University Press, 1977).

27. There is, of course, a huge literature in economics on trusts, monopolies, oligopolies, mergers, and consolidations. A series of relevant articles and a thorough twenty-nine-page bibliography of recent work in the field may be found in Eleanor M. Fox and James T. Halverson, eds., *Industrial Concentration and the Market System: Legal, Economic, Social and Political Perspectives* (American Bar Association Press, 1979). See also Harvey J. Goldschmid et al., eds., *Industrial Concentration: The New Learning* (Boston: Little, Brown, 1974); Robert H. Bork, *The Antitrust Paradox: A Policy at War with Itself* (New York: Basic Books, 1978), chaps. 8, 10, and 13; Edwin Mansfield, ed., *Monopoly Power and Economic Performance: The Problem of Industrial Concentration,* fourth ed.(New York: Norton, 1978); and Yale Brozen, *Concentration, Mergers, and Public Policy* (New York: Macmillan, 1982).

28. Of the scholars listed in note 29, Averitt, Eichner, Galbraith, Oster, and Piore are economists; Chandler and Porter are historians; Berger is a political scientist; and Beck, Horan, Tolbert, Hodson, Kaufman, and Fligstein are sociologists.

29. Robert T. Averitt, *The Dual Economy: The Dynamics of American Industry Structure* (New York: Norton, 1968). Other authors have invented their own nomenclature to denote phenomena similar to center firms: for example "the megacorp" in Alfred S. Eichner, *The Megacorp and Oligopoly: Micro Foundations of Macro Dynamics* (New York: Cambridge University Press, 1976); the "multiunit business enterprise" in Chandler, *The Visible Hand;* and, simply, "Big Business" in Porter, *The Rise of Big Business, 1860–1910.* John Kenneth Galbraith's "technostructure," used in *The New Industrial State* (Boston: Houghton Mifflin, 1967) is a related concept. In each case, the author's purpose is specifically to distinguish the phenomenon from its antecedents: the single-function, labor-intensive, "peripheral" firm without sufficient resources or power to affect the behavior of other firms.

Other sources on the idea of industrial dualism—that is, the concept of a center (or core) sector versus a peripheral one—include Suzanne Berger and Michael J. Piore, *Dualism and Discontinuity in Industrial Societies* (Cambridge: Cambridge University Press, 1980); E. M. Beck, Patrick M. Horan, and Charles H. Tolbert II, "Stratification in a Dual Economy: A Sectoral Model of Earnings Determination," *American Socio-logical Review*, vol. 43 (October 1978), pp. 704–20; Beck, Horan, and Tolbert, "The Structure of Economic Segmentation: A Dual Economy Approach," *American Journal of Sociology*, vol. 75 (March 1980), pp. 1095–1116; Beck, Horan, and Tolbert, "Industrial Segmentation and Labor Market Discrimination," *Social Problems*, vol. 28 (December 1980), pp. 113–30; Gerry Oster, "A Factor Analytic Test of the Theory of the Dual Economy," *Review of Economics and Statistics*, vol. 61 (February 1979), pp. 33–39; and Michael J. Piore, "Labor Market Segmentation: To What Paradigm Does It Belong?" *American Economic Review*, vol. 73 (May 1983), pp. 249–53.

Critical analyses of the concept of dualism include Randy D. Hodson and Robert L. Kaufman, "Circularity in the Dual Economy: Comment on Tolbert, Horan, and Beck," *American Journal of Sociology*, vol. 86 (January 1981), pp. 881–87, with rejoinder from Tolbert, Horan, and Beck, ibid., pp. 887–94; Robert L. Kaufman, Randy Hodson, and Neil D. Fligstein, "Defrocking Dualism: A New Approach to Defining Industrial Sectors," *Social Science Research*, vol. 10 (March 1981), pp. 1–31; and Randy Hodson and Robert L. Kaufman, "Economic Dualism: A Critical Review," *American Sociological Review*, vol. 47 (December 1982), pp. 727–39.

All of these authors, whether pro or con on the subject of dualism, agree that industries should be conceptually segmented into something like the center versus peripheral model.

30. Chandler, *The Visible Hand*, parts 1 through 4; John Moody, *The Truth about the Trusts* (New York: Moody, 1904); William Letwin, *Law and Economic Policy in America: The Evolution of the Sherman Antitrust Act* (New York: Random House, 1965); Morton Keller, "The Pluralist State: American Economic Regulation in Comparative Perspective," in Thomas K. McCraw, ed., *Regulation in Perspective: Historical Essays* (Boston: Harvard University Graduate School of Business Administration, 1981), pp. 64–72. An exceptionally vivid discussion of the legal difficulties involved in enforcing loose horizontal combinations may be found in Louis D. Brandeis's lecture notes for a course on business law at MIT in the 1890s: see the manuscript notes, pp. 320–21, Document 9 of *A Microfilm Edition of the Public Papers of Louis Dembitz Brandeis in the Jacob and Bertha Goldfarb Library of Brandeis University* (Cambridge, Mass.: General Microfilm Co., 1978); Brandeis's views are discussed in detail in Thomas K. McCraw, *Prophets of Regulation* (Cambridge: Harvard University Press, 1984), chap. 3.

31. This process is examined in McCraw, "Rethinking the Trust Question," in McCraw, ed., *Regulation in Perspective*, pp. 11–13.

32. Ibid.; see also Lamoreaux, "Industrial Organization and Market Behavior: The Great Merger Movement in American Industry." The pioneering work of Oliver E. Williamson is relevant here. See Williamson, *Markets and Hierarchies: Analysis and Antitrust Implications* (New York: Free Press, 1975).

33. See Brandeis, Lecture Notes, pp. 324–33, see also Chandler, *The Visible Hand*, p. 357; Thorelli, *The Federal Antitrust Policy*, pp. 604–606; and James Weinstein, *The Corporate Ideal in the Liberal State: 1900–1918* (Boston: Beacon Press, 1968), pp. 63–69. On the European experience, see the essays cited in note 22.

34. This information is contained in soon-to-be-published work of my colleague Alfred D. Chandler, Jr., and I am grateful to him for allowing me to use it here.

35. Ibid.

36. For examples from the steel industry, see the *Annual Report* of U.S. Steel, 1928, p. 6 (an explicit articulation of this policy); and the list of plant closings contained in William T. Hogan, *Economic History of the Iron and Steel Industry* (three vols.) (Cambridge, Mass.: Lexington Books, 1971), vol. 2, pp. 490–93; vol. 3, pp. 892–93. For the rubber industry, see the *Annual Report* of United States Rubber for the years 1893 (p. 7), 1894 (pp. 4–5), 1895 (pp. 4–7), 1896 (n.p.), and 1902 (pp. 3–4).

37. A great deal of historical evidence suggests that tight horizontal integration was often followed by vertical integration; and that these two organizational changes often produced exceptional productive efficiencies. For example, between 1882 and 1885, the Standard Oil company, after absorbing other firms in horizontal acquisitions, concentrated production in the twenty-two most efficient of its fifty-three refineries, closing the least efficient thirty-one. This rationalization of production facilities helped to reduce the company's average cost of refining a gallon of oil by two thirds, from 1.5¢ to 0.5¢. Similarly, the American Tobacco Company, after its various consolidations and rationalizations, reduced the average wholesale price of its cigarettes from $3.02 per thousand in 1893 to $2.01 per thousand in 1899. See Harold F. Williamson and Arnold R. Daum, *The American Petroleum Industry: The Age of Illumination, 1859–1899* (Evanston, Ill.: Northwestern University Press, 1959), pp. 474–75, 483–84; U.S. Bureau of Corporations, *Report of the Commissioner of Corporations on the Tobacco Industry,* pt. 3 (Washington, D.C.: Government Printing Office, 1915), pp. 158–60. Between 1893 and 1899, American Tobacco's costs dropped from $1.74 per thousand to $0.89.

38. For a brief elaboration, see McCraw, "Rethinking the Trust Question," pp. 8–17.

39. Steven B. Webb, "Tariffs, Cartels, Technology, and Growth in the German Steel Industry, 1879 to 1914," *Journal of Economic History,* vol. 40 (1980).

40. Bruce Scott et al., "Japan D–1, from Occupation to Unprecedented Growth," in *Case Studies in Political Economy: Japan, 1853–1977* (Boston: Harvard Business School, 1980).

41. Ibid.; Chalmers Johnson, *MITI and the Japanese Miracle: The Growth of Industrial Policy, 1925–1975* (Stanford, Calif.: Stanford University Press, 1982); Ira C. Magaziner and Thomas M. Hout, *Japanese Industrial Policy* (Berkeley: University of California Institute of International Studies, 1981).

42. The American dilemma is persuasively articulated in John Zysman and Stephen S. Cohen, "Double or Nothing: Open Trade and Competitive Industry," *Foreign Affairs,* vol. 61 (1983).

"Industrial Policy" in the 1920s and 1930s

Ellis W. Hawley

In recent years, industrial policy has become a much discussed and highly controversial matter, one that has been the subject of other conferences, received much attention in the press, and been debated in a growing body of scholarly literature. Most of the debate has focused on the course that America should follow in the future, the underlying assumption being that industrial policy is something that other nations have and that the United States, depending upon one's point of view, has either failed to develop or been wise enough to avoid. Portions of the debate, however, have begun to develop a historical dimension. Those involved have started searching in the past for evidence that would help validate or refute the claims being made, finding there various arrangements resembling or approximating those envisioned by the advocates of an industrial policy. They have helped to spark a new interest in and curiosity about areas of historical experience once largely neglected as being of marginal significance; and to the further illumination of these I hope to contribute. My subject, as I conceive of it, is the degree to which the United States had or had started to develop an industrial policy during the interwar period of the 1920s and 1930s.

By *industrial policy* I mean a national policy aimed at developing or retrenching selected industries to achieve national economic goals. In this usage, I follow those who distinguish such a policy, both from policies aimed at making the macroeconomic environment more conducive to industrial development in general and from the totality of microeconomic interventions aimed at particular industries. To have an industrial policy, a nation must not only be intervening at the microeconomic level but also have a planning and coordinating mechanism through which the intervention is rationally related to national goals, a general pattern of microeconomic targets is decided upon, and particular industrial programs are worked out and implemented.

More specifically, then, I am interested in approximations to this type of action as they existed or as efforts were made to develop them from 1920 to 1940. I look first at the 1920s, focusing particularly on the approximation to such a policy reflected in the thinking and activities of the Commerce Department and its bureaucratic satellites. I shall then examine the years of the Hoover presidency, noting several relevant developments as concerns with managing change gave way to debates over how to bring about economic recovery. Finally, I shall consider the extent to which the New Deal reforms and agencies gave the United States an industrial policy in the sense that the term is now used. My argument throughout is that the United States of this period was not as innocent of industrial policy as is commonly assumed. In addition, I argue that the experience of the period confirms the view that America's political culture has had great difficulty in finding a place for such a policy; and beyond this I argue that any lessons to be drawn are not clear-cut ones, that the record is such that each side in the current debate can and probably will make use of differing portions of it.

The 1920s: Hoover and the Commerce Department

For most educated Americans, including those who have read considerable history, mention of the 1920s brings to mind images of a prosperous and complacent interlude during which a return to laissez faire was accompanied by an unbalanced growth that finally culminated in the Great Depression. What has been largely forgotten is that the decade began with a debate bearing striking resemblances to the one in which we are currently engaged. The immediate postwar years had been a time of economic troubles, a time when the economy had moved from the dislocations produced by demobilization through a feverish inflationary boom and unprecedented labor turmoil to a severe recession marked by high unemployment, numerous farm and business bankruptcies, and intensified struggles for shrunken markets.[1] Although one group of prescriptions for such ills did call for a return to laissez faire—or at least for movement in that direction through actions resembling those currently prescribed by deregulationists and supply-side economists—a second and competing group envisioned the development of new managerial capacities and the use of them to manage the disruptive forces responsible for economic instability and disorder. Impressed by what had been accomplished during the war, those on this side of the debate had embraced managerial modes of thinking resembling those of current industrial policy advocates.

As the debate had progressed, those on the return to laissez faire side had won a series of significant victories. By 1921 they had succeeded in dismantling most of the war's managerial machinery, had reprivatized most of what had been temporarily nationalized during the war period, had turned back efforts to revitalize the prewar progressive movement, and had found in Secretary of the Treasury Andrew Mellon an able advocate of their version of deregulation and supply-side economics.[2] Yet these victories had by no means driven their managerial-minded competitors from the field. On the contrary, what had also emerged by 1921, particularly among former war administrators, engineering leaders, and scientific management enthusiasts, was a confident claim that demobilization, deregulation, and privatization could go hand in hand with the building of new managerial capacities and stabilizing mechanisms. These capacities and mechanisms, so it had been and was continuing to be asserted in various public and private forums, could be built into the large-scale organizations and interorganizational relations that had become characteristic of modern capitalism in a scientific age. They could take shape and be committed to national goals, so Herbert Hoover told the Senate's Special Committee on Reconstruction in September 1920, without resurrection of the undesirable controls associated with the war system. Hoover and others were offering themselves as the master architects who with governmental and societal support could design and build this nonstatist, peacetime substitute for the war's managerial machinery.[3]

Much of this kind of thought and activity, moreover, had managed to make its way across the political line dividing the Wilson and Harding administrations. It had become the dominant mode of thought in agencies like the Forest Service, the Geological Survey, the Bureau of Mines, and the Bureau of Public Roads;[4] a version of it had become strong in the Department of Agriculture;[5] and above all, it had found a home in the Commerce Department that Hoover had now taken over and begun to reshape. Anxious to recruit Hoover as one of the "best minds" in the nation, Harding had promised to support his designs for strengthening and using the department; and the eventual result was not only the decade's prime example of bureaucratic expansionism but also an apparatus through which Hoover and his staff claimed to be developing the managerial and stabilization mechanisms needed by a modern economic order. As he had done in the wartime Food Administration, Hoover proceeded to organize a parallel structure of industry sections and industrial committees, staffing the former with volunteer specialists on leave from the private sector. As this was organized, it was also interwoven with the department's technical and service bureaus, with cooperating professional and philanthropic bodies, and with a network of local community units, again much as Hoover had structured his war control system. Set in motion, the new apparatus was soon generating a series of organizational and promotional conferences, campaigns, and follow-ups, out of which the envisioned mechanisms were supposed to come.[6]

In part the proclaimed goals were macroeconomic. There was to be more and better service for business as a whole; and, through the mechanisms it was helping to create, the department hoped both to improve the workings of market coordination and allocation and to secure a more system-conscious usage of managerial and organizational power, one that would gain for the nation the kind of efficiencies, productivity, dynamism, and long-range prospects that the market could not provide. In theory, the structure being built was supposed to provide a cooperative competition attuned to modern realities, a more enlightened monetary management, a way of discerning and publicizing overall trends and prospects, and a new set of countercyclical spending mechanisms, all serving to improve the performance of the economy as a whole.[7] The department even toyed with the idea of what would later be called an incomes policy, the idea at the time being to create a mechanism for determining scientifically the wage level that would be in the interest of the system as a whole and should therefore be adopted by socially responsible wagemakers.[8]

Yet along with this macroeconimic dimension, a notion of industrial problems or sectoral market failures justified the development of industry-specific mechanisms engaged in problem solving, market repair, or structural adjustment at the microeconomic level. Here the war experience with selective treatment of nationally vital industrial areas, Hoover's conception of himself as a trouble-shooter working with sick industries in the same way he had once doctored sick mines, and the tolerance of the American polity for exceptional case argumentation all came together to create something approaching what we now call industrial policy. Efforts were made to develop industry-specific mechanisms that could assist industries in need of help, either because the market in such areas was in need of repair or supplementation or because previously established regulatory mechanisms were now producing irrational industrial behavior. Along with these efforts were others seeking an apolitical planning and coordinating mechanism capable, as Congress and the parties were thought not to be, of making such intervention a rational and coherent instrument for attaining national economic goals. Expected to fill this role was what Hoover staffer Edward Eyre Hunt called the "cooperative committee and conference system," which amounted in practice to an interacting network of industrial statesmen, volunteer specialists, functional representatives, and affected interests that the department regarded as a kind of national economic council engaged in differentiating sound measures from the unsound.[9]

What eventually took shape here was not, of course, a full-fledged industrial policy apparatus of the kind described in recent studies of France or Japan. Although some of those involved thought of themselves as engaged in "national planning,"[10] one could point to no document as a national plan, to no officially recognized planning agency, or to no prestigious corps of national planners grounded in long-established political institutions. Nor did anyone have the same kind of power to dispense rewards and impose penalties. The planners had no readily controllable kit of tax favors, special financing, governmental guarantees, and legal exemptions with which to implement their designs; and there was little prospect that they would soon acquire one. The antistatist ideology of the leading figures in the enterprise, the association of such tools with the undesirable aspects of wartime control, the need to accommodate the period's return to laissez faire impulse, and the resistance of traditional political institutions and arrangements to power grabs by would-be technocrats all made such acquisition highly unlikely. What the enterprise proposed to rely upon amounted chiefly to moral leadership, selective technical assistance, appeals to science, personal and departmental imprimaturs, and networks for mobilizing and bringing to bear private power and social pressures.

Yet if the commerce secretariat of the 1920s was not a full-fledged industrial policy apparatus, one can find in its organization and activities a number of striking analogues to what students of French or Japanese industrial policy have described. In its bureau structure and organized interpenetrations and commingling of public and private agencies, it resembled the institutional complex centered in Japan's Ministry of International Trade and Industry. In the ongoing whirl of activity produced by its cooperative committee and conference system, it had a feature analogous to MITI's deliberation councils or the concensus building mechanisms of French indicative planning. In its notion of a national service composed of industrial statesmen and privately-based public men, one finds something of an analogue to the elite corps of officials at the center of the French and Japanese structures. And in its efforts to establish power centers alternative to political parties and to keep the political establishment contested by such parties small, it embraced a kind of corporatist thinking that one also finds in France and Japan.[11] At times, moreover, it did seem, despite its ideological aversion to statist coercion and the political and cultural obstacles involved, to be reaching for something closer to the tool kits available in current industrial policy models. In 1922 Hoover tried to add a mechanism empowering it to grant selective antitrust exemptions, somewhat as the war agencies had done;[12] and at various times he tried to secure for it an institutionalized voice in tariff setting, procurement decisions, subsidy dispensation, and the use made of government property and credit.[13]

In operation, this approximation to the industrial policy model did help to develop several industry-specific mechanisms featuring the kind of business-government collaboration and rationalization strategies now commonly associated with a developmental as opposed to a regulatory interventionism.[14] It showed for a time that such mechanisms could be established and recognized as legitimate in sectors other than those connected with defense or national security, leaving a record in this respect that current discussions often ignore.[15] Although space does not permit a detailed examination of all of these industry-specific mechanisms, it seems appropriate at this stage to look briefly at a few of the ones featured in recent historical scholarship and make some general observations about them.

Industry-Specific Mechanisms

In general, the industries for which the Hoover apparatus attempted to develop such mechanisms were those that had, for one reason or another, been designated as problem industries. In part, this designation meant that they had attracted the concern and attention of politicians. As used by the Hooverites and those associated with them, however, it also meant that they were industries in which market failure, improper regulatory intervention, or inability to benefit from generalized promotional programs had created impediments to industrial progress and thus to the efficient working of the industrial organism toward what Hoover called "its only real object—maximum production."[16] Among them were such basic materials industries as lumber, such consumer durables industries as housing, such energy industries as petroleum, coal, and electrical power, such transport industries as railroads and shipping, such new industries as aviation, radio, and motion pictures, and such fundamental industries as agriculture.

The industry-specific mechanism that Hoover seemed proudest of, the one that he regarded as "Exhibit A of the government by co-operation," was the new complex of associational activity developed for a lumber industry plagued by backwardness and waste and seemingly incapable in the form that it had entered the 1920s of providing the nation with efficient and responsible management of a basic resource. Put together at a series of organizational conferences, the first of which was held in 1922, the complex eventually consisted of two interlocking committees, the Central Committee on Lumber Standards and the National Committee on Wood Utilization, through which those making the market in the field were to join with departmental officials to forge an improved marketing system in which efficient, progressive, and responsible entrepreneurship would be rewarded. In particular, they would come to and implement agreements in regard to standardization, material usage, and forestry techniques; and each of these areas had a whirl of activity that Hoover and his aides interpreted as movement toward the intended goal. If any of the self-congratulatory publicity could be believed, the new mechanism was helping to move the industry from the problem category to the one labeled "exemplary." The lumber industry was now, said Hoover, on "the path of righteousness."[17]

In part the concern of the Hoover apparatus with lumber was linked to a simultaneous concern with another problem area, namely that of building and housing. Here, as Hoover analyzed it, was another industry plagued by waste and backwardness and seemingly unable, without special assistance, to develop the mass markets that would allow it to install new production technologies and fulfill its latent capacity to make the United States a nation of homeowners. Here, too, the department helped to develop a new complex of associational activity, centered in this case in a new Building and Housing

Division staffed by volunteer specialists and linked through committees to industry, community, professional, and civic education groups. The complex focused its efforts partly on waste elimination that could reduce production costs, partly on securing trade agreements, consumer values, and regulatory and institutional reforms that could make the kind of market that was needed; and in both lines of activity it was by 1928 boasting of a long list of achievements. If building and housing was not yet behaving like automobiles, it was supposed to be on the way and capable with further improvements of playing its proper role in the nation's economic and social progress.[18]

Throughout this period efforts were also made to shape the demand for building and housing so that it would serve as a balance wheel for the economy as a whole. The idea in general was that those contemplating building should be encouraged to defer action during cyclical upswings and to take it when the economy turned downward. This procedure was supposed to be in both their interest and the national interest. Attempts to create a mechanism that would get them to see this and enable them to act on the insight did not meet with much success, however. The Commerce Department was not empowered to manage governmental building in this fashion, as Hoover and other proponents of the idea hoped that it would be. It learned that although the building and housing industry welcomed campaigns to get building underway in recession periods, it strongly resented those trying to stop it during cyclical upswings, particularly those campaigns that Hoover mounted to dampen the boom of 1923. Furthermore, hopes that a new American Construction Council, formed in 1922, could build a consensus within the industry for this kind of construction planning were never realized. The council never amounted to much more than a paper organization.[19]

With the consumer durables industry often held up as a behavioral model, namely that of automobiles, the commerce secretariat showed relatively little concern. Here, it was believed, the industrial structure that had emerged and the grant-in-aid complex through which a modern highway system was being created were both working well. With the backwardness and irrationality of other parts of the transportation system, however, and with some of the social costs attendant on the development of "automobility," there was concern. The result, by mid-decade, was another complex of associational activity, centering in a transportation division linked through a network of committees to industry associations and concerned private groups. Among its products were a system of regional shipping boards, designed to work with the railroads for purposes of eliminating periodic car shortages; an apparatus for promoting uniform traffic control laws; and another for promoting highway safety measures. Also offered were schemes for railroad reorganization, a national waterway plan, and rationalization of the support system for the merchant marine; but these designs were never successfully implemented.[20]

In addition, the department early embraced the view that the situation in aviation constituted another national problem that it should help to resolve. The nation, it felt, urgently needed a new air service, which was essential both to economic progress and to national defense. The market to support one, it believed, could be developed if the industry were properly assisted in reducing accident rates, overcoming irresponsible adventurism, changing public misperceptions, and upgrading its equipment. Such were the goals of a parallel structure of industry committees and departmental task forces that took shape in the mid-1920s, and they remained the goals of what amounted to a union of the Aeronautical Chamber of Commerce with Hoover's Aeronautics Branch following the passage of the Air Commerce Act in 1926. To the usual complex of associational activity there was added in this case what Hoover saw as a foundation of constructive regulatory law developed through sincere cooperation between the public and private sectors, and as of 1928 the mechanism's architects could argue that a national problem was being resolved through what might now be called market-conforming methods.[21]

Two other new industries for which the department helped to develop problem-solving mechanisms were those of radio and motion pictures. In the former case it saw a great new resource best developed by relying on the practicality and progressiveness of private initiative yet having characteristics that made this potentially productive of resource spoilage, time-consuming legal hassles, and serious social abuses. A mechanism was needed to prevent this from happening; and in its efforts to forge one, the department sought both a regulatory charter and a cooperative alliance or pool capable of securing conformance to extralegal arrangements. The ultimate outcome was the Radio Act of 1927, establishing a Federal Radio Commission that in its initial form functioned largely as a departmental extension.[22] In the latter case, an industry regarded as a problem because of its offenses to good morals and controversial marketing practices, the department hoped to achieve a similar kind of ordered liberty by encouraging the self-regulatory machinery being developed by Will Hays and the Motion Picture Producers and Distributors of America. In 1926 the department began to encourage self-regulation through a motion pictures unit that in effect was both a part of the Hays organization and a part of the Bureau of Foreign and Domestic Commerce.[23]

Still another problem sector to which the commerce secretariat gave a good deal of attention was that composed of the fuel or energy industries. This began with a concern about oil shortages and efforts to create a cooperative mechanism that could ensure access to oil outside the United States.[24] It continued with concerns about the functioning of the oil market, particularly with its tendencies to encourage destabilizing behavior and wastage of an unrenewable resource. A search for appropriate mechanisms to develop a better market began in earnest in 1924, proceeding chiefly through a Federal Oil Conservation Board of which Hoover was a member, and becoming particularly enamored with the idea of promoting "unitization."[25] At the same time, much attention was given to the power question, notably at a series of superpower conferences through which the department kept trying to develop a new institutional framework that could turn industrial developers, public regulators, and regional planners into a cooperative alliance for fostering economic and social progress.[26] From 1921 on, the problems of a coal industry plagued by persisting overcapacity and attendant competitive and labor disorders received similar attention. Here the department toyed with technological solutions involving the conversion of coal to other forms of energy, with a scheme for what might now be called a rationalization cartel and with the idea of using labor organization as an instrument of industrial rationalization. It was unable to implement any of these designs, however; and what it was able to provide in the way of aids for orderly marketing did not seem to be of much help. Throughout the period coal remained a "sick" industry.[27]

Finally, the Hoover apparatus also became deeply involved in trying to solve what Americans in the 1920s called the farm problem. Here it tended to agree with the view that agriculture was both a fundamental industry and an important producer of social virtue. Hence, the continued malfunctioning of the sector could have serious negative implications both for the industrial organism as a whole and for the quality of American society. It saw the kind of protectionism being sought by the period's farm organizations as also likely to have serious negative effects, however. Protectionism would lead in all likelihood to a stifling of technical and organizational progress and leave the country with a sector of industrial backwardness for which it would have to pay both in new regulatory costs and in food and fiber bills. The sector needed new institutions through which the market could again be made into a force encouraging progressive individualism. In schemes for a system of agricultural marketing associations, for a progressive-minded tariff revision, and for more imaginative uses of agricultural credit, schemes that the farm groups kept rejecting as unworkable or as designs for business domination, the department offered concrete suggestions as to what the new institutions should look like and how they might be established.[28]

The commerce secretariat in the 1920s, then, was engaged in a wide variety of industry-specific operations that when taken as a whole did have a certain coherence. Probably they can also be credited with some contribution to better economic performance. The measures used by those involved allowed them to boast of a number of successes; and while these were clearly designed to put the best face possible on the situation, the bias was probably not great enough to negate all of the boast. Yet even by such measures, there were also clear cases of frustration and failure. One thinks particularly of the cases of coal, the railroads, electrical power, and the agricultural sector. Nor does the experience suggest that those functioning as the elite of national servants in the interventionist machinery were always able to identify the arrangements capable of improving an industry's economic performance. In

71

their thinking about agriculture, for example, or in their general misreading of the latent progressiveness waiting to be tapped and organized in such traditionally unprogressive areas as lumber, housing, and coal, they proceeded from premises that subsequent experience would show to be largely untenable.

The evidence from the 1920s, I would argue, also suggest that while the ongoing organizational and managerial revolutions had made a certain kind of industrial policy possible, America's culture and polity still contained elements that were strongly resistant or downright hostile to its establishment and operation. The nation, after all, had originated in a revolt against attempts at economic management through a centralization of imperial policy making. It had in the nineteenth century developed its own form of the modern state, one that sought national coordination and modernization not through an officialdom inherited from a monarchical past but through a court system run by modernizing lawyers, a mass party system built on patronage dispensation to local developers and competing interests, and a market system designed to release and discipline the energies of modernizing entrepreneurs. The nation had also developed as major features of these systems an aversion to autonomous bureaucratic power, a legal code stressing individual over group rights, and a marked preference for seeking the public good through adversarial proceedings and arm's length bargaining—a tradition that had much to its credit in achieving equity and minimizing corruption. Outside of government, the nation had developed a group life and a set of popular cultural symbols that did not correspond very closely to those assumed in the Hooverian formulations. The assumption there was of a group and popular life becoming increasingly enlightened, responsible, and system conscious, thus providing the social raw material from which the envisioned rationalizing and stabilizing mechanisms could be coaxed and set in operation. What had to be dealt with, all too frequently, however, was a group life geared to the competitive pursuit of narrow and specific interests and a citizenry that was still capable of being mobilized, at least in part, by anticorporate, populistic, or libertarian symbols and values.

All of these features of the nation's institutional and cultural life were obstacles to what the Commerce Department and its allies were attempting, and in various ways they limited and shaped the extent to which the America of the 1920s could have an industrial policy. The form the industrial policy apparatus took and the kind of men charged with it reflected the need to accommodate or placate such political and cultural resistance. The difficulties encountered in attempts to build and legitimize cooperative mechanisms said much about the continuing strength of individualistic, entrepreneurial, and adversarial traditions and ideals. The relations of the apparatus with Congress, with the courts, with other parts of the executive branch, and with fragmented or refractory industrial groups, particularly at times when those in charge of it reach for powers that depended on affirmative action by these other institutions, all indicated that the American situation was a long way from the kind of institutional deference characteristic of such relationships in the Japanese and French models.[29]

A final point concerns the difficulty of keeping the mechanisms that were created from abandoning their developmental functions and turning into protectionist mechanisms engaged in perpetuating inefficient structures or providing shelter from adverse economic forces. A tendency in this direction seemed to be built in just as some current critics of industrial policy have suggested it is today; and in the end most of the Hooverian creations that survived would follow this path. On the other side, however, this tendency was greatly accelerated by failure at the macroeconomic level and the search for shelters pending the recovery of aggregate demand. Given proper action there, the tendency might possibly have been resisted and elements to contain it built into the mechanisms. Although this resistance seems unlikely, had no great contraction occurred after 1929 the task would certainly have been easier.

Policy during Hoover's Presidency

With Hoover's elevation to the presidency in 1929, one might expect to find the United States moving toward a more fully developed industrial policy. Initially, Hoover did seem to have something of this sort in mind. One of his projects in 1929 called for a more formalized national economic council resembling those proposed in current industrial policy bills. As envisioned, the council would institutionalize an ongoing deliberation among the leaders of the major economic groupings, the administrators of the government's economic departments and agencies, and outstanding individuals recognized for their public mindedness.[30] Another project was governmental reorganization that, had it been successfully accomplished, would have made developing and implementing an industrial policy considerably easier. Envisioned here were not only greater institutional support for the work of the commerce secretariat and better managerial tools for the White House but also a remaking of the Interior, Labor, and War departments so that the government's public works, land management, and social welfare programs might be more effectively used to supplement its work with organized industrial groups.[31]

In addition, Hoover did use the power of the presidency to further several of his earlier designs for dealing with problem industries and sectors. Most notably, he secured the passage in 1929 of the Agricultural Marketing Act, establishing a Federal Farm Board organized along corporative lines and equipped with lending and managerial powers that it could use to build a system of agricultural marketing associations and other market stabilizers. In operation, the Federal Farm Board would prove to be a major fiasco, partly because it got involved in futile efforts to contain depression forces but also, it

73

seems, because American agriculture was sadly deficient in the kind of cooperative spirit, managerial talent, and good organizational raw material that the board needed to build its envisioned marketing system.[32] In actions of lesser magnitude, the new administration helped to consolidate the arrangements that had been worked out for the radio industry, secured new legislation under which federal airmail contracts were to help rationalize the aviation industry, and made further efforts to develop appropriate mechanisms for making the oil market serve the public good. Its solution for oil now was unitization promoted under an interstate compact and leasing reforms, but at a national oil conference in 1929 it learned that this solution was not supported by much of what had now become a badly divided and highly contentious industry.[33]

There were, then, some efforts to carry through on what had been done or attempted before 1929. As things turned out, however, this preoccupation did not remain central to the Hoover administration for very long. The great economic problem after October 1929 was not the wastes or inefficiencies attendant upon malfunctioning market and regulatory structures in particular industries but rather a failure of aggregate demand that was not setting in motion systemic adjustments needed to correct it. The overriding concern, as this failure persisted and the economy kept contracting, was with forging mechanisms that could correct this macroeconomic disorder. Although there was some talk of technological solutions involving the creation of new industries or export solutions to be achieved by efficiencies enhancing national competitiveness, the search for a corrective never moved very far along either of these two paths. Instead, the search tended to stay with the macroeconomic prescriptions coming from the commerce secretariat in the 1920s, seeking through cooperative action to sustain mass purchasing power and reassure potential investors, keep the monetary and credit systems in working order, turn destructive competition into the kind facilitating systemic adjustments, and activate such balance wheels as construction spending and latent foreign demand.

Hoover's first recovery program, to be more specific, featured the formation of cooperative organizations to inhibit wage-cutting, dispel gloom, and stimulate construction spending. Such were the purposes of the organizations formed in the wake of a series of business conferences and also of some arms of the President's Emergency Committee for Employment created later in 1930. At the same time the administration resisted various anticompetitive moves and proposals, continuing to distinguish here between the need to restrain destructive competition and efforts to escape the socially beneficial kind. When recovery still failed to come, the administration then argued that the necessary adjustments had been made but that recovery was being held back by developments abroad, threats to the monetary system, and adverse political factors. Another set of organizations became necessary to overcome these obstacles and allow recovery to proceed; and in its efforts to create these the administration brought forth the international stabilization mechanisms of 1931, the new credit institutions established in the first half of 1932, and the system of banking and industrial committees organized in August and September of 1932. It also embraced the view that deficit reduction through tax increases would help to remove psychological impediments to recovery, a line of thought and action for which it has, of course, been much criticized since.[34]

The Reconstruction Finance Corporation (RFC) established in early 1932 was intended not as an agency of industrial policy but as a temporary tool for carrying the financial structure through a crisis period and overcoming irrational preferences for greater liquidity. It was, to be sure, modeled on the War Finance Corporation of 1918; it had the kind of powers that might have been used for industrial policy implementation; and it became marginally implicated in industry-specific efforts to resolve the farm, housing, and railroad problems. Its major purpose, however, was to make available emergency credits for institutions in temporary trouble but presumably capable, if so assisted, of playing the roles they had been assigned in national economic recovery and future economic progress. It was never tied to the kind of wartime machinery used to select particular industries for promotion or retrenchment or even to anything resembling the Commerce Department apparatus of the 1920s. Nor did it try in any systematic way to reform the capital structures of the aided institutions.[35]

On balance, then, the Hoover presidency seems to have been years of setback or at least of minimal progress for the idea of what is now called industrial policy. Certain developments might have been pulled together and built into something approximating the industrial policy model. They were not pulled together, partly, one suspects, because of the continuing cultural and political obstacles in the way of doing so but also because they were not widely seen, either by Hoover or others, as ways to overcome the systemic disorders reflected in the persisting failure of aggregate demand. The remedies for these disorders seemed to lie in other forms of organization building, particularly in tools for unleashing and sustaining proper spending and credit flows. Preoccupied with trying to create and make use of these, the administration had little energy left for supply-side difficulties that now seemed of secondary importance. Besides, the administration could argue, tackling those difficulties was futile until the macroeconomic disorder was remedied.

The New Deal

With the advent of the New Deal in 1933, there was notably less reluctance to use the powers of the state as tools of economic management. The continuing crisis had reduced societal and business resistance to the idea, discrediting in the minds of many both the notion of natural correctives and that of coaxing new ordering mechanisms from the group life of the private sector. Unlike the Hooverites, the New Dealers believed that statist bureaucracies could be made into effective tools and that the nation had reached a point at which it should resurrect the more statist elements of the war system. Yet, as during the Hoover period, the focus was still on trying to end the depression by unleashing and sustaining proper spending and credit flows, not on putting idle resources to work by moving them into the likely industries of the future or making existing industries more internationally competitive; and the hostility of the culture and polity to the kind of planning now associated with the industrial policy model was probably greater during the New Deal period than it had been earlier. If the period brought a rapid growth of the administrative state, it also brought an upsurge of interest group activity, mass political activism, and anti-establishment attitudes that made it extremely difficult for the new state to become a planning state applying a new rationality to its microeconomic interventionism.[36] Hence, that the New Deal state, as it took shape in 1933–1939, never developed much in the way of an American industrial policy should come as no real surprise.

This is not to say that thinking along this line was absent from the period or from the processes out of which New Deal laws and programs came. In the drafting process out of which the National Industrial Recovery Act of 1933 emerged, one of the provisions finally rejected would have authorized the government to pick industries to which it would give developmental assistance, using for this purpose a blend of special financing and guarantees against loss resembling that used during the war period. This was the basis of the so-called Rorty and Kent plans associated with Malcolm Rorty of American Telephone and Telegraph and Fred Kent of the New York Federal Reserve Bank.[37] Adolf Berle and others also developed schemes, which were seriously considered at several points but never adopted, for turning the Reconstruction Finance Corporation into something approaching an industrial policy agency. These schemes were for creating government-backed financial institutions that would specialize in assisting the birth and development of promising new industries.[38] In addition, efforts to equip the United States with a national economic council, often seen as a prerequisite to any kind of coherent industrial policy, persisted;[39] and in the later New Deal, a group of planners with ties to the Department of Agriculture and the National Resources Planning Board became promoters of what they called "industrial expansion" schemes. Under these an expansion board would choose potential growth industries, help them prepare expansion programs, and use governmental guarantees and tax incentives to put the programs into effect. The idea essentially was to use mechanisms similar to those in the agricultural programs for expansionary rather than contractive purposes.[40]

What one can say, however, is that the institutions envisioned in this thinking never materialized, and that while the New Deal produced a number of industry-specific laws and programs often justified as problem-solving measures that would improve the functioning of the economy as a whole, most of these emerged not from national planning or rationalizing processes but from intense political ones of the traditional sort. In the early New Deal, for example, special programs of this kind were established for agriculture, petroleum, and the railroads; and subsequently the New Deal state became involved in trying to solve the coal, shipping, aviation, trucking, housing, and electrical power problems. In some of the mechanisms created, moreover, it did employ the kind of parallel-structure bureaucracy and interpenetration or intertwining of the public and private sectors that had previously appeared in the war system and the productions of the commerce secretariat in the 1920s. But the decisions as to whether or not an industry should be in the group receiving special treatment and the kind of treatment it would receive once it was included are to be understood mostly in terms of a complex of political pressures acting on congressmen, administrators, and interest group representatives rather than the workings of anything resembling the national economic councils and planning institutions characteristic of industrial policy systems and models. Despite the enhanced role of service intellectuals in shaping some of these programs and despite intermittent efforts to create new presidential coordinating tools, the programs were the outcome, generally speaking, of the very kind of ad hoc, reactive, fragmented, and short-term policy making that proponents of an industrial policy system now find deplorable and in need of correction.[41]

What one can also say is that the national recovery strategy that came to the fore in 1933, the one manifested particularly in the industrial code system developed and administered by the National Recovery Administration (NRA), was not an industrial policy strategy. The NRA, to be sure, was modeled on the earlier War Industries Board, much as the Reconstruction Finance Corporation had been modeled on the War Finance Corporation; and the machinery created under its auspices did resemble the commodity organizations of World War I, the commerce secretariat productions of the 1920s, and the industry-specific mechanisms in the Japanese or French systems. It featured the same fusion of the public and private and the same effort to make decentralized units of industrial self-government serve the needs of the national economic system. The machinery was not, however, intended as leverage for implementing a rationally conceived and carefully coordinated program of industrial expansion in some sectors and retrenchment in others. Its aim rather was to secure, primarily through state-supported minimum wage and price floors, revisions of the legal code governing competitive practices, and the stimulation and harnessing of new organizational endeavors, an unleashing and revival of the kinds of spending and credit flows necessary to put idle men and resources to work. At least this was the aim in official policy statements and in the guidelines for approving and administering codes. In practice, as various studies have pointed out, the machinery was also used to create or strengthen industrial shelters for those seeking merely to survive until the return of better economic weather.[42]

If the NRA experience has relevance for the industrial policy question, then, it lies not in any attempt on its part to give the United States an industrial policy but rather in what it can tell us about the working of a type of bureaucratic machinery resembling that through which current proposals are apparently to be implemented. That machinery relied heavily on the technical and administrative resources of the private sector, partly because the government lacked the kind of bureaucratic resources capable of making and implementing industrial codes, but also because, as in current thinking, the private sector was to provide the needed managerial capacity without producing statification and big government. The experience during the NRA period should perhaps be a warning against using such machinery for similar managerial projects. One might argue, of course, that conditions have changed, that more careful attention to the inclusion of safeguards and the limitations imposed by industrial structure and incentives could make such machinery workable,[43] or that the ability to make it workable is of an entirely different order than it was in 1933 or 1934. Under the conditions of the time and in the form it actually took, however, the machinery was ineffective and highly problematic. It relied on agencies of implementation that had the autonomy and incentives to distort what was intended. It intensified industry divisions and concerns about a redistribution of power, the result being a program that was torn and enfeebled by bitter and continuing policy conflicts. It produced the antithesis of what its creators had said it was going to produce, namely a new era of intense business-government conflict rather than one of fruitful cooperation. And not surprisingly, it could not secure the conditions that were supposed to bring recovery.[44]

The NRA experience also illustrates, one might conclude, the failure of either the economic crisis or the continuing organizational and managerial revolution to overcome those elements in the culture and polity that were hostile to national planning bureaucracies of any sort. An older set of populist, republican, and entrepreneurial symbols proved to be potent weapons in the political wars that swirled around the creation and operation of the code system. Although the NRA did stimulate a good deal of new organizational activity, this activity produced conflict-oriented organizations fighting to advance particular interests and secure proper shares in a pluralistic order rather than organizations that could become working parts of the planning system devising and implementing national plans. As an attempted planning system, the NRA structure proved unable to develop satisfactory roles for organized labor, for the social constituencies that have idealized small business or consumer sovereignty, for lawmakers outside the agency's administrative domain, and for its central corps of governmental and business administrators. It became an agency engaged mostly in political brokering and political damage control rather than the organization and operation of a planning system; and the fact that it did so may say something about the likely fate of any attempt to develop the planning systems envisioned in current proposals for an industrial policy. It promises to be anything but an easy task.[45]

In a sense the later New Deal was a product of this heightened pluralism and the accompanying inability to legitimize a planning organization or achieve fruitful business-government cooperation. Out of these came what Otis Graham and others have called the broker state as opposed to a planning state, a state "intervening in an ad hoc and piecemeal fashion on behalf of those groups with sufficient political and economic power to obtain assistance."[46] With the emergence of the broker state came both a further distancing of America's microeconomic interventionism from the kind envisioned in the industrial policy model and a shift to new recovery strategies compatible with such a state's capacities—to strategies, in other words, that downplayed the need for a planning organization and stressed instead the spending and credit flows that could be released through appropriate fiscal policies, politically feasible antitrust action, and an organizational promotion aimed at strengthening labor and consumer groups and thus achieving greater balance in the interplay of economic power. The broker state structure and orientation, moreover, proved strong enough to withstand and defeat the new planning impulses that appeared during the period, particularly those seeking to equip the president with new planning tools, to create new regional planning agencies, and to organize recovery from the recession of 1937 through new exercises in national or industrial planning. As economic conditions worsened again in late 1937 and early 1938, some support developed both for a new economic concert similar to that attempted under the NRA and for the previously noted industrial expansion schemes. What emerged, however, were a new spending program, increased antitrust activity, and a large-scale inquiry into the monopoly problem. Not until the approach of war created openings for a previously legitimized kind of planning organization did the New Deal state enter upon a period of coexistence with another national managerial apparatus that would leave a considerable legacy for the postwar period.[47]

Thus the New Deal experience, when taken as a whole, seems to offer further evidence attesting to the strong and continuing resistance of America's culture and polity to the uses of state and private power envisioned in the industrial policy model. One can find in that experience several impulses toward establishing the envisioned institutions, indicating that they had become the answer for certain segments of the society and political order; and if one looks hard enough, one can find examples of microeconomic intervention that offer some encouragement for those who insist that such institutions can be effective in the American context and can be prevented from developing protectionist and antidemocratic features. Otis Graham, for example, finds such encouragement in the developmental successes of the Tennessee Valley Authority, in the postdepression performance of American agriculture, in the changes wrought by the Rural Electrification Administration, and in the research activities of the National Resources Planning Board. Thomas McCraw finds at least a bit of encouragement in the regulatory successes of the Securities and Exchange Commission; and others have had kind things to say about the system of oil management that came to center in the Texas Railroad Commission.[48] Generally speaking, however, the period's would-be developers of mechanisms approximating those in current industrial policy models found themselves engaged in an exceedingly difficult and frustrating enterprise, one that not only involved repeated setbacks and disappointments but also helped to stimulate a new activism embracing antimanagerial values, usher in a period of intense business-government conflict, and release organizational and political energies that made a mockery out of the designs for concerted action and system-conscious coherence.

Conclusion

The historical experience reconstructed here seems to suggest, then, that the United States has not been untouched by managerial impulses and designs resembling those from which national industrial policies have sprung, but that its culture and polity have made it a place where the envisioned uses of state and private power have been difficult to institutionalize and legitimize. Such policies could be pursued to a considerable degree in wartime; but the managerial impulses following World War I had to accommodate themselves to demands for a return to laissez faire and traditional forms of governmental activity. They could produce the apparatus through which Hoover's commerce secretariat claimed to be equipping society rather than the state with a much-needed managerial capacity, an apparatus that in significant ways resembled those associated with industrial policy models; but they could not produce full-fledged planning institutions equipped with the sort of reserve powers that had been given to several war agencies and enjoying the kind of deference that such institutions have had in the more successful forms of capitalist planning. Although the coming of the depression and the New Deal brought a new willingness to enlarge the role of government and reestablish some of the wartime instruments, they also brought a parallel development of new political and institutional barriers against planning operations of the industrial policy type. In practice the NRA and RFC became agencies engaged in providing protection and trying to restart spending flows rather than agencies organizing growth through strategic interventions at the microeconomic level. Except for a few areas, in which exceptional political circumstances produced special outcomes, the new American state became a broker and compensatory state rather than a planning or developmental one.

On the basis of that experience, one might possibly argue that a workable industrial policy for the United States can be both conceived and implemented. One finds in it evidence of strong managerial impulses, potentially harnessable for such purposes; and one can find instances of an interventionism that brought achievements of the kind celebrated by industrial policy advocates. Presumably, given the will and the accumulation of knowledge since the New Deal era, these instances could be greatly multiplied. The experience also suggests, however, that doing these things would be anything but an easy task and that attempting to do them may bring forms of group and political behavior making the task more difficult and enhancing the likelihood that the end product would be reduced economic welfare and retreats from the democratic ideal rather than the reverse. Before making the attempt, one informed by such experience would seem obliged to argue, there should not only be an exceptionally strong case for taking action but also a thorough exploration of options more compatible with the persisting antimanagerial components of America's polity and political culture.

Notes

1. For details see John D. Hicks, *Rehearsal for Disaster: The Boom and Collapse of 1919–1920* (Gainesville: University of Florida Press, 1961); and George Soule, *Prosperity Decade: From War to Depression, 1917–1929* (New York: Rinehart, 1947), pp. 81–106.

2. On these matters see James R. Mock and Evangeline Thurber, *Report on Demobilization* (Norman: University of Oklahoma Press, 1944); Burl Noggle, *Into the Twenties* (Urbana: University of Illinois Press, 1974); David Burner, "1919: Prelude to Normalcy," in John Braeman et al., eds., *Change and Continuity in Twentieth-Century America: The 1920s* (Columbus: Ohio State University Press, 1968); and Lawrence L. Murray, "Andrew W. Mellon, Secretary of the Treasury, 1921–1932: A Study in Policy," Ph.D. diss., Michigan State University (1970).

3. Herbert Hoover, in U.S. Senate, Select Committee on Reconstruction and Production, *Reconstruction and Production* (66th Congress, 3d session, 1921), pp. 625–27. I discuss this development in *The Great War and the Search for a Modern Order* (New York: St. Martin's Press, 1979), pp. 45–55. See also much of the other testimony in *Reconstruction and Production;* Edwin T. Layton, *The Revolt of the Engineers* (Cleveland: Case Western Reserve University, 1971), pp. 170–204; Glenn Frank, "Self-Governing Industry," *Century Magazine,* vol. 98 (June 1919), pp. 225–36; and Edward Eyre Hunt, "Reconstruction," in Box 19, Hunt Papers, Hoover Institution Archives, Stanford, California.

4. See George T. Morgan, *William B. Greeley: A Practical Forester* (St. Paul, Minn.: Forest History Society, 1961), pp. 39–52; Lawrence Hamilton, "The Federal Forest Regulation Issue," *Journal of Forest History,* vol. 9 (April 1965), pp. 2–11; Bruce E. Seely, "Engineers and Government-Business Cooperation: Highway Stan-

dards and the Bureau of Public Roads, 1900–1940," *Business History Review*, vol. 58 (Spring 1984), pp. 66–77; and Joseph A. Pratt, "Creating Coordination in the Modern Petroleum Industry," *Research in Economic History*, vol. 8 (1983), pp. 179–215.

5. See Donald L. Winters, *Henry Cantwell Wallace as Secretary of Agriculture, 1921–1924* (Urbana: University of Illinois Press, 1970), pp. 109–44.

6. I have discussed the remaking of the Commerce Department in "Herbert Hoover, the Commerce Secretariat, and the Vision of an Associative State, 1921–1928," *Journal of American History*, vol. 61 (June 1974), pp. 116–40; the structure of the wartime food organization in "The Great War and Organizational Innovation: The American Case," a paper presented at the Davis Center Conference on World War I, Princeton University, January 21, 1984; and the initial efforts to create stabilizing mechanisms in "Herbert Hoover and Economic Stabilization, 1921–1922," in *Herbert Hoover as Secretary of Commerce* (Iowa City: University of Iowa Press, 1981), pp. 43–79. See also Joseph Brandes, *Herbert Hoover and Economic Diplomacy* (Pittsburgh: University of Pittsburgh Press, 1962); Peri Arnold, "Herbert Hoover and the Department of Commerce," Ph.D. diss., University of Chicago (1972); and Ross T. Runfola, "Herbert C. Hoover as Secretary of Commerce, 1921–1923," Ph.D. diss., State University of New York at Buffalo (1973).

7. On the macroeconomic dimension see Evan Metcalf, "Secretary Hoover and the Emergence of Macroeconomic Management," *Business History Review*, vol. 59 (Spring 1975), pp. 60–80; Carolyn Grin,"The Unemployment Conference of 1921: An Experiment in Cooperative Planning," *Mid-America*, vol. 55 (April 1973), pp. 83–107; and my "Herbert Hoover and Economic Stabilization." See also Edward Eyre Hunt, "Recent Economic Changes in the United States" (1929), Hunt Papers, Springfield, Ohio.

8. See especially Edward Eyre Hunt to Charles Merriam, January 29, 1924; Hunt to Joseph Willits, October 26, 1924; Hunt to Beardsley Ruml, October 31, 1924; Hoover to Arthur Woods, September 26, 1924; and memorandum entitled "Bases of Agreement" (no date, but apparently 1924), all in Box 27a, Hunt Papers, Hoover Institution Archives.

9. Edward Eyre Hunt, "The Cooperative Committee and Conference System," December 14, 1926, Hunt File, Commerce Department Section, Hoover Papers, Hoover Presidential Library, West Branch, Iowa.

10. Edward Eyre Hunt, "National Planning for Avoidance of Unemployment," *American Federationist*, vol. 34 (September 1927), pp. 1063–65; Hunt, "Planning: A Bird's-Eye View of Recent Experience," Hunt Papers, Springfield, Ohio.

11. My understanding of the Japanese and French systems is based primarily on Chalmers Johnson, *MITI and the Japanese Miracle: The Growth of Industrial Policy, 1925–1975* (Stanford, Calif.: Stanford University Press, 1982); Ezra F. Vogel, *Japan as Number One* (Cambridge: Harvard University Press, 1979); Robert S. Ozaki, "How Japanese Industrial Policy Works," in Chalmers Johnson, ed., *The Industrial Policy Debate* (San Francisco: ICS Press, 1984), pp. 47–70; and Stephen S. Cohen, *Modern Capitalist Planning: The French Model* (Cambridge: Harvard University Press, 1969).

12. See draft of desired legislation, attached to David Wing to Richard Emmet, June 19, 1922, Trade Association Statistics File, Commerce Department Section, Hoover Papers. See also Robert Himmelberg, "Relaxation of the Federal Anti-Trust Policy as a

Goal of the Business Community, 1918–1933," Ph.D. diss., Pennsylvania State University (1963), pp. 121–22.

13. The story of these expansionary efforts and the bureaucratic conflicts generated can be documented from materials in the Reorganization of Government and Commerce-Reorganization files, Commerce Department Section, Hoover Papers. See also my discussion in "Herbert Hoover, the Commerce Secretariat, and the Vision of an Associative State."

14. For a discussion of the distinction, see Johnson, MITI, pp. 305–19.

15. See, for example, Ozaki, "How Japanese Industrial Policy Works," p. 68.

16. Foreword to Federated American Engineering Societies, *Waste in Industry* (New York, 1921).

17. I discuss the lumber developments in "Three Facets of Hooverian Associationalism: Lumber, Aviation, and Movies, 1921–1930," in Thomas K. McCraw, ed., *Regulation in Perspective* (Cambridge: Harvard University Press, 1981), pp. 95–123. See also William G. Robbins, *Lumberjacks and Legislators: Political Economy of the U.S. Lumber Industry, 1890–1941* (College Station: Texas A & M University Press, 1982), pp. 112–32.

18. The building and operation of the complex can be followed in memoranda and correspondence now deposited in the Building and Housing File, Commerce Department Section, Hoover Papers. See especially "Federal Activity in Promotion of Better Housing Conditions and Home Ownership" (1923), and "Better Homes and Decreased Costs," January 11, 1928.

19. See Edward Eyre Hunt, "Business Cycles and Unemployment," October 1, 1927, Box 21, Hunt Papers, Hoover Institution Archives; Grin, "Unemployment Conference of 1921"; Rose C. Field, "Industry's New Doctors," *New York Times*, June 4, 1922; Hoover to Harding, March 2, March 17, 1923, Box 6, Harding Papers, Ohio State Historical Society, Columbus, Ohio; "Secretary Hoover Advocates Curtailment of Public Building Construction," *Engineering and Contracting*, vol. 59 (April 25, 1923), pp. 921–22; Franklin D. Roosevelt to Hoover, May 17, 1923; Hoover to Roosevelt, May 24, 1923; Hoover to Lawrence Richey, June 18, 1923; Porter Moore to Hoover, June 23, 1923, all in Construction File, Commerce Department Section, Hoover Papers. In the face of protest in 1923, Hoover insisted that he had attempted only to delay federal construction. This was technically true, but in various ways he was encouraging efforts to create a mechanism for shaping private decisions as well.

20. Hoover, "Railroad Reorganization," April 1923; Hoover, Address to the Transportation Conference, January 9, 1924, both in Railroad Consolidation File, Commerce Department Section, Hoover Papers; Hoover to Coolidge, November 22, 1923, Coolidge File, Commerce Department Section, Hoover Papers; "Report of Committee on Matters Affecting the Merchant Marine," December 29, 1924, Committee File, Commerce Department Section, Hoover Papers; Hoover, Statement before House Rivers and Harbors Committee, January 30, 1926, Waterways File, Commerce Department Section, Hoover Papers; "Report of the National Conference on Street and Highway Safety," March 25, 1926, Conference—Traffic Safety File, Commerce Department Section, Hoover Papers.

21. I have discussed these developments in some detail in "Three Facets of Hooverian Associationalism," pp. 108–15. See also David Lee, "Herbert Hoover and the

Development of Commercial Aviation, 1921–1926," *Business History Review*, vol. 58 (Spring 1984), pp. 78–102.

22. The best discussion of the radio developments is in Philip T. Rosen, *The Modern Stentors: Radio Broadcasters and the Federal Government, 1920–1934* (Westport, Conn.: Greenwood Press, 1980), see especially pp. 47–76, 93–112. See also Glenn Johnson, "Secretary of Commerce Herbert C. Hoover: The First Regulator of American Broadcasting," Ph.D. diss., University of Iowa (1970).

23. See my "Three Facets of Hooverian Associationalism," pp. 115–19; Bureau of Foreign and Domestic Commerce, *Annual Reports: 1926*, pp. 13, 45–46; *1927*, pp. 41–42.

24. Michael J. Hogan, "Informal Entente: Public Policy and Private Management in Anglo-American Petroleum Affairs, 1918–1924," *Business History Review*, vol. 48 (Summer 1974), pp. 187–205.

25. Kendall Staggs, "Herbert Hoover and the Petroleum Overproduction Problem, 1926–1932," M.A. Essay, University of Iowa (1984), pp. 7–11; Federal Oil Conservation Board, *Report to the President* (1929).

26. John Lathrop, "Hoover's Super-Power Plan to Solve Many Fuel Problems," *Boston Globe* (April 23, 1922); Hoover to Coolidge, November 16, 1923, Coolidge File, Commerce Department Section, Hoover Papers; Hoover to E. B. Whitman, October 20, 1923; Hoover, Statement to Superpower Conference, October 13, 1923, both in Superpower File, Commerce Department Section, Hoover Papers.

27. See my "Secretary Hoover and the Bituminous Coal Problem," *Business History Review*, vol. 42 (Autumn 1968), pp. 253–70. See also James P. Johnson, *The Politics of Soft Coal* (Urbana: University of Illinois Press, 1979), pp. 108–23; Hoover, "Plan to Secure Continuous Employment and Greater Stability in the Bituminous Coal Industry," May 9, 1922, Coal File, Commerce Department Section, Hoover Papers; and Lathrop, "Hoover's Super-Power Plan to Solve Many Fuel Problems."

28. See James H. Shideler, "Herbert Hoover and the Federal Farm Board Project, 1921–25," *Mississippi Valley Historical Review*, vol. 42 (March 1956), pp. 711–29; and Joan Hoff Wilson, "Hoover's Agricultural Policies, 1921–1928," *Agricultural History*, vol. 51 (April 1977), pp. 335–61; Hoover, transcript of remarks to Business Man's Agricultural Conference, April 15, 1927, Agricultural File, Commerce Department Section, Hoover Papers.

29. On the institutional deference in the Japanese and French systems, see Johnson, *MITI;* and Cohen, *Modern Capitalist Planning*. As evidence for the lack of this kind of deference in the United States of the 1920s, one thinks particularly of the relations between the commerce secretariat and the congressional farm and rivers-and-harbors blocs, between it and established bureaucratic groups in the Treasury, state, interior, and agriculture departments, between it and a number of adversary-oriented regulatory and judicial bodies, and between it and such refractory industrial groups as the hardwood lumber manufacturers and the southern coal operators. See again my "Three Facets of Hooverian Associationalism"; "Herbert Hoover, the Commerce Secretariat, and the Vision of an Associative State"; and "Secretary Hoover and the Bituminous Coal Problem." On the pre-1920s American state and the development of adversarial and pluralistic traditions, see Stephen Skowronek, *Building a New American State* (Cambridge: Cambridge University Press, 1982) and Thomas K. McCraw, "Business and Government: The Origins of the Adversary Relationship," *California Management*

Review, vol. 26 (Winter 1984), pp. 33–52.

30. See Hoover to Robert Lamont, May 17, 1929, and memorandum entitled "Industry Conference," in Commerce Department File, President's Subject Files Collection, Hoover Papers; and Julius Barnes, "Notes for an Autobiography," Drawer 7, File 2, Barnes Papers, Duluth, Minnesota. See also my discussion of the project in "Herbert Hoover and American Corporatism, 1929–1933," in Martin L. Fausold and George T. Mazuzan, eds., *The Hoover Presidency: A Reappraisal* (Albany: State University of New York Press, 1974), p. 105.

31. See the discussion in Barry D. Karl, "Presidential Planning and Social Science Research: Mr. Hoover's Experts," *Perspectives in American History,* vol. 3 (1969). The specific plans for reorganization can be found in the Government Departments File, President's Subject Files Collection, Hoover Papers.

32. See David B. Miller, "Origins and Functions of the Federal Farm Board," Ph.D. diss., University of Kansas (1973); and Martin L. Fausold, "President Hoover's Farm Policies, 1929–1933," *Agricultural History,* vol. 51 (April 1977), pp. 362–77.

33. For details on these actions, see Rosen, *Modern Stentors,* pp. 127–44; my "Three Facets of Hooverian Associationalism"; Staggs, "Hoover and the Petroleum Overproduction Problem"; and Robert F. Himmelberg, *The Origins of the National Recovery Administration* (New York: Fordham University Press, 1976), pp. 100–103.

34. I discuss the establishment and evolution of these recovery measures in considerable detail in "Hoover and American Corporatism"; and *The Great War and the Search for a Modern Order,* pp. 182–212. See also Himmelberg, *Origins of NRA,* pp. 88–180; Albert U. Romasco, *The Poverty of Abundance: Hoover, the Nation, and the Depression* (New York: Oxford University Press, 1965); and David Burner, *Herbert Hoover: A Public Life* (New York: Knopf, 1979), pp. 245–83. For Hoover's thinking about the need to develop a new growth area and what in particular might be done to secure a sound basis for such growth in meeting the need for better housing, see Hoover to Roy Young, March 24, 1930, Public Statements File, Hoover Papers.

35. The best work on the origins and early operations of the RFC is James S. Olson, *Herbert Hoover and the Reconstruction Finance Corporation, 1931–1933* (Ames: Iowa State University Press, 1977). See especially pp. 24–61, 116–19. See also J. F. Ebersole, "One Year of the Reconstruction Finance Corporation," *Quarterly Journal of Economics,* vol. 47 (May 1933), pp. 464–92.

36. On this the arguments in Barry D. Karl, *The Uneasy State: The United States from 1915 to 1945* (Chicago: University of Chicago Press, 1983), pp. 111–81, seem to me persuasive.

37. Himmelberg, *Origins of NRA,* pp. 197–200.

38. *Business Week,* February 24, 1934; March 24, 1934; November 17, 1934; and April 2, 1938; Adolf A. Berle, "Banking System for Capital and Capital Credit," May 23, 1939, Statements to Commission File, Temporary National Economic Committee Records, National Archives; Ellis W. Hawley, *The New Deal and the Problem of Monopoly* (Princeton, N.J.: Princeton University Press, 1966), p. 321.

39. U.S. Senate, Committee on Manufactures, *Discussion of a National Economic Council* (75th Congress, 3d session, 1938); Coordinator for Industrial Cooperation, *Council for Industrial Progress* (1936); Kim McQuaid, "The Business Advisory Council of the Department of Commerce," *Research in Economic History,* vol. 1 (1976), pp. 171–81.

40. Arthur Dahlberg et al., *Recovery Plans* (TNEC Monograph 25, 1940), pp. 103–10; Mordecai Ezekiel, *Jobs for All through Industrial Expansion* (New York: Knopf, 1939); Hawley, *New Deal and Monopoly,* pp. 172–84.

41. I discuss these industry-specific programs in some detail in *The New Deal and the Problem of Monopoly,* pp. 205–46. See also Richard S. Kirkendall, *Social Scientists and Farm Politics in the Age of Roosevelt* (Columbia: University of Missouri Press, 1966); Theodore Saloutos, *The New Deal and Agriculture* (Ames: Iowa State University Press, 1983); Gerald D. Nash, *United States Oil Policy, 1890–1964* (Pittsburgh: University of Pittsburgh Press, 1968), pp. 128–56; Earl Latham, *The Politics of Railroad Coordination, 1933–1936* (Cambridge: Harvard University Press, 1959); Johnson, *Politics of Soft Coal,* pp. 217–38; Philip J. Funigiello, *Toward a National Power Policy: The New Deal and the Electric Utility Industry, 1933–1941* (Pittsburgh: University of Pittsburgh Press, 1973); National Resources Planning Board, *Housing: The Continuing Problem* (1940).

42. See Bernard Bellush, *The Failure of the NRA* (New York: Norton, 1975); Hawley, *New Deal and Monopoly,* pp. 19–146; Michael M. Weinstein, *Recovery and Redistribution under the NIRA* (New York: North-Holland, 1980).

43. Thomas McCraw has argued that the Securities and Exchange Commission was successful in making such machinery workable and utilizing it to achieve public policy goals. See Thomas K. McCraw, "With Consent of the Governed: SEC's Formative Years," *Journal of Policy Analysis and Management,* vol. 1 (1982), pp. 346–70.

44. See the works cited in footnote 42. See also Leverett S. Lyon et al., *The National Recovery Administration* (Washington, D.C.: Brookings Institution, 1935); Committee of Industrial Analysis, *The National Recovery Administration* (House Document 158, 75th Congress, 1937); Theda Skocpol and Kenneth Finegold, "State Capacity and Economic Intervention in the Early New Deal," *Political Science Quarterly,* vol. 97 (Summer 1982), pp. 255–78.

45. On the unanticipated organizational activity and how it helped to produce the arrangements characteristic of the post-1934 New Deal, see especially Francis M. Perna, "The National Recovery Administration: The Interest Group Approach to Economic Planning," Ph.D. diss., Cornell University (1981). See also my discussion in *The New Deal and the Problem of Monopoly,* pp. 72–110.

46. Otis L. Graham, Jr., *Toward a Planned Society* (New York: Oxford University Press, 1976), pp. 65–67.

47. See Graham, *Toward a Planned Society,* pp. 31–68; Karl, *Uneasy State,* pp. 155–81; Hawley, *New Deal and Monopoly,* pp. 383–438; Barry D. Karl, "In Search of National Planning," Paper presented at meeting of the Organization of American Historians, April 7, 1983; and Hawley, "A Partnership Formed, Dissolved, and in Renegotiation: Business and Government during the Franklin D. Roosevelt Era," in Joseph Frese et al., eds., *Business and Government* (Tarrytown, N.Y.: Sleepy Hollow Press, 1985).

48. Otis L. Graham, Jr., "The Planning Idea from Roosevelt to Post-Reagan," in Lawrence E. Gelfand and Robert J. Neymeyer, eds., *The New Deal Viewed from Fifty Years* (Iowa City: Center for the Study of the Recent History of the United States, 1984), pp. 1–19; McCraw, "With Consent of the Governed"; Introduction to Chalmers Johnson, ed., *The Industrial Policy Debate*.

Commentaries

James Fallows

I am here as a journalist rather than a historian. So my charge is to consider some of the connections between the historical patterns we have heard about in these discussions and even more so in the papers and the process now underway in calls for industrial policy.

I am struck by the many similarities between industrial policy as it has been practiced or advocated in the past and what we are now hearing. One of those similarities, of course, is the extent to which the desire for industrial policy is a craving that dare not speak its name because it is so much at odds with other traditions in the American political and economic tradition, especially the desire for a market economy.

Similarly, there is the recurrent pattern that calls for industrial policy arising from the dislocations of specific troubled industries and the desire to cope with that. There is the constant tension, both over the past two centuries and now, between these somewhat contradictory diagnoses of the problem— one diagnosis being overcapacity, the other diagnosis being the need for increased productivity.

Finally, there is a similarity in the mild hypocrisy of many of those who oppose industrial policy because, as Professor Wildavsky has pointed out, in the market economy they are often bedecked with many subsidies that even the most buccaneer, free marketeers end up getting from the state.

But with those similarities noted, I also am struck by a difference in today's political economy of industrial policy and what I have heard about the past two centuries. In describing this difference I speak from my experience as a reporter over the past year or two as I have traveled to the regions where the calls for industrial policy are most often heard; that is, I have been in the Upper Midwest in the manufacturing states extensively for the past year or two and also in some of the more booming Sun Belt states.

Although Professor Wildavsky's suggestion of a tripartite model of ways to think about industrial policy is useful and makes sense, his suggestion that many of the Left's calls for industrial policy come out of a concern for fairness and equality of result slightly misstates the political point. If fairness and equality of result and condition were the main propulsive factors in politics now, we would see a much greater emphasis on racial issues and the problems of the black lower class, for example, which has the least equal result of the American population. One hears much less discussion of that when one talks about industrial policy than one does of blue-collar, unionized workers in the Upper Midwest. And the concern is not so much fairness as it is ways of responding to a change that many of these workers perceive as profoundly inimical to their interest.

It is possible to overstate the degree of regional, industrial, and techno-logical change going on in the United States, but it is still occurring. On the whole, people are still leaving the northern manufacturing states and moving to southern states. People are leaving jobs in heavy manufacturing industries and taking up jobs in service industries.

There is a change in the technical emphasis in the manufacturing process, and the question is, Should these connected changes be welcomed and encouraged or resisted, shunned, and feared? I believe that the most fervent calls for industrial policy come from people in that latter category, who are upset about the direction of these connected technical, geographic, and economic changes and want to impede them.

They are concerned for several reasons. One of the reasons is strictly geographic. If one talks at length with people who are most concerned about the decay of the industrial Upper Midwest, what seems to be on their minds is their distaste for Phoenix or Miami or Houston. There is something unpleasant to them about those sterile Sun Belt communities. So that is probably the least rational but the real reason, a geographic distaste for the rise of the Sun Belt and the decline of the Upper Midwest.

One interesting note on this point, I think, was a book published about ten years ago called *Power Shift,* by Kirkpatrick Sale. It is a book that at the time I thought was an extremely vulgarized treatment of this northern versus south-ern change because it reeked of distaste for everything in the South. It suggested as the prototypical Sun Belt citizen Beebee Rebozo as against, say, John Kennedy as the prototype of the northern citizen. But I think some of that attitude is still significant.

A more profound concern, perhaps, is that of community. Over the past sixty or eighty years relatively stable manufacturing communities have grown up around the steel mills of South Chicago and similar establishments throughout the Upper Midwest. Those communities are obviously in the midst of extreme turmoil. People who have lived in one house for fifty years no longer can find a way to support themselves there. So this sense of community and the various human costs of disrupting a community and locating it someplace else are also part of the concern.

A third concern is political. There is a deep and often unspoken fear among many, many Democrats that the political consensus of the Upper

Midwest, the coalition that has been useful since the New Deal, cannot be recreated. If the people who are part of this coalition in Detroit and Chicago go to Los Angeles or Houston or to a small town in Michigan or in Wisconsin, they will no longer join the same coalition. This is part, many Democrats feel, of a secular decline in the coalition that has been so important to them.

The main reason for concern, however, is the connection of economic effects upon this subject population—that is, unionized, blue-collar workers —and what the technical and geographic changes mean for them. Without spending much time on this subject, I am greatly impressed with the number of times I have heard, from machinists in Chicago or unemployed auto workers in Flint or others, the deskilling argument that has been a popular feature of Marxist analysis, especially for the past ten years. That argument is that the introduction of technology into automation will displace the most skilled workers first and lead to a widely polarized society and that capitalists desire to take the skill out of jobs so they can more easily dominate the work force. This is the pattern that many people see in industrial automation.

This is connected similarly to the now fashionable—that sounds more sneering than I mean to be—idea of a two-tiered society. This type of analysis labor unions especially have put out in the last year or two: exposure to international competition, the introduction of automation will lead to a society made of doctors and McDonald's hamburger servers without any middle class of people with relatively well-paying blue-collar jobs.

There is a similar fear about the rise of a service economy as part of the same pattern.

I would like to go into all of these points at greater length, but I cannot here. My point is that this process of change, which seems so profoundly threatening for all these different reasons to many people who have been important to the Democratic party, looks very different to people with other interests in other parts of the country. To them the same change in technology and the same opportunities in world trade are the sources of opportunity for their new industries. The argument about industrial policy, then, reflects the side of this cultural, economic, geographic divide on which people find themselves.

What people in the threatened class mean when they speak of industrial policy is something to impede, regulate, or dampen the change that they see as being so threatening. Industrial policy means big public spending programs for highways so that one can buy more steel. It means trade protection. It means plant-closing loss and so on, whereas to their counterparts in Austin or San Jose industrial policy means opening up the Japanese market for semiconductors or computers so they can sell more of their wares.

That to me is the cultural tension, the cultural politics of industrial economy: now, not so much concern strictly for fairness, but a very understandable reaction of a class that sees itself in decline.

Herbert Stein

When I first encountered these papers I felt like the man in the French play who realized at an advanced age to his surprise that he had been talking prose all his life. I had previously thought of industrial policy in a certain context; and I had written about it; and what I thought industrial policy was was something that we do not now have, something that has been proposed by people like Robert Reich, Felix Roette and Lester Thoreau, Lane Kirkland, Gary Hart, and at an earlier stage Fritz Mondale, each of whom had reasons for being on that side that I thought I could understand and that I was against, not only because they were for it and because we did not now have it, but for other reasons.

Now I discover that at least in two of these three papers industrial policy is something we have always had. According to Aaron Wildavsky, industrial policy is economic policy. That's the first sentence in his paper. And that thought really has set me reeling because it made my being against industrial policy difficult.

Although I did recently write in the summary of my forty-six years in Washington that economic policy is random with respect to the performance of the economy; thank God, there is not much of it.

Now, Mr. McGraw also seems to identify industrial policy as government intervention in the economy, and he shows that we have always had it. As I read him—I may be misreading him—he considers that a good thing, too.

Mr. Hawley is the only one of the three authors who has a view like mine of what industrial policy is: that is, it is something different from several selective, discreet, ad hoc interventions in the economy. It has the notion of a comprehensive plan, a certain devotion to a big picture of the future welfare of the economy, a certain aura of science about it. I think that is the aura being commonly attached to the notion of industrial policy today. And that is what we do not have and I do not think we are going to have and I do not think we want.

I would like to make a brief comment on one aspect of Mr. McGraw's paper before giving my own view of what the situation is. The impression I get from Mr. McGraw's paper is that he thinks the policy of protecting domestic industry and dumping the product on the rest of the world is a way to efficiency and growth. The most obvious thing to say about that policy is that every country cannot carry it out at the same time. Economists do have a certain prejudice for a cosmopolitan outlook that makes accepting that kind of prescription for policy difficult for them. Even aside from that prejudice, if one looks only at the interests of a single country, the basic fact is that that country cannot protect all of its industries and dump the products of all of them on the rest of the world. A country operates with a certain limited supply of resources; and, if it protects some industries and thereby diverts resources into them, it diverts resources away from other industries.

Economists have recognized for a long time that in principle a possibility exists that a governmental decision to protect certain industries and divert resources to those industries will in the long run give a better result in the market allocation of the resources. This is an old infant-industry argument. The question is whether government can on the whole be expected to choose the industries for the best results.

The opposition to this whole line of policy from people like me is based not so much on an economic argument as on a political proposition that the government will not choose the right industries. That is a subject on which it would be useful to have the considered view of political scientists; but I just express a prejudice, perhaps also based on my long tenure in Washington.

Now I would comment on the proposition that this kind of protectionist policy is an explanation of the apparent success of several economies from time to time, most recently the Japanese economy. Well, that explanation may be true; but of course we have all heard many explanations for the success of the Japanese economy. They have a high savings rate. They do not devote a large portion of their gross national product for defense. They have a very strong work ethic. They have something that makes them very good at mathematics. They have small fingers. I do not think we yet know which of these explanations is the correct one; so I am a little reluctant to accept the explanation that protectionist policy has been a major positive contribution.

My view of the industrial policy situation or the government interventionist situation is that there has always been a good deal of government intervention in the U.S. economy. Originally this was mainly at the state and local levels, but it became increasingly a federal function. Probably in absolute terms, as measured by the pages in the *Federal Register* or by the number of employees in the federal regulatory agencies, this intervention has grown over the years, although I do not know whether historians have any way of measuring whether we have more intervention now than we did earlier.

In any case, these measurements are certainly not very good, and they do not really measure what we are interested in. I do not think we are interested in how much intervention there is. We are interested in the degree of freedom in the economy and the extent to which the economy approximates a competitive model. In that dimension the degree of freedom is increasing, and we are coming closer to the competitive model of the economy despite the increase in the size of government intervention somehow measured.

That is because what determines the degree of freedom is not—and the closeness to the competitive model is not—the amount of intervention but things like the size of the market, the costs of information, the costs of transportation, the mobility of the labor force, the technological advance, the production of substitutes for all existing products, and the opening of the international market. The net of those forces has been and continues to be to increase the competitivness and the freedom of the market. I said something like this recently on a program in which I was on a platform with one of the leading libertarian economists of this country, and he said, "Well, but you can't go into the post office business."

It occurred to me that I really had no desire to go into the post office business in the first place. As a matter of fact, however, we have an increasingly large number of firms that are in the post office business with overnight mail delivery, and we will have more and more as we begin to communicate everything by computer network. So technology is even breaking down that limitation on the freedom of enterprise.

What has been going on right along is a race between certain forces making for more government intervention and forces making for a freer market, and on the whole the forces making for the freer market have been gaining.

Now, the questions that should be of interest to political scientists are, What determines and what limits the speed of government expansion and is the limit that determines the balance of the outcome different here than elsewhere? I would like to learn from political scientists about an American view of how things should be that is other than the outcome of the struggle among well-informed self-interests. I really do not get much of an answer to that question out of quotations from Jefferson and Hamilton, for one thing, because that was a long time ago and, for another, because I do not know whether they are representative of the operational political culture of their time.

I can imagine 200 years from now people quoting Ronald Reagan and Fritz Mondale and political scientists saying that is what the American people thought in 1984. Although I will not be around to testify on that, I guess I will leave a little note saying that is not the way I thought.

Nevertheless I do believe that, when all the interests are laid out on the table, there is an American attitude, a certain aversion to the spread of government intervention and a particular aversion to this kind of comprehensive, pseudoscientific planning, the approach that I identify with industrial policy. I think that is what Professor Hawley is also saying. Something resists that explicit comprehensive planning notion even though it is rather receptive to lots of particular interventions.

There may be a simpler explanation that has nothing to do with the political culture. It may result from the fact that the only people who have any self-interest in this overall planning system are a bunch of professors who think they would be the ones to run it, and they just do not have much political clout.

James T. Patterson

As a historian I would like to reflect a minute on what we can learn from history.

I see a certain underlying consensus, although perhaps the individual paper givers do not, in these three papers in answer to this question of what we can learn about the potential for industrial policy from history. I see that, particularly in the twentieth century, much in American political culture has operated and probably, since I am struck by the continuity rather than the break, will continue to operate to inhibit the political realization of industrial policy in the comprehensive planning mode.

Professor McCraw talks about the importance of what he calls a tentative and reluctant tradition of industrial policy in the United States. I think that is not a bad phrase. While we have had manifestations on the part of Herbert Hoover and other people who have attempted to promote some kind of comprehensive, coordinated or corporatist industrial policy, these have been rare. They have been on the political fringes. They have been, as in the case of Hoover, quickly overturned by economic circumstances, the crash and the Depression of 1929 and the 1930s. I would like to underline two reasons—explicit as well as implicit in the papers—this has been so to show the historical underpinning for the day's talk.

Two important strands in twentieth-century popular American political culture have inhibited and will continue to inhibit industrial policy. The first of these is the continuing strength, particularly on the Left, of what historians have called the populist, progressive, New Deal tradition.

Historians are well aware that there were striking differences between these groups of people—the populists, the progressives, the New Dealers. Indeed, there were striking differences within each of these groups; the discontinuities are real, and the political sources of support were often very different. But dating back at least to the Jacksonians is an underlying continuity of a strong hostility in America (perhaps elsewhere, although I suspect stronger here) in the popular mind to special interests, special privilege. In the minds of many twentieth-century Americans, those special interests and special privileges have been indelibly associated with large-scale business enterprise—the trusts, the monopolies, Standard Oil, the American business community—as if it were a monolithic, undifferentiated evil force in American life.

This feeling has been extraordinarily strong. One sees it particularly clearly in the first forty years of the twentieth century when many spokesmen from the Left, particularly from the plains and the western states, brought to their political ideology a hostility not only to big business but also to big government and brought the antimonopolistic tradition into the mainstream of

American life. They were politically effective on many occasions.

This tradition has definitely lost its visibility in the last forty years, but I think in the popular level it continues to exist and to inhibit any policies that could be considered as somehow representing an alliance, a league, or—worse yet—a conspiracy between government and big business.

The second of these strands is a corollary; it represents widespread popular doubts all through the twentieth century (again a continuity) toward the state and more particularly toward government employees, whether they be elected officials or, perhaps worse yet, faceless bureaucrats, paper-shuffling, irresponsible experts, economists, or academics.

This feeling is of course shared by many of the business interests, but it goes much beyond that and militates against the likely adoption of any comprehensive national planning. On the one hand, one has a distrust of business; on the other hand, one has a distrust of business's presumed partner, the government, in such an enterprise of planning.

Professor Hawley speaks of the durability of a "set of populist, Republican and entrepreneurial symbols" in American life. I like that phrase, too, and I think it expresses this doubt about government.

I speak as someone who has written books largely responsive to and sympathetic with the progressive tradition in American history. I would in some ideal world like to see us able to develop a comprehensive national industrial policy, but I do not think that the record of American history in the twentieth century suggests that there is much support in the political culture and in the popular mind for this kind of development. I therefore do not expect to live to see it.

Part Two
Industrial Policy in
International Perspective

Introduction

The second group of papers analyzes industrial policies from a comparative international perspective. Other political economies have dealt, and are dealing, with the challenges that have produced the calls for industrial policies in the United States; their experiences, like that of this country, have been shaped by their individual political institutions, cultures, and practices. Thus, to gain the added dimension of an international perspective, AEI commissioned papers on the politics of industrial policy in five industrial nations: France, Great Britain, West Germany, Japan, and Italy.

France

Stephen Cohen, Serge Halimi, and John Zysman note that "since 1945 France can legitimately be called a strong state, one that has decided to be permanently involved in the conduct of economic affairs and that has created the adequate tools to make this involvement possible." Their paper, "Institutions, Politics, and Industrial Policy in France," traces the evolution of French interventionist policy from the Great Depression through the first years of Socialist leadership under President François Mitterand. The authors concentrate on the role of political and institutional factors in the development of French industrial policy, highlighting the system's strengths and weaknesses. They also provide an insightful analysis of the 1981 Socialist electoral victory and subsequent implementation of the "nationalization policy" and evaluate the impact of these changes on the future of French industrial policy.

Although many believe active government involvement in the economy to be a longstanding feature of French society—a product of "étatism" dating back to Louis XIV—the authors argue that this perception conflicts with the facts. The government's role in the economy was "only occasionally a commanding one" and "the entanglements of industry and state at the turn of the century were limited." Comprehensive government economic intervention only fully emerged after World War II. Before the end of the war, "economic liberalism was . . . the orthodoxy of the Republic."

The devastating impact of the 1930s Depression, the shock of the so-called Great Humiliation of 1940, and the destruction during World War II combined to solidify public support for modernization in France. The interventionist ideology adopted to achieve that goal "grew not from some intellectually compelling theory but because practical alternatives were limited." Entrepreneurship, capital, and other essential ingredients for modernization were in short supply at the end of the war. Further, note the authors, the disgrace of Vichy's collaboration with Hitler "excluded any reactionary path and discredited conservative parties and institutions," aiding the Left politically and the case for interventionism. Together these factors produced a major ideological and institutional transformation following the war—the formation of the "dirigiste" consensus. This transformation was "held together by the junction of three major evolutions—the attribution to the state of vastly increased economic responsibilities, the appearance of new political and economic institutions, and the emergence of a younger generation of new leaders."

The institutional structure and the character of French industrial policy implementation, according to the authors, show considerable continuity from 1945 through 1980, despite major political transformations. Institutionally, economic decision making is dominated by a strong, centralized executive branch. Parliament's limited role in economic policy formation, evident in 1945, was formalized by constitutional changes in 1958 and continues today. A well-trained corps of professional bureaucrats forms a selective civil service, responsible for policy formation and implementation. The indicative plan and the credit-based, administered-price financial system have been the major interventionist instruments for the state, although the plan has steadily declined in importance. Control over funds in the economy, beginning with the allocation of the Marshall Plan money, represents the most important vehicle for industrial policy implementation.

Insulated from detailed parliamentary influence and in control of the financial system, the executive bureaucratic structure has at least two advantages when forging industrial policy. First, bureaucrats do not have "to take into account the micropolitics of interest group demands" and "can discriminate against a politically powerful segment of the population" when forming policy. Second, their isolation from legislative politics removes much policy making and policy implementation from the public realm and permits the state to act "without always provoking a national political debate."

Overall, the French system has worked remarkably well, the authors argue. Since 1945 France has enjoyed unprecedented economic prosperity. French industrial policy measures have worked best when addressing industries in which competition is limited, returns from investment are slow, and markets are controlled by the state. Not surprisingly, the state has faired less well in ventures in which markets and products change rapidly.

The 1981 Socialist victory and initiation of the nationalization policy marks a turning point in the evolution of French industrial policy. Indeed, the authors argue, it may mark the rebirth of economic liberalism in France. "The nationalizations were political symbols. Given the extraordinary interventionist capacity built up and refined by the conservatives, there was no technical need for the move." The nationalization policy, the authors maintain, was a political move that largely failed. "By acquiring ownership of companies and banks it could already control, the state ripped asunder the shadowy world in which it operated beforehand." It placed government intervention in full view of the public, making it alone responsible for the economic problems originating in key sectors. What is more, the Socialist move increased government accountability during troubled economic times. "The unlikely outcome of Socialist nationalizations," they conclude, "may then well have been the destruction of a general . . . consensus around the notion of a state-managed economy."

Great Britain and West Germany

In his two papers, "British Industrial Policy" and "West German Industrial Policy," Jeffrey A. Hart describes the organizational structure for economic policy making and examines the historical development of industrial policies in each country. He then turns his attention to specific British and German government initiatives in three sectors—steel, automobiles, and information technology—both to illustrate larger industrial policy trends in each country and to reveal some of the strengths and weaknesses of these policies. Professor Hart's papers not only offer an informative and insightful introduction to British and German industrial policies but also provide the added benefit of direct comparative analyses at the sectoral level to enrich our understanding.

In his paper on British industrial policy, Hart states: "The key to understanding British industrial policy is understanding the general weakness of British firms in international competition." British industrial policy consists of a series of ad hoc and reactive policy initiatives designed principally to improve the performance of British industries and firms in international competition. This pattern of reactive interventionism, furthermore, has been a consistent feature of British economic policy for at least a decade and a half. Despite proclaimed ideological differences concerning the roles of government and the market, he argues, both Labour party and Conservative party governments have responded to industrial crises in a similar fashion. Hart attributes this continuity in British industrial policy to public expectations and political pressures produced by the strong interventionist legacy of the 1960s —a legacy that even ardent free-market advocate Margaret Thatcher has been unable to ignore completely. Britain's decentralized institutional structure for economic policy making also helps explain continuity in policy.

Though on the surface the British government appears structurally suited for industrial policy formation and implementation, Hart argues, the distribution of economic policy making authority is sufficiently fractured to discourage or prevent broad-based industrial policy initiatives of the regional or sectoral types. Five principal institutional actors share responsibility for industrial policy making in Britain: (1) the prime minister and Cabinet, (2) the Treasury, (3) the Department of Trade and Industry, (4) the National Economic Development Council (NEDC), and (5) the British Technology Group (and its predecessors). The last three, further, are structured specifically to promote "industrial democracy" in the policy-making process and have, as a result, frequently sacrificed efficiency for consensus building. Hart states that the NEDC, for example, has been criticized for making the government's role "too equal with that of management and labor" and has been branded, as a consequence, the "institutionalized recreation of pluralistic stagnation." Britain, in short, has a "tradition of decentralized authority for industrial policies" that operates against comprehensive industrial policy programs and in favor of ad hoc industrial policy measures.

The historical evolution of British industrial policy shows that, contrary to what might be expected, the interparty rivalry between Labour and the Conservatives explains little about industrial policy development in Britain since the late 1960s. Despite their ideological aversion to industrial policy, several Conservative governments bowed to political pressures and chose the interventionist path enough times "to make one question the firmness with which Conservatives were likely to pursue their preferred policies." Hart states that the "Labour party, on the other hand, has not always been a bastion of support for government intervention generally and industrial policy specifically." He maintains that failures associated with the National Plan experiment in 1964 and Tony Benn's industrial policy attempts in 1974–1975 dampened initial Labour enthusiasm for Socialist policies. Thus, instead of well-defined oscillations in policy initiatives paralleling the shifting political fortunes of each party, we find a general pattern of "growing mutual acceptance on the part of Labourites and Conservatives of a policy that rescues large failing firms deemed crucial to the overall economy, provides investment capital and other support for high-technology industries (especially microelectronics), manages the state's portfolio primarily with an eye to obtaining a reasonable return on investment (except in the case of major rescues), and otherwise leaves things pretty much to the private sector."

Professor Hart's closer examination of British government policies in the steel, automobile, and information technology sectors provides support for the existence of this pattern in British industrial policy since the late 1960s. This review of sector-specific policies and developments also offers some insight into the strengths and weaknesses of the British system in dealing with problem industries and firms. Hart argues that the British state appears better equipped to promote emerging growth industries like microelectronics than to resurrect declining industries like steel and automobiles. One explanation, he suggests, is that heavily protected industries or state enterprises delay "capacity reduction because of their insulation from short-term economic pressures" and, as a result, do not adjust well when faced with declining fortunes. State-protected or -owned firms, however, can assume greater risks and "can be successful in increasing investment where private enterprises have a history of overcaution," perhaps giving them an advantage in growth industries or sectors.

In his second paper, which examines the West German case, Hart characterizes German industrial policy as "combining a low degree of centralization of government institutions for making industrial policy with a highly centralized 'corporatistic' or 'concertative' bargaining system, especially during crises." Germany, he argues, resembles Britain and the United States in its decentralization of decision-making authority and France and Japan in its bargaining arrangements. The Federal Republic of Germany, in contrast to Britain, has a strong tradition of market-oriented, noninterventionist economic policies. The federal government traditionally maintained a "hands off" posture with regards to troubled firms, leaving rescue operations to the banks or to regional governments. During the post-OPEC period, however, pressures generated by, among other things, increased international competition have caused the German government also to intervene increasingly in industrial crises. The Germans still view federal government intervention as a measure of last resort, and German initiatives still tend to shun "ownership" solutions in favor of indirect measures.

Industrial policy-making authority in Germany, states Hart, is also decentralized (perhaps even more so than in Britain) and serves to discourage broad-based industrial policy programs. Economic policy-making responsibility is divided among the chancellor's office, the German Bundesbank, the Ministry of Economics, the Ministry of Research and Technology, the Sachsverständigenrat (Council of Experts), and the regional governments. The German central bank, or Deutsche Bundesbank, in contrast to the British system, resembles the U.S. Federal Reserve Bank in its structural independence, holds sole control over monetary policy, and acts as an institutional brake on elected officials' authority. "State governments," Hart notes, "have considerable power, and economic policy in the Federal Republic is truly federal." Finally, strong ties between the German banks and industry reduce the need for federal government involvement at the firm or industry level—informal ties significantly absent in Britain's merchant banking system.

German economic policy, argues Hart, has evolved over the past thirty years from relatively noninterventionist policies to much more ambitious forms of intervention. Policies from 1950 through 1967 can be summarized by four basic principles embodied in the then popular notion of a "social market economy": (1) the state should rely on the competitive market and avoid government economic planning; (2) the state's role was to promote competi-

CARL A. RUDISILL LIBRARY
LENOIR RHYNE COLLEGE

tion; (3) while countercyclical economic measures were acceptable, monetary tools should be used and "inflationary" demand-style Keynesian policies avoided; and (4) the free market and libertarian polity were mutually dependent and reinforcing. The two major political parties, according to Hart, were in "basic agreement" on the planning versus competition issues and the "social market economy" program until the 1966–1967 recession. Nineteen sixty-seven witnessed the formation of the grant coalition between the Social Democratic party and the Christain Democratic Union, an economic policy shift toward Keynesian demand management, and the formation of an informal bargaining process called "concertation" (uniting trade unions, management, the government, and the Bundesbank principally for wage negotiations). Nineteen seventy-three and the OPEC crisis brought yet another shift in the focus of debate and actual economic policies as sectoral and mesoeconomic interventions were seriously considered and eventually adopted. Finally, government involvement in industry crises increasingly emerged as a feature of German industrial policy after 1975. Hart attributes the government's willingness to intervene to new policy instruments that made such intervention possible, to the vulnerability of German banks to a growing number of firm failures, to the number and importance of firm failures resulting from increasing international competition and some firms' bad strategies.

Sector studies, again, illustrate general trends in German industrial policy. In all three sectors, the Germans avoided intervention, preferring solutions by the banks or the regional governments or both. When the government finally intervened, it chose indirect measures to achieve its goals. In the case of steel, for example, the German government avoided nationalization and "relied primarily on its ability to sanction mergers and to provide grants, loans, and loan guarantees." These sector examples show that this German approach has produced both successes and failures. One weakness of the German strategy, Hart argues, is that, once deciding to intervene, the government tends to get "much more involved than it had ever intended." Another weakness is that "because the banks have incentives to rescue ineptly managed but very large firms, government intervention tends to be very costly." Professor Hart concludes that "the main lesson of German industrial policy is the need to match public policy to the market conditions and industrial capacities existing in specific industries."

Japan

Chalmers Johnson opens his analysis of Japanese industrial policy with a warning that "Japanese institutions of government and business are themselves quite different, and have quite different histories and functions, from those of the Anglo-American world; and these differences directly influence the kind of government-business relationship that exist in Japan." Citing a leading scholar on Japan, he states further:

> Terms such as "competition," "private industry," or "free enterprise," commonly used in discussions of Japanese business, conjure up in the minds of readers in English quite different images from existing realities of Japanese business. "Collusive rivalry," "semiprivate industry," "quasi-public enterprise," respectively might be more apt expressions, precisely because their Western referents are unclear.

Johnson then describes four basic institutional "realities" that form the backdrop to the political economy of Japan and that present a great contrast to the situation in the United States. First there is the existence of a state bureaucracy that is highly respected, that is made up of the "best and the brightest," and that wields broad discretionary powers. Conversely, the Japanese parliament or Diet is the weakest of all the industrialized nations under scrutiny; made up of a high proportion of former bureaucrats, it reigns but does not rule. A third background element in the Japanese political economy is a triangular alliance among big business, the bureaucracy, and the parliament. Big business itself is organized in oligopolies of bank- and trading-company-based conglomerates that subordinate profit to market share. Finally, the Japanese legal system is modeled more on Continental European tradition than on Anglo-American common law; it thus eschews detailed contracts and adversarial relations in favor of ad hoc agreements and arrangements backed by administrative guidance from the bureaucracy.

Johnson analyzes five institutions (or policies) that form the basis of a government–business-shaped industrial policy. First, the Fiscal Investment and Loan Plan is an investment budget wholly in the hands of the bureaucracy. It amounts to about 40 percent of the general account budget and 6 percent of gross national product in a given year. It finances, among other things, retreats from declining sectors and advances into high-risk, new high-technology sectors. Second, 250 state organs known as deliberation councils form the institutional base for public-private consultation. The most famous and important of these is the Industrial Structure Council attached to the Ministry of International Trade and Industry (MITI). This council is the approval body for MITI's long-range "vision plans" for the future structure of Japanese industry. Third, antitrust and monopoly policy in Japan has developed on a highly pragmatic, ad hoc basis, with the guiding principle being the impact of industrial structure on Japan's place in international competition. Thus the Japanese have developed a complex combination of cartelization and competition that defies Anglo-American theory and practice but that is a key element in their industrial competitiveness. Fourth, they have created a complex group of incentives and disincentives for industrial location, avoiding what Johnson characterizes as the "chaotic (and damaging) process" of the shift to the Sun Belt in the United States. Fifth, they have developed a highly sophisticated R&D policy that is concerned above all with the process of taking scientific and technological breakthroughs and getting them to market quickly through cost reductions, quality controls, and improved production and design techniques. "This commercial orientation of much of Japan's public investment," he concludes, "is a critically important part of the government-business relationship, and one that is growing rather than declining in importance."

After reviewing in some detail the role of MITI in promoting overall economic direction and in targeting and assisting key industrial sectors, the paper concludes with four recommendations for nations trying to compete with Japan: (1) learn from Japan's experience but do not try to copy it exactly; (2) bring one's own macroeconomic policies under control first; (3) avoid protectionism at all costs; and (4) inhibit political influence on economic policy making.

Italy

Devoting his commentary to a brief analysis of the changing relations between state-owned and private enterprises in Italy, Mario Schimberni first traces the historical development of the publicly owned industry sector in Italy from the early 1930s to the present. He then offers a set of recommendations to improve the functioning and effect of Italian industrial policy in the future. The government, he notes, must concentrate its focus only on essential objectives when formulating policy. The government must also learn to rely more on private industry and market mechanisms to achieve policy goals. "There is in Italy today," concludes Schimberni, "a new climate of opportunity for private industry, an opportunity that industrial leaders must now seize for the good of the Italian economy."

Commentaries

Robert Pastor. "These papers," begins Robert Pastor in his commentary, "not only help us to see how other governments relate to their domestic economies but also force us to question certain assumptions governing our own relation between the government and the private economy." Specifically, evidence presented in the papers challenges three common assumptions in the United States—assumptions that derive support from neoclassical economics: (1) that government intervention in the economy is inherently inefficient and impedes economic development; (2) that state companies are inefficient and drain public resources; and (3) that long-term economic planning fouls up the economy. "All the papers do suggest that these three assumptions are tenuous at best." Chalmers Johnson's warning about generalizing the lessons of one country's experiences, he argues further, should be turned around. "We are really talking about whether or not these basic assumptions that Americans hold have a specific validity, which pretends to a universality, or whether or not they have any validity at all." Comparative economic study enables us to test the universality of these principles. Pastor urges additional, more detailed comparative study to ascertain better the necessary qualities for successful government intervention.

Howard J. Wiarda. Howard J. Wiarda concludes the second panel discussion by summarizing the large and diverse set of questions raised by the studies on the individual countries. He states that while the papers provide valuable insights into the evolution and status of country-specific industrial policies, they fail to establish adequate comparative measures to evaluate these policies rationally. Indeed, he argues, the papers indicate a lack of consensus on such fundamentals as the definition of industrial policy itself. He concludes that "we need comparative indexes, comparative measures for evaluating industrial policy" and encourages their development.

Institutions, Politics, and Industrial Policy in France

Stephen S. Cohen, Serge Halimi, and John Zysman

*The issue is not whether France's economy will be directed or not.
The only choice is between an indecisive direction implemented by a
number of pilots each of whom follows his track, and direction
under the authority of a single and good pilot.*

MICHEL DEBRÉ, 1938

*The political change of 1981 has had at least one positive effect: a
large majority of Frenchmen now agrees to criticize the excesses of
state power and to demand more individual responsibility.*

RAYMOND BARRE, 1983

The perception that France is a strong state, one that can exert industrial leadership, is widespread. It is also accurate. Since 1945 France has legitimately been called a strong state, one that has decided to be "permanently involved" in the conduct of economic affairs and that has created the adequate tools to make this involvement possible. This involvement goes much beyond the traditional mix of quotas, subsidies, and cartels; the government has become a marketplace player with a system that hinges on a specific set of institutional arrangements. The executive branch has been freed from detailed microintervention by parliament. The elite administration is a self-contained system, almost a social caste, with considerable discretion in implementing its purposes or those set by the party in power. Administrative discretion is combined with instruments that permit the administration to allocate funds within the economy. Those interventionist instruments are rooted in a credit-based, administered price financial system.

Many believe this system to result from *etatisme*, some unfathomable yet

This essay draws heavily on Stephen Cohen, *Modern Capitalist Planning: The French Model*, Rev. ed. (Berkeley: University of California Press, 1977); and John Zysman, *Governments, Markets, and Growth: Financial Systems and the Politics of Industrial Change* (Ithaca, N.Y.: Cornell University Press, 1983).

still permanent feature of French society and character. The understanding, though common, is misplaced. The French state has, no doubt, played a continuing role from Louis XIV to François Mitterrand; but with industrial action, this role has only occasionally been a commanding one. Interventionism in recent years has grown, as powerful and practical justifications have made it compelling. Were the interventionist pressures to lose some of their power and the institutional framework some of its effectiveness, the statist consensus would no longer be ensured.

These interventionist elements result from the perceived need to face a situation of backwardness and to muster the instruments of an economic take-off. France's ideology and institutions have not been built on the logic of Anglo-Saxon laissez faire.

The mixed economic performance of the French state strengthened under Socialist tenure has led to some unraveling of the *dirigiste* consensus. The recent Socialist nationalizations had little to do with the desire to increase state control as a means of facing a crisis situation, a crisis to which the Left believed economic liberalism offered no acceptable answers. The nationalizations took place in the context of an existing and sophisticated apparatus to conduct industrial policy that gave the state great power. By acquiring ownership of companies and banks it could already control, the state ripped asunder the shadowy world in which it had hitherto operated. It thereby transformed its intervention into a public issue. The unlikely outcome of Socialist nationalizations may then well have been the destruction of a general—though recent and unspoken—consensus around the notion of a state-managed economy. Most interesting at the moment, then, are not the institutions of intervention but the politics swirling around the institutions.

Industrial Policy before and during World War II

Before 1981 every significant thrust toward an increased role of the state in the economy was closely associated with the perception of a failure of economic liberalism. Often there were quite serious problems, dramatized by a major economic disruption or a political collapse. Indeed, France's strong state was set up in the twentieth century to change the nation's production profile. Capitalist development had been slow and uneven. An interventionist ideology grew not because some theory was intellectually compelling but because the practical alternatives were limited. The state hardly ever intervened to redistribute the wealth produced by private companies; it intervened after World War II to recreate a wealth that had disappeared, to build industries that were in shambles, and to restore a nation that had been defeated.

The mythology of a French economy continuously dominated by the state notwithstanding, the entanglements of industry and state at the turn of the century were limited. The demands of a protracted World War I illuminated the inadequacies of French industry. The end of the war and, more important, its successful outcome led to a "return to normalcy": the prewar status quo was vindicated and then consolidated by France's eventual victory. At the time, economic liberalism was called the "orthodoxy of the Republic,"[1] a republic rooted in the countryside, in the small town, and in small business. French bureaucrats were trained in a private school, and the French state had few tools and little desire to intervene systematically and continuously in the economy.

The Great Depression of 1930, the great humiliation of 1940, and the great destructions of World War II dramatically challenged this orthodoxy. Beginning in 1932, French intellectual elites took notice of a growing backwardness of France's economy vis-à-vis other nations, especially Germany. Entangled in the sibling ideologies of smallness and stability, France was becoming a caricature of Malthusianism: a declining and aging population, tiny agricultural plots and industrial units, protection against the winds of change. Stuck in its preference for craft over industry, snuggled behind a Maginot Line against German invasions, dependent on electric power which came from Germany, France was asking for the humiliation that was soon to follow. The strength of this liberal, yet still premodern, consensus is apparent in that the Great Depression was not enough to shatter it. Even the leftist Popular Front, which took power in 1936, did not dare to nationalize any substantial portion of French industry. It only applied some stimulus, which today would be called Keynesian, to an economy ill fitted to respond.

When World War II broke out, it did so on what Charles de Gaulle called a "hopelessly laggard economy." Within five weeks, the French superpower was unequivocally trounced, and its armies had capitulated in disgrace. At this juncture, two vastly different options could be contemplated. Neither included a continuation of past economic policies so thoroughly discredited by the extreme weakness they had brought upon the country. The first path was a truly reactionary one, blaming the defeat not on the lack of modernization but, rather, on its very existence. Modernization had supposedly destroyed French fiber and its set of sturdy traditional values. France, this side argued, had to be punished for its industrial arrogance and brought back where it belonged: the small family farm with its plot of land, its plow, and its cow. The state should be strengthened to see to it that no disruptive force could again challenge this enjoyable paralysis. Eighty-four-year-old Philippe Pétain, proud of his bygone military glory, became, symbolically enough, the head of that state. His huge popularity at the time said much about the deep longings of the French: security, sedateness, and sleep.

This strategy collapsed when servitude to Germany became part of the package. Resistance fighters had no trouble pointing out that Pétain's choices led him to accept the subservience of France to a stronger Nazi Germany.

For the Resistance, embodied by de Gaulle, France had to catch up instead of blissfully slipping further backward on the road to modernity. It had to make the right choice between industrialization and oblivion. The humiliation of 1940 had doomed the prewar mix of French-style liberalism (which bore little resemblance to the British version) and stability; the disgrace of Vichy's collaboration with Hitler excluded any reactionary path and discredited conservative parties and institutions (the church and the business community) whose attitude during the war had been objectionable at best. In the face of the collapse of past ideologies and elites, the opportunity was great for a determined young elite to redraw the French economic and political landscape. Given the strength of the Left at this time, the scope of the reconstruction task, and the bitterness over past experiences emphasizing stability or gradualism, one is hardly surprised that 1944 saw an unprecedented attempt to centralize if not socialize economic power and to awaken French society.

Without the defeat of 1940, such a shift would have been inconceivable. The interventionist temptation was at last acted upon because of the elimination of those who would have resisted it. A policy of development and growth would be initiated with the belief that only the state could secure and sustain its momentum. In the eyes of the modernizers, the magnitude of the reconstruction task at hand and the absence of any alternative entrepreneurs meant there were no choices. This point needs emphasis because it says much about the difference between the nationalizations of 1945 and those of 1982. When François Mitterrand decided to "complete the unfinished process opened by Charles de Gaulle," the challenge to be faced appeared less dramatic, the resistance to nationalization was greater, and alternatives existed. In 1945 the consensus for state activism was broad and lasting; in 1982 it was narrower, and it quickly evaporated.

Les Trente Glorieuses

The thirty years that followed World War II witnessed an unprecedented economic prosperity ("les Trente Glorieuses") as well as the ebb and flow of state intervention. But the ebb was high and the flow, low. French economic policy since the war has been marked by a statist mode of policy making. It may be less visible when a booming economy no longer requires close direction, it may be more apparent when a cyclical downturn pushes some companies to bankruptcy thereby increasing state leverage to reorganize ailing industries; it is always there. Elsewhere we have reconstructed the political process that built this system, the story in which the state gains the opportunity to pursue its ideology and the instruments to implement its ambitions. We will now examine the prevailing situation as it existed in 1981 before French Socialists decided to increase the vast powers of the state substantially. The economic institutions of 1945 were not identical to those of 1980; a thirty-year evolution of tinkering and construction had taken place. But we do indeed believe that the continuity is real, notwithstanding major political transformations. In contrast, as we shall show later, the nationalizations of 1982 represent such a strengthening of *direct* state control that they reduce the sophistication of the interventionist system and release the oppositions to a *dirigiste* industrial policy that had successfully been contained beforehand.

Until the oil crisis of 1973, France's economy underwent major transformation and spectacular expansion. Broadly speaking, these changes can be ascribed to an institutional and ideological revolution. Ideologically, the elite consensus around a "stalemate society" had been broken after 1945 and replaced among those responsible in the government with a born-again fervor for economic modernization. Institutionally, the state stopped being the referee of a sluggish game, becoming instead the coach, player, and ball. Needless to say, these two evolutions are closely interrelated. Without a new ideology, the institutions of *dirigisme* would not have appeared; without these institutions, the ideology would not have prevailed. Because the list of problems that had to be addressed during those years was quite spectacular, without a strong state a successful resolution of the stalemate—the defeat of those who supported a traditional economy and traditional approaches to managing it—would have been remote. Entrenched special interests, an outdated network of distribution, cartels and lack of competition, a backward agriculture, timid businessmen, subsidized inefficiency; everywhere, everybody was in search of a profit without risk in the womb of a protected environment. Many of these people understood a strengthening of the state to mean more effective protection, when in fact the stronger state forced them to change or to disappear. For those who engineered the change this misunderstanding was not unfortunate; by the time the truth became clear, it was too late for the victims, however.

The institutional and cultural transformations that took place after 1945 were held together by the junction of three major evolutions—the attribution to the state of vastly increased economic responsibilities, the appearance of new political and economic institutions, and the emergence of a younger generation of leaders. A statist ideology pervaded the bureaucracy and gave it the desire to transform French society; a new set of institutions enabled the executive to shelter its bureaucracy from conservative interest-group pressures; and a sophisticated set of instruments for state control of the economy offered the bureaucracy the tools it needed to act. Ideology motivated the action, politics weakened the opposition, and institutions permitted the implementation.

It is difficult to overestimate the major ideological transformation France underwent after World War II, from the previous republican orthodoxy of small villages and a seasonal pace of life to the theme of modernity and change. The interventionist attitude played a dominant role only because it alone seemed able to rid France of the shackles of her backwardness. The marriage of modernization and state intervention seemed obvious at the time;

it was not, however, cast in concrete. Today's loss of confidence of French society in an economic progress brought upon by the state and the resurgence of an ideology of private entrepreneurship amply demonstrate that fact. But in 1945, there was no enterpreneurial spirit to speak of and a lot of enterprise to show. France had the opportunity to change everything that had made her weak. In addition to the desire and the opportunity, it had the elites that modernization required. After a few years, many thought, modernity would trickle down into the life of the average Frenchman who remained more stunned than excited by the change. As Jean Monnet, a leader of French planning, once said, "Behind a tractor, a farmer will never think again as he used to when he was behind a horse."[2]

Still, in the process of fundamentally transforming France, farmers, like most Frenchmen, were pushed more often than they jumped. The pushers were part of this new generation, which suddenly occupied an overwhelming position of power in French society after the old elites had gone underground, discredited by their unquestionable failures before the war and by their questionable behavior during the war. Besides youth, these new elites brought with them a Saint-Simonian fascination with industrialization and scientific progress, an unconcealed hostility toward political parties tied to specific clienteles, and more generally a devotion to the idea of public interest. According to them, this public interest could best be served by a *dirigiste* system adroitly mixing rationality and elitism—that is, the cult of elites, which like them knew what this public interest was. These men and their ideological successors, trained in the schools from which they were recruited for state service and later in which they taught, have been in power since 1945. To make sure that the ideas these elites held so dearly would not fade away, a heavily ideological school was set up and given a lock on the recruitment of whoever was expected to count in French society. Although the National School of Administration (ENA) graduates fewer than two hundred students a year, its alumni include the current prime minister, both leaders of the opposition, and nine of the twenty managers named by the Left to head nationalized companies. Until 1945, a private institution, l'École Libre des Sciences Politiques, was responsible for grooming French elites in the idea that state intervention always meant the defense of narrow societal interest at the expense of the average taxpayer. After 1945 the ENA taught the supremacy of technocracy and state-led growth over economic liberalism and the ineptness of a generally Malthusian business community. The shift did not lead to any democratization of the elites, but the ideology with which they pervaded state and society could hardly have been more different.

The modernizing elite, trained in common schools, found its base in the state administration, the civil service. The elite positions were filled from within the privileged corps, the *Grands Corps d'État*. Entry into these corps—crosses between unions and gentlemen's clubs—came upon graduation from ENA and a second school, Polytechnique. Those new bureaucratic elites, however, would not have found their nationalist fervor very useful except for a constitutional battle that removed their major competitors—French legislators—from the arena of effective policy making. Because of the parliamentary nature of the French system, before 1945 state intervention essentially meant the allocation of subsidies to electoral lobbies. Likewise ministries represented specific constituencies (such as officers by the Ministry of Defense and farmers by the Ministry of Agriculture) more than they were agents of a coordinated state intervention. The turn toward a presidential system took place only in 1958; it has been accentuated ever since. The decline of parliamentary power over economic policies, however, long preceded that turn. If parliamentarians had the nominal power to supervise the growing entanglement of the state in the economy, they were not even close to having the expertise and the staff actually to control what was taking place. As new economic institutions mushroomed and gained power, this handicap became formidable.

In 1958 a new constitution, inspired by Charles de Gaulle, accentuated the power of the executive by stripping away from the parliament its nominal power and relegating deputies and senators into positions of virtual impotence. We need not detail or describe the devices that achieved such a result; it is enought to say that the legislature completely lacks the institutional power and the technical expertise to exert any influence on the day-to-day operations of French economic policy. When, in 1978, the French government de facto nationalized the steel industry, the parliament was not even consulted. Five years later when the executive completely reorganized the electronics industry, deputies kept debating what seems to be in France an eternal subject of vain controversy: the rights and obligations of religious schools. Examples of that kind could be endlessly recounted. This insulation from parliamentary pressure and influence has at least two advantages for the French bureaucracy. First, not having to take into account the micropolitics of interest group demands to which parliaments are usually responsive, bureaucrats can discriminate against a politically powerful segment of the population. Second, because decisions are made in executive offices and not after roll calls, the state can intervene without always provoking a national political debate. Economic policies therefore are removed from the public realm, and they keep a low visibility.

Having a purpose, having a team, and being free from outside interference, is not enough, however, to permit effective intervention. A specific set of tools of intervention were put in place. Like other countries, France used the instruments of taxes, public spending, and price controls. In each case, the use of these instruments for purposes of economic policy was somewhat new despite the assertions of those who claimed a history of constant intervention in France. It took World War I for the country to introduce an income tax; it took the Depression and World War II before France used public spending for purposes other than the mere payment of the debt and of the essential missions of defense, justice, and education. At any rate, these instruments are fairly common in all countries and do not require a detailed explanation, with the possible exception of price controls, which can mobilize the equivalent of a real army controlling 200,000 stores and verifying five million price tags in less than a week.[3] Still the role of all these traditional devices has remained fairly constant in French economic policy.

What does need to be explained because of its specificity and its importance in the conduct of French industrial policy is the institution of indicative planning and the organization of the financial system. Both have played decisive—and twin—roles. Though the glory of planning essentially belongs to the past, the role of finance still looms enormously large.

Planning can be the epitome of the bureaucratic dream. During the late 1940s and early 1950s, however, it was to express the agenda of the nation through a process of collective research and proposition organized democratically. But when the first plan was set up, it had less to do with social experimentation than it did with distributing limited resources (mostly American aid) to a devastated economy. In theory, planning was indicative. In conformity with the rationalist orientation of the French bureaucracy, planners believed that if they could only justify their priorities, everybody would follow them. As Jean Monnet said, "Our plan will not impose anything on anybody."[4] In fact, the indications carried considerable weight thanks to the funds to which they were attached in a country starving for credit. The alliance between the Planning Commission and the Treasury probably did more for the implementation of the plan than did any pedagogy of modernity. Gradually, however, planning lost its power. First, a substantial economic growth reduced the commission's opportunities to restructure ailing industries. Second, France's growing entanglement in the world economy and the sophistication of a booming market made long-term predictions more difficult because of the number of variables planners could no longer control. Managing the unpredictable is more difficult a task than organizing a closed system. The sixth plan could not forecast the quadrupling of oil prices, which completely reshuffled French economic data, any better than the seventh and the ninth plans could anticipate that the value of the dollar—the currency with which France has to pay 40 percent of its imports—was to increase by an average of 20 percent every year between 1980 and 1984.

In 1965 the preamble to the fifth plan addressed the issue squarely: "Is planning useful in an economy where, after a period of war and reconstruction, the mechanisms of market and competition have found a new vigor? Is a plan still possible?"[5] Upon its arrival to power, the Left tried to revive the old magic and did in fact elaborate a new, decentralized plan. Planning rhetoric flowed endlessly to the general indifference of the public. Two facts spoke louder than words, however. François Mitterrand named his archrival Michel Rocard minister of planning and, in July 1984, offered the job to the Communist party, which was so little flattered that it turned the job down.

Whereas the plan was publicly discussed and sometimes (although less and less) executed, the decisions of a state-controlled financial system remained in the shadows of executive secrecy and carried a lot of weight. One can argue that state-led industrial intervention has essentially depended on the selective allocation of credit made possible by a credit-based, price-administered system. This influence of the state was certainly facilitated by its ownership, following the nationalizations of 1945, of the three major banks. State control, however, extended beyond the banks it owned to the credit system in its entirety and, through credit, to the economy as a whole. The interventionist capacities of the French state rested as much on financial as on administrative arrangements.

Because of the various degrees of self-financing of investments from industry to industry, the extent to which determining the credit policies of financial institutions mattered was bound to vary. Still, the existence of a narrow securities market compelled every major industry facing economic difficulties or undergoing a program of improving its capital equipment to turn to banks for the funds they needed. Through banks, these industries were once again meeting the state and its priorities. Located in the Ministry of Finance, the Treasury (*Tresor*), composed of elite bureaucrats trained by the ENA, controlled not only the money supply but also the allocation of credit, capital markets, and investments in general. By using the banks it owned or controlled as intermediaries between itself and private companies, the Tresor could influence industrial policies without appearing to be in command. Of course, the state could act directly by using the large pool of funds it controlled to map the industrial strategy it, along with the Planning Commission in years following World War II, had selected. Increasingly, however, this direct intervention was replaced with a more sophisticated type of influence relying on banks and parapublic institutions.

Whenever necessity arose, the Tresor could assemble the pool of funds required to restructure an industry by urging the cooperation of banks either nationalized or not. As one official said: "The funds are always there." Echoing his cocksureness, a banker confirmed, "They do not ask all the time but, when they do, it is difficult to refuse." One instance no refusal took place was in 1978 during the rescue of the steel industry. The Tresor urged parapublic institutions to buy shares of this lame duck and thereby was able to raise $2 billion, temporarily keeping the industry alive. The result of this intervention was that steel became de facto nationalized at a time when a rhetoric of economic liberalism was in full swing. We must emphasize that the arm-twisting policy of the Tresor was in no way confined to parapublic institutions; it extended to private banks.

After 1945 the Ministry of Finance had become the center of French economic policy, endowed with powers going far beyond its traditional prerogatives of taxation and budget allocation. By a loose control of the money supply, it was in a position to use inflation as a tool to dissolve political conflict; by its use of the fear of inflation, it was able to scale down programs implemented by other ministries; by its command of credit allocation, it had "moved from the position of banker of the budget to that of banker of the economy."[6] To handle all of these responsibilities, it had been given a staff whose technical expertise nobody could match.

Overall, these state policies (ownership, control, influence) had been quite successful. Nationalized companies such as Renault, Air France, and EDF were largely responsible for the technological innovation that took place. The state proved to be a remarkably gutsy entrepreneur, willing and able to undertake large, high-risk investments. The outcomes that were achieved would have been unlikely without its intervention. No less important, private businessmen began to emerge from their self-destructive Malthusian cocoon. Impressed with the successes of public companies and enticed by the subsidies the state had to offer, they increasingly chose expansion over extinction.

Nonetheless, many of the industrial projects undertaken in insulation from both participatory policies and market forces failed. From the Concorde to Fos, from *Le France* to *La Villette*, the list represents a significant amount of wasted money. Stuck with what Alain Touraine recently called a "railway vision of modernization," the French state often believed that "any good engine would carry any train, anywhere, at any speed."[7] Because they created industrial sectors that did not grow on the basis of their competitiveness, interventionist tools worked best only when addressing activities in which competition was limited, returns from the investment slow, and markets controlled by the state (such as nuclear power, energy, and space). When, however, the state dealt with sectors dominated by fast-changing markets, intense competition, and endless lines of products, the results proved to be mediocre at best (electronics). Here bureaucratic controls proved too heavy, too rigid, and too slow. In other words, success had less to do with the tools French authorities decided to use than it had with the adequacy of these tools to the task.

To summarize the interventionist apparatus as it stood in 1981: At the core were a state administration, substantially insulated from detailed parliamentary influence, and a credit-based administered price financial system dominated by the administration. The plan that held a privileged position in the structure was the home base of a group of young modernizers who altered the purposes and ideological premises of French state action. That plan did not survive, but the system endured and served the varied purposes of conservative governments in the quarter century from de Gaulle's return to power in 1958 to Mitterrand's victory in 1981.

115

By gambling that, in 1982, the tasks at hand required more and not less of the kind of state intervention that had brought France back from industrial insignificance after 1945, the French Left made a daring move.

Nationalization Following Mitterrand's Election (1982)

After the election of François Mitterrand to the presidency of France, the Left implemented a large program of nationalizations. It constantly referred to the precedent of de Gaulle's nationalization following World War II and pointed to what it perceived to be their successful economic outcome to justify the move. No matter how negatively one assessed the economic legacy of Raymond Barre, however, one could hardly argue that it had much in common with the rubble of 1944 and that it thus required the same medicines. The justifications given to the nationalizations of 1982 were, however, to be nearly identical to those used to explain the same process thirty years before, leaving aside desire to punish the companies that had collaborated with the Nazis. In 1981 the French state, commanding the economic tools it did not possess immediately following World War II, had the option of using them instead of creating new, maybe superfluous, and therefore expensive tools.

Political victory of the Left aside, the analogy between 1944 and 1981 was dubious indeed. In the first case, progressive forces had the opportunity to dramatize an economic disaster and to take advantage of the collapse of economic liberalism. In contrast, not only would "economic disaster" sound grossly hyperbolic in 1981, but also, and more important, the ideology of economic liberalism was on the upswing, bolstered by the tradition of French elites to equate modernity with the imitation of the trends developing in the United States. This surge of popularity for economic liberalism was somewhat concealed by the electoral triumph of the Left; but, as soon as the honeymoon of the new Socialist president came to an end, this ideology reasserted itself with a vengeance. Socialists were in no position to afford many mistakes lest the interventionist consensus disintegrate. Newly nationalized companies were challenged to perform successfully and to be managed flawlessly. Results fell far short of these expectations.

In February 1982, nine major industrial companies and all thirty-five banks with assets above one billion francs were officially nationalized. The state now exercised direct control over 30 percent of the sales, 24 percent of the industrial labor force, and 50 percent of the investments. The move marked the apex of state influence in the economy.

Though the real explanation of these new nationalizations was political, the reasons advanced to justify them were essentially economic. According to the Left, French private companies had demonstrated their inability to prevent the deepening of the economic crisis and the deindustrialization of the country. To react against this trend, the state had the responsibility to stand up for the revival of France through the revival of industrial investment and economic growth. The first part of the argument was not a difficult one to make given the relative mediocrity of the French economic performance at the time. Unemployment was at an historic high, industrial jobs were disappearing at an annual rate of 100,000, and overall investment levels were sustained only because of the steady pace of capital expenditure in public companies (essentially due to the hugely expensive nuclear program). Unsurprisingly, the Left derived from this grim assessment the indictment of a conservative government and its laissez-faire policies. In response to this passivity, French Socialists opposed a program of activism and optimism based on a strong state leading the way to an industrial renaissance. The leftist government wanted to nationalize so that it could use the powers of the state, from salesmen to researchers, from financiers to customers, as a means of energizing a lagging industrial base. Nationalizations were construed as "an electroshock and not a tranquilizer."[8] In a substantially different context, all this was a near perfect repeat of the theme of 1944. Industrial machismo was in full swing.

The nationalization of the banks that were still privately owned was part of the same project. Bankers, it was argued, kept favoring short-term profitability and real estate investments instead of lending industry the credits it needed to modernize. Being state owned would supposedly ensure the banks' compliance with the expansionary objectives of the state. Here one has to point out that the argument was somewhat lame. Given the extent to which banks, even privately owned, were controlled by the state, it is difficult to see what prevented the political executive from having them discriminate between various demands for funds in accordance with the objectives of the nation, as those objectives were defined by the Tresor. Moreover, the biggest banks were already nationalized and did not seem to have adopted a credit policy so markedly different from that for which private financial institutions were blamed.

A purely defensive rationale for nationalization was maybe less attractive than the dynamic, forward-looking one that was popularized, but it was also more real. The de facto nationalization of steel, three years before the Left came into power, was only one example of a series of conservative industrial interventions. The companies had to be subsidized to survive, but the subsidies were so large that they could be justified or organized only by nationalization. The conservative government of Giscard d'Estaing gave the reorganization a different label, but it was nationalization. Seen in that light, the move of 1982 represented what Mitterrand called "a weapon to defend French production."[9] Nationalizations simplified the process of rationalization that could prove necessary whenever a company had to be restructured. Equally, from the Left, could the state continue to bail out ailing companies and offer them the funds to modernize, while excluding itself from the future profits stemming from these investments? Nationalizations at least offered a reasonable answer to that problem. They were also thought to be indispensable if the

117

Socialist ambition to move away from an industrial strategy of *crèneau* (market niche) to one of *filière* (vertically integrated sectors) was ever to take place.

Still, for a leftist government not to give a social content to its most significant policy decision would have been odd. The policy was infused with social content in two ways. First, nationalizations were to guarantee social protection against economic disturbances. According to the Left, by putting the burdens of adjustment on workers and the poor, the market demonstrated its inadequacies and threatened social cohesion and social peace. Second, nationalizations were expected to strengthen the weakest labor movement in western Europe. This assumption was based on the evidence of a greater rate of union membership in nationalized companies. More important, the inclusion of unions on the board of nationalized companies—where representatives of the state always hold a majority—would empower the unions through the access to information. In itself this labor reform was mild by European standards, but it was significant in a country in which labor unions had consistently been refused any responsibility and had been granted an unusually limited number of rights.

Here those who engineered the social breakthrough were not without ulterior motives. Because labor unions favored the principle of nationalization, they were expected to do their best to see it succeed economically. If economic success meant moderation in wage demands, the Left would certainly find nothing wrong with that.

When all else was said, however, a pragmatic argument settled the discussion: "In France nationalizations work. Look at Renault, look at the banks: out of the ten biggest in the world, three are French and have been nationalized for the last thirty years."[10] Because they worked, nationalizations could be multiplied.

Compelling as they were, however, these economic justifications provide a poor insight into the decision of 1982. In fact, the decision was essentially political. Throughout its tumultuous history, the French Left had asserted its commitment to change and formed the common ground between its feuding parties (Communist and Socialist) by stressing in a symbolically potent way its desire for structural reforms. Nationalizations represented this symbol of a break with the past of that much desired *rupture avec le capitalisme* (break with capitalism). Without them, *le changement* would not be much of a change, and France's "new model of development" would not materialize. In sum, the Socialist party thought it had to nationalize simply to prove that it was the true Left and not just another kind of social democratic force. The economic explanation was sketched *after* the political decision had been made.

Nationalizations were political symbols. Given the extraordinary interventionist capacity built up and refined by the conservatives, there was no technical need for the move, which was a substantial gamble. The economic policy of the Left, a mixture of Keynesianism and nationalization, was from the onset premised on a French expansion in the context of a worldwide recovery. It was expected to improve profit margins throughout the country. Improved profits would, in turn, permit industrial investments, the modernization of the economy, and added social benefits for French workers. Without the anticipated growth, everything would be much more difficult, including the demonstration that nationalizations work.

According to a governmental newsletter, two conditions had to be met to show that the nationalizations were successful: "financial profitability before the end of 1985" and "the type of management autonomy required by an industrial environment in which quick decisions have to be made." The problems of the new interventionist policy could not be expressed any more eloquently than by juxtaposing those two conditions. "Autonomous managers" had to eliminate financial losses by the end of the year, which happened just to precede major elections in which nationalizations were to be a major campaign issue. The requirement was far from simply rhetorical. To ensure that managers would not construe their autonomy too literally, 1985 was also the year when the terms of these managers had to be renewed. The decision to set a deadline for profitability was also surprising because the Left had in the past repeatedly condemned the objective of short-term profitability as a mistaken concept—a mistaken concept that, incidentally, nationalizations were supposed to remedy.

Mistaken or not, to understand the impatience of French Socialists to see that deadline for profitability implemented was not difficult. Nationalized companies were absorbing money at an alarming rate. The state had paid thirty-five billion francs in compensations to expropriated shareholders merely to gain the right to absorb a flow of red ink totaling no less than fifty billion over three years. Many of these firms were functionally bankrupt before the nationalizations. They were propped up by disguised intervention before the election. Indeed, the real winners from nationalizations were the stockholders, whose holdings in several companies that might have been considered bankrupt would otherwise have been worthless. Had the steel industries been nationalized after the election rather than before, many private fortunes would have been preserved. The conservatives—not needing to prove that they did not intend to eliminate private property—could be tougher brokers.

Nationalizations, of course, gave no direction or strategy to intervention. At first, the industrial policy was multidirectional, asserting that as it was "there is no doomed sector, there are only outdated technologies."[11] This principle was soon to be abandoned when the till of the state could no longer afford financial largesse toward hopelessly lame ducks. The resources expected from economic growth never appeared, as a sputtering recovery had to be doused by an austerity program made necessary because of growing trade and budget imbalances. Given the limited resources of the state and the large amount of funds that had to be poured into the expanding deficits of public companies, the original commitment to invest in the industries of the future could not be met. In 1984, offsetting the losses of the steel industry alone drew over a third of the capital resources the government could allocate to nationalized companies. That amount was more than the whole *filière electronique* received, even though it had been dubbed "the number one priority of the industrial policy." The assistance for development had largely been devoted to subsidy. When he was asked to assess the wisdom of the 1982 nationalizations, Jacques Delors, then finance minister, answered, "they have brought into companies lacking resources a strong and responsible shareholder."[12] In short, the state now paid the bills.

For their part, critics of the move lost no time theorizing once again that public subsidies were in fact dampening incentives to move out of declining sectors into expanding ones. What would have been left of French industries had all the declining ones been phased out was of course a question to which everyone knew the answer: not much. Therefore, once again, the state played its role of industrial Red Cross.

The financial difficulties of newly nationalized companies were all the more important insofar as they threatened to translate into a structural shift, reinforcing the interventionist nature of French industrial policy. Beginning with financial losses, the traditional cycle led to state subsidies allowing struggling companies to survive and then, logically, ended with state controls to supervise this use of public funds. Despite the claims of conservative critics, the cycle was not premeditated, and the ways to break it were hard to implement. Cutting subsidies would have meant accepting the collapse of critical industries and the loss of many jobs, a situation likely to tear apart the French social fabric. Subsidizing without control implied enabling private and public managers to count on an unrestrained access to the limited funds of the public treasury.

High-flying rhetoric of the conservative opposition aside, however, the Left could not be exonerated from some responsibility for the beginning of the cycle, the fact that companies were losing money. To the extent that the companies (especially those in the public sector) were asked, even by the conservatives, to perform several functions, the economic rationality of which was debatable, then financial losses were not totally self inflicted. If it could be demonstrated that the difficulties companies faced were actually caused by the many costly obligations—generally with a social purpose—they were expected to meet, then the terms of the debate would significantly be altered. As one (fired) manager argued, "The state demands too much from companies to enable them to live alone; it gives them enough to let them survive. Therein lies the logic of an administered economy."[13]

In theory, there were no state demands. Maybe to erase the powerful image of managers of nationalized companies named after a cabinet meeting, Socialist officials stated and reaffirmed their commitment to managerial autonomy. From the minister of economic planning's statement that "state owned does not mean state controlled,"[14] to Matignon's industrial adviser's contention that "the main strategy is to have no strategy, to let the managers decide what they want,"[15] reassurances abounded. They were capped by the much-publicized presidential warning to a minister of industry he would eventually fire because of excessive interventionism: "The demand of a coherent industrial policy is incompatible with a meddlesome bureaucracy." Even official statements included a hedging line to this proclaimed full autonomy. Autonomy had to be "compatible with the objectives of French industrial policy,"[16] which, among other things, included employment and the "reconquest of domestic markets." The nationalization bill of 1982 was even more straightforward: "The mission of public companies is the achievement of the economic and social objectives of the government." If it were otherwise, one must acknowledge, the meaning of nationalization would be completely lost. The state could not be expected to buy—at an expensive price—exclusive or majority control of major companies just to let them operate freely. Therefore, the promise of full autonomy—which even private companies had rarely enjoyed in the French system—sounded hollow from the very beginning.

Just because control was logical does not mean that it was necessarily healthy. It was definitely not healthy when some nationalized companies saw their profits confiscated so that the budget deficit could be reduced, when they were forced to use these profits to acquire politically sensitive debt-ridden businesses, or when they were required to make a profit to bolster the case of an embattled government before an election. Unfortunately, all these things took place. In 1982 banks were required to alleviate the pressure on the Treasury by using their profits to lend six billion francs (at 7 percent interest) to ailing companies. The previous year, Laurent Fabius, then budget director and now prime minister, channeled the earnings of the telecommunications sector into the general budget. In 1983 Fabius, then minister of industry, fired Albin Chaladon when he refused to spend Elf's profits to buy two money-losing chemical companies. Compagnie Generale d'Electricité was hardly luckier; it too had to acquire a couple of ailing companies to save jobs. Except for contributions to the deficit, none of this of course was new.

Both the state control of enterprises never quite free to manage themselves and the politically motivated expenditures of public funds to rescue unprofitable companies and stem unemployment predate the election of 1981. What nationalizations made possible was the correlation of the two: the use of public industries to achieve centrally defined societal goals. The stagnant economy could not but reflect negatively on the successful image nationalizations had maintained and support the growing perception that the saying "nationalizations work" was not quite true.

Concerning the banking industry, the point of knowing whether or not "nationalizations work" did not make much sense. Seeing significant change from the addition of the last 10 percent of deposits outside state-owned institutions but not outside state control would have been difficult. Opposition leaders charged that the move had facilitated discrimination against the credit requests of private businesses crowded out of the market by the priority given to the financial needs of public companies. The criticism ignored the fact that such a complaint had repeatedly been made by small businesses in the past and was part of the litany of recriminations, including *les charges écrasantes* (high taxes), French patrons ritually made whenever they were about to lobby for protection or for a subsidy. With respect to banks, the change was the absence of change, as François Mitterrand himself acknowledged. After having watched a report on a small company forced into bankruptcy because a nationalized bank had refused a loan, the French president reacted by noting wearily: "Private banks were doing the same before; nationalizations have made no difference."[17]

What Mitterrand said was not entirely accurate, however. The decision to transform into public ownership the public control the state already exercised over banks introduced a politically potent issue for the opposition: the fear of "creeping nationalizations." Whenever a bank requested a stake in a company it would rescue, the government was accused of seeking to expand its control through its banks. The case of Creusot Loire demonstrates how this request could lead to cynical charges. This private company had lost money in thirteen of its fourteen years of existence. When, again, it requested financial aid, the formerly private Suez Bank logically asked for an equity position in the company as a condition for help. In the French system, it probably would also have done so as a private bank. Creusot Loire used Suez's nationalization to reject at first the terms of the loan, equating them with creeping nationalization. Nothing could better illustrate the bind in which the government had tied itself. Either its nationalized banks acted to protect their investments, and the state was accused of economic hegemonism; or the banks did not so act, and the state was blamed for having an irresponsible business attitude toward its banks.

On the one hand, the politically motivated argument of creeping nationalization made the expansion of nationalized companies difficult. On the other hand, legal impediments against public divestitures prevented those companies from selling unnecessary subsidiaries as a means of improving their capital base, a necessary move given the difficulties the state had in fulfilling its promises of funds. Without breathing room, the public sector was threatened with a difficult survival in a closed and stagnant world. To make matters even worse, France's European neighbors, generally committed to economic liberalism, were skeptical about any close cooperation with a country known for its nationalized companies and its penchant for bureaucratically constructed industrial policies.

Nationalization in Disrepute

In 1983 it became clear that the financial revenues of economic growth, which were expected to smooth out all the creeking mechanisms of state control, would not be forthcoming. Advocates of the French model of development could have blamed macroeconomic problems for the failure of nationalizations and could have expected that, were growth to surge, their strategy would eventually be vindicated. Most of them, however, did not choose this easy way out. Gradually the realization dawned on the Left that industrial difficulties could not simply be ascribed to a sluggish pace of economic growth. The mixture of centralization, voluntarism, and bigness that for so long characterized the French model of development and pulled the country out of oblivion had finally met its limits.

In reaction to this latest stalemate in French society, a new ideology began to invade political speeches and flooded economic analysis. French elites competed with one another in the quest for the mantle of thoroughbred liberalism. Economic Darwinism, the chilly winds of which were to invigorate a stagnant society, was dutifully advocated. Denationalization became a synonym of courage; *fonctionarisation*, a symbol of cowardice. Beyond the clutter, something significant was happening. Economically, state intervention had not succeeded; ideologically, it was collapsing. French Socialists were paying for their mistakes, three of which could be easily identified. Each one compounded the other, any one of them would have sunk the strategy of 1981.

In the 1950s and 1960s economic modernization meant the displacement of farmers and small shopkeepers; in the 1980s it has implied the shedding of labor in traditional industries. During the 1950s and 1960s the political Right was in power; in the 1980s, the Left has been. In each case, the ruling coalition had to modernize against its social base. Whereas the first modernization took place with the twin advantages of booming economic growth and an industrial backwardness mapping the way to the future, the current transformation has lacked both these assets. Now nothing smooths the transition, little indicates where it will lead, and the opposition is substantial. This much the Left could have anticipated even before it began to stumble. Given that, from the onset, a policy of stringent protectionism was rejected, the necessary adjustments to an environment of international competition could neither be prevented nor postponed. To expect that these adjustments would not involve pain was wishful thinking. If they did, as they did, political wisdom pointed to the necessity of keeping the hand close to the chest, closing plants, and laying off workers invisibly. Instead, the Left transformed every industrial choice

123

into a public issue, a subject for open debate, even though the outcome of this discussion was known long before the talk had started. Nationalizations may have been candid insofar as they disclosed the (somewhat hidden beforehand) magnitude of the state control over the economy. In troubled economic times, that type of candor is hardly politically shrewd.

The second mistake concerns the issue of an unsteady control. Increasing governmental supervision of the economy was certainly bad politics, although it could conceivably have been good economics. Then, however, the government had to know what it wanted instead of swinging from one priority to another when it was not simultaneously asserting contradictory objectives. In three years, France has had five ministers of industry and at least three different policies. One day unemployment is the target, and inflation the price to pay to reduce it; another day the fight against inflation becomes the number one priority, and rising unemployment is an accepted risk. One day businesses have their prices frozen, and the Treasury makes up for lost revenues; another day reducing taxes becomes the objective, and, to slash budget subsidies, companies are allowed to charge their real costs. One day failures are blamed on foot dragging—when not simply sabotaged—by the business community; another day the culprit becomes a meddlesome bureaucracy stifling managerial initiatives.

No policy, no matter how competent its implementers, could have resisted this indecisive leadership, this succession of shifts. This situation was intensified because, no matter what it did, the French Left, suspected by its conservative opposition of being inept at handling the economy, had constantly to convey the impression that it was logical in its approach and consistent in its strategy. Put to such a test, past conservative governments would not have fared very well. Fortunately for them, their economic competence was often more a matter of trust than one of record. The Mitterrand administration would not be so fortunate, and any mistake it did or shift it undertook quickly became magnified. The so-called conversion of French Socialists to supply-side economics was therefore bound to erode their credibility significantly—a lot more, at any rate, than would former Prime Minister Raymond Barre's economic liberalism be derided after a de facto nationalization of the steel industry or, in another country, a conservative president be weakened by an economic recovery generated and sustained by the public deficits he once vowed to eliminate before he actually quadrupled them. Instead of a lopsided scrutiny, had such a leniency been applied to French Socialists, their policy and their contradictions would have met with more understanding.

The third mistake we wish to identify relates to the understanding Socialists have had of what were to be their industrial goals, insofar as some of them have remained constant. The emphasis on bigness and the attempt to imitate a misunderstood Japanese industrial strategy immediately come to mind. If one has been corrected, the other has yet to be recognized. Clinging to a vision of industry borrowed from "Modern Times," the French Left, and the Right before it, have long equated modernity and bigness, cottage industry and survival of the past. Today we can conceptually grasp why these equations are not necessarily correct.[18] Statistics speak louder than insights, however. Since 1974, in terms of job creation, growth, profitability, and investments, small- and medium-sized companies have consistently outperformed larger units.[19] They adjust better, and they appear—and disappear—faster. The lessons are unambiguous, and they demonstrate that no unemployment policy will succeed unless small businesses hire the surplus labor shed by larger companies. Either the government must encourage the creation of small businesses, or it will have to take into account what has made them successful and expand the cottage model of management to big units. Given that this model includes several characteristics that are anathemas to labor unions (lower pay, lesser job stability), such a choice could involve a significant cost for the Left. Simply put, compounding the transition from traditional to modern, the shift from big to small would seriously undermine the already narrow electoral base of the Left. The temptation of bigness therefore remains, and with it the usual tendency of the French bureaucracy to nationalize along the lines "one skill per company, one company per industry." This type of nationalization would supposedly structure French industry in such a way to make it internationally competitive.

Single national champions such as Télécommunications de France (CGE) and Electronique de France (Thomson) were set up as there already was one Electricité de France. Was that not the lesson of the Japanese experience? Unfortunately the French Left misread the Japanese experience. They saw a similar set of administrative and financial institutions. They noted extensive set intervention in pursuit of economic development and industrial competitiveness. The conclusion that they drew was that the tactics the Japanese used were similar in character to the tactics that the French state had employed. When the French state had intervened in the Gaullist years in pursuit of detailed objectives, it had used administrative power to shape a series of national champions, one or at most two French companies in a sector that could be internationally competitive. The champion would be protected at home to be competitive abroad. The core of the notion was to use political power to override market developments and push them in a different direction. The Japanese in fact used internal competition, a form of controlled competition, as a policy instrument. They shaped and structured the domestic competition and used international market signals to guide their choices. The Japanese tried to ride with the market, to navigate the waters of competition. The contrast in tactics could not have been greater.

Conclusion

The failure of the Socialists' industrial strategy not only left open to challenge the structural transformations they had enacted; it threatened the very existence of an interventionist economic policy that had merely been dramatized by the additional nationalizations of 1982. Today France is the scene of a keen competition for the crown of "most dedicated liberal." Socialists, including François Mitterrand himself, have joined the fray looking for ways "to rid France of this interventionism Frenchmen live with since their very birth."[20] Still the competition mostly opposes conservative leaders each of whom wants to be seen as the greatest "denationalizer."

From the minimalist position advocating the sole denationalization of the banks acquired in 1982 to the maximalist stand of those who, at last count, wanted to privatize the unemployment agency, the gap is significant. The debate, however, is not particularly enlightening as it carefully avoids the major issues, which will have to be addressed. For instance, who will purchase these companies sold by the state? Either they continue to lose money; and then public opinion presses for the sale, but no buyer volunteers. Or they start to make profits, in which case buyers are found but the public no longer wants to sell. In other words, unless conservatives elaborate their position, French voters are unlikely to be persuaded by a platform that wants to sell what works and keep what does not.

There should also be a lot of skepticism regarding the conservative theory now equating economic crisis to an excess of state intervention stifling the activities of private businesses.[21] In France, rather than preventing entrepreneurial initiative by its action, the state has often intervened to compensate for the absence of such initiatives. The unpopularity of Socialist economic policies may be warranted, but it should not be such that it allows analyses that bear little relation to the facts made plain by history.

When conservatives were in power, the French Left was embroiled in ideological and often esoteric economic arguments. Those arguments did not help when 1981 came and, with it, the responsibility actually to manage the economy. Now that the Left governs the country, conservatives seem to have occupied the ground of ideological futility. Talks of denationalization have replaced discussions of increased state control. Today like before, however, the same deafening silence strikes whomever wants to shift the terms of debate from the form to the substance. Unfortunately, structural religiosity is a poor substitute for an informed discussion on the objectives of French industrial policy.

Notes

1. Richard Kuisel, *Capitalism and State in France* (New York: Cambridge University Press, 1981), chap. 1.

2. Jean Monnet, *Memoires* (New York: Doubleday, 1978), pp. 305–306.

3. "Le Blocage des prix et des salaries," *La lettre de Matignon* (Paris: June 1982).

4. Stephen Cohen, *Modern Capitalist Planning,* pp. 3–10.

5. Kuisel, *Capitalism and State in France.*

6. F. Bloch-Laine, *Profession fonctionnaire* (Paris: 1976), p. 103.

7. Alain Touraine, "L'Avant 1986," *Intervention No. 8,* p. 15.

8. Jean Le Garrec, *Le Nouvel Observateur,* October 10, 1981.

9. François Mitterrand, press conference, October 1981.

10. François Mitterrand, press conference, October 1981.

11. J. P. Chevenement, *Le Point,* June 1982.

12. Jacques Delors, *Le Nouvel Observateur*, May 1984.

13. A. Chalandon, "Denationaliser pourquoi?" *Le Monde,* July 12, 1984.

14. M. Rocard, *Business Week,* January 10, 1983.

15. C. Mandil, *Business Week,* January 10, 1983.

16. P. Dreyfus, *Le Point,* February 22, 1982.

17. Mitterrand, "7 Sur 7" (television program), January 1984.

18. Charles Sabel, *The Division of Labor* (New York: Cambridge University Press, 1982).

19. M. Delattre, *Economie et statistique,* October 1982.

20. François Mitterrand, *Liberation*, May 10, 1984.

21. J. Chirac, *Le Figaro Magazine*, April 14, 1984, p. 105.

British Industrial Policy

Jeffrey A. Hart

[In Britain] industrial policy is largely reactive. The management of industrial crisis in Britain tends, therefore, to comprise a set of negatives. On the government's side, there are no regional programs for industrial adaptation, no anticipatory loan financing— only rudimentary sectoral reconstruction—and no lame duck rescue agency (the IRC and NEB were both formally concerned with "viable" enterprises).[1]

Industrial policy in Britain on the whole has been characterized by its liberal, voluntarist, and cooperative approach.[2]

The British approach to industrial policy combines an overall market-oriented mythology with several poorly coordinated attempts at centralized administrative guidance. The key to understanding British industrial policy is understanding the general weakness of British firms in international competition. The reaction of the state to this generalized weakness has taken many forms, most of which have not been considered worthy of permanent institutionalization nor of generalization to or rationalization at the level of the whole economy. The generally ad hoc or reactive nature of industrial policy in Britain before the early 1970s came at a high cost. The state had to become more interventionist than anyone except the most ardent socialists ever intended. Even British conservatives, like Margaret Thatcher, have had to yield to the pattern of the past in dealing with industrial crises, despite their belief in the benefits of privatization, deregulation, and competition. The main difference between the United States and Britain is not in the mythology but in the practice, and the practice has been primarily the result of the state's belated response to weakness.

This chapter was written for presentation at a conference on industrial policy at the American Enterprise Institute, Washington, D.C., October 1, 1984, organized by Claude Barfield. Thanks are due to John Freeman for his extensive comments on that version of the chapter. Further helpful comments were provided by Claude Barfield and Howard Wiarda. The current version was written in April 1985.

The lessons that the United States can learn from the British example therefore are mainly those having to do with successful and unsuccessful modes of coping with the weakness of specific industries and firms in states with a tradition of decentralized authority for industrial policies. In this respect, the British case offers examples all along the spectrum of failure-success. Only in the past two years or so can one even vaguely identify British steel policies as realistic (it is hard to call the consequences of rapid rationalization "success"); but British policies toward the microelectronics industry have resulted in the nurturing of at least one enterprise, Inmos, which has become one of the few truly innovative European firms in that industry. The subsequent privatization of Inmos may be considered scandalous; but its creation and early growth were no mean feats, given the intense international competition in microelectronics. As in the discussion of other large industrial countries, this chapter will combine descriptions of overall economic and industrial policies in both crisis and noncrisis periods with a more detailed look at policies in specific industrial sectors. The three sectors to be singled out (for reasons spelled out later) are steel, automobiles, and information technology.

Organization of the State

The British government is at first glance well equipped with formal institutions for the making and implementation of industrial policy, but in fact the power for making economic policy generally is quite widely distributed among various conflicting agencies. The most important actors are (1) the prime minister and his/her cabinet, (2) the chancellor of the Exchequer (henceforth the Treasury), (3) the Department of Trade and Industry, (4) the National Economic Development Council and related agencies, and (5) the British Technology Group (and its predecessors the Industrial Reorganization Corporation and the National Enterprise Board).

The Treasury. The advantage of the Treasury in industrial policy formation is its connection with the Bank of England, which makes it authoritative on questions of government financing of industrial projects. In the 1975 reorganization of the Treasury, an Industrial Policy Group, headed by the undersecretary of the Treasury, was formed. Although this group survived the change in government in 1979, it was not much used by Sir Geoffrey Howe, the first chancellor of the Exchequer in the Thatcher administration. Its main function is to monitor the expenditures of the Department of Trade and Industry. The Industrial Strategy Staff Group, an interministerial group, is chaired by the representative from the Treasury and includes representatives of other ministries, the Confederation of British Industries (CBI), the Trade Unions Congress (TUC), and the National Economic Development Council. This group functions mainly to discuss the industrial consequences of government regulation.[3]

The Department of Trade and Industry. In 1964 the Labour government created a Department of Economic Affairs (with an industrial policy division) to formulate and implement a national plan and a Ministry of Technology to deal with what Harold Wilson called the "white heat" of the technological revolution in industry. With the demise of the national plan in 1966, the Ministry of Technology was upgraded and the Department of Economic Affairs downgraded. In 1969 the Ministry of Technology absorbed the Ministry of Power, and some of the responsibilities of the Board of Trade were shifted to it. In 1970 the Conservative government merged the Board of Trade and the Ministry of Technology into the Department of Trade and Industry.

The Department of Trade and Industry was divided into a Department of Trade and a Department of Industry by the Wilson government after the election of 1974. The Thatcher government reunited the two departments again in June 1983. The Department of Trade and Industry is organized primarily along sectoral lines, employing experts in each major branch of industry to monitor developments, to administer aid programs, and to provide the minister with proposals for policy initiatives. The Department of Trade and Industry by its very nature is a highly politicized agency providing one of the more important conduits for the expression of the interests of manufacturing firms and unions to the government.[4]

The Department of Industry was responsible for managing the government interests in British Steel, the Post Office (and later British Telecom), British Leyland, Rolls Royce, British Aerospace, and the National Enterprise Board. It was therefore the locus of many important industrial policy decisions. Nevertheless, it played a subordinate role generally to the Department of the Treasury in overall economic policies and was often challenged and overruled by other agencies. Industry generally adopted a quasi-protectionist perspective while the Treasury traditionally defended the value of the pound on international currency markets and the Department of Trade perceived itself as the principal "guardian of free trade" within the British government. The merger of Industry and Trade by the Conservative government in 1979 was probably designed to rein in the protectionist tendencies of Industry.[5]

The National Economic Development Council. The National Economic Development Council (NEDC) was established in 1962 by the Conservative government during a period of slow economic growth. It has a somewhat complex organization. The council itself is a broad overarching body to summarize and reconcile the work of the ten Economic Development Committees (EDCs) and the thirty Sector Working Parties (SWPs) with the help of the secretariat-like National Economic Development Office (NEDO). At every level of the NEDC (except the NEDO) there are representatives of the government, the trade unions, and management. At the council level, the trade unions are represented by the TUC while business is represented by the CBI. These are the most important national union and business organizations. The main animus behind the NEDC-NEDO-SWP complex is the belief that getting government representatives, union leaders, and firm managers together periodically for an exchange of views is valuable. Andrew Shonfield criticized the government's role in NEDC as being too close to that of management and labor: "It behaved as if it were an interest group arguing its case with equal partners who were expected to have other interests."[6] Gerald Dorfman called the complex the "institutionalized re-creation of pluralistic stagnation."[7] It was clearly one of several concertative arrangements set up by the British state to provide channels of access for labor and management to industrial policy making.

The SWPs (also called "little Neddies") produce documents periodically summarizing the status of their particular sector and recommending a set of governmental policies to improve that status. The SWPs represent firms that account for roughly 40 percent of total manufacturing production.[8] As Wilks argues, "Governments in practice have been reluctant to abolish the 'talking shop' of the NEDC, which supplies one of the few arenas for consensus generation."[9] In addition to consensus building, the NEDC provides an alternative way of obtaining information about industries to the more traditional, bureaucratic model provided by the Department of Trade and Industry. By the same token, it is more suited to industrial lobbying because of the direct role taken by industrial representatives on SWPs and the NEDC itself.

The British Technology Group. The British Technology Group (BTG) is the latest incarnation of a series of quasi-governmental entities designed by the British government to promote the growth of high-technology concerns. The first in the line was the Industrial Reorganization Corporation (IRC), which was set up in 1966 with an initial capital fund of £150 million. The IRC was active in the 1960s but was abolished by the Conservative government after the 1970 elections in its "u-turn over industrial policy."[10]

In 1975 the Labour government established the National Enterprise Board (NEB) as a state-owned holding company for the management of state-owned enterprises. Members of the board were to be appointed by the secretary of state for industry, with chairman and reporting chairman to be selected from the private sector. There were to be eight or nine other members, four of which were to be selected from the trade unions. The initial borrowing authority of the NEB was £1 billion. The authorizing statute for the NEB was the 1975 Industry Act, which instructed the NEB to promote "industrial democracy" while also achieving a high (15–20 percent) return on its investments. The NEB was unable to do either; it focused primarily on promoting

131

TABLE 1

ASSETS, RETURN ON ASSETS, AND NUMBER OF COMPANIES
MANAGED BY THE NATIONAL ENTERPRISE BOARD, UNITED KINGDOM,
1976–1979

Year	Assets (millions of £)	Return (%)	Number of Companies
1976	959	11.8	13
1977	1132	11.4	33
1978	1576	11.3	46
1979	1502	4.8	68

SOURCE: Wyn Grant, *The Political Economy of Industrial Policy* (Woburn, Mass.: Butterworths, 1982), p. 105.

the growth of high-technology firms that had difficulty getting private financing. Of course, it inherited from the Department of Industry the task of managing the government's interests in British Leyland, and this job distracted the NEB somewhat from its activities in other areas. Nevertheless, several of the NEB's firms did respectably, and it was able to obtain a reasonable return on its investments, given the general background of recession and decline (see tables 1 and 2).

The initial portfolio of the NEB included 10.1 percent of the shares of British Leyland, Britain's largest automobile firm; 50 percent of the elec-

TABLE 2

NATIONAL ENTERPRISE BOARD SHAREHOLDING, UNITED KINGDOM, MARCH 1976

Company	Business	NEB Share (%)	Cost (millions of £)	Date Acquired
British Leyland	automotive	98.9	695	Feb. 1976
Cambridge Instruments	electronic	79.7	6	Feb. 1976
Albert Herbert	machine tools	100.0	36	Feb. 1976
Rolls Royce	jet engines	100.0	203	Feb. 1976
Brown Boveri	engineering	20.0	3	Mar. 1976
ICL	computers	24.4	12	Feb. 1976

SOURCE: Michael Parr, "The National Enterprise Board," *National Westminster Bank* (February 1979), p. 55.

TABLE 3
INVESTMENTS BY NATIONAL ENTERPRISE BOARD–BRITISH TECHNOLOGY GROUP, UNITED KINGDOM, 1980
(millions of £)

Firm	Business	Amount
Inmos	semiconductors	21.0
NEXOS	office automation	16.0
Cambridge Instruments	electronics	15.0
Data Recording	electronic equipment	15.0
Wholesale Vehicle	leasing	11.0
British Underwater	engineering	7.0
United Medical	medical	6.0
Argon Viewdata	teletext	4.5
Insac	software	4.0
Monotype	printing	3.5
QI Europe	NA	2.0
Total		105.0

NOTE: NA = not available.
SOURCE: Michael Davenport, "Industrial Policy in the United Kingdom," in F. Gerard Adams and Lawrence R. Klein, eds., *Industrial Policies for Growth and Competitiveness: An Economic Perspective* (Lexington, Mass.: Lexington Books, 1983), p. 345.

tronics firm, Ferranti; and 25 percent of the shares of Imperial Computers Limited (ICL). NEB was responsible for setting up two high-technology firms in the late 1970s: Nexos and Inmos. Nexos was supposed to develop a line of office automation software while Inmos was charged with the development and production of advanced semiconductor devices.

The Labour government also established an Advisory Council for Applied Research and Development (ACARD) to advise the cabinet on policies to promote research and development. One of the first major recommendations of ACARD was to centralize decision making in the area of information technology. In 1980 the Thatcher government created a minister of state in the Department of Industry to deal with information technology.

The Thatcher government abolished both the IRC and the NEB in 1979 and replaced them with the BTG. Management of British Leyland was taken away from the BTG and given back to the Department of Industry in the 1981 Industry Act.[11] The Thatcher government announced a general policy of privatization, which in this case translated into the selling of state-owned shares of private companies. In 1980, for example, the government sold its interest in Ferranti for $75 million. Even the Thatcher government, however, saw some value in continuing to promote high technology through the BTG, as table 3 demonstrates.[12]

Wyn Grant suggests a reason for the Thatcher government's acceptance of the BTG: "The NEB as an organization is particularly suited to pursuing those industrial policy objectives concerned with efficiency and international competitiveness, rather than the employment objective which necessarily looms large in regional policy."[13]

Competition policy in the United Kingdom, as in most other large industrial countries, is rather weakly enforced. The Monopolies and Mergers Commission is the main responsible agency; but many major mergers have been actively promoted by the state (especially in the days of the IRC), and few mergers have been referred to the Monopolies and Mergers Commission for rulings.

Organization of the Interests

Labor is relatively powerful in Britain and is roughly comparable to labor in Germany in its influence in policy formation and implementation. The formal organization that aggregates labor interests is the TUC, a confederation of 112 unions organized mostly along craft rather than industry lines. Connections between the TUC and the Labour party are quite close (as in the case of the Deutsche Gewerkschaftsbund—especially the IG Metall—and the Social Democratic party (SPD) in Germany). Labor has consistently supported initiatives in the past two decades to institutionalize industrial policy making. In 1980, for example, the TUC–Labour party Liaison Committee advocated an expanded industrial policy based on a combination of comprehensive planning, an upgraded NEB, establishment of a National Investment Bank, and greater use of import controls.[14] To those who have followed the recent pronouncements of the AFL–CIO and the Democratic party, these policy proposals will sound quite familiar. Partly because labor is powerful, the state is organized to incorporate labor views in economic and industrial policy making but also to insulate certain areas of policy (especially macroeconomic and trade policy) from too much influence.

Business is represented primarily by the CBI, which aggregates the views of industry-specific associations with some tendency to weigh more strongly the views of the largest and most profitable firms in Britain.

Britain's merchant banking system has prevented the emergence of the kind of bank-manufacturing alliances that exist in Germany. The British system lacks the extensive system of personal contacts, close supervision of financial accounts, large shareholdings in specific firms, and bank memberships on supervisory boards of firms that typify the German system. The Bank of England plays a coordinating role in crises, and, increasingly, large banks like Barclays and Midland participate in rescue operations as lead banks; but Britain is still far from the so-called universal banking of Germany.[15]

The Evolution of Industrial Policy

The politics of industrial policy in the United Kingdom might seem at first glance to be primarily an outgrowth of interparty rivalry. The Conservative party and its allies are ideologically hostile to industrial policy. For example, in a 1977 policy document of the Tories, the following statement can be found:

> Should government have an industrial policy at all . . . ? Of course government must have an economic policy . . . but an economic policy that is not primarily directed to creating the conditions in which wealth-creating industry . . . can develop and flourish is bound to fail. An "industrial policy" which consists largely of interference, tinkering, and providing palliatives for structural defects is no kind of substitute for it.[16]

Despite the general ideological hostility to industrial policy, several Conservative governments have found themselves faced with decisions to accept forms of government intervention or to suffer major political costs. Although in some cases they still chose the more politically costly noninterventionist path, a sufficient number of exceptions made one question the firmness with which Conservatives were likely to pursue their preferred policies.

One example would be the passage of the 1972 Industry Act by a Labour-dominated Parliament and its acceptance by subsequent Conservative governments. The 1972 act gave wide latitude to the Department of Industry in dealing with governmental rescues of large private concerns. It also established a set of industrial development advisory boards, which were essentially corporatist institutions to help the government arrive at goals for industrial policy. This idea was quite consistent with the economic policy policy goals of the Heath government.[17]

Another example of Tory industrial policy initiatives is the Finance Act of 1972. That piece of legislation established a system of accelerated depreciation of all investments in new plants and equipment (see table 4). An allowance of 54 percent of the value of investments was permitted in the first year and 4 percent in subsequent years.[18] Thus Conservatives had accepted both concertative and supply-side investment policies in the early 1970s, policies that were also acceptable to the Labour party.

The Thatcher government, admittedly, came into office with a greater determination than earlier Conservative governments to undo the interventionist and statist policies of the previous Labour governments. Even they, however, did not insist on the rapid privatization of state-owned companies, nor did they abandon the institutions set up in the late 1970s to promote high-technology industries:

> Sectoral policies in Britain have been embraced by both sides of the equation. The Thatcher government is belatedly financing micro-

135

TABLE 4
ESTIMATED REDUCTION IN BRITISH CORPORATION TAXES DUE TO 1972 FINANCE ACT, ALL MANUFACTURING, FISCAL YEARS 1974–1982
(millions of 1985 £)

Fiscal Year	Amount
1974/1975	1450
1975/1976	2090
1976/1977	2060
1977/1978	2650
1978/1979	2800
1979/1980	2810
1980/1981	3220
1981/1982	2285

SOURCE: Department of Industry, as cited in Michael Landesman, "The Effects of Industrial Policies in the U.K., 1973–1981," paper delivered at a conference on industrial policies and structural adaptation, ISVEIMER, Naples, April 21, 1983.

electronics, information technology, and robotics on the one hand, and successive governments have facilitated planned rationalization in textiles, steel and other declining sectors on the other.[19]

The Labour party, on the other hand, has not always been a bastion of support for government intervention generally and industrial policy specifically. The left wing of the Labour party and their allies in the trade union movement have long supported a socialization of production through state investment and other forms of governmental participation in the economy. Disillusionment with the national plan experiment in 1964 and with Tony Benn's stab at industrial policy making in 1974–1975, however, forced party leaders to reformulate their views.

Labour's shifting perspective on industrial policy is best seen by considering the following three periods: (1) 1964–1970, (2) 1975–1979, and (3) 1980 to the present. In the first period, the Labour government of Harold Wilson tried to formulate and implement a national plan, but the devaluation of 1966 ended that experiment and gave further impetus to alternatives to planning, especially government support for research and development and the establishment of concertative bodies for specific industrial sectors within the framework of the NEDC. In this case, macroeconomic realities imposed themselves in such a way as to disillusion moderate members of the party from traditional socialist approaches to economic policy.

In the second period, another leftist experiment—this time focusing on the promotion of state enterprises under Tony Benn's management of the

Department of Industry—ended badly, thus creating the basis for further policy experimentation and ideological revisionism. The prime minister personally took charge of preparing the 1975 Industry Act, in part a reaction to the Conservative's 1972 Industry Act, and was influenced in this by a socialist economist named Stuart Holland. The 1975 act established the NEB (its main lasting achievement), reduced the protectionist and interventionist elements of the earlier act, and helped to create the basis for a new agency to encourage foreign investment in the United Kingdom. Also, Tony Benn was replaced as minister of industry by Eric Varley, a man much more in line with the prime minister's way of thinking.[20]

Also in this period, the Labour government implemented an Accelerated Projects Scheme. Between April 1975 and June 1976, this program funded 111 projects with £72 million in direct assistance and £568 million in project costs. The main idea was to use the state to encourage investment in areas that the state deemed important (a sort of "pick the winners" state investment policy). This project was succeeded in 1976 by the Selective Investment Scheme (SIS), which was designed to attract both domestic and foreign private investment in the United Kingdom.[21] By June 1979 SIS had received 742 applications and by March 1980 had offered £106.5 million to 166 projects and allocated £1 billion for future investments. Compared with the tax benefits given to manufacturing in the 1972 Finance Act, the SIS looks extremely small.

In 1978 the Labour government was confronted with the imminent collapse of the Chrysler (UK). This crisis will be discussed at greater length below under the head of policies toward the auto industry. The important point for now is that the Labour government used Section 8 of the 1972 Industry Act to justify its expenditure of public funds to prevent the liquidation of Chrysler (U.K.). This part of the act left the handling of the state's participation in financial restructurings of "major" enterprises on the brink of collapse to the discretion of the chancellor of the Exchequer. It was included in the 1972 act because of the difficulty that previous governments had had in passing enabling legislation for earlier restructurings—Rolls Royce being the main exemplar. Industrial assistance to the private sector (mostly to prevent firm failures) under sections 7 and 8 of the 1972 Industry Act grew sharply from 1975 to 1979 (see tables 5 and 6).

The misfortune of Labour was that many of these otherwise well-designed and probably intelligent programs came under the scathing criticism of the Conservatives as, mostly in desperation, the Labour government used them increasingly to bail out failing firms in the late 1970s. A careful analysis of the distribution of funds shows a decided tendency to favor mature and declining industries at the expense of the more buoyant.[22] The Conservatives came into office in 1979 with the goal of undoing much of the Labour government's innovations, and they immediately closed down SIS. They also

TABLE 5

GOVERNMENT ASSISTANCE TO PRIVATE SECTOR INDUSTRY, UNITED KINGDOM,
FISCAL YEARS 1972–1979
(millions of 1979 £)

Budget Category	1972/ 1973	1973/ 1974	1974/ 1975	1975/ 1976	1976/ 1977	1977/ 1978	1978/ 1979
Regional development grants	610	560	500	450	420	340	350
Section 7 of 1972 Act + NEB + Local Authority Act	50	80	120	550	330	480	360
Shipbuilding Aerospace and R and D	520	600	630	500	290	30	70
Total	1180	1240	1250	1500	1040	850	780

SOURCE: Grant, *The Political Economy of Industrial Policy*, p. 53.

converted the NEB into the BTG and gave the BTG the task of privatizing the industries under its control. The Conservatives did not undo everything. They did not insist on the immediate privatization of the holding of the BTG (to have done so would have been foolish). They kept the Labour government's schemes for promoting the microelectronics industry: the Microelectronics Industries Support Program (MISP), the Microprocessor Applications Project (MAP), and the Product and Processors Development Scheme (PPDS). Although these were relatively small programs, they helped make British manufacturers more aware of opportunities for applying microelectronic technology. There was a doubling of government spending for microelectronic R and D between 1978–1979 and 1979–1980.[23] Also the programs continued to use the economic development committees and sector-working parties set up by Labour under NEDC in the 1970s (especially as they had fewer direct political links to the trade unions).[24]

The Thatcher government shifted away from sector-specific policies back to the more traditional regionally focused policies of dealing with the effects of industrial decline. In December 1979, they designated several new areas as "special development areas," which made them eligible for Regional Development Grants.[25] Also, the Thatcher government implemented a new program of designating enterprise zones that could qualify for special government grants to local governments to upgrade buildings for use in attracting new investment or to purchase shares of local firms undergoing financial difficulties.

The Thatcher government, like some previous governments, had to face several industry crises: in steel, computers, and automobiles. Thatcher's chancellor of the Exchequer, Geoffrey Howe, was decidedly lukewarm on industrial policy as was her first minister of industry, Sir Keith Joseph. The

TABLE 6

DIRECT GOVERNMENT SPENDING FOR INDUSTRIAL POLICY,
UNITED KINGDOM, 1981–1982
(millions of £)

Department	Amount
Department of Industry	
Regional Development	695
Science and Technology Assistance	212
Selective assistance to firms	62
NEB/BTG	41
Support for	
British Leyland	620
Rolls Royce	193
Steel	100
Shipbuilding	82
Concorde	32
Other Departments	
Northern Ireland	403
Scotland	180
Wales	104
Department of Energy	292
All Others	67
Total	3083

SOURCE: Wyn Grant and Stephen Wilks, "British Industrial Policy: Structural Change, Policy Inertia," *Journal of Public Policy*, vol. 3 (February 1983), p. 21.

subsequent minister of industry, Patrick Jenkins, was more pragmatic, however, especially with respect to the continuing rescue efforts for British Steel, British Leyland, and ICL.[26] The Thatcher government's desire to extricate the government was expressed fully in the cases of Laker and DeLorean motors but was not allowed to get in the way when these larger crises occurred.

Thus, although some reversals have occurred as one government has succeeded another, the general pattern seems to be one of growing mutual acceptance on the part of Labourites and Conservatives of a policy that rescues large failing firms deemed crucial to the overall economy, provides investment capital and other support for high-technology industries (especially microelectronics), manages the state's portfolio primarily with an eye to obtaining a reasonable return on investment (except in the case of major rescues), and otherwise leaves industry pretty much to the private sector. The two parties have both accepted the continuing decentralization of administrative authority over industrial policies. While there was oscillation over the merger of trade and industry ministries, authority remained essentially fragmented with Treasury maintaining a great deal of veto power over the actions of the Department of Industry, the NEB, the BTG, and other such agencies. Concertative mechanisms for bargaining with and obtaining information from employer and union interests have persisted since their introduction in the 1972 Industry Act. Thus much continuity, a recognizable pattern, exists in British industrial policy of the past decade and a half.

I turn now to a closer examination of British industrial policies in specific sectors. The three sectors to be examined are steel, automobiles, and information technology (with a special focus on semiconductor components). These sector-specific cases will help to establish further the existence of continuity in British industrial policy. The examination of sector-specific crises demonstrates the reactions of the government to crisis. Differences across sectors will be investigated, especially those differences that concern the dynamism (potential for growth and technological change) and internationalization of firms in the sector.

Policies for Steel

British steel policies must be viewed in light of the general global overcapacity problem in the world steel market. Britain, like many other countries, had to manage the shrinkage of its steel-making capacity, especially in the late 1970s and early 1980s, because of recession, the decline in the demand for steel exports, and the reduced use of steel in manufacturing generally. The British steel industry in the middle and late 1970s was more of a disaster than that of other countries because of a major push to increase capacity just when demand took a major downturn. British policies of the early 1980s were much more realistic and effective than those of the 1970s. So the overall story is one of painful learning.

The problem begins after World War II. The British steel plants had done yeoman service during the war, but they were growing obsolete. Britain had many relatively small steel firms, most with very old plants. The macroeconomic policies of British postwar governments in maintaining a high value of sterling relative to other currencies had a dampening effect on the competitiveness of British exports, from which the British steel industry, like all the others, suffered to some extent. In addition, the management of the British steel industry was relatively conservative. When the Japanese and German steel industries were rapidly adopting new technologies, like basic oxygen furnaces and continuous casting, the British industries stuck with open hearth furnaces and an emphasis on liquid steel processing.[27]

Nationalization of the Steel Industry. Leftists in the Labour party focused on the steel industry as a key to their efforts to socialize the economy. In 1950 they nationalized the industry, but in 1953 the Tories denationalized it. This early attempt must have had the effect of discouraging private investment in the industry. After fourteen years of sluggish performance, the Labour government renationalized the industry again in 1967—Labour took that long to regain a majority in the House of Commons. Fourteen of the largest bulk steel producers were consolidated into a state enterprise called the British Steel Corporation (BSC). BSC controlled 92 percent of British steel production and was at the time the third largest producer of steel in the world (by weight). It employed 270,000 people and produced 23.3 million tons of steel in its first year of operation.[28] There remained 210 private steel firms in the domestic market, most of which were quite small. Only two relatively large firms were left to compete with BSC: GKN and Johnson Firth Brown.[29]

In 1967 BSC steel relied on open hearth furnaces to produce 57 percent of its raw steel (a rather high percentage compared with Germany and Japan, but not too different from the United States). Subsidization of the industry began in earnest in 1968. The BSC had inherited plants on more than sixty major sites. Many of these were in bad shape. Nevertheless, the first financial task was to pay for the nationalization itself. The BSC found itself owing the former shareholders a debt of around £1.2 billion. The British government helped to pay this debt by passing the 1969 Iron and Steel Act, which wrote off some of BSC's debts and made up the difference with public revenues in the form of government loans. Subsidies subsequently took the form of a policy of forgiveness in repaying the dividends for those loans (called public dividend capital).

New Investments Create Overcapacity. In 1970 the newly elected Conservative government contemplated splitting BSC into two smaller firms but decided instead to undertake a careful study of the industry and BSC's prospects. This study resulted in a white paper published in 1973 calling for a "Ten Year Development Strategy" for steel. A £3 billion expansion program was suggested for the modernization of old plants and the construction of five modern facilities to raise steel-making capacity to 30 million tons per year (about double the current level). The basis for this recommendation was the belief on the part of the Department of Trade and Industry staff that demand for steel both domestically and in export markets was rising rapidly and that BSC had an excellent opportunity to profit from that increasing demand by modernizing and augmenting its productive capacity.[30] Although BSC's profits had been low, its early problems might have been due more to price controls imposed by the Iron and Steel Board than to inherent deficiencies in the firm itself.

In retrospect, the stupidity of this plan is crystal clear. Yet one must recall that the early 1970s was a time of economic boom and of shortages of raw materials. When demand for steel slumped after the 1973 OPEC price increases (in the United Kingdom demand dropped from 19.5 million tons in 1973–1974 to 15 million tons in 1974–1975), the foolishness of expansion became evident, and the newly elected Labour government scaled back the size of the expansion. Unfortunately, the damage had already been done. BSC had begun to build major facilities at Scunthorpe, Lackenby, Ravenscraig in Scotland, and at Llanwern and Port Talbot in South Wales. Once begun the building was hard to stop because both parties had to satisfy important political constituencies and because British leaders were constantly aware of the threat of devolution of Scotland and Wales.

The result of the building of the new facilities were overcapacity. The new plants helped Britain become less reliant on domestic ores and coking coals (more expensive than and inferior to imports) because they were coastal. They should have allowed BSC to take advantage of the economies of scale available to plants using the basic oxygen process; however, these particular plants were scaled down to a size somewhat smaller than that required to realize maximal economies of scale—primarily for political reasons. Nevertheless, the new plants were sure to result in greater productivity, lower energy costs, and generally more internationally competitive production. Unfortunately, the stagnation of both domestic and export markets resulted in political pressures to keep the older and less efficient plants open, thus forcing the new plants to operate unprofitably at low levels of capacity utilization.

What should have happened, of course, was the shutting down of the older plants. Politically closing these was difficult because the whole effort had been sold originally as an expansion of capacity rather than as a modernization of existing capacity. The unions opposed closing older plants; the local communities that were involved did so as well. Fourteen ministers on the Labour cabinet in 1976 represented constituencies threatened by plant closures.[31] Thus big losses began for BSC in 1975 and continued through 1978. Imports increased their share of the British market from 5 percent in 1970–1971 to 20 percent in 1977–1978. BSC's share of the British market declined from 70 to 55 percent during the same period (see table 7).

BSC's huge operating losses required government subsidies to increase rapidly so that the firm could continue to meet its loan obligations. In 1977 BSC's chairman, Sir Charles Villiers, began to close obsolete plants and to reduce capacity. The firm continued to suffer large losses, however. In 1978 the minister of industry, Eric Varley, published a white paper on steel, *The Road to Viability*, which recommended drastic cuts in investment and production for BSC. Although the Labour government rejected these recommendations, nevertheless the BSC workforce was reduced by 44,000 between 1974 and 1979. BSC was near bankruptcy by the time the Thatcher government came to power in mid-1979.

The Thatcher Government Reduces Capacity. In June 1980, Sir Charles Villiers wrote to the minister of industry, Sir Keith Joseph, to ask for an additional subsidy for BSC of £400 million for fiscal year 1980–1981. The

TABLE 7
BRITISH STEEL CORPORATION LOSSES AND DECLINES IN MARKET SHARE, 1970–1979

Year	Profit/Loss (millions of £)	Market Share (%)	Import Share (%)
1967/1968	(19)		
1968/1969	(23)		
1969/1970	12		
1970/1971	(10)	70.4	5.6
1971/1972	(68)	66.0	9.6
1972/1973	3	63.7	12.1
1973/1974	39	62.2	13.2
1974/1975	73	58.0	15.7
1975/1976	(255)	55.7	18.2
1976/1977	(95)	55.0	19.1
1977/1978	(443)	54.8	20.4
1978/1979	(309)	54.1	19.4
1979/1980	(545)		
1980/1981	(668)		
1981/1982	(358)		
1982/1983	(1330)		

NOTE: Figures in parentheses are losses.
SOURCES: Iron and Steel Trades Confederation, *New Deal for Steel* (London: 1980), pp. 26 and 58; Keith Ovenden, *The Politics of Steel* (London: Macmillan, 1978), p. 170; British Steel Corporation, BSC Annual Reports and Accounts 1981–1982, p. 45; "British Steel Says Rivals Also Seek U.S. Steel Pact," *Wall Street Journal* (March 30, 1983), p. 3.

normal disaster at BSC had been compounded by a major strike. The alternative, according to Villiers, was liquidation. Immediately after the strike was settled, the Thatcher government recruited Ian MacGregor, at that time a partner of the firm of Lazard Freres in New York, to replace Villiers as the chairman of BSC. Despite the strong ideological objections to such a bail out on the part of the minister of industry, the subsidy request was granted in September 1980. An additional £110 million was granted in November 1980. An implicit *quid pro quo* for Sir Keith Joseph must have been a "get tough" policy on the part of the new chairman.

As soon as he took over in July 1980, MacGregor recommended a further reduction of the workforce by 20,000 and a reduction in production of 0.6 million tons per year.[32] At that moment, BSC was losing about $4 million a day.[33] Between January 1980 and May 1981 the workforce was reduced by 62,000.[34] MacGregor continued or accelerated several reductions planned by Villiers. Between 1977 and 1981, fifteen mid-sized steel works were closed, as were thirty-one of the existing forty-nine blast furnaces in the public sector.[35] The total work force was eventually halved from 160,000 in 1980 to around 80,000 in 1981. The combination of layoffs and plant closures drastically increased the productivity of the remaining operations. BSC continued to sustain losses, but the losses were reduced. Furthermore, the 1981 Iron and Steel Act provided for a write-off of £3.5 billion of BSC capital with a reserve of £1 billion for future purposes deemed fit by the chairman. MacGregor asserted that maintaining production capacity at around 14.4 million tons would be possible, but people were concerned that low operating levels at the Ravenscraig plant would eventually lead to its closure.

The 1982 recession produced another increase in BSC's losses, and the Labour party began to criticize MacGregor and the Thatcher government for their policies. One issue was the rather large payments made to Lazard Fréres in compensation for the services of MacGregor while he was on loan to BSC ($1.2 million as of July 1980 and further payments depending on the length of employment with a ceiling of $3.3 million).[36] Also, government subsidies rose again in fiscal year 1983 to $871 million from $497 million the year before.[37] When MacGregor announced that he would retire as BSC chairman in August 1983 to run the National Coal Board, the head of the British Mineworkers, Arthur Scargill, referred to him as "the American butcher of British industry" and "a hatchet man." Nigel Lawson, chancellor of the Exchequer, said that "hatchet men are a great deal cheaper than this." MacGregor himself said that he was not a "butcher" but "a plastic surgeon trying to redeem the features of aged properties which need some kind of face lift."[38]

Another tempest brewed when Ian MacGregor announced in April 1983 that BSC and U.S. Steel were contemplating an arrangement whereby BSC would sell U.S. Steel slabs made at the Ravanscraig plant in exchange for a $100-million investment by BSC in the U.S. Steel Fairless (Pennsylvania) plant. This move simultaneously angered the United Steel Workers (who objected to a concessionary wage arrangement that would have been part of the deal), those people in the United States who were critical of subsidization of the British steel industry (that is, most of the Reagan administration), the Commission of the European Communities (which saw the deal as possibly unraveling a larger deal made between the United States and Europe limiting European steel exports to the United States), and those British citizens who found the spectacle of BSC making direct foreign investments in the United States with its largely government-subsidized revenues somewhat hard to take. The economics of this deal looked good; the politics stank.[39]

Regardless of what one may think of Ian MacGregor, the story of British steel policies is not a happy one. The Thatcher government pursued an adjustment policy, which shifted most of the adjustment costs onto the workers, whereas previous governments had avoided adjustment because they were not sure it was necessary. Some element of this earlier approach still exists in the policies of the Thatcher government. In March 1982 the Thatcher government announced that it had instructed BSC to keep all five of its integrated plants open for the next three years, despite the fact that it had not allocated sufficient funds for this purpose.[40] When an attempt was made to close the Ravenscraig plant in the summer of 1983 before the elections, the government blocked it not to arouse discontent on the part of Scottish nationalists.

The lessons here are fairly simple: (1) Avoid expanding production capacity just before a decline in demand; (2) reducing overcapacity quickly when demand declines may be kinder in the long run than doing it slowly; (3) most democratic political systems will opt for the slow reduction of overcapacity; and (4) state enterprises can be successful in increasing investment when private enterprises have a history of overcaution, but they are also likely to contribute to delays in capacity reduction because of their insulation from short-term economic pressures. The British have learned all of these lessons, which have all been painful, especially for the workers.

Policies toward the Auto Industry

The British auto industry grew up in the 1920s and 1930s under an imposing set of tariff barriers but with relatively no restrictions on the entry of foreign firms, in this case the two American giants, Ford and General Motors, which began to manufacture in the United Kingdom in the 1920s. General Motors purchased Vauxhall in 1925. Ford's large plant at Dagenham was constructed in 1931. In 1945 foreign exchange restrictions limited the ability of British firms to set up their own overseas manufacturing facilities. Thus the British firms were imperfectly sheltered at home while effectively prevented from internationalizing at a crucial time. As a consequence, many rather small British manufacturers emerged only to become victim to later waves of internationalization and scale economizing in the global auto industry.

The first glimmering of what was to come was the merger of Austin and Morris in 1952 into BMC. This merger was prompted by increasing competition from Ford; but, because of less-than-alert management, opportunities for rationalization of production were overlooked, and the firm continued to produce in various small and inefficient plants. The Austin Mini, Austin's innovative front-wheel-drive vehicle, was introduced in the late 1950s and was a technical but not financial success. The larger domestic firms were able just to hold on to their shares of the market, but profit margins deteriorated steadily.

> [The] boom of the early sixties created an overexpansion of the motor industry without a rationalization of industrial structure. This was particularly harmful for the UK motor industry in that, by 1965, the European motor industry experienced overcapacity, so intensi-

145

fying international competition. The failure to rationalize meant that between 1965 and 1969 the UK motor industry consisted of manufacturers who were too small and failed to exploit potential economies of scale.[41]

In addition, the government used the auto industry in the 1950s and early 1960s as a weapon in its fight against regional concentration of industry, thus encouraging the building of more small and inefficient manufacturing facilities in underindustrialized regions.[42]

In 1965 BMC purchased Pressed Steel, the only large independent supplier of auto bodies in Britain. When this purchase occurred, smaller firms like Rover and Jaguar clearly saw that they would have to cooperate with BMC or other large firms to survive. Leyland purchased Rover at the end of 1965; and BMC and Jaguar formed a joint venture called British Motor Holdings (BMH), which left Jaguar with considerable autonomy but guaranteed access to BMC's auto bodies. Thus by the end of 1965 only two major British-owned firms or groups, Leyland and BMH, were left.

During the recession of 1967, the financial weaknesses of Standard-Triumph became apparent, and it was taken over by Leyland. Chrysler purchased a 70 percent share in Rootes in 1967 with the permission of the British government. Rootes would have had to close had there been no purchaser; and only Chrysler, at this point desperate for an outlet in Europe, was willing to purchase such a firm. The IRC held 15 percent of the shares of Rootes until 1973, when Chrysler purchased the remaining 30 percent of outstanding shares. (Ford had purchased 100 percent of Ford (U.K.) in 1960.)

The Formation of British Leyland. In 1968, the continuing weaknesses of Leyland and BMC led the government to encourage the merger of those two firms into the British Leyland Motor Company. The IRC provided £25 million in loans for retooling as an added incentive. The traditionally independent-minded management of the auto firms was quite upset about this injection of government capital, and several executives resigned; but the head of British Leyland, Don Stokes, was amenable to the arrangement and was later rewarded by the Labour government with the deputy chairmanship of the IRC in 1969. British Leyland was thus freed from close supervision and scrutiny by the IRC.

British Leyland in 1968 was a very large firm. Its $1.9 billion in sales compared favorably with Volkswagen ($2.5 billion) and Fiat ($1.7 billion). It was building too many models, however, and its output was low given the number of workers employed. It took 185,000 workers at British Leyland to produce the $1.9 billion in sales. The same number of workers at Chrysler (U.S.) produced $5.7 billion in sales. Some people have suggested that the earlier mergers had been partly to blame: that Morris injected Austin with inefficiency in 1952 and that BMC had done the same to British Leyland in 1968.[43]

The early 1970s were boom years for British Leyland and a period of relative nonintervention on the part of the Tory government. This idyll was ended by two unforeseen catastrophes. British Leyland decided to make a major investment to increase capacity in 1973 (£500 million) just before the OPEC-induced recession that was to follow shortly. In March 1974, Tony Benn became minister of industry. The difficulties experienced by British Leyland during this period led the Ministry of Industry to undertake a series of discussions with Chrysler (U.K.) concerning the possibility of a merger between British Leyland and Chrysler.[44] After the passage of the 1975 Industry Act, one of the first industries to receive financial assistance from the NEB was British Leyland. One of the first to be denied was Chrysler (U.K.).

Lord Ryder, the first director of the NEB, issued a report in 1975 arguing that the government should be willing to back British Leyland financially to the tune of £2.8 billion over eight years. The argument was premised on the feasibility of British Leyland's remaining a mass producer of automobiles, which required both a rationalization of existing facilities and an expansion of capacity.[45] According to John Barber, deputy chairman and managing director of British Leyland: "We do not have the volume to compete with the real giants in the cheap end of the market."[46] Harold Wilson, agreeing with this assessment, accepted the Ryder report and issued the following statement: "The Government has decided that Britain must remain in the world league so far as a British owned automobile industry is concerned."[47] In this way, British Leyland became a state enterprise.

Shortly after the Ryder report was issued and accepted, the Central Policy Review staff published its own report on the auto industry suggesting that British auto manufacturers needed to internationalize by forming links with other European firms to meet the challenges of international competition. The policy review staff underlined the problems of too many models and plants but was quick to point out that merely increasing production of fewer models would not solve the problems of British firms. To realize economies of scale, production needed to be increased but not at the expense of overly reducing the number of models offered for sale (that is, they had correctly perceived the problems of Volkswagen). The policy review staff report had a particularly important influence on later government policies toward Chrysler, as we shall see.

The Collapse of Chrysler (U.K.). 1975 was a busy year for automotive policy, not just because of the two reports discussed above, but also because of the near collapse of Chrysler (U.K.). The crisis was a long time coming, but the precipitating event was a message sent in October from the chairman of Chrysler (U.S.), John Riccardo, to the British government announcing that Chrysler "would start liquidating Chrysler (UK) from the end of November . . . unless Her Majesty's government in the meantime took it over."[48]

147

Chrysler (U.K.) lost $35 million in 1974 and $71 million in 1975. Neither the NEB nor British Leyland were interested in purchasing Chrysler (U.K.), and even the Ministry of Industry favored liquidation initially (but only if combined with import controls). The cabinet objected, however, to import controls, while the Scottish Office strongly opposed the closing of the main Chrysler plant at Linwood. Because they were concerned about Scottish nationalism and the threat of devolution and because the closure of Chrysler (U.K.) would threaten arms sales to Iran (Chrysler [U.K.] had just completed an assembly plant there), the cabinet decided to rescue Chrysler (U.K.) with £72.5 million in loans and £90 million in loan guarantees.

The end of the Chrysler story is a sad one. In 1977 Chrysler (U.K.) was taken over by Peugeot/Citroen. Following the suggestions laid out in the policy review staff report of 1975, the government had first promoted greater integration between Chrysler (U.K.) and Chrysler (Europe)—especially Chrysler (France). When Peugeot purchased Chrysler's European interests in 1977, the British government made no objection to the inclusion of Chrysler (U.K.). The Linwood plant, never cost efficient since its construction in 1960–1962, at the insistence of the Board of Trade closed forever in June 1981, displacing 5,000 workers (a shadow of the original work force). Chrysler (U.K.) now became Talbot under the direction of Peugeot (now called PSA). In 1982–1983 Talbot received £50 million in loans from the British government.[49]

Continued Weakness at British Leyland. The 1975–1977 period was one of continuing weakness at British Leyland as well. "By 1979 Ford (UK), Vauxhall, and Chrysler (UK) had all become very much integrated into the European motor industry—a development encouraged by the Chrysler (UK) bail-out—whilst BL had become a secondary junior league producer."[50] Don Stokes, the managing director, was not a forceful individual and was replaced in 1977 by Michael Edwardes, who immediately asked and received support for a major reduction in the size of the work force, the number of plants, and the degree of centralization of management of the firm. He also won greater managerial independence from the NEB and implemented a new policy of establishing performance targets for divisional managers. He began a round of tough bargaining with the unions for wage restraints and was successful, especially after the beginning of the Thatcher government, in getting a series of wage restraint agreements.[51] In 1979 British Leyland made a deal with Honda to coproduce a mid-sized car that would be sold both in Europe and in Japan. This car would have a Honda engine, gearbox, and transmission with a British Leyland body and other components. In that same year, the government increased the flow of funds to British Leyland to £1,205 million.

During the campaign in 1979, the Tories had pledged to continue aiding British Leyland. This pledge helped them to win in important constituencies

TABLE 8
SHARES OF THE UNITED KINGDOM DOMESTIC MARKET FOR
NEW AUTOMOBILES, 1968–1980
(percent)

	1968	1973	1980
British Leyland	40.6	31.9	18.2
Ford	27.3	22.6	30.7
General Motors	13.2	8.0	7.2
Talbot	10.2	9.7	9.4
Imports	8.7	25.8	40.5

NOTE: A problem exists with these data because of the strange distinction made in British statistical sources (mainly the Society of Motor Manufacturers and Traders) between captive imports and other imports. Captive imports are those marketed by firms already manufacturing in the United Kingdom. It is estimated that about half of the "imports" to the United Kingdom in 1979 were captive imports. The 1980 figures include captive imports under the appropriate United Kingdom firm's market share.
SOURCE: George Maxcy, *The Multinational Motor Industry* (London: Croom Helm, 1981), p. 221; European Research Associates, *EEC Protectionism: Present Practice and Future Trends* (Brussels: 1982), p. 144.

like Birmingham, Oxford, and Coventry. They showed themselves willing after the election to support British Leyland. In January 1981, Sir Keith Joseph announced that British Leyland would receive £990 million in aid. This aid was to help the company launch a new model called the Minimetro. In addition, the 1981 Industry Act increased the borrowing limit of the Department of Industry to permit the department to cover its lending needs to British Leyland after the transfer of responsibility for British Leyland from the NEB to the Department of Industry.[52]

In March 1981 British Leyland reported a loss of £535 million in the financial year.[53] British Leyland's work force in the United Kingdom dropped from 176,000 in 1977 to 96,000 in 1981. Its share of the U.K. domestic market had dropped from 40.6 percent in 1968 to 18.2 percent in 1980 (see table 8). The end of this decline was not in sight. By no stretch of the imagination, by no conceivable rhetorical flourish, could this record be interpreted as a success. Yet British Leyland was still there.

Again, the best explanation of British industrial policy in a specific sector, as in steel, lies in the weakness of its domestic firms. The intervention of the government has become massive and has bridged the ideological chasms separating the Labour government of Harold Wilson and the Conservative government of Margaret Thatcher. More continuity than discontinuity exists here, and it is all depressing. Perhaps I can end on a more upbeat note with my third case—information technology.

Policies toward the Information Technology Industry

Again, the underlying condition for British policy is the weakness of domestic firms. In this case, however, the type of intervention that the government has chosen has been somewhat more effective in promoting the growth, and not preventing the adaptive adjustment, of firms in the industry. The case of information technology illustrates the more general point made by John Ikenberry in his work on U.S. energy policies that each country, with its own characteristic set of governmental institutions and state-society links, has distinctive capabilities for responding to the needs of certain industries for supportive governmental policies.[54] Each state has "comparative advantages" depending on the industry in question. Apparently states and societies like those of Britain and the United States have the right characteristics for promoting innovation in information technology whereas the states and societies of France and Germany, for example, do not.

An increasingly important member of the family of industries included under the rubric of information technology is the microelectronics industry (information technology encompasses computers, office automation, telecommunications, consumer electronics, and electronic components). Access to innovations in microelectronics components, especially advanced products such as microprocessors and random-access memories, is crucial to the competitiveness of "downstream" industries. For this reason most industrialized countries in recent years have begun to focus their policies on promoting domestically owned microelectronics industries. The microelectronics industry began with a strong connection with military defense. The United States and the United Kingdom have the highest percentages of government research and development devoted to defense of the five largest industrial capitalist countries (see table 9). The fates of private firms like Plessey, Ferranti, and GEC in Britain have been tied to government defense policies at least since World War II. Like the microelectronics industries of other major

TABLE 9

GOVERNMENT RESEARCH AND DEVELOPMENT ALLOCATED TO DEFENSE,
1961–1967
(percent)

Period	United States	United Kingdom	France	Germany	Japan
1961/1962	71	65	44	22	4
1971/1972	53	44	28	15	2
1976/1977	51	46	30	12	2

SOURCE: Robert F. Wescott, "U.S. Approaches to Industrial Policy," in Adams and Klein, *Industrial Policies for Growth and Competitiveness*, p. 110.

150

countries, the degree of dependence on military applications has decreased, but a strong link still exists.

The first item to be discussed is British policy toward the information technology industry as a whole. Next the stories of two state enterprises, ICL and Inmos, will be told. Then some generalizations will be made about the role of government policy in information technology, especially in microelectronics.

Policy toward the Industry as a Whole. The United Kingdom has 4 percent of the world information technology market. The information technology industry in the United Kingdom has been growing at a rate of 12 percent annually. The United Kingdom's domestic market is increasingly dominated by foreign-owned firms. In mainframe computers, for example, IBM is dominant (as in most of the rest of the world) (see table 10). In semiconductors, the number-one firm is Texas Instruments, followed by Philips (based in the Netherlands but with large holdings of former United Kingdom-owned firms like Mullard) (see table 11).

The main British firms in the information technology industry are Imperial Computers Limited (ICL), General Electric Company (GEC—only a faint connection with General Electric in the United States), Standard Telephone and Cables, Ltd. (STC), British Telecom, Mercury, Thorn-EMI, Ferranti, Plessey, and Inmos. ICL, British Telecom, and Inmos are state-owned firms. GEC, STC, Thorn, Plessey, and Ferranti are private; but GEC, Plessey, and

TABLE 10

SHARES OF THE UNITED KINGDOM DOMESTIC MARKET FOR
MAINFRAME COMPUTERS, END OF 1976
(percent)

Firm	Share of Market
IBM	47.2
ICL	26.7
CII-HB	8.5
Burroughs	6.1
Univac	6.0
NCR	3.0
CDC	1.3
Others	1.4

NOTES: Of the above, only ICL is British owned. Detail may not add to 100 percent because of rounding.
SOURCE: M. Delapierre, L. A. Gerard-Varet, and J. B. Zimmerman, "The Computer and Data Processing Industry," in H. W. de Jong, ed., *The Structure of European Industry* (Amsterdam: Martinus Nijhoff, 1981), p. 269.

TABLE 11
SHARES OF THE UNITED KINGDOM DOMESTIC MARKET FOR SEMICONDUCTORS, 1962–1977
(percent)

	1962	1968	1973	1977
Texas Instruments	13	23	18	22
Philips	49	22	17	18
Motorola	NA	6	14	11
ITT	2	7	13	8
GEC	7	4	NA	6
SGS	NA	14	3	3
Ferranti	10	5	4	1
Others	19	19	32	31

NOTE: Of the firms above, only GEC and Ferranti are British owned. Detail may not add to totals because of rounding. NA = not available.
SOURCE: Giovanni Dosi, *Technical Change and Survival: Europe's Semiconductor Industry* (Brighton: Sussex European Research Center, 1981), p. 75.

Ferranti are highly dependent on British military contracts.

Again the problem is the weakness and the smallness of British firms and a growing penetration of foreign-owned firms and imports into the British market. According to a study published by the Information Technology Economic Development Committee (of NEDC), "the U.K. information technology industry now has such a small share of world markets that it can no longer continue to invest adequately in product development, in marketing or in production facilities."[55] The global sales of IBM were more than sixteen times the total sales of ICL. The sales of AT&T were twenty times the sales of Plessey. The level of import penetration in information technology had reached the high level of 54 percent by 1982–1983.[56]

The Alvey Report. In 1982 the British government commissioned a report on the information technology industry, which posed the problem as follows:

> The issue before us is stark. We can either seek to be at the leading edge of these technologies; or we can aim to rely on imported technology; or we can opt out of the race. The latter we do not regard as a valid option. Nor is the reliance upon imported technology practical as a general strategy, though we cannot be completely self-sufficient either. . . . The only sensible option . . . is to share in the future growth and development of the world IT sector . . . in specific targetted priority areas.[57]

The Thatcher government accepted the recommendations of the Alvey Report and the Electronic Components SWP for a special government-funded research program for advanced information technology aimed at matching, at least on a small scale, the efforts of the United States and Japan in this area. In September 1984 the Alvey Research Program announced the funding of thirty-four research projects, the total for this phase of the program being around $83 million. About half of that amount would go to Plessey, GEC, and STC. The program is supposed to run for five years with a total expenditure of $483 million.[58] The Alvey Research Program is the latest in a series of British efforts to promote the information technology industries. I will briefly examine the history of these earlier programs.

Policies of the 1950s and 1960s. In the 1950s, the British government encouraged the growth of the domestic computer industry primarily because of the needs of its Atomic Energy Agency for advanced computers. The National Research and Development Corporation (NRDC) was in charge of these efforts. In 1954 the Development of Inventions Act gave the NRDC more flexibility by extending the period in which the NRDC had to become self-supporting. In 1957 the NRDC initiated a project for the development of supercomputers. The principle contractor was Ferranti, along with the Department of Electrical Engineering at Manchester University. As a result of these efforts, Ferranti developed the ATLAS model, which turned out to be more successful in the British market than its main competitor, IBM's STRETCH model.[59]

In the 1960s, the Labour government during its period of developing a British industrial strategy increased the amount of government funding of research and development and encouraged the mergers which led to the formation of ICL. The IRC financed ICL initially with a loan of £3.5 million. In 1968 ICL received an additional dose of public R and D aid of £13.5 million, another £40 million in 1972–1973. The government adopted a preferential purchasing policy for government computers to favor ICL. In 1967 the government started buying shares in ICL; by 1969 it owned 25 percent of the shares.[60]

The NEB Promotes Information Technology. Nineteen seventy-eight was a particularly important year for policy initiatives in information technology. In one of its last major transactions, the NEB purchased 75 percent of the shares in a fledgling microelectronics firm called Inmos. The firm was founded by Iann Barron and two Americans, Richard Petritz and Paul Schroeder. These three held onto 5 percent of the shares of the firm. Petritz, formerly an employee of Intel, saw some opportunities for a start-up firm to produce very fast microprocessor chips (later called transputers). The founders approached the NEB with their ideas and were able to secure the support of the Labour government. Petritz became the chief executive officer of the firm, which

153

decided to build two plants—one in South Wales to produce 64K DRAMs (Dynamic Random Access Memories) and one in Colorado to produce 16K static RAMs and 64K DRAMs. By 1984 Inmos had 844 employees in the United States and 544 in the United Kingdom.[61]

The Electronics Components SWP in NEDC complained to the government about the purchase of Inmos without adequate consultation. They were concerned about the government's sponsorship of new competitors. Shortly after receiving these complaints, the Labour government announced two new programs, MISP (Microelectronics Industry Support Program) and MAP (Microprocessor Applications Project).[62] MISP was designed to help domestic firms come up to global standards in the manufacturing of integrated circuits. The program was relatively small: only about £24 million was to be spent. In fact, even that small amount was not spent during the five years allocated for the program. The firms questioned the emphasis on standardized as opposed to customized circuits implicit in the funding criteria.[63]

MAP was designed to increase the familiarity of British manufacturers generally with the microelectronics technology so that they would increase the use of that technology and thereby increase demand for domestic microelectronics and information technology products. In 1977 a survey by the Department of Industry had shown that only 5 percent of British firms were aware of developments in microelectronics. The MAP offered a series of training sessions for British industrialists that were quite well attended: 133,000 attended MAP awareness seminars by 1982.

The Privatization of Inmos and ICL. In 1979 the Thatcher government continued MISP and MAP but revised the previous governments' policies toward ICL and Inmos. As part of its overall policy of privatization, the Thatcher government instructed the British Technology Group (successor to the NEB) to look for private purchasers for its shares in ICL and Inmos. This instruction created an interesting political controversy between the Conservative and Labour parties because of the Labour party's firm belief that the policies of 1976–1979 had been responsible for maintaining some credible alternative to IBM (in the case of computers) and for making Britain the only country in Europe with an independent domestically owned mass producer of integrated circuits (Inmos). Peter Shore, Labour MP and shadow cabinet member, said that "to abandon public ownership now would be no more than ideological spite."[64]

Despite Labour objections, the Thatcher government proceeded with its plans. Kenneth Baker, the new minister of information technology, criticized the previous government's policies: "The previous government saw the NEB as a major interventionist instrument that could start up new ventures and buy companies that were about to collapse and save them . . . . [The problem is that] civil servants aren't very good at that sort of thing."[65]

The irony of this statement was that the NEB and its predecessors had been set up in such a way as to minimize the influence of civil servants in industrial policy making. The members of the board of the NEB were primarily industrialists. Perhaps the belated recognition of this fact made the Thatcher government able to replace the NEB with the BTG without abandoning the idea completely.

The BTG dismissed Richard Petritz as chief executive officer on Inmos in July 1983 and replaced him with Sir Malcolm Wilcox. The first offer to come in was from AT&T, soon after its deregulation in the United States. AT&T had recently purchased a 25 percent stake in Olivetti. It wanted the Inmos plant in South Wales to ensure access to European Community markets and to avoid the 17.5 percent tariff on microelectronic imports.[66] AT&T offered $69 million for 60 percent of Inmos's shares in February 1984. AT&T also offered to put an additional $96.6 million into the plant in South Wales for retooling and said it would transfer the seventy-person Inmos design team, which was working on the transputer, to the control of ICL. The British government was not pleased with this offer since it had already invested over $140 million in Inmos and wanted at least to recover that sum from the sale. In addition, Inmos itself was opposed to the sale, as were the BTG, Sinclair, and ICL, all of whom wanted Inmos to remain in British hands. Peter Shore of the Labour party called the deal "technological treason," while David Owen of the SDP called it "little short of lunacy."[67] The bid was rejected soon after it was made simply for being too low. Merrill Lynch had estimated that a public offering of Inmos shares would bring in around $270 million.[68]

The firm had lost around $78 million cumulatively by the end of 1983, so there was still substantial sentiment among Thatcherites to sell it.[69] A parliamentary debate in June 1984 resulted in the passing of an amendment endorsing privatization of the firm.[70] Soon after this debate, Thorn-EMI offered $13.8 million for slightly less than 10 percent of the shares of Inmos. Inmos and the BTG welcomed the offer because it was a gesture of support and would help to counter offers from foreign firms like AT&T. Also in June Inmos was approached by a consortium of Dutch interests that wanted to finance the building of a new chip-making facility in Limburg for about $69 million.[71] While this offer was another shot in the arm for Inmos, it nevertheless conflicted with the company's plans to build another plant in the United Kingdom. In any case, the BTG had the right to veto the arrangement.

In the latest development, Thorn-EMI offered to buy the BTG's 75 percent of Inmos shares for $124 million. It was expected to purchase the remaining shares for around $39 million, but the offer to the BTG was not contingent on this purchase. Thorn had just submitted an unsuccessful bid of around $1.12 billion for British Aerospace. A merger of Thorn and British

Aerospace would have created a firm with $6.95 billion annual sales. GEC also offered to purchase British Aerospace, a merger that would have created a military industrial giant with $11 billion in annual sales accounting for about 25 percent of the expenditures of the British Defense Ministry.[72] When British Aerospace rejected the bid from Thorn, GEC announced that it might not go ahead with its bid because of the prospect of objections from the Monopolies and Mergers Commission.[73] It was rumored that Ferranti and Plessey were pushing for a hearing of the Monopolies and Mergers Commission if the deal went through.[74] When Thorn upped its bid for Inmos to $165 million in August, Inmos accepted; and the merger took place.

The privatization of ICL was concluded with a successful bid from Standard Telephones and Cables (STC) of $561 million in August 1984. Thus ended a long and not terribly successful experiment in state entrepreneurship. In its last years, ICL had undergone some severe financial difficulties. The big losses began in December 1980 and continued through 1981. The Thatcher government had replaced the managing director of ICL with an American named Robb Wilmott, formerly the manager of Texas Instruments (U.K.), who concluded a series of arrangements with Fujitsu to get access to Fujitsu chips and to market Fujitsu IBM-compatible mainframes in the United Kingdom and in Europe. A series of loans and loan guarantees from the government were required to prevent bankruptcy of the firm until it returned to profitability in 1981–1982.[75]

STC had been founded in 1880 as an agency for Western Electric. In 1925 it was acquired by ITT. ITT cut its stake in STC to 85 percent in 1979 and then to 35 percent in 1982. STC bought about 10 percent of the shares of ICL at the end of July 1984 in a "dawn raid" and then offered £350 million for the rest of shares needed for control. ITT approved because it saw the bid as a necessary counterpart to the arrangement between IBM and Rolm (another computer/telecommunications linkup). The ITT holding in STC created some political opposition to the STC-ICL merger, but the Thatcher government approved the deal anyway when ITT announced that it planned to reduce its share of STC from 35 to 25 percent (which meant a 26–27 percent share in the STC-ICL merged company).[76]

The merger mania of the summer of 1984 was a joint function of the desire of the Thatcher government to privatize and of the large cash holdings accumulated by the more dynamic British firms during the recovery of 1983–1984. The image one obtains from a close examination of these financial transactions is not one of a dead industry, but rather of one appearing to be undergoing some reinvigoration. The growing concentration of ownership may be a worrisome development; but, given the size of the internationally competitive firms in the same industry, Britain apparently is not alone in this development. In microelectronics and information technology, the British case seems to demonstrate a fortuitous combination of more than usually realistic state entrepreneurship and hasty privatization. Possibly a state-owned Inmos and ICL might have done well by themselves. A Thorn-Inmos and STC-ICL may do better, but it is probably too early to tell.

Conclusion

The British case is a strange one. As in the case of Germany, we have to distinguish between ideology and practice. We must also consider variation in results of government policies across industrial sectors. The British state has been alternately interventionist and market oriented with respect to domestic business. The peculiar combination of concertative and interventionist institutions set up under both Conservative and Labour governments lends some continuity to policy. So does the overall weakness of British firms in international competition; a legacy of earlier policies of the defense of the pound in international currency markets. The result is that the British state seems relatively better organized to make intelligent industrial policies in the high-technology microelectronics and information technology fields, less well organized for making policy for declining industries like steel and autos.

Notes

1. Stephen Wilks, "Liberal State and Party Competition: Britain," in Kenneth Dyson and Stephen Wilks, eds., *Industrial Crisis: A Comparative Study of State and Industry* (New York: St. Martin's Press, 1983), p. 139.

2. Michael Davenport, "Industrial Policy in the United Kingdom," in F. Gerard Adams and Lawrence R. Klein, eds., *Industrial Policies for Growth and Competitiveness: An Economic Perspective* (Lexington, Mass.: Lexington Books, 1983), p. 340.

3. Wyn Grant, *The Political Economy of Industrial Policy* (Woburn, Mass.: Butterworths, 1982), p. 28.

4. Ibid., p. 29; Stephen Wilks, "Liberal State and Party Competition: Britain," p. 135; and "Ministerial Marionettes," *The Economist* (October 22, 1983), p. 53.

5. Wyn Grant, *The Political Economy of Industrial Policy*, pp. 31–35.

6. Andrew Shonfield, *Modern Capitalism: The Changing Balance of Public and Private Power* (New York: Oxford University Press, 1969), pp. 151–52.

7. Stephen Blank, "Britain: The Politics of Foreign Economic Policy, The Domestic Economy, and the Problem of Pluralistic Stagnation," in Peter Katzenstein, ed., *Between Power and Plenty* (Madison, Wisc.: University of Wisconsin Press, 1978), pp. 98–99.

8. Michael Davenport, "Industrial Policy in the United Kingdom," p. 341.

9. Stephen Wilks, "Liberal State and Party Competition: Britain," p. 137.

10. Martin Holmes, *Political Pressure and Economic Policy: British Government, 1970–1974* (Woburn, Mass.: Butterworths, 1982), p. 37; Wyn Grant, *The Political Economy of Industrial Policy*, pp. 77–78; and John Zysman, *Governments, Markets and Growth* (Ithaca, N.Y.: Cornell University, 1983), pp. 216–17.

11. Wyn Grant, *The Political Economy of Industrial Policy*, pp. 109–110.

12. Stephen Wilks, "Liberal State and Party Competition: Britain," p. 135; Michael

Davenport, "Industrial Policy in the United Kingdom," pp. 344–46; and Barnaby J. Feder, "Inmos: A Success for Britain," *New York Times* (July 14, 1984), p. 32.

13. Wyn Grant, *The Political Economy of Industrial Policy*, p. 115.

14. Ibid., p. 21.

15. Kenneth H. F. Dyson, "The Politics of Economic Management in West Germany," *West European Politics*, vol. 4 (May 1981), pp. 60–61; and Zysman, *Governments, Markets and Growth*.

16. Wyn Grant, *The Political Economy of Industrial Policy*, p. 14.

17. Ibid., p. 49.

18. Michael Davenport, "Industrial Policy in the United Kingdom," p. 333.

19. Stephen Wilks, "Liberal State and Party Competition: Britain," p. 131.

20. Wyn Grant, *The Political Economy of Industrial Policy*, pp. 45–50.

21. Ibid., p. 51.

22. Michael Landesman, "The Effects of Industrial Policies in the U.K., 1973–1981," paper delivered at a conference on industrial policies and structural adaptation, ISVEIMER, Naples, April 21, 1983, table 1.

23. Wyn Grant, *The Political Economy of Industrial Policy*, p. 84.

24. Michael Davenport, "Industrial Policy in the United Kingdom," p. 342.

25. Wyn Grant, *The Political Economy of Industrial Policy*, p. 79.

26. Stephen Wilks, "Liberal State and Party Competition: Britain," p. 134.

27. Jonathan Aylen, "Plant Size and Efficiency in the Steel Industry: An International Comparison," *National Institute Economic Review*, no. 100 (May 1982), pp. 209–210.

28. Ibid., p. 73; Robert Lubar, "An American Leads British Steel Back from the Brink," *Fortune* (September 21, 1981), p. 89; Patrick Messerlin, *The European Industrial Adjustment Policies: The Steel Industry Case* (Brighton: Sussex European Research Centre), p. UK1; and Anthony Cockerill, "Steel and the State in Great Britain," *Annalen der Gemeinwirtschaft*, vol. 49 (Oct./Dec. 1980), p. 447.

29. Jonathan Aylen, "Innovation in the British Steel Industry," p. 201.

30. Josef Esser, "Sozialisierung als beschaeftigungspolitisches Instrument? Ehrfahrungen mit der verstaatlichen Stahlindustrie in Europa," *Gewerkschaftliche Monatshefte*, vol. 31 (July 1980), pp. 448–51; Wyn Grant, *The Political Economy of Industrial Policy*, p. 93; and Jonathan Aylen, "Plant Size and Efficiency in the Steel Industry," p. 74.

31. Ibid., p. 227.

32. Wyn Grant, *The Political Economy of Industrial Policy*, pp. 93–94.

33. Robert Lubar, "An American Leads British Steel Back from the Brink," p. 88.

34. Jonathan Aylen, "Innovation in the British Steel Industry," p. 68.

35. Ibid., p. 69.

36. Robert Lubar, "An American Leads British Steel Back from the Brink," p. 88.

37. "British Steel Says Rivals Also Seek U.S. Steel Pack," *Wall Street Journal* (March 30, 1983), p. 3.

38. Robert L. Muller, "Britain Names Ian MacGregor Coal Board Chief," *Wall Street Journal* (March 29, 1983), p. 39.

39. Frederick Kempe and Thomas F. O'Boyle, "British Steel Says It May End Some Subsidies," *Wall Street Journal* (April 6, 1983), p. 2.

40. J. J. Richardson and G. F. Dudley, "Steel Policy in the UK: The Politics of

Industrial Decline," (unpublished manuscript, European University Institute, Florence, Italy, 1984).

41. Peter J. S. Dunnett, *The Decline of the British Motor Industry: The Effects of Government Policy, 1948–1979* (London: Croom Helm, 1980), pp. 94–95.

42. Daniel T. Jones, *Maturity and Crisis in the European Car Industry: Structural Change and Public Policy* (Brighton: Sussex European Research Centre, 1981), p. 108; and Stephen Wilks, "Liberal State and Party Competition: Britain," p. 142.

43. Peter J. S. Dunnett, *The Decline of the British Motor Industry: The Effects of Government Policy, 1948–1979* (London: Croom Helm, 1980), p. 101.

44. Stephen Wilks, "Liberal State and Party Competition: Britain," pp. 143–46.

45. Peter J. S. Dunnett, *The Decline of the British Motor Industry*, p. 133; and George Maxcy, *The Multinational Motor Industry* (London: Croom Helm, 1981), p. 228.

46. Ibid., p. 220.

47. Ibid., p. 228.

48. Peter J. S. Dunnett, *The Decline of the British Motor Industry*, p. 136; Stephen Wilks, "Liberal State and Party Competition: Britain," p. 142; and Michael Moritz and Barrett Seaman, *Going for Broke: The Chrysler Story* (New York: Doubleday, 1981), p. 187.

49. Stephen Wilks, "Liberal State and Party Competition: Britain," p. 147.

50. Peter J. S. Dunnett, *The Decline of the British Motor Industry*, p. 169.

51. Daniel T. Jones, *Maturity and Crisis in the European Car Industry*, pp. 48–49.

52. Wyn Grant, *The Political Economy of Industrial Policy*, pp. 109–110.

53. Ibid., p. 95.

54. John Ikenberry, "State Power and the Politics of Adjustment: U.S. Responses to the Oil Shocks and the Development of Governmental Comparative Advantage" (Ph.D. diss., University of Chicago, 1984).

55. James Fallon, "Says U.K. Losing Share of World Info. Tech. Market," *Electronics News* (September 10, 1984), p. 20.

56. Ibid.

57. United Kingdom, Department of Industry, *A Programme for Advanced Information Technology* (London: HMSO, 1982), p. 14.

58. James Fallon, "Says U.K. Losing Share of World Info. Tech. Market," p. 20.

59. P. Drath, M. Gibbons, and R. Johnston, "The Super-Computer Project: A Case Study of the Interaction of Science, Government, and Industry in the UK," *Research Policy*, vol. 6 (1977), pp. 2–34.

60. M. Delapierre, L. A. Gerard-Varet, and J. B. Zimmerman, "The Computer and Data Processing Industry," in H. W. de Jong, ed., *The Structure of European Industry* (Amsterdam: Martinus Nijhoff, 1981), p. 271; and Stephen Wilks, "Liberal State and Party Competition."

61. James Fallon, "U.K. Unit Hits Inmos for Investment in U.S.," *Electronic News* (May 21, 1984), p. 73; and Barnaby J. Feder, "Inmos: A Success for Britain," *New York Times* (July 4, 1984), p. 25.

62. Wyn Grant, *The Political Economy of Industrial Policy*, pp. 64–65.

63. Ibid., pp. 64 and 86; and Giovanni Dosi, *Technical Change and Survival: Europe's Semiconductor Industry* (Brighton: Sussex European Research Centre, 1981), p. 37.

64. Barnaby J. Feder, "Inmos: A Success for Britain," p. 25.

65. Beth Karlin, "Britain's State-Run Microchip Maker Setting Plans to Seek Private Financing," *Wall Street Journal* (July 13, 1983), p. 34.

66. Beth Karlin, "Inmos of U.K. Rejects Offer from AT&T," *Wall Street Journal* (February 21, 1984), p. 33.

67. "AT&T Technology Offers $80M for 2 Inmos Plants; We Invest $96M in Wales Unit," *Electronics News* (June 25, 1984), p. 1.

68. "Thorn-EMI Will Buy a 76% Share in Inmos," *New York Times* (July 13, 1984), p. 26.

69. James Fallon, "U.K. Unit Hits Inmos for Investment in U.S.," p. 73.

70. "AT&T Technology Offers $80M for 2 Inmos Plants," p. 1.

71. James Fallon, "Dutch Seek Local Inmos Facility," *Electronics News* (June 4, 1984), p. 71.

72. James Fallon, "GEC, Thorn Continue Fight to Buy British Aerospace," *Electronics News* (June 11, 1984), p. 18.

73. James Fallon, "British Aerospace Rejects Thorn EMI's $1B Bid," *Electronics News* (June 18, 1984), p. 64.

74. Barnaby J. Feder, "A Partner for British Aerospace," *New York Times* (June 18, 1984), p. 32.

75. Wyn Grant, *The Political Economy of Industrial Policy*, p. 98; and Stephen Wilks, "Liberal State and Party Competition," pp. 148–55.

76. James Fallon, "ITT to Reduce Ownership in STC to Less Than 25%," *Electronics News* (September 10, 1964), p. 27.

West German Industrial Policy

Jeffrey A. Hart

Introduction

West German industrial policy differs from that of all the other large capitalist industrial countries in combining a low degree of centralization of government institutions for making industrial policy with a highly centralized "corporatistic" or "concertative" bargaining system, especially during crises. Germany is like the United States and Britain in its governmental decentralization, more like France and Japan in its bargaining arrangements. This system is often praised for its ability to maintain economic stability (especially low inflation and unemployment rates) while ensuring labor peace. It has been criticized for its failure to incorporate more marginalized sectors of the working force into the mainstream German society and for undermining the legitimacy of the major parties and interest groups. As in the industrial policies of all the other large capitalist countries, one must distinguish the normal policy-making process from that which exists during crises. Therefore, the narrative below will start with a description of the institutions that are responsible for industrial policy making along with some historical background on them. Some attempt will be made to identify the elements of continuity not just in the institutions themselves but also in the justifications for government intervention in general. Then several cases of major industrial crises and the politics of crisis resolution will be discussed. The conclusion will attempt to synthesize the lessons learned from studying both normal and crisis policy making.

Thanks are due to the American Enterprise Institute for partial funding of the research for this chapter, and in particular to Claude Barfield for organizing the AEI conference on industrial policy, held in Washington on October 1, 1984, at which an earlier draft was presented. Peter Katzenstein, Alfred Diamant, and Gerd Junne provided helpful comments on that draft.

This chapter omits any detailed description of European industrial and regional policies that affect Germany. Inclusion of European policies would help to provide a more complete picture of German policies. The reader may wish to obtain this additional information by reading the author's forthcoming work on industrial policies, *Atlantic Riptides*.

Background on the German Institutional Setting

The most important government institutions for a discussion of economic and industrial policies are the chancellor's office, the Bundesbank, the Ministry of Economics, the Ministry of Research and Technology, the *Sachsverständigenrat,* and the regional governments. As in all large capitalist nations, the government institutions work within a wider policy network, which includes the political parties, the unions, employer associations, and other private actors. This section will focus only on government institutions to provide some background for the uninitiated. Those already familiar with German governmental institutions may want to skip to the next section.

The chancellor of the Federal Republic is in a key position to propose new policies, especially as the chancellor often is also the head of the largest party in the ruling coalition. But the chancellor must win approval for all legislative changes in the parliament and has limited control over certain parts of the bureaucracy, as in many other industrial democracies. A particularly important limit on the chancellor's policy-making power in economic policy is the high autonomy of the German central bank, the Bundesbank.

The Deutsche Bundesbank (a central bank that also coordinates the activities of the regional banks and is autonomous from the rest of the federal government) has sole control over monetary policy. It was created under the occupation in 1948 and was modeled after the U.S. Federal Reserve System. The Bundesbank in Frankfurt, however, serves as a true central bank unlike any of the branches of the Federal Reserve System in the United States. The board of directors *(Zentralbankrat)* of the Bundesbank is composed of the directors of the Bundesbank and the presidents of the central state banks *(Landeszentralbanken).* The Landeszentralbanken have no real independence, unlike the state banks *(Landesbanken),* but are merely administrative units of the Bundesbank. Members appointed by the federal government have eight-year terms. The long terms are designed to ensure that the Bundesbank can be quite independent from the chancellor and the ruling party if it chooses to be.[1]

The Ministry of Economics shares control over fiscal policy with the Ministry of Finance. The Ministry of Economics has been headed by relatively conservative political figures since World War II. Ludwig Erhard was the master of economic policy during the Adenauer administration. At that time the Ministry of Economics had no real rivals for control over economic or industrial policy in the federal government. In 1972, however, the creation of the Ministry of Technology and Research presented the Ministry of Economics with a rival of considerable importance. The Ministry of Technology and Research developed an elaborate research planning system and was given authority over administering various technical aid programs for specific industries. During the 1970s, the majority of this aid went to the nuclear energy programs and to the state governments.[2]

The *Sachverständigenrat* (which roughly translates as Council of Experts) was created in 1963 to produce an annual report on the economy. Composed mostly of academic economists, it tends to take a relatively conservative (that is, neoclassical) view toward economic policies. It disapproves of too much involvement of the government in domestic economic affairs and favors maintaining liberal free trade policies in external economic affairs. The Sachverständigenrat was an early proponent of national-level bargaining between management and labor allocating wage increases according to productivity criteria. The federal government appoints its five members to a term of five years.[3] It has lost much of its influence in recent years.

Antitrust or competition policy is the province of the *Bundeskartellamt* (Federal Cartel Office). Antitrust administration, however, is pretty much a paper tiger—or at least it has been until quite recently. The Kartellamt can be overruled by the minister of economics on any ruling.

Finally, no one could describe the formal institutions for economic policy in the Federal Republic without reference to the state governments. These governments have the power to collect taxes (but not to set rates), to distribute state revenues (a certain percentage of which come from federal income taxes) according to the mandate of state assemblies, and to use state banks (Landesbanken) for development and aid purposes. The result is that the state governments have considerable power and that economic policy in the Federal Republic is truly federal, yet the state governments remain subordinate to the federal government in many important areas.

The Evolution of Economic and Industrial Policy in Germany

German economic policy is strongly market oriented. The main goals pursued are increased growth, price stability, low unemployment, and external equilibrium.[4] When a trade-off has had to be made in macroeconomic policies between price stability and increased growth, the general response of the German government has been to favor price stability.[5] The evolution of German industrial policy has been affected by macroeconomic cycles. The period between 1950 and 1967 was one of relatively high average growth with swings between fast growth and recessions. Recovery from World War II and membership in the European Economic Community accounted for a large proportion of the growth in this period. Besides price stability, macroeconomic policies stressed promotion of exports through a somewhat undervalued exchange rate for the mark.[6]

During the 1950–1967 period, the ruling parties, the Christian Democratic Union/Christian Social Union (CDU/CSU) and the Free Democratic Party (FDP), favored a market-oriented and generally noninterventionist approach to economic policy; and even the Social Democratic Party (SPD) moved in this direction after the Bad Godesburg Program of 1959. The economic policies of the CDU were consistent with the widely accepted notion of a social market economy or *Soziale Marktwirtschaft*. This concept, originally coined by Professor Mueller-Armack and adopted by the Freiburg School of economists who influenced Ludwig Erhard (economics minister between 1949 and 1963 and then chancellor from 1963 to 1966), embraced four basic principles: (1) a focus should be on the general desirability of competition in the economy, and central planning should be avoided; (2) the most important role of the state in the economy was to promote competition and avoid monopolies; (3) anticyclical policies should be adopted by the government, but the manipulation of the money supply was more desirable than Keynesian demand management because of the possible inflationary effects of the latter; and (4) a competitive market economy and a libertarian political system went hand in hand, and both needed to be maintained.[7]

The major opposition party, the SPD, differed in some major respects with the program above. After 1959, however, on economic planning in the face of real competition, they were in basic agreement. The Bad Godesburg Program of 1959, for example, states the following: "Free competition and free initiative of entrepreneurs are important elements of Social Democratic economic policy. . . . The Social Democratic Party is in favor of the free market whenever real competition exists."[8] The paragraph continues, however, to invoke planning as a necessary response to domination of markets by individuals or groups to "preserve the freedom of the economy." The SPD opposed cartels during the Adenauer administration when the CDU favored them. The SPD stressed consumer and worker interests in competition and free trade during this period.[9]

The recession of 1966–1967 was a major turning point in many respects because it was the beginning of the end of CDU control of the federal government. The German Bundesbank, angered by an increase in public spending preceding the 1965 elections, implemented highly restrictive monetary policies in August 1964 and maintained them for eighteen months. The resulting recession was quite marked. The gross domestic product decreased by 15 percent, and the number of unemployed increased by 140,000. In all of Europe, only Germany experienced such a deep recession at this time. The Bundestag responded with the Stability and Growth Act of 1967, which mandated countercyclical policies on the part of federal authorities to avoid future shocks of this sort.[10] The German political system, and especially the SPD, began to perceive a need to increase governmental intervention to reduce the effects of business cycles.

In 1967 the grand coalition (combining the CDU and the SPD) government initiated an informal process called *konzertierte Aktion* (concerted action), which brought together representatives of the government, the Bundesbank, the major employer groups, and the trade unions to establish a greater degree of consensus on economic policies (and especially on wage policies).

Through this mechanism the SPD/FDP coalition government intervened actively after 1969 in national wage negotiations to avoid strikes. At the end of the 1960s a short burst of wildcat strikes and an increase in labor militancy had occurred. *Konzertierte Aktion* ended in 1977 when the unions withdrew in opposition to the contesting in the Constitutional Court by the German Employers' Association of the 1977 Codetermination Act. They decided also at this time to pursue more actively the goal of *Mitbestimmung* or codetermination (in the form of effective worker representation on supervisory boards of corporations) and humanization of working life.[11] In 1978 the *Industrie Gewerkschaft Metall* (henceforth IG Metall, the main union of the auto and metal workers) first called for a thirty-five-hour work week to maintain levels of employment during a period of rapid increases in productivity.[12] IG Metall was concerned that jobs lost in traditional manufacturing industries because of technological rationalization of production would not be replaced elsewhere. It was also concerned that the rationalization of production might produce extremely unpleasant working environments. Thus both the thirty-five-hour week and the humanization of the workplace goals stemmed from fears about the effects of the introduction of new production technologies.

The 1966–1973 period was one of intense debate within the SPD on planning and *Strukturpolitik* (structural policy). Although the SPD/FDP coalition's economics minister, Karl Schiller, added the concept of global steering —a German version of Keynesian demand management—to the policy lexicon after the 1966–1967 recovery, some members of the SPD pushed for more ambitious planning and sectoral industrial policies.[13] These were mainly the young socialists and SPD technocrats, a not very powerful wing of the party. Nevertheless, one of the results of their efforts was the establishment in 1972 of the Ministry of Research and Technology (BMFT).[14] The BMFT became, through its ability to allocate credit to specific firms, the main institutional focus of sectoral industrial policy in Germany.

The OPEC price increases of 1973 put a temporary end to the experiment with Keynesian policies as the Bundesbank, with the concurrence of Economics Minister Helmut Schmidt, again used restrictive monetary policies to reduce inflation through induced economic recession. When Schmidt became chancellor in 1974, a reflationary package was introduced against the advice of the Sachsverständigenrat.[15]

At this point, the domestic debate over the economy changed its focus. Whereas previously the main debate had been between the advocates of intervention and those of nonintervention, now the debate was between those who wished to stick with macroeconomic policy interventions and those who preferred additional sectoral or mesoeconomic interventions. The oil price increases created a major problem of adjustment for German industries. The higher price of energy had an immediate and negative effect on those industries that were highly dependent on energy as an input: that is, most of the heavy manufacturing and durable goods industries in Germany. There was an immediate call for government aid for the promotion of alternative energy production and energy-conserving technology. In 1974, even the bastion of neoclassical economics and the most prestigious of the five main economic think tanks in Germany, the Kiel Institute for the World Economy, began to point out that German economic problems were not merely cyclical but structural in nature. Problems in textiles, shoes, and clothing industries would spread to other parts of the economy. Some economists at Kiel began to advocate sector-specific policies not inconsistent with the mandate of the BMFT. "Sectoral policy seemed to go along with the emphasis on selective competitiveness, increased research and development, and a new international division of labor articulated by the Kiel School."[16]

The economists at Kiel were not alone, however. In 1976 the chancellor's office received a report from the Swiss consulting firm PROGNOS on the structural sources of unemployment in Germany.[17] This report, together with the arguments of the Kiel economists, helped to create an impetus for more sector-specific industrial policies.

The main opposition to sector-specific policies came from the FDP leadership, in particular Count Otto von Lambsdorff, the minister of economic affairs. The FDP preferred macroeconomic measures, such as tax reductions, to mesoeconomic ones. The SPD view prevailed on the question of research on structural trends. In 1977, the government decided to approve such research, and in 1978 the five economic think tanks (IFW in Kiel, DIW in Berlin, HWWA in Hamburg, RWI in Frankfurt, and IFO in Munich) were asked to prepare annual structural reports.[18]

Also, in the summer of 1978, the government decided to inject the sum of DM13 billion into the economy to stimulate growth. The BMFT came up with an ambitious proposal for directing DM12 billion for research and development in five specific sectors: (1) ecology and environmental improvement, (2) humanization of the work place, (3) alternative energy technology, (4) water treatment, and (5) general promotion of innovation. Again the FDP opposed the sector-specific measures, whittling back considerably the increase to BMFT funding.[19] In 1978–1979, the government enacted a large tax reduction for business amounting to around DM8 billion in 1978 and DM10 billion in 1979.[20]

In other words, the FDP views on how to stimulate the economy prevailed over those in the SPD who preferred a structural approach. The effect of tax reductions was dramatic: an increase of 14 percent in investments in plant and equipment.[21] The economic recovery spurred by this investment was interrupted, however, by the second OPEC oil price increases in 1979.

After the 1979 OPEC price increases, the Schmidt government returned to the traditional deflationary policies advocated by the Bundesbank and the Ministry of Finance. The resulting recession was prolonged by the restrictive monetary policies adopted by the Reagan administration in 1981. Even before the recession of 1980–1982 several German industries began to suffer difficulties that forced them to approach the government for assistance. Previously the German government dealt with bankruptcies and plant closures in a hands-off manner. Rescues of firms in trouble were generally handled either by the major investment banks or the regional governments (sometimes both acting together).[22]

Increasingly after 1975, the federal government itself began to intervene in industry crises. The first major case was the steel industry in the Saar valley in the middle and late 1970s. The next two examples are the rescues of AEG in 1979 and 1982. For the purposes of comparison, the case of the rescue of Volkswagen will also be discussed below. The general argument to be made here, however, is that the German government became more involved in resolving industry crises in the late 1970s and early 1980s for the following reasons: it had adopted new policy instruments that made such intervention possible; the German banks became vulnerable to the increasing number of firm failures;[23] and the number and importance of firm failures increased because of heavier international competition and bad firm strategies. Thus intervention became both necessary and possible for the federal government to a greater extent than it had been in the past twenty years (see tables 1, 2, and 3).

The increased involvement of the German federal government in rescues and the general increase in expenditures for entitlements led directly to a

TABLE 1

TOTAL WEST GERMAN FEDERAL AND REGIONAL GOVERNMENT AID,
SELECTED CATEGORIES, 1974 AND 1983
(billions of 1985 DMs)

	1974	1983
Industrial	7.2	9.4
Coal	2.9	1.3
Manufacturing	4.3	8.1
Other	48.1	15.1
Housing	—	7.4
Regional	—	4.6
Stock purchasing	—	3.1
Total	55.3	24.5

SOURCES: Juergen B. Donges, "Industrial Policies in West Germany's Not So Market-Oriented Economy," *The World Economy*, vol. 3 (September 1980), p. 196; "Down to Earth: A Survey of the West German Economy," *The Economist* (February 4, 1984), p. 11.

TABLE 2

Subsidies to the West German Industrial Sector, Federal and Regional Governments, 1966–1978
(millions of 1985 DMs)

Year	Grants and Loans	Tax Allowances	Total
1966	692	2608	3300
1967	1107	3799	4906
1968	1230	3826	5056
1969	867	4800	5667
1970	1077	5449	6526
1971	1024	6686	7710
1972	1149	7670	8819
1973	1605	7926	9531
1974	2054	8513	10567
1975	1935	7613	9548
1976	1796	7975	9771
1977	2272	7784	10056
1978	2588	8044	10632

Source: National Economic Development Office, *The West German Economy* (London: September 1981), p. 88. Original source is the Seventh Subsidy Report of the West German federal government.

TABLE 3

West German Federal and Regional Government Subsidies to Specific Industrial Sectors, as Percent of Value Added, 1974 and 1980

Industry	1974	1980
Railways	72.9	82.5
Agriculture, forestry, and fishing	40.7	31.7
Coal mining	17.8	17.2
Office machinery and computers	6.9	4.5
Telecommunications	2.3	2.0
Motor vehicles	0.8	0.6
Iron and steel	0.6	0.4

Source: Andrew Black, *Industrial Policy in W. Germany: Policy in Search of a Goal?* (Discussion Paper in Industrial Policy), (Berlin: International Institute for Management, June 1984), p. 21.

conflict within the SPD/FDP coalition between Chancellor Helmut Schmidt and Minister of Economics Count Otto von Lambsdorff. The immediate cause of the breakup of the coalition in 1982 was an open letter from von Lambsdorff to Schmidt concerning his disagreement with Schmidt about the continued growth of subsidies and entitlements expenditures. Von Lambsdorff and Schmidt also had open conflicts over the role of the minister of research and technology (especially his use of public funds to support Siemens).[24] Thus the internal debate over the direction of economic and industrial policies was a key factor in the fall of the SPD/FDP coalition and the election of a new CDU/FDP coalition government in 1982.

To summarize, German economic policy evolved over the past thirty years from the relatively noninterventionist policies implicit in the concept of *Soziale Marktwirtschaft* to much more ambitious forms of intervention. The first point of transition was 1966, when the German system moved decisively toward a Keynesian demand management and anticyclical policy (interrupted in 1973 and 1979 by periods of monetaristic orthodoxy). Major parts of the German government remain committed to this approach. Another turning point occurred in 1973 when the OPEC oil price increases provoked a serious turn toward structural policies and, in particular, the use of state-controlled investment funds to promote specific new technologies. That year was also a period of increased institutional openness to reducing the costs of adjustment to firms and workers during a period of rapid change in relative prices and in technologies. From 1973 to 1979, the German government came close to adopting what we might call a supply-side economic policy, especially toward the end of that period when it used tax reductions for businesses to spur investment. The failures of these policies led in 1982 to the crisis that broke up the SPD/FDP coalition and replaced it with the more conservative CDU/FDP government. Not enough time has passed since 1982 to make firm judgments about the differences between the CDU/FDP government and its predecessors. Yet, as I will try to demonstrate below, there seems to be more continuity than discontinuity in its overall economic and industrial policies.

Policies for the Steel Industry

In 1945 the occupation authorities confiscated two major German enterprises: IG Farben (a huge chemical combine) and the Krupp steel complex. The British military trusteeship controlled the iron and steel production of occupied Germany. The Allies planned to dismantle the Nazi-created Salzgitter iron and steel works, but they abandoned these plans when the workers protested. Labor unions were suppressed until 1947, when German workers were permitted to organize at the zonal level. France, like Russia, wanted to limit permanently the ability of Germany to resume its previous world leadership position in steel production. This aim was expressed in French proposals for the internationalization of steel production in the Ruhr Valley. The French position on this matter helped to create political support later for the creation of the European Coal and Steel Community.

The United States, in contrast, was initially concerned primarily in breaking up the large combines in steel (and other industries), to deconcentrate control over production in a sort of internationalization of U.S. antitrust laws. The United States succeeded in codifying this goal in the Potsdam Agreement, which called for the breaking up of trusts and cartels in postwar Germany. The Vereinigte Stahlwerke, created during the Weimar years and second only to Krupp in importance in the Nazi steel industry, was broken up into thirteen smaller firms. But the United States relaxed its position on the reconcentration of German industry in 1947–1948 as the Cold War got underway. "It was one of the basic ideas underlying the Marshall Plan that an enhanced economic recovery of Western Europe crucially depended on the economic development of Germany."[25] So even the less ambitious policy of deconcentration lost its initial appeal to the occupation forces.[26]

How the Germans stood on these issues was clear from the beginning. They believed that deconcentration of the steel industry would prevent it from resuming its prewar eminence. Thus the immediate response to the occupation efforts at decartelization was the formation of the *Walzstahlkontore* (steel consortia), which coordinated production of the small firms created by the breakup of the larger combines so that they could continue to take advantage of scale economies.[27] The *Kontore* were partly the creation of the German banks. The occupation authorities realized that the deconcentration of control over steel production required the deconcentration of banking as well. The smaller banks formed after 1945 quickly began to merge into larger financial institutions, however. Of particular importance for the steel industry was the emergence of the Deutsche Bank, which had its directors on the supervisory boards of almost all of the major steel firms.[28]

In 1962–1963, after a period of rapid growth, a crisis developed owing to an overcapacity of production of several million tons. The lead banks for the steel industry (especially the Deutsche Bank) persuaded Mannesmann to stop the planned increase in production of sheet steel in exchange for an eight-year contract with Thyssen for the supply of slabs for Thyssen's new sheet steel production.[29] Thus the German banks reverted quite early to their traditional role in structuring the nature of competition and specialization within the steel industry.

The next major crisis occurred in 1967, at the same time as the general economic recession. The Krupp steel works had been allowed to resume operations during the early days of the Cold War. In 1967 the president of the Deutsche Bank, Herman Abs, took over the management of the firm. The president of Thyssen, Dr. Sohl, made a statement at this time which helps to explain the position of the industry: "We don't want state intervention that submits our industry to external influences. . . . We hope that the time when prices and incomes in our sector were considered political factors belongs to the past."[30] Thus the firms preferred bank intervention to state intervention as a way of limiting the politicization of the industry. The banks had strong financial incentives to intervene. The state had an ideological stake in avoiding overt intervention. Thus the major actors at this point agreed on a policy of bank-led restructuring.

Also in 1967 the *Walzstahlkontore* were replaced with the *Rationalisierungsgruppen* (rationalization groups). The Northern rationalization group, for example, consisted of Kloeckner, Peine-Salzgitter, and Maximilianshütte. Kloeckner had invested in a major way in engineering and technology. It owned 26 percent of Korf Engineering, which owned a method of direct reduction. Using the crude steel products supplied by Peine-Saltzgitter and Maximilianshütte, Kloeckner tried to carve out a niche for itself in the markets for specialty steels. In 1977 Kloeckner purchased a controlling share of Maximilianshütte. Thus, even though Kloeckner eventually ran into financial difficulties in the 1980s, one can argue that the existence of the rationalization groups contributed to the reconcentration of control over steel production.[31] In 1960, for example, the two top German firms controlled only 23 percent of production; by 1984 they controlled 52 percent.[32]

In the early 1970s, a Dutch holding company called Estel, jointly owned by Hoesch Werke AG (a German steel firm that was not doing very well) and Hoogovens BV (the largest Dutch concern), was established. Hoogovens gained access to the German market in this way in exchange for new investments made in Germany through Estel. This was the first major attempt by the German industry to deal with problems of specific firms by internationalizing control.[33]

The next major crisis occurred in 1977. The Deutsche Bank again took a leading role in a second restructuring of Krupp. This time three other banks along with the federal minister of economics were involved in the bargaining. One result was the so-called Krupp discount—a lower interest rate paid by the firm to its major lenders, which amounted to no less than a private subsidy.[34] The small steel firms of the Saar Valley were also particularly hard hit. Between 1974 and 1977, employment fell by 6,000 workers. In 1977 two firms—Roechling Burbach and Neunkircher Eisenwerke—threatened layoffs or bankruptcy. This threat began a round of negotiations involving the firms, the state and federal governments, the unions (especially IG Metall), and eventually the Luxemburg-based enterprise, Arbed.

The restructuring plan that emerged in 1978 was quite complex. Arbed agreed to take control of the Saar Valley firms in exchange for a one-time infusion of DM1 billion in aid from the federal government. The IG Metall agreed to this control even though it meant a drastic reduction in jobs in the industry (9,000 over five years to be precise) because the union received guarantees of jobs for certain workers and social aid for those who would be displaced. Adjustment assistance also was to come from the European Community under article 56 of the Treaty of Rome, and arrangements would be made to allow older workers to retire early without losing their pension benefits. Production capacity declined by 20 percent as a result of the closing down of the least efficient units.

This restructuring plan was a hard pill to swallow, but it seems to have had some of the desired effects. Unemployment in the region decreased from 7.6 percent in 1977 to 6.6 percent in 1980.[35] Nevertheless, by November 1982, Arbed was in financial trouble. Chancellor Kohl was faced soon after his election with the possibility of bankruptcy of the firm. A special bridging loan of DM2.2 billion was arranged with some brokering on the part of the federal government to avoid the loss of 30,000 jobs in the Saar. By 1982 the unemployment level in the region had soared to 12 percent.[36]

The 1977–1978 steel crisis also affected the Estel group and therefore the Ruhr Valley firm Hoesch. During the crisis the German government decided not to give loans to nonnational companies (companies less than 100 percent German owned), so Estel was left out of the picture. In addition, the success of the Estel venture depended on further movement toward implementing the Werner Plan, which had stabilized exchange rates between the German mark and the Dutch guilder, but no such further movement was forthcoming. Thus by 1982 the Estel venture was dead. Hoesch was incorporated into a new grouping of Ruhr Valley firms.

Bargaining over rationalization of the Ruhr was also complex, and had not yet resulted in a stable solution by the end of 1984. The first step was taken by Krupp and Hoesch in 1981 in negotiations to form a firm called Ruhrstahl. This idea was supported by the IG Metall union and by state and federal economics ministers. By June 1982 Ruhrstahl approached the federal government with requests for assistance of DM14 billion. In January 1983 three mediators were appointed by the federal government to recommend a course of action for the Ruhr Valley. They suggested that the five Ruhr firms should merge into two groups: a Rhine group composed of Thyssen and Krupp and a Ruhr group composed of Hoesch, Kloeckner, and Salzgitter. Aid from the federal and state governments would be given, but only DM3 billion would be needed. This solution was opposed by IG Metall and the North-Rhine Westphalian government.

By March 1983 Kloeckner was nearly bankrupt.[37] Thyssen had refused to merge with Krupp because of the demands of Gerhard Stoltenberg, the finance minister, that Thyssen pay cash to cover differences in valuation between the two firms. The lead banks were very unhappy with the decisions of Thyssen's chairman, Dieter Spethmann, because Thyssen would be ineligible for state subsidies as a result of the collapse of the merger deal. Thyssen lost $173.7 million from September 1983 to September 1984, the majority of which was accounted for by losses at its American subsidiary, the Budd Company, purchased in 1978.[38]

The steel industry of Germany, like that of all other major industrial countries, went through a period of great difficulty in the late 1970s and early 1980s. Attempts at internationalization in the Saar were only partially successful. The same could be said about attempts to rationalize by the formation of regional groups in the Ruhr. The problems of the Ruhr, of course, were much more important quantitatively than those of the Saar, since the Ruhr was where the largest and most modern steel-making facilities were located. The German federal government was increasingly involved in negotiations for the restructuring of the industry. Neither the banks nor the state governments were capable of handling it alone. Nevertheless, the German government avoided either nationalizations or restrictive trade measures in its efforts to assist the industry. It relied primarily on its ability to sanction mergers and to provide grants, loans, and loan guarantees.

Policies for the Auto Industry

The German auto industry, as in many other countries, is an oligopolistic industry dominated by a small number of firms: Volkswagen, Ford, BMW, Opel (the German subsidiary of General Motors), Daimler Benz, and Porsche. BMW, Daimler Benz, and Porsche produce high-priced autos only, while Volkswagen, Ford, and Opel produce autos at the lower prices. Because German drivers drive fast and tend to calculate lifetime costs of owning an automobile, they seem to be somewhat less inclined than consumers in other countries to buy the less-expensive but less-well-built Japanese exports. Nevertheless, Japanese imports currently account for about 10 percent of the domestic market (see table 4).

The auto industry is an important source of export revenues for Germany. Roughly half of its export revenues in the early 1980s were accounted for by exports of motor vehicles. Net exports of motor vehicles produced a trade surplus of DM58 billion in 1982. The importance of motor vehicle industry in creating employment and export revenues combined with the relative strong international competitiveness of German firms has reinforced the general tendency of the German federal government to defend free trade at home and abroad. While one expects to see free trade policies meshing with noninterventionist domestic economic policies, in Germany the state has been deeply involved in the evolution of the industry. The best example of this involvement is the state's relations with Volkswagen, the largest German firm.

The Case of Volkswagen. The role of the German government in the auto industry is shaped to some degree by the origins and importance of Volkswagen in the German industry. Volkswagen was started in 1939 under the

173

TABLE 4

SHARES OF FIRMS IN THE WEST GERMAN DOMESTIC AUTO MARKET, 1980
(percent)

Firm	Market Share
Volkswagen	30.3
Opel	16.9
Ford	10.4
Daimler	10.2
BMW	5.7
Renault	4.7
Fiat	3.6
Toyota	2.4
Nissan	2.1
Mazda	1.9
Honda	1.8
Other	10.0

SOURCE: European Research Associates, *EEC Protectionism:* Present Practice and Future Trends (Brussels: 1982), p. 144.

tutelage of the Nazi government. After negotiations with Ford and General Motors failed to produce an agreement satisfactory to the National Socialist government, it "asked" several German firms, including Porsche and Daimler, to help the state form a new firm to produce a "people's car." The German government wanted to demonstrate that Germany could produce mass consumption items like automobiles that could compete eventually on a world scale. In the meantime, they were prepared to subsidize the development of this capability through direct state aid and investment and through the establishment of a system of forced savings under which families would periodically set aside small sums to qualify for a vehicle at a later date. The workforce of the Volkswagen plant at Wolfsburg (near the current border with East Germany) was mostly German, but already in 1939 Italian workers were imported through an agreement between Hitler and Mussolini.

After World War II, Volkswagen was allowed to continue production. In 1960, 60 percent of the shares of Volkswagen were offered to the public. The federal government retained a 20 percent share of the stock as did the state government of Lower Saxony (Volkswagen is still 40 percent government owned). The state intervened occasionally during times of crisis but otherwise left the firm mostly to its own devices. In this respect, the German government does not differ much from the governments of the other major industrial countries.

Volkswagen made its success with a single model, the Beetle. In the

1960s Germany made major inroads into foreign markets with that model, and prospects for Volkswagen looked very rosy. The Japanese auto producers were already gaining, however. Volkswagen became vulnerable eventually because of its slowness to develop new models. Although the firm tried to deal with this problem by purchasing Audi from Daimler Benz in 1965 and NSU in 1969, the firm still remained highly dependent on the Beetle. The resistance to such mergers by minority stockholders of acquired firms produced fairly intense political resistance to further acquisitions and resulted in the dismissal of Kurt Lotz as head of Volkswagen in 1971. Rudolf Leiding, who replaced Lotz, tried to introduce some new models. By 1974, however, the firm was in severe financial trouble as a result of increased competition in foreign markets and difficulties in making the transition from single-model to multimodel production. In addition, the floating of the mark after 1972 reduced the trade advantages of an overvalued currency for all German exports, especially automobiles.

During the period of transition, Leiding had called for wage restraints from the auto workers. This appeal made him extremely unpopular with the IG Metall, which had five of the seats on the supervisory board (*Aufsichtsrat*) as a result of the campaign in the late 1960s for codetermination. The displeasure of the workers was expressed also through the SPD coalition government. Leiding himself stated that maybe he had "underestimated the influence of the Federal and Lower Saxony SPD governments who are part-owners of VW." In 1974 Leiding was replaced by Toni Schmuecker, a man who had been in charge of the reorganization of the Rheinstahl firm in the early 1970s and was trusted by the SPD and the unions.[39]

In 1974 Volkswagen sales fell by 11 percent. The firm was heavily dependent on exports. In 1973, 70 percent of production was exported; by 1975 this figure fell to 56 percent. A decline in demand in the United States provoked by the 1974 recession and increased competition from Japan created severe difficulties for Volkswagen exports to the United States, its most important foreign market. Volkswagen had begun to set up plants for overseas production in Belgium, Brazil, Yugoslavia, Mexico, Nigeria, and South Africa. The capital outlays required for these ventures were substantial, and the return was not always good. Although growth was buoyant in oil-producing countries like Mexico and Nigeria, it was sluggish elsewhere.

The government of Lower Saxony and the representative of the IG Metall cochaired the supervisory board of Volkswagen in 1974. The firm secured an agreement with IG Metall to a reduction in the work force of 40,000 workers (roughly one-fourth of the total) in exchange for a system of layoffs distributed across different plants and a general avoidance of plant closures. Some of these workers were Turks, who had to leave Germany after being laid off. Italian workers could not be expelled from Germany under the Treaty of Rome, so they were offered general severance payments. The government of

Lower Saxony and the federal government agreed to implement a special program for regional assistance to provide for dismissed German workers. Finally, older workers were encouraged to make extensive use of early retirement provisions to reduce the size of the workforce. By 1976 Volkswagen was back in the black.[40]

Since 1974 Volkswagen has successfully introduced a number of new models including the Rabbit (or Golf as it is called in Europe). It has made major investments in production facilities in the United States (not yet earning much money)[41] and has begun a joint venture with Nissan to produce a new model called the Santana. This model would be sold in Japan and Southeast Asia, and Volkswagen expects to benefit greatly from increased access to Asian markets, Nissan's marketing expertise, and advanced automotive components produced in that region. Volkswagen had a 50 percent market share of the auto market in Brazil in the late 1970s, which has declined in recent years to around 40 percent. Brazil, however, has become an increasingly important supplier of components for Volkswagen's assembly operations in other countries. In 1983 Volkswagen signed an accord with the Spanish national firm SEAT to produce several models in Spain.[42] Thus Volkswagen has made major steps toward internationalization to supplement its strategy of diversifying its model lines.

The Auto Industry in General. German governmental policies toward Volkswagen demonstrate the general preference of the federal government for letting the state governments and the major banks preside over most restructuring exercises; but when that policy fails, as in 1974, the federal government steps in smartly. The German autoworkers union, IG Metall, is unusually deeply involved in policy making for the firm, both through its representation on the supervisory board (a result of the campaign for *Mitbestimmung*) but also through its influence along with the allied SPD in the Lower Saxony and federal governments. This overall pattern seems to have worked reasonably well in the case of Volkswagen and perhaps for the German auto industry more generally.

BMW had serious financial problems in the late 1950s but was restructured by the Bavarian state bank (which is controlled by the CSU) along with its major private lenders: another example of the general preference of the federal government for allowing the state govenments and the banks to do the restructuring.[43]

Even foreign subsidiaries seem destined to go along with the general pattern. That is, all auto firms operating in Germany are relatively free of effective federal government intervention in normal times, while remaining subject to the actions of banks, unions, and local governments. The Ford Motor Company, for example, did not want to allow the IG Metall to represent its workers or to join the main association of German auto firms, the *Verband der Deutsche Automobilindustrie* (VDA), when it began to increase production in Germany in the 1960s. IG Metall, however, organized the main Ford plant in 1962, thus forcing the company to join the German auto employers' association or forgo the advantages of bargaining at the national rather than the plant level for wage contracts.

Ford also planned to build a green field plant in Dortmund in the late 1960s to be near its major steel suppliers. The steel firms controlled the land in the area, however, and refused to sell to Ford because they feared that Ford would bid up wages in the region.

Not only does the German government avoid involvement in restructuring unless all else fails; it tends in assisting the industry more generally to avoid targeting and industry-specific measures in favor of more diffuse promotional activities. An example of this preference is the CAR 2000 program administered by the federal Ministry of Research and Technology. The purpose of this program is to subsidize the development of exotic technologies relevant to the automotive industry by the federal funding of projects proposed by the firms themselves for models not under current development. The German government is comfortable with this sort of fuzzy policy, uncomfortable with French or Japanese style of administrative guidance.

Policies for Microelectronics

Although the German auto industry has been overall a pillar of strength, and therefore relatively autonomous from state intervention except during temporary crises, the same cannot be said for the German microelectronics industry. Germany is Europe's biggest market for semiconductors (32 percent in 1980; 29 percent in 1983); yet only Siemens to date has managed to compete with the other major suppliers in Europe, where it still is fourth after Philips, Texas Instruments, and Motorola. In addition, Siemens was unable to foresee developments in demand to produce the right types of circuits. A Siemens executive has "ruefully" described the past decade of chip making as "10 years of dismal failure."[44] Much of its recent marketing success is due to second sourcing of Intel chips.[45]

Other signs of general weakness in markets related to the microelectronics field exist. Siemens, for example, was marketing Fujitsu mainframe computers because it had been unable to develop competitive systems on its own. IBM dominated the German market for mainframes, and the Japanese were their main challengers in that market.

IBM defeated both Siemens and AEG (the other large German firm in the electronics field) in November 1981 for a $22.5 million contract to build a videotext system for the Bundespost (post office). Although IBM had some problems with this contract, experiencing several delays and cost overruns, for the Bundespost to award such a contract to a foreign bidder was unusual.

177

The biggest crisis in microelectronics so far did not involve Siemens, however, but its nearest German competitor, AEG-Telefunken. The story of the near collapse and rescue of AEG is an important addition to the overall picture of state-societal links in Germany. It illustrates again the general tendency of the state to avoid involvement in rescues unless absolutely needed and the relatively important role played by the private banks in the system.

The Case of AEG-Telefunken. AEG is a firm with deep roots in German industrial history. An early innovator in radio and electronics, it was always the main rival of Siemens in Germany. By the 1970s, AEG had become a highly diversified holding company with equity participation in nuclear engineering, consumer electronics, and various other businesses. In 1983 it was Europe's fourth largest electronics concern and the world's twelfth largest electronics firm.[46] It employed 120,000 workers, more than 100,000 in Germany. AEG played a crucial role in establishing Germany as a major industrial nation. Thus its fall from grace in the late 1970s and early 1980s was rather a shock to most Germans. Part of the problem can be traced to the mid-1970s when AEG and Siemens, who were partners in the nuclear engineering concern, Kraftwerk Union, had to take major losses in the restructuring of that firm. For AEG, the cost was between DM1 billion and DM1.5 billion.[47] The main problem, however, was that AEG had failed to see that its consumer electronics business could not compete with foreign firms. It delayed too long in diversifying out of consumer electronics and shoring up its other businesses. It also had serious weaknesses in microelectronics (see table 5).

AEG paid no dividends after 1973. Losses in 1979 amounted to around DM1 billion. On October 24, 1979, the chief executive officer, Walter Cipa, informed the Aufsichtsrat of the firm that big problems existed and that major layoffs of employees were likely. The next day, the IG Metall representatives of the organized workers at AEG issued a press release reporting the large anticipated layoffs and opposing them. Representatives of major shareholders accused IG Metall representatives on the Aufsichtsrat of leaking confidential internal information, and the union representatives defended themselves by arguing that the management's first recourse was always to lay off people rather than to do something more creative to maintain levels of employment.

On November 8, 1979, four AEG representatives met with the minister of economics, Count von Lambsdorff, and the minister of finance, Hans Matthoefer, to convince them to involve the federal government in resolving the problems of AEG. Their efforts were to no avail. On December 4, 1979, a rescue plan put together by the major banks under the leadership of the Dresdner and Deutsche Banks was announced. This plan included a major write down of the nominal value of AEG shares, a restructuring of its debt, the layoff of 12,000 employees, the closure of a gas turbine plant, and a "solidar-

TABLE 5

AEG PROFITS AND LOSSES, 1970–1979
(millions of DMs)

Year	Profits/Lossses
1970	105
1971	79
1972	45
1973	94
1974	− 664
1975	− 77
1976	397
1977	8
1978	− 347
1979	− 968

SOURCE: Doug Anderson, *AEG-Telefunken, A.G.* (Cambridge: Harvard Business School, 1981), p. 20.

ity contribution" of German manufacturing firms (an agreement to purchase DM 200 million–450 million of unsecured debentures at less than the market rate of interest).[48]

The banks were anxious to avoid federal government intervention, and so were many firms. At the time a German businessman made the following observation:

Small firms get into trouble all the time and go under. But a business of this size can't be allowed to fail. The State won't let it. We saw that the United States did not abandon Chrysler and Canada won't abandon Massey-Ferguson either. We were therefore of the opinion that in Germany, as well, the State would not allow a company like AEG to go bankrupt. We concluded that if we wanted to preserve our economic system we had to make an attempt to save the company without leaving that task to government.[49]

Concern that the failure of AEG would reduce competition in the German market still further was also expressed. But the problem of not encouraging other large firms to expect bailouts was also clearly recognized and handled by the not terribly generous terms of the rescue.

In 1980 Hans Friderichs of the Dresdner Bank was elected chair of the *Vorstand* (board of directors) and brought in a new manager for the firm, Heinz Duerr, who had previously run Bosch, a producer of automobile components and electronic products. AEG, along with Bosch and Mannesmann, made some new investments in telecommunications, and the situation began to look a little brighter for the firm. In the summer of 1982, however, AEG rejected an offer from GEC (a British heavy electrical equipment firm) for 40 percent of AEG's capital goods business, and the value of AEG stock fell precipitously.

By July 1982 the firm was once more on the edge of bankruptcy. A new rescue was devised, this time with direct involvement of the federal government. The government came up with DM1.1 billion in credit guarantees and 85 percent of a package of DM0.6 billion export credits. The banks agreed, as a result of government guarantees, to grant DM1.1 billion in new credit to the firm. The firm itself filed for "composition" (*Vergleich*), which is roughly equivalent to reorganization on chapter 11 of the bankruptcy laws in the United States. Composition is possible in Germany only if write-offs of debt are less than 65 percent of existing debt and 75 percent of all creditors agree to the package. A writer for *The Economist* made the following observation about this rescue:

> West Germany's way of financing industry puts most of the burden of rescues onto the banks for two reasons. The universal banking system makes banks more deeply committed to industry than elsewhere. And the government's *laissez faire* approach to industrial finance leaves banks to pick up the tab when things go wrong.[50]

The final episode to this sad story is the sale of AEG's consumer electronics subsidiary, AEG-Telefunken, to the French firm, Thomson-Brandt, in March 1983. This sale came about largely as a result of the blocking of the sale to Thomson of a somewhat larger German consumer electronics firm, Grundig, by the German Cartel Office. While the official story was that the purchase of Grundig would reduce the level of competition in consumer electronics to an unacceptably low level, the fact that Philips owned 24.5 percent of Grundig and that Grundig was a major purchaser of semiconductors produced by Siemens had a lot to do with the opposition of the federal government to the Thomson-Grundig deal.

In spite all of this trouble, AEG is not dead as a semiconductor producer. In 1982 the components production wing of AEG, Telefunken Elektronik Gesellschaft (TEG), formed a joint venture called Eurosil with the United Technologies Corporation and the Diehl Group and took an 85 percent share. This joint firm owned a new plant for the production of advanced semiconductor devices. TEG is a major supplier for Volkswagen and BMW and United Technologies' subsidiary Mostek is an important supplier of CMOS and NMOS circuits in Europe, while Eurosil supplies components to the watch and telecommunications firms of Europe. Therefore AEG may be able to recover some of its lost glory in league with its new partners.

The Belated Promotional Policies of the Federal Government. The German

TABLE 6

SHARES OF FIRMS IN WEST GERMAN SEMICONDUCTOR MARKET,
1986, 1972, AND 1978
(percent)

Firm	1968	1972	1978
Siemens	22	26	21
Valvo (Philips)	25	18	15
Texas Instruments	16	12	13
AEG Telefunken	9	12	9
SEL (ITT)	10	8	7
Motorola	6	7	6
SGS-Ages	6	3	3
Other	6	14	26

SOURCE: Giovanni Dosi, *Technical Change and Industrial Transformation* (London: Macmillan, 1984), p. 159.

electronics industry is not just Siemens and AEG. One must also include Valvo (Philips), Bosch, SEL (ITT), Nixdorf, IBM-Germany, Texas Instruments, and Motorola as important actors in Germany and Europe generally. German-owned firms are clearly in a weak position overall, however (see table 6). For this reason Uwe Thomas, director of electronics research of the German Ministry of Technology and Research said in 1982: "The main emphasis of this ministry is to see what we can do in strengthening the application of microelectronics."[51]

A large percentage of the R and D funds previously went for research on mainframe computers; insufficient attention was given to the development of advanced microelectronic devices. Accordingly, the ministry budgeted $190 million for this purpose to be spent over 1982–1985.[52] More important, the ministry spent $1.4 billion to advance German semiconductor and computer research in 1974–1979, a program that unfortunately failed to achieve the desired results. One of the problems with the ministry's approach was its overreliance on aid to the two largest firms: Siemens and AEG. Roughly $1.3 billion went to Siemens, $0.4 billion to AEG (see table 7).

Total BMFT research and development funds remained constant in relation to GNP (around 0.7 percent) between 1974 and 1981. The funds devoted to promotion of high-technology industries (see the column in table 7 dealing with Economic Services/Industrial Promotion) accounted for a nearly constant 22–24 percent of the total. Thus, despite the desire of the minister of Research and Technology to increase the emphasis on high technology in R and D spending, as of 1981 he had not been able to prevail against opposing forces, mainly in the form of the minister of economics.

TABLE 7

RESEARCH AND DEVELOPMENT SPENDING BY THE WEST GERMAN
FEDERAL MINISTRY FOR RESEARCH AND DEVELOPMENT, 1974–1981
(millions of 1975 DM)

Year	Economic Services/ Industrial Promotion	Energy	Defense	Environment	Basic	Total
1974	1699	1331	1493	155	1641	6319
1975	1679	1557	1455	192	1535	6418
1976	1542	1348	1551	191	1391	6023
1977	1418	1462	1488	179	1319	5866
1978	1511	1611	1560	201	1386	6269
1979	2023	1884	1591	261	1317	7076
1980	2033	1867	1385	251	1331	6867
1981	2044	1882	1206	224	1291	6647

SOURCE: BLACK, *Industrial Policy in W. Germany*, p. 10.

The resignation of von Lambsdorff from that ministry in 1984 might have removed one of the more effective obstacles to a shift in German research policy. The replacement of von Lambsdorff with a minister more interested in promoting small- and medium-sized firms allowed the minister of research and development to make several changes that many previous ministers had advocated.

The most recent five-year program, for 1984–1989, called for the expenditure of $1.2 billion to support research on integrated circuits, data processing, and industrial automation. The minister of technology and research, Heinz Reisenhuber, defended these efforts: "If we want to be internationally competitive and create new jobs, we absolutely must use the big potential for innovation and growth in [electronics] technology."[53]

Part of the overall strategy for promoting German microelectronics was the use of state agencies like the Bundespost and Bundesbahn to purchase more advanced technological products. The Bundespost met with firms like Siemens and AEG before establishing specifications for purchasing contracts for telecommunications equipment. IBM's ability to penetrate this system was a testimonial to its technological strength and political savvy.

On the whole, however, the German policy is one of letting the firms do whatever they can on their own to meet the international competition. In case of problems, the banks take the first step to rescue the larger firms. The government steps in only when it must and tries to limit itself to loan guarantees rather than giving direct subsidies. This approach has not been completely bankrupt. AEG is still alive, Siemens seems to be prospering, and several new and smaller firms like Nixdorf are finding market niches in which to grow and prosper. The Germans have learned the lesson of not becoming too dependent on national champions to lead them out of industrial crises; they have studiously avoided administrative guidance of the French or Japanese varieties.

Conclusion

German industrial policy is a strange mixture of decentralized control with increasingly ambitious goals. The growth of the capacity of the federal government to intervene in specific regional and industrial crises has been substantial, but the government remains firmly committed to allowing other social actors (especially the banks) to try their hand at resolving crises before it gets involved. The case of steel highlights the weaknesses of this strategy. (1) The government has eventually become much more involved than it had ever intended. (2) Because the banks have incentives to rescue ineptly managed but very large firms, government intervention tends to be costly when it occurs. (3) The older and younger workers pay a larger share of adjustment costs than the workers in the midrange. The case of automobiles shows that the combination of strong firms and avoidance of administrative guidance go hand in hand to produce desirable results, as the rapid adjustment of Volkswagen to changed world market conditions attests. The case of semiconductors shows how wrong pursuing a national champions policy can be when the national champions experience a chronic inability to catch up to the global leaders. It also shows that the German government learned this lesson well in the 1980s.

German industrial policy, therefore, is much like U.S. industrial policy (and the elephant in the classic joke about the blind men)—what you see depends on where you look. To identify German policy with any extreme on any descriptive continuum, however, would be a big mistake. Merely to say that German policy works would also be a mistake. It works for some people and some industries some of the time. It has gone through major evolutionary changes since 1945. The main lesson of German industrial policy is the need to match public policy to the market conditions and industrial capacities existing in specific industries.

Notes

1. Peter A. Hall, "Patterns of Economics Policy among the European States: An Organization Approach," in Steven Bornstein, David Held, and Joel Krieger, eds., *The State in Capitalist Europe* (London: Allen and Unwin, 1983), pp. 10–12; and Jeremiah

M. Riemer, "Alterations in the Design of Model Germany: Critical Innovations in the Policy Machinery for Economic Steering," in Andre Markovits, ed., *The Political Economy of West Germany* (New York: Praeger, 1982), p. 60.

2. Jonathan Story, "The Federal Republic—A Conservative Revisionist," *West European Politics*, vol. 4 (May 1981), p. 64; and Josef Esser and Wolfgang Fach with Kenneth Dyson, "'Social Market' and Modernization Policy: West Germany" in Kenneth Dyson and Stephen Wilks, eds., *Industrial Crisis: A Comparative Study of State and Industry* (New York: St. Martin's Press, 1983), p. 122.

3. Karl-Georg Zinn, "Politik und Sachverstandigenmeinung—Sachverstaendigenrat und Council of Economic Advisers im Vergleich," *Gewerkschaftliche Monatshefte*, vol. 29 (March 1978), p. 181; Kenneth H. F. Dyson, "The Politics of Economic Management in West Germany," *West European Politics*, vol. 4 (May 1981), p. 36; and Jeremiah M. Riemer, "Alterations in the Design of Model Germany," pp. 68–69.

4. Gerhard Wagenhals, "Industrial Policy in the Federal Republic of Germany: A Survey," in F. Gerard Adams and Lawrence R. Klein, eds., *Industrial Policies for Growth and Competitiveness* (Lexington, Mass.: D. C. Heath and Company, 1983), p. 247.

5. Michael Kreile, "West Germany: The Dynamics of Expansion," in Peter Katzenstein, ed., *Between Power and Plenty* (Madison, Wisc.: University of Wisconsin Press, 1978); and Peter Hall, "Patterns of Economic Policy among the European States."

6. Eric Owen Smith, *The West German Economy* (London: Croom Helm, 1983), p.27.

7. Ibid., pp. 19–20; and Ernst-Juergen Horn, *Management of Industrial Change in the Federal Republic of Germany* (Sussex: Sussex European Research Centre, 1982), pp. 6–8.

8. Kenneth H. F. Dyson, "The Politics of Economic Management in West Germany," p. 37.

9. Jeremiah M. Riemer, "Alterations in the Design of Model Germany," p. 81.

10. Peter A. Hall, "Patterns of Economics Policy among the European States," p. 16; and Jeremiah M. Riemer, "Alterations in the Design of Model Germany," p. 60. Nevertheless, in the spring of 1973, prior to the OPEC oil price increases, the Bundesbank adopted restrictive monetary policies, again contributing to a general recession (although this time in company with most of the OECD countries).

11. Josef Esser and Wolfgang Fach with Kenneth Dyson, "'Social Market' and Modernization Policy," pp. 107–108.

12. Wolfgang Streek, "Qualitative Demands and the Neo-Corporatist Manageability of Industrial Relations: Trade Unions and Industrial Relations in West Germany at the Beginning of the Eighties," *British Journal of Industrial Relations*, vol. 14 (1981), p. 151.

13. Josef Esser and Wolfgang Fach with Kenneth Dyson, "'Social Market' and Modernization Policy," p. 106.

14. Kenneth H. F. Dyson, "The Politics of Economic Management in West Germany," p. 35.

15. Ibid., pp. 43–44.

16. Jeremiah M. Riemer, "Alterations in the Design of Model Germany," p. 76.

17. Hans Besters, *Neue Wirtschaftspolitik durch Angebotslenkung* (Baden-Baden: Nomos-Verlag Gesellschaft, 1979), p. 29.

18. Ibid., p. 29; and Gerhard Wagenhals, "Industrial Policy in the Federal Republic of Germany," p. 254.

19. Stephen Woolcock, *Industrial Policy in the European Community* (M.Phil.

Diss., University of Edinburgh, 1980), p. 97; Hans Besters, *Neue Wirtschaftspolitik*, pp. 30–31; and Guido C. Goldman, "The German Economic Challenge," in Andre Markovits, ed., *The Political Economy of West Germany: 'Modell' Deutschland* (New York: Praeger, 1982), pp. 14–15; see also table 5–3.

20. Kenneth H. F. Dyson, "The Politics of Economic Management in West Germany," p. 47.

21. Guido C. Goldman, "The German Economic Challenge," pp. 19–21.

22. Christopher Wilkinson, "Trends in Industrial Policy in the EC: Theory and Practice," paper prepared for delivery at a meeting of the Centre for European Policy Studies, Brussels, June 1983; and Kenneth H. F. Dyson, "Introduction," in Kenneth Dyson and Stephen Wilks, eds., *Industrial Crisis: A Comparative Study of State and Industry* (New York: St. Martin's Press, 1983), p. 41.

23. Ibid., pp. 53–55.

24. Josef Esser and Wolfgang Fach with Kenneth Dyson, "'Social Market' and Modernization Policy: West Germany," p. 109.

25. Ernst-Juergen Horn, *Management of Industrial Change*, p. 13.

26. Eric Owen Smith, *The West German Economy*, pp. 13–17.

27. Domenico Moro, *Crisis e ristrutturazione dell'industria siderurgica italiana* (Varese: Giuffre Editore (1984), p. 88.

28. Andrew Shonfield, *Modern Capitalism: The Changing Balance of Public and Private Power* (New York: Oxford University Press, 1965), p. 255; and Eric Owen Smith, *The West Germany Economy*, p. 17.

29. Andrew Shonfield, *Modern Capitalism*, p. 256.

30. Jean G. Padioleau, *Quand la France s'enferre* (Paris: Presses Universitaires de France, 1981), pp. 161–62.

31. Domenico Moro, *Crisis e ristrutturazione*, pp. 95–96.

32. Ibid., p. 88.

33. Ibid., p. 95.

34. Josef Esser and Wolfgang Fach with Kenneth Dyson, "'Social Market' and Modernization Policy," p. 114.

35. Gerhard Ollig, "Staat und Stahl in Deutschland," p. 434; and Josef Esser and Wolfgang Fach with Kenneth Dyson, "'Social Market' and Modernization Policy," pp. 112–13.

36. Ibid., p. 114.

37. Ibid., pp. 112–13; and John Tagliabue, "Kloeckner Pulling out of German Steel Plan," *New York Times,* (March 15, 1983), p. 21D.

38. John Tagliabue, "Thyssen's Difficulties with Budd," *New York Times* (March 28, 1984), p. 29; and Daniel F. Cuff, "Thyssen's Big Push to Revitalize Budd," *New York Times* (April 9, 1985), p. 29.

39. Eric Owen Smith, *The West German Economy*, p. 209

40. Josef Esser and Wolfgang Fach with Kenneth Dyson, "'Social Market' and Modernization Policy," pp. 114–18.

41. "The People's Car Struggles to Change Gear," *The Economist* (October 24, 1981), pp. 65–66.

42. John Tagliabue, "Seeking to Restore the Magic at VW," *New York Times* (March 25, 1984).

43. Eric Owen Smith, *The West German Economy*, p. 209. The federal government does not always, strictly speaking, let state banks do the rescuing. Given the predominance of the CSU in Bavaria, and of Franz Josef Strauss in the CSU, national party politics project to some extent onto the policies of the state banks of certain states. Thus, and only thus, could one explain the recent DM1 billion loans from the Bavarian

state bank to the East German government.

44. "Siemens is Set to Take on the World in Integrated Circuits," *Business Week* (August 6, 1984), pp. 64–65.

45. Gerd Junne, "Multinationale Unternehmen in 'High Technology' Sektoren order wie gut ist die Strategie vom guten Zweiten?" in Peter H. Mettler, ed., *German Multinationale* (forthcoming), pp. 11–14.

46. Josef Esser and Wolfgang Fach with Kenneth Dyson, "'Social Market' and Modernization Policy," p. 118.

47. "Banking on Recovery: A Survey of International Banking," *The Economist* (March 26, 1983), p. 49; and Doug Anderson, *AEG-Telefunken, A.G.* (Cambridge, Mass.: Harvard Business School, 1981), case 1–381–187, p. 9.

48. Ibid., pp. 1–2.

49. Ibid., p. 16.

50. "Banking on Recovery: A Survey of International Banking," p. 50.

51. "Last Chance Tactics of European Chip Makers," *Business Week* (June 28, 1982), p. 117.

52. Ibid.

53. "Bonn's Late Push in the High Tech Race," *Business Week* (April 9, 1984), pp. 43–44.

The Institutional Foundations of Japanese Industrial Policy

Chalmers Johnson

In writing about the Japanese government-business relationship, one must first issue the warning to beware the usual meanings of English-language terms and to be prepared to use familiar words such as *parliament* or *bureaucracy*, in a new way. The leading legal authority in the United States on Japan, Dan Henderson of the University of Washington's Law School, states:

> Terms such as "competition," "private industry," or "free enterprise," commonly used in discussions of Japanese business, conjure up in the minds of readers in English quite different images from existing realities of Japanese business. "Collusive rivalry," "semi-private industry," "quasi-public enterprise," respectively, might be more apt expressions, precisely because their Western referents are unclear.[1]

Thus the first point to make is that the Japanese institutions of government and business are themselves quite different, and have quite different histories and functions, from those of the Anglo-American world; and these differences directly influence the kind of government-business relationship that exists in Japan.

Let me cite a few of the most important differences, which I will expand on later. First, the Japanese state bureaucracy, particularly the economic bureaucracy concentrated in the ministries of Finance, International Trade and Industry, Agriculture, Transportation, Construction, and Posts and Telecommunications, and the Economic Planning Agency, is an intrinsic meritocracy. Service in any one of these ministries is the most prestigious occupation in the country, and the senior public service is drawn primarily from the top 20 percent of the best law school in the country, that of Tokyo University. These men originate virtually all national policies, control the three unconsolidated national budgets, retire early and move on to top positions in business and politics (a process that is called *amakudari,* or descent from heaven, and that is directly opposite to the movement of talent in the United States from the boardrooms of private corporations *to* the government), and maintain legendary old-boy connections with each other during and after their period of public service. The state bureaucracy, particularly the economic bureaucracy, has supplied many of the most important prime ministers of postwar Japan, and has been a source of political recruitment that is unknown and close to unimaginable in the United States.[2]

Second, the parliament of Japan—the assembly of elected representatives of the people (known as the Diet)—is constitutionally the "highest organ of state power" (article 41 of the Constitution of 1947); but in practice it is one of the weakest parliaments among all the advanced industrial democracies and certainly weaker than the U.S. Congress, which is the strongest such institution in the world. In postwar Japan an informal relationship between the Diet and the economic bureaucracy has developed in which the Diet reigns but the bureaucracy actually rules—or, to describe the situation another way, the bureaucracy makes policy, and the Diet merely rubber-stamps it. This relationship is unstable and constitutes a moving target. The present is a phase of relative Diet ascendancy; for example, tax policy, which was under firm bureaucratic control and not subject to political influence during most of the postwar period, is more in the hands of the ruling conservative political party today than in the past. The relation between the Diet and the economic bureaucracy is a cyclical one, however; the bureaucracy always regains influence in times of economic crisis, such as during postwar reconstruction or after the oil shock of 1973. To cite one example of Diet weakness, the bureaucracy's budget has been modified by the Diet only three or four times since the creation of the Liberal Democratic Party (LDP) in 1955, and these modifications have always involved relatively minor changes in defense appropriations.[3]

Third, big business in Japan maintains a skewed triangular relationship with the other two main power centers, the bureaucracy and the Diet. Big business keeps the LDP in power by supplying enormous funds to the leaders of conservative factions (whose actual electoral constituencies are normally rural). This relationship is important because since 1948 uninterrupted single-party dominance in Japan has been prerequisite to bureaucratic initiative and leadership.

Japan's single-party reign has not had the stultifying consequences of single-party rule in places such as the Philippines largely because Japan's LDP learned how to replace the head of the party, something it does with great frequency, through internal factional struggle. The party keeps itself in power through quite open subsidies to Japan's farmers, who are vastly overrepresented in the nation's system of electoral constituencies. At the same time, such payoffs to farmers have had powerful income redistribution and equalization effects and have eliminated rural poverty, which was the major source of instability in prewar Japan.[4] One consequence of the LDP's long reign—

which shows no sign of ending soon unless the Americans destroy Japanese agriculture in the name of market opening—is fairly frequent corruption scandals by politicians who have abused their access to the LDP-bureaucratic-big business nexus. The main advantage that Japan gets from its single-party system is simply than it allows for "solving problems with an eye to the economic system, rather than to a particular category of citizens."[5]

As we indicated earlier, the Diet tries, on occasion, to direct the bureaucracy; but this effort is weakened by the presence of large numbers of former elite bureaucrats within the ranks of conservative politicians. (Currently, about 20 percent of the Diet members are exbureaucrats.) The bureaucracy, in turn, supports the interests of big business, but it is not subservient to business because business financial support flows to the party. The bureaucracy supports big business primarily because it is interested in securing the economic welfare and economic defense of Japan as a whole.

Fourth, the Japanese legal system derives from the Continental European tradition rather than from the Anglo-American common law tradition. This derivation means that economic law, lawyers, detailed contracts, and adversarial relations are relied on much less in Japan than in other open economic systems. Perhaps most important, and differing from both the Continental and the Anglo-American traditions, administrative law is markedly underdeveloped in Japan. If a Japanese thinks that the executive branch has exceeded its mandate or is interpreting a law in an undesirable manner, he will not easily obtain relief by turning to the courts, which are also notoriously slow. The *trend* is toward an increased reliance on administrative law, as seen in the pollution suits of the 1970s, but this reliance is not yet sufficiently advanced to make much of an impact.[6] Instead, bureaucratic power in Japan is checked by intense competition among the various ministries, by the use of Diet members to obtain advantages for particular groups (rather than to establish general policy), and through the practice of administrative guidance—meaning ad hoc, not legally binding agreements and arrangements between the bureaucracy and its clients to achieve common goals.

I will summarize the discussion to this point. The Japanese government is extremely intrusive into the privately owned and managed economy, but it intrudes through market-conforming methods and in cooperation rather than in confrontation with the private sector. Japan's economic bureaucracy is probably the most powerful in any contemporary capitalist democracy, but it is also the smallest, cheapest, and imposes the lightest tax burden. With the exception of certain political sacred cows, such as the publicly owned railroads and rice-price supports for Japan's farmers, the economic bureaucracy tries to avoid subsidies, preferring instead the use of loans, seed money, tax breaks, and ad hoc benefits to promote its policies.

In talking about any goverment-business relation, the issue is never government intervention in the private sector. *All* governments intervene in their economies for various reasons, such as consumer protection, social welfare, national defense, and so forth. The key considerations in intervening are the functional priorities of a government. The first priority of the Japanese government in the private sector is not protectionism or neo-mercantilism (as in France) or regulation (as in the United States, with the exceptions of the defense and agricultural sectors) or welfare (as in Sweden or the Netherlands). Japan's first priority is, above all, developmental—meaning that the government tries to secure Japan's economic livelihood through public policies based on such criteria as long-term dynamic comparative advantage and international competitive ability. The Japanese government's most important contributions to the economy are think-tank functions and supervision and coordination of the structural changes necessary to keep Japan competitive in world markets.

One needs to know a lot more about the Japanese government and business community to understand and adapt to the relation between them. Some of what one needs to know are the following. (1) The outlook between public and private managers is similar because of similar educational experience. There is a lack of pronounced class, ethnic, or religious divisions in Japan; and the populace is aware of Japan's vulnerabilities and of its need to trade because it is an overpopulated, highly industrialized set of islands situated close to both China and the Soviet Union, with almost no natural resources. (2) Japanese big business is an oligopoly, organized into bank- and trading company-based conglomerates or industrial groups (*keiretsu* in Japanese, descendants of the prewar *zaibatsu*), which means that profit considerations often take a lower priority to such criteria as market share, capital formation, research and development, and long-term market penetration. (3) Japan's enterprises still obtain most of their capital via bank lending rather than by the sale of equity shares, which means that Japanese managers are much less influenced by shareholders or securities analysts than in other systems, that they are much more influenced by the monetary policies of the central bank than in other systems, and that bailouts or reconstructions of the Lockheed or Chrysler types are common and not particularly controversial in Japan because banks and the government cooperate to protect their investments. (4) The history and norms of Japanese labor relations, which result in intense enterprise loyalties, show an almost total absence of interfirm transfers but very extensive intrafirm transfers, enterprise unionism, and norms of consensus formation rather than majoritarianism in both governmental and enterprise decision making. Many of these aspects of Japanese business are already familiar to Americans, and most of them have been extensively described in the numerous recent books in English on the Japanese political economy.[7] I therefore want to turn instead to several concrete institutions of the government-business relation that are rather less well known to foreigners but that constitute the heart of the matter for Japanese officials and businessmen. Following this discussion one can begin to see the real dimensions of the Japanese political and economic challenge to nations such as the United States.

Government-Business Institutions

FILP. The first of these institutions is the Fiscal Investment and Loan Plan, which I am going to call FILP. This is the investment budget, or what one analyst has called the "shadow budget." Earlier I referred to three unconsolidated national budgets in Japan. One of these is the General Account budget and the other is the Special Accounts. The third is FILP, a budget for government investments and loans in high-priority sectors, and it is totally controlled by the bureaucracy. In recent years the FILP has been about 40 percent of the size of the General Account budget and about 6 percent of gross national product (GNP), so we are talking about significant sums of money in government hands. The chief use of these funds is to finance the ninety-nine (as of 1984) public corporations in Japan, as well as the innumerable foundations, associations, and promotional organizations that serve as intermediaries between the government and the private sector. One of the most important of these institutions, funded by the FILP, is the Japan Development Bank (JDB), created in 1951. It makes loans that serve governmental development policies, such as for new energy sources, for so-called structural finance to promote mergers and rationalization in declining sectors, and for research and development (R and D) in risky areas, such as the fifth generation computer. The JDB's influence is primarily not monetary but indicative. A JDB loan does not begin to cover all the costs of a project; it is, however, a signal to the entire financial and business community that a particular project has been targeted by the government and is a sector that all growth-oriented enterprises should get into, given the government's track record in targeting.

The source of funds for the FILP is the postal savings system, meaning the nationwide system of tax incentives and administered interest rates that encourage small savers to put their money into government accounts, where they are held in trust and invested by officials of the ministries of Finance and International Trade and Industry (MITI). Japan's extraordinarily high rate of savings from personal disposable income—today about 18 percent and the highest rate among comparable economies—is something to be explained not by culture, natural frugality, or the family system, but by public policy and powerful incentives. The Japanese save because of the low welfare commitment of the government—it is said that the well-run Japanese household will have a full year's salary available in liquid savings accounts—and because the government makes it easy and profitable for people to save at their local post offices. Under current tax law, an individual's interest on the first ¥ 9 million (about $40,000) in postal and commercial savings accounts combined is tax exempt. This situation means the postal savings system is also the main source

191

of tax evasion in the country, since a person could, in theory, open a separate account at every post office in the country. The Ministry of Finance has recently tried to fill in this loophole, but it abandoned the idea when it discovered that strict enforcement would drive a lot of savings abroad or into gold and would, in effect, kill the goose that lays the golden eggs. During 1984 the ministry merely noted the existence of 217,260,000 tax-free deposit accounts at commercial financial institutions and 326,790,000 at post offices. These figures work out to an average of five such accounts for every man, woman, and child in Japan.[8] The postal savings system alone controls assets about four times those of the world's largest commercial bank, the Bank of America—which is a considerable financial institution to be totally in the hands of the bureaucracy for public investment and which is generally beyond the influence of pork-barrel politics.[9]

Among the many advantages that Japan gets from its FILP and savings systems are the ability to finance much larger General Account deficits than in other countries, the ability to administer interest rates by pegging them to the postal savings rate, the ability to service the national debt cheaply by keeping interest rates artificially low, and the ability to make government loans to deserving projects based on their merit rather than on political influence or lobbying.

On May 29, 1984, the Japanese and United States governments accepted the report of the Japan-U.S. Working Group on Yen/Dollar Exchange Rate Issues to liberalize the Japanese capital market and to internationalize the yen. When the measures in the report are fully implemented several years from now, regulated interest rates in Japan on very large deposits will be replaced with market rates; and foreign financial institutions will have greater access to the Japanese market in such fields as trust banking. Equally important, the measures will deregulate yen financing and yen investments in the Euroyen market by foreign firms and foreign financial institutions. These reforms undoubtedly will increase external demand for the yen and may thereby increase its value vis-à-vis the dollar, which should make Japanese products less price competitive against American goods in international commerce. At any rate, that is the theory behind these complex and arcane maneuverings. None of these measures, however, will have an immediate effect (and only an ambiguous longer-term effect) on the domestic Japanese financial structure and on the postal savings system. Equally important, although the Ministry of Finance entered into the agreement of May 29, 1984, the Ministry of Posts and Telecommunications controls the postal savings system, and the Postal Ministry has a different conception of the goal and the pace of financial liberalization than the Ministry of Finance.[10]

Deliberation Councils. The second set of institutions I would like to mention is the approximately 250 permanently operating forums for public-private consultation on important issues. These forums are known collectively as *shingikai*, or deliberation councils, and they bring together under the auspices of a particular ministry the leading industrialists, journalists, academics, and representatives of consumer groups to consider and approve government policies before they are implemented. In a sense the deliberation on laws and policies that goes on in U.S. congressional committee hearings occurs in Japan outside the Diet and in forums where representation and procedures are much less subject to political influence or media exploitation.

The deliberation councils take up many important subjects, including tax policy, capital liberalization, the price of rice, and educational reform; but their importance is perhaps best illustrated by MITI's blue ribbon panel for approving its policies, the Industrial Structure Council (*Sangyō Kōzō Shingikai*). Its functions are the management of industrial policy as a whole, including the promotion of new managerial practices, policies for depressed industries, targeting of new, higher-value-added industries, and so forth. The public-private agency approves MITI's famous "long-term vision plans" for economic development. (These plans, incidentally, are not a state secret but are readily available at any government bookstore in Tokyo—and in English translation.) The *shingikai*, combined with the formal institutions of Japanese big business, such as the Federation of Economic Organizations (*Keidanren*), give the Japanese government a power of consultation and coordination with the private sector that is smooth, continuously in operation, and much more easily controlled than the lobbying and political action committees that the American government-business relationship generates.

During 1984, the Japanese deliberation councils and particularly the Industrial Structure Council figured prominently in the newest and potentially most damaging dimension of the Japanese-American trade war—namely, the so-called transparency issue. This issue refers to the excellent job Japan does in Washington of monitoring the United States government, of lobbying congressional committees in a timely and appropriate way, and of hiring American law firms and senior officials recently retired from office to propound Japan's point of view. By contrast, the United States does not even seem to understand clearly how the system in Tokyo works. There is no question that this discrepancy actually exists.[11] The argument is over *why* it exists.

Japan may simply have done a better job in learning English (and the vocabulary of American politics) and in adapting to the market it is trying to penetrate than the Americans have done with regard to the Japanese market. But perhaps also, as American trade negotiators have charged, the American system is much more transparent than the Japanese system; and thus Japanese officials can more easily know what is going on in Washington and influence the course of events than any foreigner can affect Japan's highly private, opaque processes of decision making. For this reason, during January 1984,

193

the U.S. undersecretary of commerce for international trade, Lionel Olmer, demanded that the United States be given access to meetings of the Industrial Structure Council and permission to address them. The matter was, he suggested, merely one of reciprocity, no different from the ease with which Japanese and other foreigners can lobby the U.S. government.

In my view, the transparency issue is real. By the time a Japanese policy decision of concern to its trading partners has reached the Diet, the decision has already been made and cannot be influenced. The transparency problem could be mitigated (or, conversely, its true proportions revealed) if the Americans would devote more resources to learning the Japanese language and to developing their own independent monitoring capability on their most important ally. Even if Americans did that, however, they would still find Japanese processes of public policy making more opaque than American ones. Even if Mr. Olmer is given access to the Industrial Structure Council, he will still have no means to influence its sponsoring ministry, other ministries concerned with a particular issue, or the trade associations of an industry affected by a council recommendation. Japan, however, cannot reasonably be asked to change the entire structure of its government just to make it as amenable to influence by special interest groups as the American government is. The solution to the transparency issue thus seems to lie in creating more expertise on Japan among foreigners and perhaps in placing limitations on foreign interests' lobbying of the American Congress.

Although during the 1980s the need for American information on Japan is at its greatest intensity since World War II, the capacity to delivery that information is actually diminishing. The most recent survey of Japanese studies in the United States, prepared for the Japan Foundation and the Social Science Research Council, concludes:

> The marked growth that characterized Japanese studies . . . in the 1960s and early '70s is over, at least for the foreseeable future. Thus the number of Japan specialists at U.S. colleges and universities shows only a moderate increase since 1975 (probably not greater than that experienced by instructional staff generally); language enrollments show steady but unspectacular growth, and enrollments in courses relating to Japan appear stable. While the above results show stability or modest growth on important measures, one key indicator—funding—shows a sharp decline.[12]

Even more ominous, the report reveals that although only 1,025 Japan specialists were employed by American colleges and universities (as of 1983), the 83 most experienced of them will retire before 1988, and the prospects are that only about half of the positions they vacate will be filled with Japan specialists. Under these conditions misinformation and punditry about Japan understandably proliferate, while American business leaders have no internal capacity to evaluate either their major competitor or the misinformation being published. Those without eyes will always have a transparency problem.

Antimonopoly Institutions. Thanks to the Allied occupation after World War II, Japan got its first antimonopoly law and its so-called Fair Trade Commission to implement it. Antitrust policy and legislation, however, have always taken second place in Japan to the developmental goals of the government. This policy has meant that the government has taken international competitive ability rather than purely domestic competition as its main antimonopoly criterion and that it has been able to promote mergers, cartels, investment coordination schemes, and other forms of interfirm cooperation much more easily than other capitalist democracies have done so. The Fair Trade Commission has shown some tendency toward increased activity, particularly against so-called guidance cartels, which are forums of representatives of competing enterprises that would be illegal under the antimonopoly law except for the presence of MITI officials who legalize them. This trend appeared only during the 1970s, however, and has not seriously weakened MITI's capacity to use cartelization to promote its policies. The *kenkyū kumiai*, or research cartels, for example, are prominent today in advanced electronics and tele-communications research. Every time Japan agrees to an orderly marketing compact with the United States or the European Community, this agreement implies the creation of a domestic export cartel. MITI organizes such cartels, and it does so usually on the basis of market shares in existence when the orderly marketing compact came into effect—one reason market share looms so much larger than short-term profitability in the eyes of Japanese managers. Such cartels have been consistently ruled legal in Japan, regardless of the stipulations of the antimonopoly law.

Despite this toleration for cartels, as well as elaborate governmental regulation of different industries and extensive cross-share-holding within the bank-based industrial groups, there is not necessarily less competition in Japan than in the United States. To the contrary, there may very well be more competition. This subject is highly complicated and controversial, but Japan seems to have much to teach the rest of the capitalist world about how to maintain competition in advanced, highly oligopolized market economies. What is Japan's secret? It has, of course, numerous elements; and different analysts will produce different lists. My list is as follows:

• Governmental targeting of industries for the future and subsequent measures to reduce the risks of development generate cut-throat competition among the industrial groups to enter all such industries, while their financial strength and diversification make them able to do so.

• Governmental protection from foreign competition is extended only for developmental purposes, not for permanent security (except for agriculture); and in the case of declining industries, performance goals (such as scrapping

195

excess capacity) are always extracted in return for public assistance.[13]

• Japan's labor relations, by emphasizing enterprise rather than trade unionism, provide strong incentives for the whole labor force to compete on every dimension, including wage restraint when necessary.

• Bankruptcies of all but the largest firms are commonplace. Even when large, politically potent firms are bailed out, old management is nevertheless ruthlessly weeded out (the rebuilding of Mazda Motors during the late 1970s is a good example).[14]

• The high debt-to-capitalization ratios that prevail throughout Japanese industry mean that management is much more attuned to the long-term growth interests of its bankers than the short-term profit interests of its stockholders. Most of the "secrets of Japanese management" are based on such structural features of the economy rather than on any unusual managerial techniques.

• Japan's overall dependency on imported resources and its extensive information-gathering-and-processing capacities in government and the general trading companies mean that Japan is better informed about international competition and more prepared to meet it than less internationalized economies are.

Perhaps the most important point about the maintenance of competition in Japan is how undoctrinaire the Japanese are about it. They consistently ignore the opinions of economists and lawyers on the subject of antitrust and make most of their decisions on an ad hoc, case-by-case basis. In direct contrast to the United States, the Japanese government is normally promerger, whereas the private sector often resists mergers because of the managerial and union difficulties involved. In the United States virtually all mergers are initiated by the private sector and are usually resisted by the government. Even so, the Americans seem to be deeply hamstrung by their laws and theories concerning competition. As Stuart Eizenstat, former President Carter's chief domestic advisor, recently stated:

> If the antitrust laws ever seemed to make sense, they appear topsy-turvy now. One arm of the government approves a $10 billion merger between Texaco and Getty Oil, and two relatively healthy companies in a healthy industry, and a General Motors-Toyota joint venture between two strong corporations in a recovering but concentrated market. Then another arm of the government turns down a merger between LTV and Republic Steel, one of which is on the economic ropes, in an industry which has been in a long-term structural decline and may need mergers to survive—and then reverses itself a few weeks later under heavy pressure. All of the preceding is occurring while yet another branch of the government, the Congress, moves to block another set of mergers in the oil industry, even though these mergers create less concentration than the already sanctioned Texaco/Getty merger.[15]

By contrast, Japan's antitrust policy violates most tenets of Anglo-American theory and practice on the subject, and that seems to be the key to its success.

Industrial Location Institutions. In the United States we have the wholly ad hoc and often chaotic process known as the "shift to the sunbelt"—a process that often damages the places receiving new industry, such as Denver or Phoenix, as much as the places losing it. By contrast, Japan has created a complex of powerful incentives and disincentives for industrial location, cost cutting, rationalization of transportation, and workers benefits, which are extremely profitable to industry. In some cases this policy has meant that the government has made available to industry free of charge improved coastal land and industrial parks built at public expense. These policies are formulated and implemented in Japan through the Industrial Location and Environmental Protection Bureau of MITI; through similar bureaus in the ministries of Construction and Transportation; through such powerful public corporations as the Japan Railway Construction Corporation, the Honshu-Shikoku Bridge Authority, and the Regional Promotion and Facilities Corporation (all extensively funded by FILP); and through local governments.[16] Needless to say, the task is made easier because Japan's government does not have a federal structure. The central government is able to implement its policies with only minor local opposition (one famous recent exception being the creation of the new airport at Narita). The benefits of Japan's industrial location and relocations policies are today available to foreign-affiliated firms or subsidiaries and can greatly facilitate the financing of a foreign advance into Japan.

Industrial Research and Development. As is well known, Japan pursues a policy of "engineering R and D"—meaning that it is concerned above all with taking known scientific and technological discoveries and commercializing them by engineering into them quality controls, cost reductions, improved production techniques, and innovative designs. To do this Japan graduates annually more engineers than the United States, even though its population is only half that of the United States.[17] Government support for research and development (R and D) specifically takes into account the commercial and industrial relevance and the growth potential of various projects. The governmental units responsible for Japanese R and D are the Ministry of Education, which funds academic researchers; the Science and Technology Agency, which is concerned primarily with atomic power and space research; and, above all, the Agency of Industrial Science and Technology, an integral part of MITI and the operator of the most important governmental laboratories as well as the main R and D policy maker.

This pattern of public R and D policy can be contrasted with that of the United States, which—in areas other than national defense—pursues a policy of "Nobel Prize R and D," institutionally isolates its R and D from industrial and commercial concerns, graduates annually more chemists and physicists than Japan, and implements its civilian R and D through the National Science Foundation, a governmental agency run by (and for) professors. Needless to say, the United States wins many more Nobel Prizes than Japan, but Japan provides a much larger and more powerful engineering establishment to nourish its civilian industries. Many more chief executive officers in Japan have engineering backgrounds, in contrast to the business administration or financial educations of the majority of American chief executive officers. Interestingly enough, two of the five postwar presidents of Keidanren, the top business community post in the country, were engineers. This commercial orientation of much of Japan's public R and D investment is a critically important part of the government-business relationship, and one that is growing in importance.

This sketch of some of the institutions of the Japanese political economy is not intended to be exhaustive. I have introduced it here to illustrate the range of institutions found in Japan and to suggest the quality of thought that lies behind them. The different priorities and political principles found in Japanese government, as contrasted with those of the United States, seem to me to be the key to the highly controversial and even emotional debate in the English-speaking world about the Japanese economic challenge to the market economies of North America and Western Europe. No one disputes the *record* of Japan's high-speed economic growth, which lasted for about two decades during the postwar era and was then followed by a decade of slower but still impressive expansion of both production and productivity. Equally important is Japan's record of orderly shifts of industrial structure, first from labor-intensive, light industry to capital-intensive, heavy industry and currently to knowledge-intensive, high-technology industry. Everyone knows that Japan is the world's largest manufacturer of automobiles, that it controls well over half of the world's market share for some important types of microelectronic components, and that other very rapidly growing capitalist economies of East Asia are explicitly modeling themselves on the Japanese economy. The dispute is about precisely what these facts mean, above all, what the political and intellectual implications for Japan's competitors are.

Political and Economic Implications

Virtually the entire Western community of professional economists is united on one point: Whatever the data from Japan may be, they must not be allowed to challenge the prevailing theoretical paradigm of how market economies work. Professional economists are fundamentally hostile to comparative economics. They conceive of their field as a theoretically and mathematically based science, one that seeks and allegedly has discovered a few universal laws, and in which comparative studies would be as irrelevant as they would be in, say, physics. Economists are uninterested in the thought that the *Wealth of Nations* actually concerned only one nation.

In recent times comparative economics has had a brief flurry of interest as an adjunct to the study of Soviet-type socialism; but as the Soviet economy began to falter, so too did comparative economics.[18] One would have supposed that the arrival on the scene of the Japanese-type economies would have reinvigorated comparative economics, but this has not happened (yet). Instead, most professional analysis of the Japanese economy "sees the basic source of Japan's economic growth as lying in a vigorous private sector, energetically, imaginatively, and diligently engaged in business, productive investment, and commercially-oriented research and development and in the saving to finance those activities."[19] The discrepancy between the performance of Japan and of other, no less diligent and energetic market economies during various parts of the postwar period is explained by a vast range of temporary or contingent factors: the especially propitious environment in which Japan found itself (that is, the same postwar environment as all other American allies), mistakes by Japan's competitors in the management of their enterprises, Japanese "free rides" of various kinds on the backs of American scientists or taxpayers, secrets of Japanese management (namely the search at the Harvard Business School for such secrets in Musashi Miyamoto's *Book of Five Rings*, a 1643 treatise on swordsmanship), Japanese workaholism, "creative Confucianism" in East Asia, and so forth. Economic punditry, however, steadfastly avoids analysis of the Japanese government-business relationship for the simple reason that the comparison with the United States would likely be damaging to both local theory and local practice.

As the American trade balance in manufactured goods with Japan inexorably worsens each year, and as one quick fix after another (for example, elimination of nontariff barriers, pressures against the "undervalued yen") is attempted with no change, the professional economics approach has started to lose credibility. It simply does not and perhaps cannot account for the numerous discrepancies between theory and practice that are now commonplaces of daily life in either Japan or the United States (such as the differences in the cost of capital in the two countries and Japanese savings behavior during periods of high inflation). This weakness of pure economics has produced a resurgent interest in the West in political economy, particularly in professional schools of business and in departments of political science. By political economy I mean an analysis of economic phenomena based on the explicit recognition of the indivisibility of economics and politics—a view that has as its corollary the understanding that economic theory is a totally utopian subject unless and until it is translated into the real world through institutions.[20] (As a practical matter this view also means that any discussion by political or business leaders in either Washington or Tokyo of the "glories of the free market" or of the "need to restore macroeconomic fundamentals" is purely ideological and probably designed to camouflage their real intentions.)

Even when they bear the same names—"labor union," "public corporation," or "stockholders"—the institutions of modern capitalism vary greatly among systems. There is no theoretical way to show what the institutions of capitalism ought to be. One can only show through comparative analysis the consequences, both intended and unintended, of particular institutional configurations. Equally important, the hypotheses of economic theory are not simply manifested in institutions; such institutions also have political foundations and political consequences that have their own theoretical rationales. The institutions that actually exist in a modern capitalist system owe as much to a nation's history as they do to either economic or political theory, which is not to say that such institutions are in any sense sacrosanct but only to indicate one of the kinds of knowledge that is needed if a nation wants to reform its institutions.

As should by now be obvious, I place myself in the school of political economists. I do not contend that Japan has repealed the laws of economics, nor do I hold that the Japanese government in general or any individual agency of it in particular was the exclusive author of the postwar economic miracle. I do contend that the Japanese have put together the political and economic institutions of capitalism in ways that differ from the Anglo-American model and that this Japanese configuration has many different tradeoffs, not all of which have as yet become fully manifest to either the Japanese or Japan's competitors. The most obvious tradeoff is that in return for lesser levels of political participation than those prevailing in the United States, Japan has obtained a comparatively more effective and more efficient public economic policy.[21]

Industrial Policy

Embedded in Japan's institutional structure is something called industrial policy. Adopting a Japanese-type industrial policy without also adopting Japanese-type institutions is not possible, which suggests at the outset that Japan cannot be a model for the United States. The responsibilities, endowments, and political traditions of the United States differ too much for that. It does not follow, however, that a competitor of Japan could not match Japan's industrial policy within a different institutional setting. Certainly during World War II and again today the United States has succeeded in matching and excelling its military enemies without copying their institutions. This is what, on the economic front, industrial policy is all about.

Industrial policy means initiating and coordinating governmental activities to lift the productivity and competitiveness of a whole economy and of particular industries in it. As a set of policies, industrial policy is the complement, the third side of the economic triangle, to a government's monetary and fiscal policies. Industrial policy is first of all an attitude and only then a matter of technique. Above all it means the infusion of goal-oriented, strategic thinking into public economic policy. There is no such thing as a government's not having an industrial policy, in the sense that any agency controlling 20 to 30 percent of the gross assets of an economy will have a profound effect on the markets within that economy. The issue is whether a government's industrial policy will be ad hoc, incoherent, and run by and for insiders or whether it will be consistent, long-term, and run for the sake of future generations.

Industrial policy has its own macro and micro aspects. At the macro level it provides governmental incentives for private saving, investment, research and development, cost cutting, quality control, and improvements in labor-management relations and in the appropriate education and reeducation of the labor force. At the micro level it seeks, on the one hand, to identify those technologies that will be need by industry in ten to twenty years and to facilitate their development and, on the other hand, to anticipate those technologies that will decline in importance and to assist in their orderly retreat or to support them on extraeconomic grounds (for example, domestic food supply or weapons for defense). Micro industrial policy is also popularly known as "industrial targeting."[22]

In Japan, macro industrial policy has been of much greater if unheralded importance than industrial targeting. Japan's genuine successes with targeting have depended as much on the macro environment created by industrial policy as on the concrete policy measures intended to promote or support particular industries. Macro industrial policy à la Japan is not a matter of some new or esoteric technique of government; it is rather an emphasis on economic fundamentals in public policy making and the use of the criterion of international competitive ability in evaluating *all* governmental programs. The formulation and implementation of industrial policy in Japan depend as much on its depoliticization to the greatest degree compatible with democracy as on any economic mode of thought. Japan has been able comparatively to depoliticize its industrial policy because of widespread public awareness of Japan's dependency on imports for most of its fuel, food, and raw materials.

The Role of MITI. Japan's MITI has the primary, although not the exclusive, responsibility for formulating and executing national industrial policy. Concretely, what has MITI done in the past, and what does it continue to do today? In the broadest sense MITI does four things:

First, it makes medium-term econometric forecasts concerning the development of and the needed changes in the Japanese industrial structure. Within this framework, it sets up goals that it believes the private sector must achieve if Japan is to remain competitive. These indicative plans, or "visions" as the Japanese call them, involve specific comparisons between Japan and its various foreign competitors of cost structures for different scales of production for each important industry. The major criterion (among many employed) in making industrial policy judgments is still income elasticity of demand, as it has been since the early 1950s.

Second, MITI arranges for the preferential allocation of capital to selected strategic industries. It does this through the governmental and semigovernmental banks; and the Ministry of Finance guides the commercial banks to coordinate their lending policies with MITI's industrial policies. Financial support of an industry also implies guidance (not control) by MITI. This guidance is usually indirect and subtle. For example, during 1984 the ministry exercised its influence over the biotechnology industry through preferential financing and ideas it disseminated to the unions of laboratory researchers at the various pharmaceutical companies.[23] Among MITI's most recent financial beneficiaries are so-called venture capital enterprises, which the ministry supports through the Small and Medium Enterprise Agency (an organ of MITI), the Japan Development Bank, and the 1983 law it sponsored to create "technopolises" in Japan—that is, new research cities modeled on California's Silicon Valley and aimed at stimulating synergistic influences among adjacently located high-tech businesses.[24]

Third, MITI targets those industries it believes Japan must develop in the future and creates a package of policy measures to promote such development. In the past, MITI's prime promotional measure was protection against foreign competition in the Japanese home market. This protection was achieved through foreign exchange control (until 1964), protective customs duties (until the late 1970s), control of foreign capital investment (until about 1976), and control of imports of foreign technology (until 1980). As Andrea Boltho, formerly with the Organization for Economic Cooperation and Development in Paris, states, "Relative to other industrialized countries, Japan's effective tariff rates were higher, her quota system more comprehensive, and the ingenuity of her hidden trade barriers on manufactured imports and subsidies to manufactured exports almost certainly greater."[25]

Since the early 1980s MITI has abandoned protectionism (although the culture and habits of protectionism continue with only slightly declining force in the general trading companies, regardless of official policy). Contemporary promotional measures stress financial assistance, tax breaks, incentives given through administrative guidance, and antitrust relief. Concerning the latter, Nobuyoshi Namiki, a former MITI official and one of its best-known theorists, defends research cartels in the targeted industries as Japan's only way to compete with the United States' much larger and richer research and development establishment. Targeting concentrates scarce resources and improves Japan's competitiveness vis-à-vis the United States in integrating basic science, applied science, production technology, and product development in the overall R and D process. "Establishing a well-defined and valid target," writes Namiki, "means that the goal has been obtained in large part."[26]

Fourth, in addition to targeting and promoting industries for the future, MITI is also actively involved with formulating industrial policies for what the Japanese call "structurally recessed industries." Some of these industries became depressed because of the global recession that followed the first oil shock (for example, shipbuilding), because of competition from the newly industrialized countries (textiles), or because of uncompetitive energy needs after the second oil shock (aluminum and petrochemicals). To create a general framework and a legal basis for governmental assistance to such industries, MITI wrote and sponsored passage by the Diet of the Special Measures Law for the Stabilization of Designated Recessed Industries of 1978, which it modified and renewed in 1983.

Designation of an industry as "recessed" under the law causes the ministry responsible for the sector of the economy in which it is located (usually MITI but, for example, the Ministry of Agriculture in the case of some chemical fertilizers) to formulate a stabilization plan for the industry. This procedure means that the ministry must forecast supply and demand (including exports and imports) for the industry on a periodic basis to measure excess domestic productive capacity and to allocate shares among enterprises for scrapping or mothballing such capacity. In drawing up these plans, the ministry must consult with an industrial advisory commission located in the Industrial Structure Council. Costs of scrapping production facilities are divided between the private sector and government, with government normally raising its share through specific import duties. The Fair Trade Commission may reject or modify ministerial plans if it considers them excessively anticompetitive; but once the commission gives its approval, the activities of enterprises in the designated industry are exempt from the provisions of the antimonopoly law.

The essence of Japanese industrial policy is the attempt by the Japanese government to engineer comparative advantage in international trade for selected Japanese industries. It does this primarily through a broad range of macroindustrial policies, but it also relies on industrial targeting to assist in shifts of industrial structure in a timely manner. On the record, as a matter of batting averages rather than of individual successes or failures, Japanese industrial policy is the best in the world. For nations trying to compete with Japan on this dimension, the response seems obvious: (1) learn from Japan the logic of what it is doing without attempting to copy Japanese institutions; (2) bring under control the macroindustrial policies of one's own nation and orient them to economic fundamentals; (3) avoid protectionism at all costs; and (4) inhibit political influence on economic policymaking—if necessary through such drastic measures as constitutional amendments stipulating a balanced budget in peacetime, ultimate tax limits, and a line-item veto for the chief executive.

Notes

1. Dan F. Henderson, *Foreign Enterprise in Japan: Laws and Policies* (Tokyo: Tuttle, 1975), p. 98.

2. On the workings of the Japanese state bureaucracy, see Chalmers Johnson, *MITI and the Japanese Miracle* (Stanford, Calif.: Stanford University Press, 1982), chap. 2.

3. See John Creighton Campbell, *Contemporary Japanese Budget Politics* (Berkeley: University of California Press, 1977), chap. 5.

4. On rural poverty in prewar Japan, see Mikiso Hane, *Peasants, Rebels, and Outcastes: The Underside of Modern Japan* (New York: Pantheon, 1982).

5. Gianni Fodella, "Economic Performance in Japan and Italy," in G. Fodella, ed., *Japan's Economy in a Comparative Perspective* (Tenterden, England: Paul Norbury, 1983), p. 26.

6. For current trends in Japanese administrative law, see Japanese-American Society for Legal Issues, "Symposium on the Oil Cartel Case," *Law in Japan: An Annual*, vol. 15 (1982), pp. 1–101.

7. For a fairly comprehensive example, see Steven Schlossstein, *Trade War: Greed, Power, and Industrial Policy on Opposite Sides of the Pacific* (New York: Congdon and Weed, 1984).

8. *Japan Economic Journal* (July 10, 1984), p. 6. For further details on the FILP, see Chalmers Johnson, *Japan's Public Policy Companies* (Washington, D.C.: American Enterprise Institute, 1978), chap. 4.

9. On March 31, 1983, deposits in postal savings accounts amounted to Y76,802 billion or $322.7 billion at US$1 = Y238, which was the prevailing rate of exchange during the spring of 1983. In addition, as of March 31, 1982 (the most recent data available), postal life insurance deposits added another Y17,567 billion ($73.8 billion) to the FILP for a total of at least Y94,369 billion ($396.5 billion). By comparison, deposits of the Bank of America on December 31, 1982, stood at $95.0 billion. Keizai Koho Center, *Japan: An International Comparison*, 1982 ed., p. 21; 1983 ed., p. 23.

10. For summaries of the movement to internationalize the Japanese financial system, see Walter E. Hoadley, "Banking and Finance: The Cost of Capital in Japan and the United States," in Chalmers Johnson, ed., *The Industrial Policy Debate* (San Francisco: Institute for Contemporary Studies, 1984), pp. 173–93; and Charles J. McMillan, *The Japanese Industrial System* (Berlin and New York: Walter de Gruyter, 1984), chap. 12.

11. See Ronald A. Morse and Edward A. Olsen, "Japan's Bureaucratic Edge," *Foreign Policy*, no. 52 (Fall 1983), pp. 167–80.

12. The Japan Foundation, *Japanese Studies in the United States: the 1980's* (Tokyo: Japan Foundation, 1984), p. 8. Also see Richard D. Lambert et al., *Beyond Growth: The Next Stage in Language and Area Studies* (Washington, D.C.: Association of American Universities, 1984).

13. Japan's policies and institutions for dealing with declining industries have not been thoroughly analyzed in English. For a good study of one industry, see Richard J. Samuels, "The Industrial Destructuring of the Japanese Aluminum Industry," *Pacific Affairs*, vol. 56 (Fall 1983), pp. 495–509. In Japanese, the most important source is Tsūshō Sangyō-shō Sangyō Seisaku Kyoku (MITI, Industrial Policy Bureau), ed.,

Sankōhō no kaisetsu (Explanation of the Special Measures Law for the Stabilization of Designated Recessed Industries [of May 1983]) (Tokyo: Tsūshō Sangyō Chōsa Kai, 1983).

14. See Richard Pascale and Thomas P. Rohlen, "The Mazda Turnaround," *Journal of Japanese Studies*, vol. 9 (Summer 1983), pp. 219–63.

15. Speech by Stuart E. Eizenstat before the Antitrust Section of the American Bar Association, Washington, D.C., March 22, 1984.

16. See Richard J. Samuels, *The Politics of Regional Policy in Japan* (Princeton, N.J.: Princeton University Press, 1983).

17. See the three-part article by Lawrence P. Grayson, "Japanese Technological Education," *Engineering Education* (December 1983, January 1984, and Februrary 1984); and Merry I. White, "Japanese Education: How Do They Do It?" *The Public Interest*, no. 76 (Summer 1984), pp. 87–101.

18. Cf. Fodella, "Economic Performance in Japan and Italy," pp. 1–2; Alexander Eckstein, ed., *Comparison of Economic Systems* (Berkeley: University of California Press, 1971); Gregory Grossman, *Economic Systems* (Englewood Cliffs, N.J.: Prentice-Hall, 1967); and Raymond Aron, *The Industrial Society* (New York: Simon and Schuster, 1967).

19. Hugh Patrick, "Japanese High-Tech Industrial Policy in Broader Context," unpublished paper for the Conference on Japanese High-Tech Industrial Policy in Comparative Perspective, sponsored by the Committee on Japanese Economic Studies, New York, March 17–19, 1984, p. 25.

20. See Harry L. Cook, "Scope and Method in Economics," paper presented to the annual meeting of the Western Economics Association, Las Vegas, Nevada, June 27, 1984.

21. For further discussion of what makes Japan different from the Anglo-American countries and a comparison between modern Japan and medieval Venice as examples of trading nations, see Chalmers Johnson, "*La Serenissima* of the East," *Asian and African Studies* (Journal of the Israel Oriental Society), vol. 18 (March 1984), pp. 57–73.

22. For further analytical details, see Chalmers Johnson, ed., *The Industrial Policy Debate*, pp. 3–26, 235–44.

23. "MITI Guides Biotech Industry," *Japan Times Weekly* (August 11, 1984), p. 11.

24. See Ministry of International Trade and Industry, *Background Information: White Paper on Small and Medium Enterprises in Japan, 1983* (Tokyo: MITI publication BI–52, 1983); Paula Doe, "Benchaa Boomu: Japanese for Venture Capital," *Electronic Business* (January 1984), pp. 98–100; *Japan Economic Journal* (July 19, 1983) (on the JDB); "The Technopolis Plan: Recent Developments," *News from MITI*, NR-289 (84–5) (March 6, 1984); and Yoshimitsu Kuribayashi, "Japan's Venture Businesses Forge Ahead," *International House of Japan Bulletin*, vol. 4 (Summer 1984), pp. 2–3.

25. Andrea Boltho, "Italian and Japanese Postwar Growth: Some Similarities and Differences," in Fodella, ed., *Japan's Economy in a Comparative Perspective*, p. 54.

26. *Japan Economic Journal* (June 26, 1984), p. 26.

State-owned and Private Enterprises in Italy

Mario Schimberni

The implementation of industrial policies takes various forms, some of which are related to the culture and traditions of different countries, which could explain why having a European community industrial policy is not easy.

I will deal with just one aspect of industrial policy, specifically the relations between state-owned and private enterprises in Italy. Italy has a so-called stable democracy with a so-called mixed economy; and I think that the Italian case can offer some ideas for you.

As I will try to show, this relation between state-owned and private enterprise is interesting, not only from the historical point of view, but also because new trends are currently emerging. The Italian economy has reached the stage in its history in which state-owned and private enterprises can begin to work together as partners in efficiently carrying out a valuable industrial policy.

Only through constructive public debate and concerted actions will we achieve this goal. To understand how we have reached this point, one must look back at the evolution of the publicly held corporations in Italy. In Italy the relation between state-owned and private enterprises is a complex one, especially when compared with that of our European neighbors.

On the one hand, we see West Germany with its more public sector, and on the other, we see France and the United Kingdom where most of the basic industries were nationalized after World War II. In Italy only the electric industry has been nationalized; yet much of our basic industries are controlled by government interests.

The formation of our public sector traces back to the Great Depression. Many of our companies became government owned during the thirties as part of the rescue operation to save Italy's three main commercial banks from failure. These banks were all holding companies for several conglomerates including electric, steel, and engineering firms, which in turn had the controlling interests in the banks that owned them. As you can see, the relation was highly intricate.

Thus, when the state took over the banks to protect the depositors, it also became a proprietor of industry. In 1933, the government established a holding agency for the acquired businesses, the Istituto Ricostruzione Industriale (IRI), and in 1953 created the other major public holding corporation, Ente Nazionale Edrocarburi (ENI).

These holding agencies operated in a mixed economy rather than in a strictly public sector. Although the government often granted industry monopolies to the businesses under its control, these companies retained certain features of their market origins, namely their legal corporate form and the minority ownership of private shareholders.

During the forties and the fifties, IRI and ENI were reorganized, creating a tier of subholding companies divided into fields of operation such as steel, engineering, and shipbuilding. At this time the state returned several companies to private control. During this period the demarcation between the private and the mixed sectors of the economy was not rigid; the distinction was one of ownership, not of organization.

In the late fifties, however, people began to look more critically at these distinctions to account for the state's presence. Under the Ministry of State's shareholdings, the state took a more active management role, establishing planning and policy-making procedures for its enterprises. As private shareholders began relinquishing their positions in these mixed companies and, predictably, as market sources dried up, the state-owned companies turned increasingly to the Italian treasury for funding.

Eventually in many—but certainly not in all—cases, assistance turned into aid. The managerial autonomy of the state-owned companies waned, and the government increased its role as operator over these financially dependent companies.

The history of Montedison reflects the reaction to this situation. Established after the nationalization of the electric utility industry in 1961, Montedison was formed by a merger between the Montecatini company and Edison electric company. The government acquired the majority holding in Montedison. After unsuccessful attempts to fit the new group into the state portfolio, the authorities sought to make Montedison private and reverse the trend toward increasing direct state intervention in business.

For various reasons related to the investment climate at the time, this privatization took place gradually, and Montedison was not truly free of government control until 1981, when the government's remaining ownership position was purchased by private investors.

We can now look back at the privatization of Montedison as a model and a turn-around for creating a new, feasible economic environment. It is not surprising, therefore, to witness today a resurgence of an ideology of private entrepreneurship among state-owned companies. But I must stress that such a spirit had existed earlier. The Montedison experience of a company in transition from public to private still provides the most interesting perspective on industrial policy in Italy.

Italian thinking about guidelines for our industrial sector has evolved. During the sixties the state-owned companies were regarded as the main instrument for implementing industrial policy simply because of their link to the government. Little thought was given to the proper use of financial support and investment incentives provided to the public sector. The government did not act to foster nonfinancial investments that would have strengthened the industrial environment.

Companies that did not use the government funds to improve their market prospects later found themselves in serious trouble. The situation worsened during the 1970s with the passage of the industrial conversion and the restructuring act. Instead of concentrating on specific objectives, this legislation has tried to encompass our entire structure, and as a result nothing has been accomplished.

As we work to improve our future we must learn from these lessons of the past. Here two points clearly emerge. First, government policy must begin to focus on essential objectives. Second, government must begin to use the contribution of the leading companies to help implement policy.

In establishing objectives, the government must identify the essentials of economic development and concentrate its action on these alone. Today the decisive effect on economic growth appears to be technological innovation. This is the essential characteristic of countries in which savings accumulate and capital markets flourish. This is not the case in Europe, particularly in Italy. In Italy, government instruments, primarily government fundings, substituted for the lack of private savings available for investment. It is important, therefore, that Italy pass an industrial policy law that commits government finance to highly innovative industrial adventures.

The other crucial point that must be addressed is implementation. If we exclude the possibility of improving the instruments that our government uses to support industry in the near term, we can look at new options. One viable alternative is to double the means for our leading industrial companies to carry out government policy. For this relation to exist, developments are necessary in two of the major areas of government intervention: agriculture and public works. These sectors have tried out new organizational forms to carry out industrial policy. The state operates exclusively through financial instruments, and its power is one of review. The operational plans drawn up by key companies in these sectors must be examined against the government's own goals.

Acting as subcontractors for the government, these main operating companies draft their plans and also manage industrial activities. Under government franchise, these operating companies contract activities to other private firms. Through these franchises the government entrusts the private concerns with the responsibility for public works and the utilities. Thus we see a new shift in the demarcation between the state-owned and the private sectors.

The relations have long ceased between the public and the private sectors by which the government provided incentives through funding and appraised the activities performed by private-sector companies. In the model I have outlined, this relation becomes much more dynamic and productive.

This arrangement by which leading private-sector companies draw up the plans of action and manage the activities that are implemented by other private firms would compensate for government's inadequacies. This arrangement would reduce the burden on government administration. Furthermore, it would give a new thrust to the process of economic and financial deregulation. Currently the Italian government has not applied this system to new areas of the industrial sector. The result is that the government has stepped up its role as a regulator and a funder, but it has not established a new relation between government and the market through effective personnel arrangements and different kinds of procedures.

So, speaking from my experience with Montedison, I can say that there is in Italy today a new climate of opportunity for private industry, opportunity that the industrial leaders must now seize for the good of the Italian economy. I conclude that in Europe the entrepreneurs are now contacting each other because all of them feel the necessity for a European community industrial policy in view of the competition from America and Japan.

Commentaries

Robert Pastor

I would like to make three brief points. First, like good comparative analyses, all of these papers not only help us see how other governments relate to their domestic economies but also force us to question certain assumptions governing our own relations between the government and the private economy.

Second, I encourage the authors to consider ways that they might further harmonize the questions they address in their papers, recognizing that the extent to which they do address similar questions is quite remarkable and useful.

Finally, I want to suggest three areas that they and others might pursue in terms of research. The major purpose of any comparative analysis, of course, is to force us to question our assumptions. In the case of industrial policy these assumptions are practically doctrine, perhaps even ideology; and they lead almost to an allergic reaction when Americans refer to industrial policy.

Leaving politics and political philosophy aside, there are three key assumptions based on neoclassical analysis. First, government intervention in the economy is inefficient and sends the wrong signals to the marketplace. Second, state companies are also inefficient; they drain public resources. Third, long-term economic planning substitutes the businessman's focus on the bottom line with the politician's and the bureaucrat's focus on extraneous social and economic objectives, which—however desirable they may be in another context—only serve to foul up the economy.

Despite the disclaimers of the authors, all the papers do suggest that these three assumptions are tenuous at best, perhaps in some places even invalid. The economic success of Japan and France, for example, is attributed largely to the nature and to the degree of government interference in the economy.

In the paper on France were many allusions to the success of state corporations and also considerable allusions to the failure of state corporations; but by no means do they imply that all state corporations are by definition inefficient.

Finally, several examples show the success of long-term economic planning. Professor Johnson has cautioned us about two things: one is applying lessons of Japan to the United States, which has different political institutions; and the second is applying even the language of the United States on free enterprise, private enterprise, or competition to Japan.

But I would turn that caution around. We are really talking about whether or not these basic assumptions that Americans hold have a specific validity, which pretends to a universality, or whether or not they have any validity at all. Second, the language now used in the United States may or may not be applicable, not only to Japan, but even to the United States.

One could argue, for example, that the United States has had an industrial policy since the birth of the Republic, although we've never called it that. We certainly had a policy on infrastructure. We have certainly regulated sectors; we call this policy regulation. We certainly have had an investment policy, which we call a fiscal policy. Perhaps we are talking about, not differences in kind between France and Japan on the one hand and the United States on the other, but differences in degree.

That statement brings me to the questions that I think are worth pursuing in the future. The paper on France is particularly helpful in pointing to possible explanations for the success or failure of different kinds of state intervention. That investigation points us in the right direction of asking, not whether an industrial policy can be efficient and effective or successful, but in what cases and in what ways might state involvement be helpful to stimulate an economy, to foster adjustment, and to obtain the various objectives that Professor Johnson mentioned.

What I found most startling—and I think future research really is required—is the extent to which the papers represent a rather massive, if disguised, assault on the key assumption about government involvement in the economy, which, as I stated previously, is that it would impede development. We have seen many cases in which government involvement can assist development. These cases need to be explored much more fully in the theoretical and also in the practical sense. In a practical way, we need to describe with much more precision the kinds of intervention in the economy in a way that would permit us to assess the results better, for example, between sectors and across nations. By so doing we would not only try to ascertain the causes of success and failure but also to identify the major issues in future international trade and investment. How might the United States need to respond to the various kinds of intervention in the economy by different countries?

To the extent that we can succeed in defining and measuring the kinds of intervention, we could take the next and most essential step toward defining the rules of the game that would harmonize and ultimately eliminate these instruments of intervention and protectionism and, at the same time, permit individual governments to address the needs they must address.

In summary, these papers help us to see opportunities for analysis and policy that perhaps have been concealed. By discarding ideology, we might be able to exploit opportunities for assisting development, adjustment, and productivity in the United States and in other countries and, more important, we might be able to negotiate what I think will be the next generation of international trade and investment problems.

Howard J. Wiarda

I will try to pull a couple of these themes together and perhaps even summarize these quite diverse papers and points of view by raising several questions.

First of all, what does industrial policy mean? Quite a number of definitions have been presented both from the Americanists in the first section and the comparativists in the second. We have examples of industrial policy as essentially market oriented, as in the United States or West Germany; as involving, to some degree at least—particularly under the present government—nationalizations in France; and as including state assistance to help promote Japanese exports. So we have quite a range of definitions of industrial policy.

Second, we have to look at the importance of history regarding industrial policy. Here I suppose the parallel would be the situation in the 1930s, both in the United States and in Western Europe, where crisis and collapse made the need to do something seem so overwhelming, both ideologically and politically. It is interesting to speculate about what parallels might exist between the present circumstances or the circumstances that we have seen the past five years or so and some of those of the early 1930s.

A third question is, Why adopt industrial policy? One could say—as Professor Johnson does—that to a degree at least it is part of the political culture in Japan. In France one could suggest that there is a long étatist tradition, although the Zysman and Cohen paper tends to downplay this particular factor. One could suggest that industrial policy grows out of necessity as a second, an alternative, explanation; that is, out of the perceived or real need for protectionism in times of economic crises (the parallel again with the early 1930s); out of perceived greater economic interdependence, worldwide; out of the political need to rationalize, structure, and control both labor and capital, which may be seen in certain instances as getting out of hand.

Fourth, what about the institutional structure of industrial policy? On one hand, industrial policy can be structured through state governments as in Germany and as planning institutions have grown at the state level in the United States. On the other hand, industrial policy in France is concentrated in the central government and in Japan is concentrated in bureaucratic industrial relations.

A fifth question, again very briefly, is, Does industrial policy work? We need measures of evaluation. To what extent does it work or fail? Are we using political or economic criteria to determine whether it works or not? Does it work better in some countries than in others and, if so, precisely why?

Sixth, who benefits? What are the political purposes of industrial policy? Is it possible that one can sort out the economic from the political purposes of industrial policy in this country and others and find out who benefits, who loses? Are there hidden agendas with which we have not yet even dealt?

Seventh, the whole argument over industrial policy involves issues that go beyond industrial policy. They have to do with the structure of American society, with the nature of our political system. What are the relations, for example, between an industrial policy in the economic sphere and the necessity that often accompanies it, at least historically, for the corporatized organization of society in the sociopolitical sphere? What about the role of the state and the extent of state power or the degree to which we or other societies wish to become bureaucratic state structures?

Finally, with regard to future work in this area, we have a good deal of work to do, first, to define our terms. What precisely do we mean by industrial policy, both in terms of different historical contexts and in terms of cross-national differences?

Second, we have to be clear about the criteria we use. There really is not a common outline, a common framework that we can use to evaluate industrial policies, their successes and failures, how they work precisely in different countries, although Professor Johnson again has done yeoman work in beginning to do these kinds of things. We need comparative indexes, comparative measures for evaluating industrial policy.

Once we have these economic and political measures for evaluating industrial policy, then we will be in a position to discuss it much more rationally and to evaluate it much more precisely.

213

Part Three
Industrial Policy and the
Major U.S. Parties

Jack F. Kemp

In a democracy, politics and economics are inextricably linked together. There is no way to discuss politics without discussing the economic climate; and, conversely, there is no way to discuss economics without discussing politics.

Indeed, the economy itself is today submerging the debate over a national industrial policy. The recovery that began in 1983—some would point to the late summer of 1982—has reduced that debate. (It is interesting that when economies are in contraction to involve oneself in the economy is awfully tempting.) In fact, one need not go back just to the debate over national industrial policy; one could go back to the late 1970s when all sorts of new ideas were coming forth from critics of the American economy.

A candidate for president in 1980 advised the country that what was needed both to reduce inflation and to expand the economy was a combination of monetary and fiscal policy simultaneously applied to the problem of stagflation—which could bring us out of inflation and bring down interest rates while increasing output, production, and investment—and to the private sector's ability to create jobs, which of course is a high social as well as economic goal.

To say that the recovery has suppressed the issue of a national industrial policy is not to suggest that the recovery is perfect, that it has reached every industry, or that it has reached all of the people who need desperately to be brought into the mainstream of our national economy. We have made a beginning, I think, in this country toward really astounding the critics, astounding our European allies. Witness that in the last year and a half 6.5 million new jobs have been created in the private sector without any degree of inflation. That occurrence was, of course, not only astounding to the French but also to many other peoples in Europe. And the French government announced that it was going to look for a reduction in the tax burden and a less regulatory climate for industry; and perhaps it could even come to the point at which it would denationalize some of the industries and banks that had been nationalized in the early 1980s.

Such is the powerful influence upon the world economy that the United States has had. Again, it is not perfect. Even in 1984 there were those who suggested that the economy was growing so strongly that we needed to take steps to slow it down lest it engender some inflation by bidding up prices as too many men and women went back to work. I frankly find that view to be barbaric in terms of the social condition it would impose upon our country, and it is bad economics as well.

I noticed in *Newsweek* that Brian Mulroney, upon taking the oath of office in Canada as the new prime minister and being asked about the big budget deficit in Canada, gave this answer: The way out of this massive deficit that we have inherited is not by any little cut or any cosmetic change. The only way out of this deficit, he said, is through economic growth—by creating new wealth, by unfettering the private sector, and by deregulation.

That is the classic prescription for an economy suffering from low rates of economic growth and high rates of inflation. Simplistic? Well, to be sure, in a short time frame it is simplistic. But behind that simple truth is a profound idea—that the source of all the wealth is people, not governments; that the way out of poverty is not through transfer payments, although transfer payment income is necessary to those who are suffering from unemployment or some problem in the economy that they themselves and their families cannot meet. But the only way out of poverty is through a job, through access to income, through access to property, through access to wealth. And the source of all wealth creation, again, is not some inanimate object, the government; it is people.

It is not even business. The source of wealth for a business is an individual man or woman whose mind is unfettered and who has the talent, the creativity, and the ingenuity to come up with new ideas. That candidate in 1980, Ronald Reagan, suggested that we should reduce the burden on the private sector's ability to grow and that we should match our reduction in tax rates and other impediments in fiscal policy by restoring a monetary policy in which the value of the dollar is predictable over time.

So it seems to me again the classic prescription, which was not just set forth by Ronald Reagan but was a readoption of an earlier prescription for economic growth in the United States, is that sound money is predicated upon measuring the value of the currency against what the currency will buy; upon less regulation of the private, entrepreneurial spirit and the enterprise of a country; upon reducing the tax burden or implementing a tax policy that will encourage working and saving—that is, labor and capital; and upon a fiscal policy that is prudent and responsible. This prescription is, of course, something that this president and his administration and those who on a bipartisan basis supported him suggested was the way out of an endemic inflation.

In 1979 we were told that inflation was here to stay. Some economists on the Left said that the only answer to inflation was an incomes policy and wage and price guidelines, which of course are euphemisms for controlling individual workers as well as those businesses that would have to succumb to such guidelines.

218

We were also told that democracy causes inflation. I can remember famous *Fortune* articles in 1978 and 1979 in which a group of conservative and liberal economists sat around a table and suggested not only that inflation was here to stay but that the cause of inflation was democracy itself. People just wanted to live too well. Of course, they told us that in 1979 when the after-tax income of the Buffalo steelworker or the Buffalo auto worker or the Colorado farmer had been steadily diminished by an inflation that was eroding the value and the purchasing power of our currency coupled with a tax system that was pushing both labor and capital, workers and entrepreneurs, into tax brackets that before had been reserved for only those in the very highest income levels.

Then a candidate for president came along and said that the answer to this situation was simultaneously to restore a sound monetary policy and to reduce the heavy burden of taxes that was an impediment to expanding the economy. This, in fact, was a restatement of John F. Kennedy's statement in the early 1960s that the major roadblock to full employment for America was the heavy burden of taxes on the backs of the American people.

It is interesting, despite all of the conventional criticism, despite all of the orthodoxy in Washington, despite all those who said cutting tax rates would be inflationary, that we ended up in late 1982, throughout 1983, and on into 1984 watching an economy really defy the—I'm now mixing my definition of classic—recent orthodoxy of the Keynesian school. In 1978 Kenneth Arrow, before he went to Stanford, said that we liberal, activist economists in the world are terribly discouraged because we cannot reconcile full employment and price stability.

And here we are in an economy with high rates of growth, without inflation, creating about 4.2 million new jobs per year. We are entering an age in which, some people predict, we will shed our industrial skin and begin new industrial expansion. We could very well be looking at a moment in the near future in our own economy in our own country in which we could actually achieve the goals of the Humphrey-Hawkins bill or the 1946 full-employment legislation, which is full employment without inflation.

That is still the goal for our national policy. And the best way of achieving that goal is to reform the tax code further, not, as Mr. Mondale has suggested, to put on a surtax as a way of reducing the deficit in 1989. The 1984 campaign is the first that I have known in history—at least in my political history—in which a president or a candidate for presidency offered to raise tax rates on everybody apparently above the income of $25,000 and put a surtax on people above $60,000 and another surtax on people above $100,000. All over the country—and I have campaigned all over the country—I found few candidates for Congress in the Democratic party embracing the candidate much less his tax policy.

It reminded me of 1972 when a Democratic congressman from Ohio was called on the phone by George McGovern's campaign manager who said, "Mr. Congressman, I've got some good news for you. Our candidate is coming to Ohio." And the Democratic congressman said, "That's great news. That's terrific for Ohio. I'll be in Louisiana, but I wish you well." The manager said, "Well, wait a minute, Mr. Congressman, we haven't told you on what day Mr. McGovern is coming to Ohio." And the congressman replied, "Whatever day McGovern comes to Ohio, I will be in Louisiana."

We had a policy, which George McGovern prescribed, to cut taxes for everybody under $17,000; it was called the Demogrant Program. McGovern dropped so precipitously in public opinion that after the campaign was over I ended up debating him, a very decent and honorable senator from South Dakota, at Vanderbilt University. I can remember asking him why he thought he was so unpopular as a result of the 1972 Demogrant Program. He said that he never realized there were so many people earning less than $17,000 in America who someday hoped to earn more than $17,000 a year.

And that is one of the basic flaws in the Mondale tax plan. The president has suggested, well, wait a minute. Here we are enjoying an economic recovery that is atypical—atypical to the extent that capital spending is up three times the normal recovery. Capital investment in new electronic equipment and high technology is up by 50 percent more than at any other point in a post–World War II recovery. Six and a half million new jobs have developed in a year and a half. Productivity is rising at 3.3 percent per year, whereas the total productivity increase in the economy of the United States from 1970 to 1979 was 0.1 percent. And there has been an entrepreneurial boom, not enough for me and certainly not enough for any of us who are looking to the economy to create jobs, but 6,000 new business starts in 1983 alone. More minorities are going into business than ever before. More women are going into business than ever before. We need more of that.

What brought the recovery about? Reducing the capital gains rate in 1978. Bill Steiger, the author, suggested that we cut the capital gains rate—I think the top rate was 49 percent in 1978. We cut it almost in half—broad bipartisan support for that—and it has brought, I think, an explosion of entrepreneurship, an explosion of venture capital, and an expansion of the equity capital so necessary to create and foster new jobs.

In the thirties the Republican party talked austerity, sacrifice, raising taxes, Smoot-Hawley tariffs, slowing down the economy apparently to finance budget deficits. And the Democratic party was talking hope at least; for whatever reason, they were talking about expanding the growth of the economy. Of course, that growth was much on the demand side.

In 1980 and 1984 the Republican party was the one opening up and thinking about our responsibilities to liberalize the trading climate of the world and to restore the classic prescription for monetary policy: to recognize that we live not in a partial economy but in a global economy. We should tie the dollar to some commodity, the value of which one can predict over a long time. Now, however, people on both sides of the aisle are talking about a new Bretton Woods international monetary system with more stable exchange rates.

I am convinced that the greatest industrial policy for the United States is to get interest rates down to single digit levels and to do that through monetary reform. The best tax policy to encourage industrialization for America would be enacting something like Bradley-Gephardt or Kemp-Kasten or some simplification of the code, broadening the tax base, and bringing down the corporate tax rate to 30 or 25 percent.

With the combination of a personal income tax rate at 25 percent and a corporate income tax rate at 25 or 30 percent coupled with efforts to protect the working poor with some modification of a flat tax approach, again in a climate of sound monetary policy and an international monetary and trading system— the linchpin of which would be a dollar backed by something of value—we would see an industrial renaissance in the United States. We would also clearly see a worldwide renaissance of economic growth, which is really what the third world needs.

We export 40 percent of all our goods to third world countries. It is desperately important that they get access to American markets. I applaud Gary Hart's resisting the protectionism and the neo-isolationism that crept into the Democratic party in the late 1970s and the early 1980s. He's been very forthright about it. I frankly think my party now represents the best chance of expanding that trading climate, opening up markets, restoring a currency that can be competitive against other currencies, and bringing down interest rates and tax rates even further.

In fact, the wonderful thing about this debate is that there will continue to be a clash of these ideas and that the Republican party will receive a mandate to bring this country once more out of the era of limits and to open up an era of illimitable opportunity, not only in this country but throughout the industrialized world.

Gary Hart

I would like to open my remarks by making four or five observations and revise those and expand upon them, if I may, in the context of the subject of this conference, namely, industrial policy.

The first observation is that we have no industrial policy. What we have in this country is a catchall, grab bag, crazy quilt, hodge-podge of individual policies that relate sometimes to industries at large and sometimes to individual companies in those industries. But that hodge-podge is based on self-interest and not on the national interest. And it is not sufficient for a leading industrial democracy to enter the eighties and nineties in competition with other, more organized industrial societies.

Second, while the world turns, old ideologies produce irrelevant debates. I will come back and describe what I mean by that observation.

Third, those old debates obscure new realities, very few of which, unfortunately, are being addressed in Congress or in the political arena this year. Those realities in some respects represent revolutions, and I think we had better begin to pay attention to them.

Fourth, the new realities require, in my judgment, structural changes. Macro policies just do not address those new realities.

Finally, let us at least have an industrial strategy even if we do not have an industrial policy.

Now, what is the situation in this country today? We are debating or discussing in this conference and there has been a lot written and said about whether or not America needs an industrial policy. Let us look at what we have. Through various tax expenditures, tax reductions, so-called incentives or writeoffs, or whatever one wants to call it, about $300 billion directly or indirectly goes into a whole variety of industrial activities in this country as of 1980 and beyond. That figure represents about 14 percent of this country's gross national product. But let us see how these resources are being allocated. In 1980, for example, out of that more than $300 billion, the government sponsored about $6 billion plus in a ship-building program, a program, by the way, that I think we need. That, however, is in contrast to less than $1 billion going into the American auto industry.

Now concerning national priorities, do we really think, in terms of this government's resources or the society's resources, that the ship-building program is six times more important than autos? I doubt it. In the same year the government allocated about $5 billion in public resources for research and development in nuclear power, and at the same time it allocated less than $1 billion in coal research for coal liquefaction and gassification. Do we really believe as a society that nuclear power is five times more important than the possibility of synthetic fuels based on coal?

In that same year public resources up to $0.5 billion were going into the timber industry, while our government was allocating zero public resources to semiconductors.

Finally, in that same year of 1980 we allocated five times more of public research and development funds to commercial fisheries than we did to new steel technologies. So we have an industrial policy; but it is about as ad hoc as any modern nation has ever undertaken, and it frankly makes little, if any, sense. Right now we have massive tax incentives for mergers and acquisitions —which presumably fall under Congressman Kemp's definition of growth, but I do not consider them productive investments—and no real requirements for tax breaks to go into productive investment. Rather we have, under both Democratic and Republican administrations, an industrial policy of bailouts and handouts.

I opposed the Chrysler bailout as I did most of the others. It was not an industrial policy; it was an ad hoc response to an immediate, urgent need. The Democrats— and I have been critical of my own party in this regard—have been a party that responds to companies, individual companies if not whole industries, that find themselves in trouble primarily because of international competition, poor management, or poor agreements among management and labor. They find themselves on the threshold of disaster; and they come, as someone once said, as a dinosaur to the public doorstep; and they say, "Feed me, or I'll die and stink up the place."

Well, that has been our industrial policy through much of the post–World War II years. But while the world turns, those in the political arena, I'm afraid—and I blame both political parties and the ideologues in both parties— are debating old ideologies that produce irrelevant debates. Right now, for example, we are fundamentally treating ourselves, too many of us, to a debate between Republicans and Democrats that is essentially between traditional laissez-faire economics and what is becoming increasingly known as redistributionism. I have been extremely critical of my own party for its desire increasingly to debate how we are going to divide the pie without any attention, or any creative attention, to how to make that pie grow larger.

And if there was one central theme that permeated the nomination process in 1984 in the Democratic party it was between those two world views—or economic, domestic views, at least—whether we should divide a stagnant economic pie more fairly or whether we ought to have policies to

223

make that pie grow (and grow not just for its own sake, if I may say so).

Growth—as Jack says that capital is people, I say that growth is not a worthy goal in and of itself for a great nation. It is growth for a purpose, growth for opportunity for those who are well and able bodied and for providing the resources for those in our society who genuinely cannot look out for themselves. That's the purpose of growth. Capital formation in the abstract does not mean a thing. And growth in the abstract does not mean a thing unless it meets at least those two needs.

One of the other parts of the irrelevant debate is that we are now in competition between old industries—namely traditional manufacturing—and new industries—namely, technology. For our thanks, those of us in the Democratic party who have focused upon the emergence of the postindustrial economy have gotten to be called Atari Democrats and lord knows what else, as if to acknowledge the emergence of a whole new economy was somehow to suggest that we could let the old economy go. Nothing could be further from the truth, and I want to come back to the synergism that must exist between that old manufacturing base and the new technologies.

There is also an irrelevant debate between those who fly the banner of opportunity and, again in the abstract, growth and those who want to talk only about social justice—that somehow this society has to choose one or the other. I think other industrial democracies in the world have proved that there is not such a tradeoff or competition but that one does not achieve social justice unless one has that growth and that opportunity. As I've already said, however, just having growth and opportunity without meeting society's needs to be a just society is to abandon a moral commitment of people to themselves.

There has also been a very counterproductive or unproductive debate from the 1970s between environmental health and economic health. I think that debate is nonsense. Somebody pays for pollution. The air, the water, and the soil of this nation are not free goods. Somebody pays. The last data I saw showed that in 1977 dirty air cost this country $11 billion in medical bills, in medication, in hospitalization, primarily on the part of those who could not look after themselves, the young and the elderly. Somebody paid. The question is the shifting of the burden of paying for cleaning up or leaving dirty that environment.

Finally, there has been a debate, which I think is also old and outdated, driven by old ideologies, between, on the one hand, central planning and governmental allocation of capital resources (in terms of industries, picking the winners if you will) and, on the other hand, the law of the jungle (removing all barriers and all controls and letting dog eat dog). If you want to drive the new entrepreneurs that Jack is talking about into the ground and destroy that entrepreneurship, the best way to guarantee that is to take all controls off, all regulations off, and completely abandon any kind of assistance in capital formation, in training of a work force that a central government can provide. But that does not mean we have to have some new, modern version of the Reconstruction Finance Corporation, a notion that a very brilliant individual, Felix Rohatyn, has proposed but with which I strongly disagree.

Then, in terms of the old debate, maybe the old debate came to an end in the early seventies—1971 or whenever it was that Richard Nixon declared himself Keynesian. Where I disagree with Congressman Kemp is that I think what we've seen—the finance or fuel of this recent recovery from a very, very deep recession in 1981, a disastrous recession—was in fact classic Keynesianism in terms of the massive 1981 tax cuts and the massive increase in government spending dedicated primarily to one government agency, many of us believe the biggest and worst bureaucracy, namely the Department of Defense.

So let us leave those irrelevant debates behind and let us focus on how those debates are obscuring what the new realities are, and let me run over what those realities are. First of all, the emergence of international competition; we cannot shove that aside, and we cannot pretend it does not exist. It is a new phenomenon, a product of the late 1960s and the decade of the 1970s, and as yet this nation has yet to respond to it. I do not think we're responding to it today in any way or to any extent that we need to do.

Second is the conservation of energy. Can anyone in this room remember in the last three and a half or four years a major speech—or any speech, for that matter—by the president of the United States on the issue that dominated the public debate throughout the 1970s, namely, energy? Not one. Our energy policy today, if we have one, is the so-called free market. Well, the free market is wonderful while demand is down, but let us see what happens when demand goes up and what that does to this nation's economy given that we have a four-year regional war in the Persian Gulf, an Islamic revolution that threatens to expand that war almost any day, and an immediate possibility of the cutoff of oil supplies.

Let us have a real international renaissance and recovery and see what that does to oil demand, see what that does to oil prices, and see what that does to our recovery. It is going to choke the recovery off—that is what. We do not have an energy policy today and until we do, we will be in serious trouble.

We have to identify another revolution, which is the postindustrial revolution. We do have a mixed economy. We do not have an economy any longer solely or primarily based on manufactured goods. We have an increasingly technological, information, communication, and finance economy, and we ought to have policies to address that. We have to acknowledge the emerging North-South opportunity and danger.

While we are transfixed by the continuing hostility between ourselves and the Soviets, the East-West conflict, and have a foreign policy that seeks to export that conflict worldwide, we are neglecting the emergence of the third world. We do not have policies to take advantage of the opening markets in

Latin America, Africa, and Southeast Asia. Until we do, we will not have long-term economic growth in this country.

Let me just add one final factor in the new realities, and that is the nuclear arms area. We are entering a crucial period of some thirty-six to forty-eight months in which technology may outrun diplomacy. This factor has little to do with industrial policy, but I think we ought to abandon the luxury of thinking that anytime we please we can resume bargaining on controlling the spread of nuclear weapons, whether the subject is the Cruise missile range and technology, the accuracy of our land-based systems, or the expansion of the nuclear arms race into space. I believe we are getting close to a position in which we do not have the luxury of diplomacy and we cannot negotiate agreements to control the spread of that nuclear capability.

The new realities in my judgment require structural changes in thinking. Macro policies, tax cuts, fiscal policy, and monetary policy do not address the new agenda in this country, namely, a deteriorating and declining infrastructure. We have no policy in this country to rebuild the public facilities and public assets.

Yet U.S. Steel two or three years ago spent $25 million diverting its heavy trucks around bridges in Pittsburgh because the bridges could not bear the weight. Well, that is not an economy that is growing and expanding. We'd better have a policy to rebuild this nation's public facilities, or we won't have long-term growth.

We ought to have policies to guarantee U.S. leadership in trade and technology. This is not going to happen accidentally, and it will not happen just because this economy, at least for the time being, is expanding. Unless we have trade policies, unless we have policies to foster American leadership in technology, we will not be guaranteed that kind of role in the world in the eighties and nineties.

I think, and Congressman Kemp thinks, we need a massive overhaul of this country's tax system. That is a profound structural problem, and the old debate and the old ideologies are not addressing it. I think the new leaders of both parties are moving close together in terms of what ought to be done, at least in outline terms.

We do not have a real urban revitalization policy or program in this country. There have, of course, been discussions about enterprise zones, and I welcome them. I have my own version of those as Congressman Kemp does. But that is only one step in what must be a national policy and program to rebuild this nation's cities. I think we obviously have to rebuild our industrial base, our manufacturing base, if for no other reason than national security.

People say, well, maybe we don't need a steel industry or an auto industry. Of course we do. Can you imagine getting involved in a conflict in Europe or in the Persian Gulf in which we had to contract with the French or the Japanese to produce our planes and tanks? Of course not. If for no other reason, we need the ability to fabricate steel and to mold that steel into weapons of war and defense.

I also think, by the way, that program of reform has to include military reform; and we are not even close to that. The institutions that defend this country need reforming badly.

Let me outline what I think an industrial policy or an industrial strategy should include at the very least. What I would call industrial modernization agreements, negotiated by the president of the United States industry by industry, steel, autos, and the rest, involving management, labor, and private capital with the government's playing the role, if necessary, of guaranteeing private loans. And those agreements ought to be industry wide, and not company specific.

We need a worker training program built around what I would propose as an individual training account, much like an individual retirement account. The employer and his employee could set dollars aside for continual reeducation and training of that worker.

I think we need to liberate institutional capital. We have hundreds of billions of dollars in pension funds and other resources that are not being used for productive investment. If we could liberalize the state and federal laws, that is an enormous pool of capital for productive investment. We need a national research and development program or policy. We do not have that today. And laissez-faire, traditional economics are not going to bring it about.

I have mentioned the tax system, which needs to reward investment, not mergers and acquisitions and not conglomerations, but productive investment, modern plants, modern equipment, and worker training. I think this country must trade much more aggressively than we do. It is not enough to resist protectionism. We need a trade policy based upon a principle, which I and others have proposed, called national treatment, particularly with the Japanese, that enables us to be a fair and aggressive trading partner.

Finally, I think we need that synergism between manufacturing and technology. Technology is not an enemy of manufacturing and vice versa. In fact, the best consumers of modern technology, the computers and so on, ought to be the steel and auto industries and others.

Those are some elements of what I think ought to be an industrial policy for this nation that avoid the shoals of central government control and planning on the one hand, and the shoals of total abdication of government responsibility, on the other.

Discussion

MARVIN L. ESCH, American Enterprise Institute: The question is, Should the industrial policies that you have enunciated have to go through Congress; and, if so, will they?

SENATOR HART: I was trying not to lay out in any kind of detail an industrial policy but to outline elements of what I would call an industrial strategy, some of which would require congressional action, some of which would not. Clearly, to create, for example, what I call individual training accounts, we would need some changes in the tax law to permit or to provide the incentives for workers and managers to set aside a few dollars of that worker's check matched by the manager and to qualify that for tax deferral or tax reduction. That would require some legislation.

The so-called industrial modernization agreements would require very little, probably some comprehensive federal capability of underwriting large-scale private loans for the specific purpose of auto or steel modernization. Frankly, the Chrysler program, which I opposed primarily because it was company specific, would be the pattern for that. That would probably require some federal authority as well.

Other elements of the strategy, making pension and institutional investment funds available for entrepreneurship and new capital formation, would require some changes in the law.

Whether such a strategy can happen or not, I don't know. I think the more recently elected officials of both parties are a lot closer together on this agenda, which is relatively nonideological, than they are on the old, outdated agenda that I mentioned.

MR. ESCH: Congressman Kemp.

REPRESENTATIVE KEMP: Well, I would like to comment briefly by saying that, first of all, the problems we were reflecting upon in the late 1970s were in large part caused by government intervention, and to criticize that intervention is not to suggest, as Senator Hart has suggested, that my position is laissez faire, not at all. But it is to suggest that we can be critical of a government that

228

got us into the position in which we had to bail out Chrysler.

Gary Hart's criticism of the bailout of Chrysler is based on the fact that the government did not bail out General Motors, Ford, and American Motors as well. At least that is what he said in his debate with Walter Mondale. It seems to me that Chrysler would never have been bailed out had we carried out policies in the 1970s that would have been procapital formation, not anticapital formation, proworker, not antiworker.

And I would suggest that to put those auto workers in Buffalo or in Detroit in 45 percent marginal income tax brackets not only had an impact upon the lives of those auto workers and their families, it also had an impact upon the cost of labor. The cost of labor in the United States has risen so rapidly that, as I understand it, a Japanese auto or steel company can get a dollar of wages after taxes to the worker for about $1.25 in pretax income; but at Bethlehem Steel in my area of Lackawanna or in auto factories in Buffalo it takes $1.90 to get a dollar of after-tax income to the worker. So the very policies that got us into the problems of the seventies are the ones being advocated in some postindustrial age. We are not in any postindustrial age. We are going through a shedding of our industrial skin, and we should apply technology to basic industry and encourage it through capital formation and lower interest rates, not go back to more of the same that got us into the mess in the first place.

MR. ESCH: Senator Hart, I think you deserve an answer.

SENATOR HART: Well, I do not think I've advocated here today going back to where we were before. In fact, my position is specifically different from going back to where we were before. As popular and convenient as it is to blame the government for everything that went wrong in the sixties and seventies, that overlooks that some companies are mismanaged; and there are mismanaged companies in this country.

REPRESENTATIVE KEMP: Why bail them out, then?

SENATOR HART: Well, precisely.

MR. ESCH: The next question.

VOICE: I'd like to pose a question to Senator Hart. One of the intriguing comparisons you mentioned at the beginning of your talk was, I believe, that the federal government spent some hundreds of millions of dollars to support the timber industry and spent nothing to support the semiconductor industry. I'd like to ask you, during that period of time, which industry do you think was more successful and what lesson do you draw from that answer?

229

SENATOR HART: It depends, I guess, on how you define success. If you mean in terms of growth and share of the marketplace in the world, clearly the latter, semiconductor industry. But, frankly, that is not guaranteed for all time because we all know what is going on in the world today; we are losing that market share, and other countries are catching up and surpassing us. We have a real problem, for example, in converting new inventions in the high-technology area into the market.

A lot of things that are being invented in this country are being produced elsewhere and marketed elsewhere, and the share of the market is being enjoyed by the Japanese, the West Germans, the French, and others.

Now, you can just say, well, that's too bad. I think it is worse than too bad. I think we ought to do something about it. Now, that does not necessarily mean a new government agency or anything of that sort. But there ought to be some way for that new entrepreneur not just to come up with a breakthrough in semiconductors or whatever but also to have some incentive and some assistance in getting that invention into the marketplace, not just for the entrepreneurs' sake but for this nation's sake.

REPRESENTATIVE KEMP: That entrepreneur does not need a government to tell him or her—

SENATOR HART: I didn't say that.

REPRESENTATIVE KEMP: Well, I'm just suggesting that you keep responding to the question on both sides of the issue. For instance, we are talking about the lumber industry versus the semiconductor industry, and you are saying that we are losing the markets in semiconductors when the evidence is contrary to that.

We are not losing the market to the Japanese in semiconductors. While they are going for a 256 RAM chip, we are moving toward chips that will expand at least by 1 billion times the capacity of a 256 RAM chip. Very frankly, it is obvious that one cannot make massive loans to industry without targeting. Someone has to do the targeting, Gary, and I would suggest it is going to be some agency or some new Reconstruction Finance Corporation, which I applaud you in publicly saying you're against; but who is going to do it?

Look at the synfuel program. Eastman Kodak goes to Tennessee, finances a project all in the private sector to produce synfuel at $30 a barrel. And we loan money to Mobil or Union Oil to produce synfuels at $70 a barrel because it was chosen by the Synfuel Corporation. It should be abandoned. We do not need to make massive subsidies to oil companies to produce in the public sector what could be done in the private sector.

MR. ESCH: Thank you, Congressman. Senator, do you have any response?

SENATOR HART: I don't remember ever saying anything about massive loans to anybody.

REPRESENTATIVE KEMP: That was number one in your industrial strategy.

MR. ESCH: Thank you. Next question.

VOICE: I'd like to ask each of the gentlemen where they disagree with the three major points that they disagree with the other on.

MR. ESCH: Congressman Kemp, you're first. At least one of the three points. Where is the major disagreement between you and Senator Hart?

REPRESENTATIVE KEMP: It is really tough to figure out what the new industrial strategy is because, on one hand, it's liberal trade and, on the other hand, it's jawboning the Japanese. On one hand, it's not picking winners and losers; but, on the other hand, point one in the national industrial strategy of Gary Hart is loan guarantees to businesses. That used to be called trickle-down economics and corporate welfare from the Left.

Today that is established Democratic policy. We have seen a manifestation of that in the synfuel program, which is not working. It is difficult to put a handle on where we disagree, except that I personally do not think it is laissez-faire economics to suggest that we should simplify the tax code, broaden the tax base, and encourage both labor and capital by bringing down the tax rates on corporate and personal income and by establishing lower interest rates.

What would be better for autos and steel would be to have a competitive currency against other currencies in the world, low interest rates to form the capital that is necessary over the long run to reindustrialize, say, steel and make it more competitive. I cannot tell whether Gary wants to lend money to the company or have it channeled through an RFC, but he's against that. Where's the money going to come from if you don't establish growth as your first condition of economic policy? To suggest that growth is somehow antisocial because it is not targeted seems to me to beg the question of how one can help the poor if the country is becoming as poor as it was in the late 1970s.

MR. ESCH: Senator, he may not have described your program quite accurately, so we will give you some time to suggest not only how you disagree with where Jack Kemp says you are but also what your own program is.

SENATOR HART: I think Congressman Kemp is having difficulty here because we are not particularly speaking the same language.

I think the major difference, Marv, would be that Congressman Kemp

231

apparently believes—I'll come back to the misrepresentations of my views—
that growth solves all problems, and I don't believe so. What I am talking
about are specific steps to be taken not just by the federal government or
Congress but also by private managers, educational institutions and a lot of
others, and private lenders to achieve certain objectives that are not just social
justice.

I mentioned national security. Is there a guarantee, is there any kind of
guarantee that this country will be competitive in the 1990s in the fabrication
of steel and the molding of that steel into vehicles, autos transferrable to tanks
and planes? Not necessarily.

And I don't know what Congressman Kemp would do about that. I don't
know what his economic policy would be if, for example, even given
increased corporate tax cuts, the American automobile or steel industry cannot
compete, if increasingly diversified conglomerates reduce their market share
of autos and steel and leave this country without the productive capability to
defend itself and, as I say in the worst case, contract out with the French or
somebody else to build our tanks and planes, which is clearly not acceptable.

We have some overriding national interests that the marketplace does not
take account of, and national security is one of those.

MR. ESCH: All right. Next question, please.

VOICE: My question is for Congressman Kemp. To what extent do you think
the current growth in the U.S. economy is a function of financing the largest
budget deficit in U.S. history? What kinds of short-term as well as long-term
consequences will result from this budget deficit? And the last question is
whether you think growth alone will get us out of the current deficit.

REPRESENTATIVE KEMP: Well, let me take the last part of your question first.
Growth is essential to reducing deficits. That has been proved in the last two
years. The only way the deficit came down in 1984 from a projected $230
billion course that was going to give us a $250 billion deficit in the year 1989
and has come down to about $170 billion or less in 1984 was through a very
strong economic recovery in 1983 and 1984, A.

B, I don't know what your growth pattern is, but mine is a lot higher than
3 percent, which is what many economists, the Congressional Budget Office,
the Office of Management and Budget, and Walter Mondale all think is about
the optimum amount of growth this economy can sustain without inflation.

If the supply siders have contributed anything to economic debate in
America, it is that growth is essential for all the social reasons that Gary
mentioned, as well as for economic reasons. Then growth is also essential for
the deficit. I think that the path we are on, although sustaining in the
intermediate period a high nominal deficit, is not so hysterical as to cause us to

follow the prescription of the national Democratic party in 1984 to raise taxes.

So if we grew at 5 to 6 percent per annum throughout 1987 and 1988, we would see by 1988 a budget generally in equilibrium.

I repeat, we cannot get America out of the red by putting American people in the red. The policies prescribed for the economy in 1984 by the president are a lot closer to getting the American people out of the red than those that have been prescribed by Walter Mondale.

One footnote is that I do not think the tax laws should be used to try to control inflation, as my distinguished opponent does. I do not think that government should intervene with tax policies such as those promoted by people who believe in a national industrial policy. I do not think that such intervention would do anything other than involve the federal government or a federal agency in the wage contracts of the auto workers in Buffalo, New York. And I think that those workers would resist that as they are resisting higher taxes at this point from the Democratic party.

MR. ESCH: Your response, Senator? Congressman Kemp suggests he is against interventionist policy, but also he's suggesting that growth will in large measure take care of the debt problem.

SENATOR HART: Well, I wish what he proposes were true. I'm afraid it is not, and I do not know very many serious economists—namely just about everybody outside the White House—who believe that growth alone will do the job. I think the key word in Mr. Kemp's formulation was "if"—if the economy in 1986 and 1987 and 1988 grows at a certain percent, then the budget will strike equilibrium. I don't know whether that means balance or it just means the deficits quit growing. In any case, I don't know. I have never heard the proposition seriously put forward that we are going to balance the budget by economic growth alone. I think all serious people in Congress and elsewhere believe that we have to change some fiscal policies.

MR. ESCH: Next? Yes.

VOICE: I wondered if Mr. Kemp would answer Mr. Hart's question about the causes of the recovery. Remember that Mr. Hart claimed that one of the causes of the recovery was the recovery from a deep recession that may have been partially induced by the policies of the current administration, that the timing of that recovery seems to be perhaps convenient.

Just to sound more balanced, I am going to ask a question of Mr. Hart, too. I wonder how your position on preservation of the auto industry for national security purposes is consistent with your opposition to the bailout of Chrysler.

MR. ESCH: I think he understands the question. Let's go back to Mr. Kemp first.

REPRESENTATIVE KEMP: Well, again, trying to put this in perspective, Senator Hart opposed cutting tax rates because they were inflationary. Now we are told in some of the editorial pages, one of which is in this town, that the deficit is leading the recovery and that it is a Keynesian, typical orthodox recovery. I don't believe that it is a typical Keynesian-led recovery. It is an investment-led recovery. It is a capital investment-led recovery.

Capital spending, according to Paul Volcker, who has testified before the Senate Finance Committee, said this recovery is atypical in that it is not consumer led. He points to the fact that consumer spending is rising at a slower rate than the growth in real GNP. Capital spending and predictions of capital spending in 1984 by most economists and most businessmen is in the high teens. This is a recovery that has been led by productivity increases not just by consumption. So I was suggesting in answer to Gary Hart that this is not a classic, or I should say an orthodox, Keynesian-led recovery. It has in large part been led by reducing the tax burden on both labor and capital.

If the growth in the economy is not high enough to bring down the deficit and to bring down unemployment, then what we need is another dose of lower tax rates, not a surtax on incomes above $60,000 or $70,000 or $100,000 in some mismanaged idea about how to soak the rich. The way to soak the rich, if that is what one is after, is to bring down the rates even further because the rich are paying higher taxes under Ronald Reagan as a percentage of the national revenue pie than they were paying in the last two decades and under the Carter-Mondale-Hart administration of 1979. I couldn't resist, Gary.

MR. ESCH: Gary, your question concerning Chrysler was about how one maintains the productive capability of a given sector without bailing out on a specific company basis. How does one choose what to support within that given sector?

SENATOR HART: Well, first of all, if the deficits do bring on a rerun of the 1981 recession, which many people predict (I hope it is not true), then I'll have occasion to talk about the Reagan-Kemp administration.

REPRESENTATIVE KEMP: What if the opposite is true, Gary?

SENATOR HART: What if? If frogs had wings, they wouldn't—

The industrial modernization agreement, which I have outlined here briefly, does not envision putting out a lot of—for that matter, even any— public capital. It is based upon private capital—if necessary publicly guaranteed on the grounds of national security, not because we want to favor the auto industry.

The auto industry is not like the turnip industry or any industry that does not centrally involve this country's national security. I think it is easy to define what industries are important to an industrial democracy, both economically and militarily. Steel and autos certainly are the leading two of those.

Now, if just cutting corporate taxes takes care of the auto industry and the steel industry, I'm all for it. But I do not think it will because those other countries are not standing still either. Frankly, in some respects their industries are better managed and better planned; and they anticipate future markets better than we do because a lot of their energies are not going into acquiring other companies and quarterly profits and things of that sort.

I am proposing that the president bring together management, labor, and capital—no Reconstruction Finance Corporation—to negotiate industry-wide the kind of agreement we had with Chrysler. My principal objection to the Chrysler agreement was that it was negotiated in desperation. It was in fact a single company bailout. It did not fit into any kind of long-term national interest that I could see except just to prevent that company from going under.

As we who debated the issue all know, the productive assets of Chrysler would have been brought up or were probably going to be bid for by other companies and managed productively and profitably. So the situation was not that all Chrysler workers were going to lose their jobs. As it was, I think 50,000 workers lost their jobs even in the reorganization.

REPRESENTATIVE KEMP: Sixty thousand.

SENATOR HART: There you are. Thank you.

REPRESENTATIVE KEMP: Sixty thousand lost jobs and lost wages.

MR. ESCH: We will have one last question, and then we will ask each gentleman to summarize as he responds to the question.

VOICE: Senator Hart, it is not clear to me that your assumption that more cooperation between business, labor, consumers, capital, and various economic factors is necessarily a good thing. In the Eastern European countries where there is centralized economic control, one has terrific cooperation between these factors. It seems to me that it is the competition between these factors that yields the information that prices contain in a free market, that allows entrepreneurs to direct capital efficiently. And it is precisely the rejection of competition and the endorsement of this cooperation that directs industrial policy advocates the wrong way.

SENATOR HART: I would just make several observations. First of all, cooperation among management, labor, and government in and of itself is not necessarily good. It does not necessarily lead to any desirable end. We compete, however, with other nations whose industries are increasingly nationally directed—we are involved in a competitive international economy, not just an economy in which General Motors competes with Chrysler and Chrysler with Ford, not just with Japanese and West German cars, but with world cars. We have to realize the world we are in.

I do not want central government planning. The kind of proposal I am talking about could be rejected by any side. If the president of the United States, a Ro^oseveltian president who has become so popular in this administration, brought together the managers of the American automobile industry, the leaders of United Auto Workers, and representatives of the private capital sector and laid out the proposed agreement—which, by the way, would not be devised by the president or the administration but would be cooperatively negotiated—any one of those people could look at it and say, "I don't like it. I'm going back to the old way of doing business."

We would rather negotiate three-year contracts and take our lumps. The president cannot order or force anybody to enter into one of these agreements. It would be done only if they all felt it were in their interest; and that would involve, in my judgment, concessions, and it would be getting something as well. For labor, in exchange for deferral of wages for a period while industries were being modernized, one could have, as I say, training agreements, individual training accounts. One could tie future wage demands to productivity or profitability of the industry. A whole lot of things can be done, but the government would not force this. It would merely propose it. Anybody could turn it down.

REPRESENTATIVE KEMP: The debate over a national industrial policy is so difficult today because it is being cast in a group of clichés. We want central planning or cooperation, but we are not going to force it on anybody. We do not want to bail out Chrysler, but we want to bail out the whole auto industry.

Look, what the auto industry needs and what the steel industry needs are lower interest rates. One can call this position laissez faire as a caricature; but my argument is that, if we continue to reform our monetary policy and bring down interest rates to where they would be normally associated with a dollar that maintained its value over a long time and if there were more stable exchange rates so that we could become more competitive in world markets, that would be beneficial not only to the world's economy but to auto and steel. What the auto industry needs is to sell about 10 million or 11 million domestic units. Auto sales are up. We need more sales. That increases the demand for steel and increases the ability of this country to put the auto and industrial sector of its economy back to work.

As far as I'm concerned, the Chrysler loan that Gary praises in terms of its cooperation and says we should apply across the board to the whole auto industry is a mistake or would have been a mistake when it was negotiated. Frankly, we lost a lot of jobs. Wages were sacrificed and I don't think the wages of the working men and women of America are causing inflation.

The cause of inflation is a monetary phenomenon. It is a decline in the value of the currency. We have to repair that. We have not accomplished that yet. The great task of the next administration is to restore stable, honest, sound fiduciary money that is guaranteed in terms of its purchasing power over a long time. Then we would have interest rates at 5 or 6 percent, not 15 or 16 percent. But the market can do a lot better allocation of the resources than can any central planner.

MR. ESCH: Let me express on behalf of the American Enterprise Institute and the people assembled two things: our appreciation that the gentleman on my left and the gentleman on my right came to join us. And let me assure you that we would look forward to having you back in many other such forums to get down to more explicit discussion on your differences, on your agreements, and on the future of our country.

Part Four
"Special Interests" and Industrial Policy

Introduction

This session of the conference was designed to examine the relation between special interest groups and industrial policy proposals. A paper by economist Mancur Olson of the University of Maryland presents a sophisticated analysis of the role and importance of special interest groups in the political and economic processes, which serves as the focal point for discussion.

Mancur Olson

The essay "Supply-Side Economics, Industrial Policy, and Rational Ignorance," by Mancur Olson seeks to "show how supply-side economics and industrial policy are largely outgrowths of right-wing and left-wing ideologies, respectively, and thus . . . also partly outgrowths of the typical citizen's rational ignorance about public affairs." Using the theories of "rational ignorance" and "collective action" developed in his earlier works, Olson examines the origins and significance of the ongoing debate about the government's role in the economy. He first reviews these theories, then outlines the basic characteristics of right-wing and left-wing ideologies, broadly defined, and evaluates them in light of the empirical evidence. Finding these ideologies deficient, he proposes alternative explanations both for the overall determinants of successful economic performance and for the underlying motivations of political choice and action. Finally, on the basis of conclusions drawn from the theories of rational ignorance and collective action and his analysis of the prevailing ideologies, Olson analyzes supply-side economics and industrial policy specifically.

"The centerpiece of ideological and political debate today is the dispute over the proper role of government." The "classical liberal" or "laissez-faire" Right, on one hand, argues that government intervention hinders economic development and individual freedom and that welfare programs reduce incentives to work and save. The Left, on the other hand, applauds government direction in the use of resources to ensure overall economic prosperity and "compassionate provision for the needs of those for whom the market does not provide an adequate income."

Despite an overwhelming preoccupation with this debate over the proper

241

role of government, Olson notes that surprisingly little attention has been given to "the question of how well each side in the debate succeeds or fails in explaining economic performance in different countries and historical periods." His evaluation, further, indicates that there is no clear relation between the role of government and economic success or failure. Given the absence of such "clear and conspicuous evidence" and the fact that "the evidence is usually not even systematically examined," he suggests that "something else" must be crucial for determining economic success and for guiding the motivations and decisions of politicians.

This "something else," maintains Olson, "is the nature of collective action in society." First, economic growth and dynamism can be directly tied to the level of "institutional sclerosis" in the society. Interest groups can serve their constituents either by encouraging an increase in the national income—a larger pie—or by achieving a redistribution of income to their members—a larger share of the existing pie. The benefits derived from a larger pie are shared equally by the whole society. A successful redistribution, however, permits members of the interest group alone to reap the full rewards of their efforts. As a result, cartelization and interest-specific lobbying are seen as means toward larger benefits for the interest group. The total pie, of course, may shrink as a consequence of the inefficiencies brought on by cartelization, but this loss is spread evenly throughout society. The interest group still achieves a net gain. As this type of activity spreads, however, society definitely loses. "Dense with organizations for collective action," the society becomes like "a china shop filled with wrestlers battling over the china and breaking far more than they carry away."

Second, the prevailing ideologies on the Left and Right do not provide a good indicator of the underlying motivation of each political group and certainly do not guide their actions once in office. "In long-stable societies like the United States," argues Olson, "most political activity is devoted to the purposes of the organized interest rather than to free markets or to the needs of the poor." Such ideologies are more often than not "devices for avoiding careful research and reflection," serving to direct the votes of the "rationally ignorant."

"Supply-side economics" and "industrial policy," continues Olson, are simply extensions of the right-wing and left-wing ideologies and should be evaluated in this light. Indeed, "these two extensions . . . are even better evidence for 'rational ignorance' than the ideologies themselves." Supply-side economics, particularly the version that proclaimed that tax cuts would be self-financing, lacked the support of most experts, and, in fact, failed to achieve this and other stated objectives. Yet public support for the supply-side ideology remains strong.

Many industrial policy proposals are similarly dubious or vague, leaving important political questions unresolved. Industrial policy measures, in addi-

242

tion, often ignore the logic of collective action itself. Would not many industrial policy structures simply strengthen the hand of organized interests? Industrial policy advocates "propose that the very foxes that have been stealing part of our productive wealth should be put in charge of the chicken coop."

Olson concludes that, despite some merits, most of the proposals on the Right and the Left do not offer sufficient bases to solve our economic problems precisely because they fail to confront "the powerful vested interests that mainly generated the problem."

Commentaries

Sidney Blumenthal. Opening the discussion, Sidney Blumenthal raises three specific criticisms against Mancur Olson's presentation. First, he questions the evidence used by Olson to show that the role of government is not the determining factor in economic performance. Blumenthal argues that this evidence is too general and too aggregated to have decisive meaning. "We should think not about government in general but government in particular" in terms of microeconomic policies when discussing industrial policy. Second, Blumenthal argues that the presence of large, strong organizations and extensive government involvement need not lead to economic stagnation and decline but on the contrary to growth and prosperity. Massachusetts, for example, has experienced an economic renaissance led by large universities, government funding, and organized interests, all in a heavily taxed environment. Third, he contends that Olson underestimates the role of real political needs in his evaluation of industrial policy and supply-side economic arguments. These proposals are not simply ideologies masking interest-specific demands. They reflect political agendas that transcend these specific interests.

Bruce Bartlett. In his commentary, Bruce Bartlett applauds Olson for providing a theoretical framework that explains why the U.S. political system cannot support industrial policies, whatever their hypothetical merits. Bartlett, however, then takes Olson to task for his "gratuitous attack on supply-side economics." Olson, he states, misunderstands both the origin and the purpose of supply-side economics. Supply-side economics evolved out of a Republican desire to reduce government's role directly, to cut taxes, and to balance the budget. A comprehensive program that attacked the welfare system, however, was politically unfeasible. Supply-side tax proposals sought, as a compromise, simply to raise revenues for a given level of taxes by fine tuning the marginal tax rates—hardly the outrageous proposition that many paint it. Further, that one can juggle the tax system to achieve larger revenues from a given tax level helps explain why Olson finds little evidence to support either ideological camp. The problem is that "the direct amount of revenue raised by

243

government is not necessarily a very good indicator of the cost . . . that that revenue-raising system imposes on the economy." Finally, Bartlett reiterates Blumenthal's contention that Olson gives undue credit to concrete political needs in his analysis.

William Schneider. Concluding the discussion, William Schneider notes that Olson's major contribution to political science was to show that political activity is not in anyone's rational self-interest. The fact of the matter, however, is that "political activity does exist and people do act in many ways that cannot be explained by their rational self-interest." Like the previous two commentators, Schneider stresses that the political component is a real and important entity that exists, in some respects, apart from the special interests that Olson finds predominantly responsible for political action. Schneider argues further that Olson fails to highlight important differences between supply-side economics and industrial policy and the ideologies that purportedly spawned their growth. Although the current debates often get bogged down by the old ideologies, both sides today seek to transcend the old "government versus antigovernment" debate. As the Kemp-Hart debate illustrates, ardent proponents of both positions share a common view of government as a problem solver that is here to stay. Supply siders see this role being played through traditional macroeconomic policies, particularly tax policies, while the industrial policy supporters envision a more direct, technocratic means of problem solving. Schneider concludes by noting that Olson's provocative notion—that the current big government/less government debate has little to do with the real problem, cartelization by special interest groups—is precisely the view of public opinion. Indeed the public has for this reason consistently voted "anti-Washington, anti-establishment in the past few elections including, somewhat paradoxically, the 1984 presidential election.

Supply-Side Economics, Industrial Policy, and Rational Ignorance

Mancur Olson

The Rational Ignorance of the Typical Citizen

Consider a typical citizen who is deciding how much time to devote to studying the policies or leadership of his or her country. The more time the citizen devotes to this matter, the greater the likelihood that a vote will be cast in favor of rational, effective policies and leadership for the country. This typical citizen will, however, get only a small share of the gain from the more effective policies and leadership: in the aggregate, the other residents of the country will get almost all the gains, so that the individual citizen does not have an incentive to devote nearly as much time to fact finding and to thinking about what would be best for the country as would be in the national interest. Each citizen would be better off if all citizens could be coerced into spending more time finding out how to vote to make the country better serve their common interests.

This point is most dramatically evident in national elections in a country as large as the United States. The gain to a voter from studying issues and candidates until it is clear what vote is truly in his or her interest is given by the difference in the value to the individual of the "right" election outcome compared with the "wrong" outcome, *multiplied by the probability a change in the individual's vote will alter the outcome of the election.* Since the probability that a typical voter will change the outcome of the election is vanishingly small, the typical citizen is usually "rationally ignorant" about public affairs.

Sometimes information about public affairs is so interesting or entertaining that acquiring it for these reasons alone pays; this situation appears to be the single most important source of exceptions to the generalization that *typical* citizens are rationally ignorant about public affairs. Similarly, individuals in a few special vocations can receive considerable rewards in private goods if they acquire exceptional knowledge of public goods. Politicians, lobbyists, journalists, and social scientists, for example, may earn more money, power, or prestige from knowledge of this or that public business. Occasionally exceptional knowledge of public policy can generate exceptional profits in stock exchanges or other markets. Withal, the typical citizen will find that his or her income and life chances will not be improved by zealous study of public affairs or even of any single collective good.

This fact—that the benefits of individual enlightenment about public goods are usually dispersed throughout a group or nation, rather than concentrated upon the individual who bears the costs of becoming enlightened—explains many other phenomena as well. It explains, for example, the "man bites dog" criterion of what is newsworthy. If the television newscasts were watched or newspapers were read solely to obtain the most important information about public affairs, aberrant events of little public importance would be ignored, and typical patterns of quantitative significance would be emphasized; when the news is, by contrast, for most people largely an alternative to other forms of diversion or entertainment, intriguing oddities and human-interest items are in demand. Similarly, events that unfold in a suspenseful way or sex scandals among public figures are fully covered by the media, whereas the complexities of economic policy or quantitative analyses of public problems receive only minimal attention. Public officials, often able to thrive without giving the citizens good value for their taxes, may fall over an exceptional mistake that is striking enough to be newsworthy. Extravagant statements, picturesque protests, and unruly demonstrations that offend much of the public they are designed to influence are also explicable in this way: they make diverting news and thus call attention to interests and arguments that might otherwise be ignored. Even some isolated acts of terrorism that are described as senseless can from this perspective be explained as effective means of obtaining the riveted attention of a public that otherwise would remain rationally ignorant.

The Logic of Collective Action

The rational ignorance of the typical voter is an example of the general logic of collective action. This logic is more readily evident when one considers organizations that lobby a government for special-interest legislation or that cooperate in the marketplace to obtain higher prices or wages. Consider, for example, organizations such as professional associations of physicians and lawyers, or labor unions, or trade associations of the firms in this or that industry, or farm organizations, or oligopolistic collusions. These are familiar examples of the many kinds of organizations, combinations, and collusions that either lobby the government or combine in the marketplace to change prices or wages.

Organizations of the kind I have listed can be understood only if one is aware of the difficulty of collective action. This difficulty arises because the benefit these organizations and groups provide their clients goes automatically to everyone in some group or category. If an association of firms wins a tariff or a tax loophole, that tariff raises the price for every firm that sells the commodity or product in question whether or not the firm contributed to the effort to win the tariff. A tax advantage or tax loophole also applies to all the firms or individuals in some category whether or not these firms or individuals supported the effort to win the tax advantage or loophole. Similarly, if one group of workers strikes to bring a higher wage in some factory or mine, all of the workers in the relevant factory or mine get the benefit of the higher wage whether or not they paid dues to the union or walked in the picket lines that made the strike successful. The same logic applies to the firms in any kind of cartel. I will not go into this subject further because I have written about it in some detail in *The Logic of Collective Action*,[1] and any reader can check the logic of my argument and the evidence supporting it in that book.

I need to use one part of this logic for purposes of the present argument, however. Since the benefits of collective action go to all people in some category or group, whether or not they supported the collective action or contributed money or time to it, no incentive for voluntary collective action in large groups exists, and voluntarily to work to obtain collective goods in the interest of one's group or class, at least in large groups, is not rational. One will get the benefits of whatever actions others undertake in any case; and, in large groups, the single individual or firm is not alone able to bring about the desired results. So large groups, at least, do not normally engage in collective action simply because of the benefits of the collective action.

The individuals in large groups do not voluntarily, in the absence of special arrangements I will consider in a moment, contribute time and money to organizations that would lobby or fix prices or wages for the same reason that the typical citizen remains rationally ignorant about many aspects of public affairs: an individual will get only a minuscule share of the benefits of anything he or she does to support an organization for collective action and only a minuscule share of any gain from doing a lot of research about which way to vote. In addition, the individual will automatically get the benefits of any contributions others make to any organization that will lobby or fix prices in his interest, and the individual will also inevitably get the benefits of any wiser public policies that result if others study the issues carefully and the nation chooses more rational public policies.

In large organizations that lobby or combine to fix prices or wages, there are special arrangements that explain why those organizations are able to attract dues-paying members. All large and lasting organizations for collective action have some special gimmicks, which I call *selective incentives*, that mainly account for their membership. The selective incentives are individualized benefits or punishments that induce individual firms or people to participate in, or help pay the costs of, collective action. They make up for the fact

247

that the collective goods or public goods that result from the collective action do not motivate rational individuals to engage in collective action. One example of a selective incentive is the element of compulsion inherent in the closed shop, the union shop, and the coercive picket line; but this example is only the most obvious. All of the large organizations for collective action that survive have some analagous arrangements. These arrangements are usually subtle, and they often provide individual benefits to those who join and participate in the organization for collective action while denying these benefits to those who do not.

When the number of beneficiaries of collective action is small, voluntary rational action may obtain collective goods without selective incentives. This is most easily evident when there are a few large firms in a relatively concentrated industry. If there are, say, three large firms of about the same size in an industry, each firm will receive about a third of the benefits of any action to get political favors or higher prices for the industry. This third of the benefits will usually be a sufficient incentive for considerable action in the interest of the industry. When the numbers in a group are small, each participant will have a noticeable effect on how well the common interest of the small group is served, and this will affect the likelihood that the others in the group will contribute. Thus those in small groups will often bargain until they agree to act to a more or less optimal extent in their group's interest. This organizational advantage of small groups—and particularly of small groups of large firms—will, as I shall later show, have important implications for public policy.

The Role of Ideology

The rational ignorance of the typical citizen that arises out of the logic of collective action suggests that simple ideologies and political slogans will play a large role in political life. Ideologies provide substitutes of a kind for detailed research and sustained reflection about public affairs. If a citizen subscribes to one of the familiar ideologies, he or she will have some guidance on how to vote and on what to say when engaged in political arguments. If spending a lot of time doing research on public affairs is not rational for the typical citizen but a left-wing or right-wing ideology can be acquired at little or no cost, then, understandably, many people would let ideology play a large role in determining how they will vote. The ideology will indicate, or at least appear to indicate, what general policy or what political party is best for people in one's own income category or social class. Clearly most of the votes cast by ordinary citizens are greatly influenced by ideology (or party affiliation, which usually amounts to much the same thing).

To be sure, the rational ignorance of the typical citizen is not the only reason that ideology plays a large role in modern life. This qualification is obvious the moment one notes that some people who are social scientists, journalists, or politicians, and have strong professional incentives to be especially well informed about public affairs, are also highly ideological. Apparently some people have psychological attributes that make them highly ideological even when well informed. Although these psychological attributes will not be examined in this paper, I shall show that they interact with the rational ignorance of the typical citizen to give the familiar ideologies and slogans an extraordinarily large role in modern society.

This paper will endeavor to show how "supply-side economics" and "industrial policy" are largely outgrowths of the right-wing and left-wing ideologies, respectively, and thus at one remove also partly outgrowths of the typical citizen's rational ignorance about public affairs. I believe, however, that one cannot properly understand how supply-side economics or industrial policy came to be politically influential ideas unless one first considers the right-wing and left-wing ideologies that mainly inspired these fashions.

Ideologies of the Right and the Left

As we all know, the centerpiece of ideological and political debate today is the dispute over the proper role of the government, particularly the extent to which it ought to aid the poorer segments of the population. From the Right, and especially the classical liberal or laissez-faire Right, the most sustained argument is that the growth of government intervention in recent times impairs economic performance and individual freedom and that overgenerous welfare-state programs intended to aid low-income people have reduced the incentive to work and to save. From the Left the most common argument is that modern society must not be fearful of using the resources and plans of democratic government to ensure that the society develops in a desirable direction and particularly to ensure that there is compassionate provision for the needs of those for whom the market does not provide an adequate income. The ideological debate that has just been described is commonplace not only in the United States but in most other countries as well, and it attracts the serious efforts of leading scholars as well as of politicians and journalists.

In view of the overwhelming preoccupation with the ideological debate to which I have just referred, it is surprising how little careful study has been given to the question of how well each side in the debate succeeds or fails in explaining economic performance in different countries and historical periods. If the Right or classical liberal side of the argument is correct, one ought systematically to find that those societies in which the role of the government is the smallest and the redistribution of income in the direction of low-income people is the least were growing the most rapidly and had the highest per capita incomes. Conversely, if the Left or the democratic socialistic side of the argument is correct, one ought to find the most impressive economic performance and the highest standard of living, at least for the poor, in the societies in which the role of government is larger and the redistribution of income to the poor presumably more generous. One can also test the familiar ideologies by looking at changes across historical periods, because in different historical periods the role of government, and the extent of income redistribution by government, has differed.

One of the few people to look at the evidence on this central debate of modern democratic societies is David Smith.[2] In a 1975 article in the *National Westminster Bank Review,* he looked at the percentages of the national income or the gross domestic product (GDP) that were used or handled by government in different developed democracies and tested the relation between this variable and the rate of economic growth in the society. What Smith found, as I see it, was only a weak and questionable association. He emphasized that this association was a negative one; those societies with the larger role for the government had a somewhat slower rate of growth. The relation was so fragile, however, that, if one omitted Japan—a special country in many ways—from the statistical test, the relation disappeared. Japan has a smaller public sector and a faster rate of growth than the other major developed democracies, and it was largely responsible for any relation that there was between the role of government and growth.

Using somewhat more recent data, Erich Weede has also found a negative relation between the share of national output taken by government in taxes and the rate of growth of per capita income, but his results are also crucially dependent on the observations on Japan.[3] Weede also tests whether a Socialist party in the government or the governing coalition affects the rate of growth, but he finds no statistically significant relation.

In a major book, *Theories of Comparative Economic Growth,*[4] Kwang Choi explores whether there is any relationship between the spending and transfer by government and variables such as the rate of economic growth and the level of investment. Choi found no strong relation between the role of government and the rate of economic growth.

One of the few other studies of this issue worth mentioning is an article by Samuel Brittan, the distinguished economic journalist for the *Financial Times of London.* In 1978 Brittan, one of the most influential advocates of monetarism and free markets in the United Kingdom, published an article on the "British disease," the slow economic growth of Great Britain.[5] In this article he argued, no doubt to the surprise of most of those who share his general approach, that one apparently cannot explain the surprisingly poor performance of the British economy in terms of the role of the state in Great Britain or the extent of income redistribution to low-income people. When one compares the United Kingdom with its European neighbors, Brittan pointed out, one finds it is not greatly different from the average of the European countries in the proportion of the nation's resources that are consumed by or handled by government. The percentage of the national income consumed and handled by government is in fact usually lower in Great Britain than in Holland, Sweden, Norway, and West Germany; but the latter countries have enjoyed a far better postwar economic performance than Great Britain has. This observation alone makes it unlikely that the role of government in Britain is the main explanation for its poor economic performance.

But Brittan brought forth even more persuasive evidence when he looked at the historical pattern in Great Britain. The British economy, he pointed out, began to fall behind the rates of growth of comparable European economies in the last two decades of the nineteenth century. At that time Great Britain and the British Empire had the closest thing to ideal laissez-faire government that the world has ever seen. The relatively slow British growth, I would add, continued through the interwar period and became all the more noticeable in the post–World War II period, when the United Kingdom was often under democratic socialistic governments and when the welfare state came into being. The poor British performance has, I would point out, become still worse under the resolutely conservative and monetarist government of Margaret Thatcher. So Britain has grown relatively slowly under laissez-faire governments, moderate conservative governments, and labor or democratic socialistic governments alike.

To make the lack of any relation between the rate of economic growth, on the one hand, and the extent of government spending and transfers, on the other, visually clear, figure 1 has been prepared. In this figure the average annual rates of growth of per capita income from 1950 to 1974 are measured along the vertical axis and the average percentages of GDP used for government expenditures plus transfers in 1955, 1965, and 1975 are shown on the horizontal axis. Since the concern in this paper is only with developed democratic countries that are relevant to the debates in this country, the countries included in the figure are those of the member nations of the Organization for Economic Cooperation and Development (OECD) for which the needed data are available. The figure makes it obvious that, except for Japan, there is no clear relation between the extent of government spending and transfers and the rate of growth. The level of government spending and transfers may, of course, have an effect on the rate of growth that has been obscured by other factors. I expect that the role of government does in fact have some effect on the rate of economic growth. Yet the evidence suggests any relation is not nearly so strong as one might expect from the overwhelming ideological preoccupation with the role of government and the welfare state.

Historical Perspective

I will now take a historical perspective, and ask in what historical periods economic growth has been most impressive, and then note what the role of the

FIGURE 1
ECONOMIC GROWTH AND GOVERNMENT SPENDING AND TRANSFERS, 1950–1975
(percent)

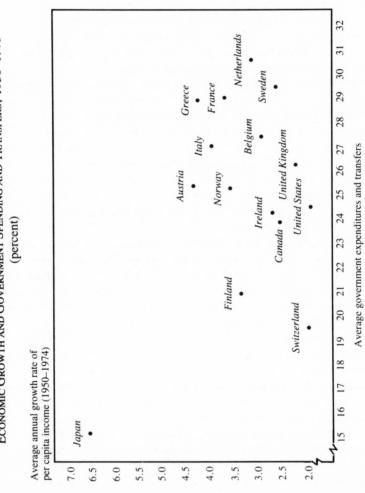

government and the extent of income redistribution has been in each of these historical periods.

If one goes back to the nineteenth century, one finds that in Great Britain (as I have already noted), to some extent in the United States, and to a lesser extent on the Continent laissez-faire policies prevailed. Great Britain and its huge empire had not only laissez faire in domestic policy but also free trade. Apart from large subsidies to the railroads, the United States had something approaching laissez faire internally, though it certainly did not have free trade, and neither did several of the countries of the Continent. Yet, the world as a whole in the nineteenth century came closer to laissez faire and free trade than it has at any other time. The nineteenth century was also a period of impressive economic performance. So this piece of evidence, taken by itself, would argue on the side of the conservative or classical liberal argument that one should limit the role of the state and be wary of the adverse effect on the incentives to work and save of redistribution to those with lower incomes.

The interwar period was quite different. Though the period between World War I and World War II did not really see the establishment of the complete welfare state—in general, that occurred only after World War II—it was still distinguished from the period before World War I by an incomparably higher level of protectionism and economic nationalism. Protectionism and high tariffs were the most striking feature of the economic history of the interwar period; even the British Empire abandoned free trade. Now, as one knows, the interwar period was a time of poor economic performance and above all of the Great Depression.

Admittedly, different things happened in different countries, and I am perhaps being too aggregative and casual in talking about the interwar period in general. So let me switch for a moment to one country, the United States. Developments here were perhaps a little simpler and easier to describe than in other countries and at the same time instructive from the point of view of the issue I am now considering.

In the United States in the 1920s the government, with the presidencies of Harding, Coolidge, and Hoover, was conservative and probusiness. Not only were these presidents conservative Republicans, but they also wanted to keep the role of the government and the transfers to the poor at a minimal level. At the same time, they supported extremely high levels of protection; the Fordney-Macomber tariffs were imposed and finally the colossally protective Smoot-Hawley tariff that passed just before the Great Depression set in. The American economy did fairly well under Harding and Coolidge and in the first months of Hoover's administration.

Then the deepest depression that the United States—indeed that the entire world—had ever seen occurred. So a substantial period of conservative and probusiness (though protectionist) government ended in a catastrophic depression. This deepest of all depressions was not really cured, though it was somewhat ameliorated, under the New Deal administration of Franklin Roosevelt; only with World War II did the American economy fully recover.

Now I turn to the period following World War II or more precisely to the period from the end of World War II until about 1970. Two facts about this period of economic history stand out above all others. First, in all of the major developed democracies, the welfare state reached its full development, and the government came to handle a significant proportion of the national income. Second, all of the major developed democracies grew more rapidly than they had ever grown before. Some—like Germany and Japan and, for a time, Italy—grew with incredible speed; but even the slowest growing of these countries, such as Great Britain and the United States, grew more rapidly than ever before. So the welfare state, on the one hand, and unprecedentedly rapid economic growth, on the other, came to the major developed economies of the West at essentially the same time. The postwar period showed the greatest increase in the peacetime role of the government, the greatest level of income redistribution to the poor, and the most rapid economic growth the world has known.

So, one must ask, was there a casual connection between large governments and the welfare state and rapid economic growth? It would seem so, but this observation does not fit with the experience of the nineteenth century; nor, indeed, does it fit with the experience of the 1970s or the present, when the welfare state has become still larger and the economic performance has turned sour. At first the welfare state and big government were accompanied by rapid economic growth, but later in the 1970s and in the present they have been accompanied by poor economic performance.

The reader may now say that the question I have raised is such a large one, and the amount of relevant evidence so colossal, that one cannot draw any conclusions without going into the matter in far, far more detail. This caution is unquestionably appropriate.

I think, nonetheless, that perhaps the detached reader will agree that no clear picture emerges from a beginning study of the evidence about the role of the state on the one hand and the rate of economic growth on the other. Given the almost universal preoccupation with the role of the government and the extent of income redistribution to low-income people, one would expect that, if either side of the ideological debate had got the matter right, there ought to be really clear and conspicuous evidence of an association one way or the other. Given the widespread interest in the issue, one would expect that someone would have shown a compelling association between the role of government and the rate of growth; but (to the best of my knowledge) no one has. If people feel strongly, as most of them do, about what the role of government ought to be in a democratic society, one would suppose that those strong convictions rested in some sort of clear and unambiguous finding about the role of the state and economic performance. That clear and conspicuous evidence, however, is not there; indeed, the evidence usually is not even systematically examined.

There is the possibility that the size and ideology of governments would have a strong impact on the standard of living of low-income people, even if they had no clear effect on the rate of economic growth or the level of per capita income. Since there are generally fewer data on the standards of living of relatively low-income people than on rates of economic growth, one must be extremely cautious in drawing any conclusions about any connection between the size or ideology of governments and the standard of living of relatively low-income people. So far as one can tell from the available studies, however, there is no strong evidence, if any at all, that the ideology or size of government is related to the standard of living of relatively poor people.[6]

Thus one may assume, at least provisionally, that something else must be crucially involved in determining the rate of economic growth and the standard of living of low-income people besides the issue around which the ideological debate revolves. If governments of right- and left-wing ideologies do not achieve what they claim they will achieve, one also has a right to suspect that their actual actions and choices are often not those that their ideologies and slogans might lead one to expect. When one sees what else is involved, and why both left-wing and right-wing are often unfaithful to the ideologies they espouse, one can come back to the familiar ideological debate and understand it in a better way. This understanding in turn will give one a fresh perspective on the debates on supply-side economics and industrial policy.

The reader may ask, "If something else is involved besides the role of government and the extent of income redistribution, what is it?" What is the something else that must be there, obscuring or denying a clear connection between the role of government and the speed of economic growth and making governments behave in ways not predicted by their ideologies?

The Nature of Collective Action

My candidate for the role of the something else is the nature of collective action in society. The difficulties of collective action may seem quite unrelated to the determinants of the rate of economic growth or the standard of living of low-income people. But that a close relation exists will be evident when I consider the incentives that organizations for collective action confront. So I will now suppose that the difficult and problematic task of organizing for collective action has in fact been accomplished for some group and that the group is now organized to lobby the government or to act like a cartel in the marketplace to influence prices or wages.

What is the incentive facing this organization that is by stipulation now organized? This incentive can best be seen by looking at an organization that, though it might be large and have many members, is still only a small part of the whole country or society in question. For the sake of simple arithmetic, I assume an organization that represents 1 percent of the income-earning capacity of a country: for example, a labor union, the members of which earn wages that are in the aggregate 1 percent of the country's national income, or a trade association of business firms, which in the aggregate earn 1 percent of the national income.

Could this organization perhaps serve its members by making the country of which it is a part more efficient and productive? In general being part of a rich and efficient society is obviously better than being part of a poor and inefficient one, so I must examine this logical possibility. A lobbying organization could, for example, lobby for measures that would make the society in which its members live and work more productive and successful. Would it have an incentive to do this?

An organization that represented 1 percent of the society would get on average only 1 percent of the benefits from making its society more productive. If the national income of the United States rises by a billion dollars because some special-interest group that is organized for collective action wins more efficient public policies, the members of the special-interest group that represents 1 percent of the country will get, on average, 1 percent of the benefits resulting from their action. Those members, however, will have borne the whole cost of whatever lobbying they have done to improve the country. If they get 1 percent of the benefits of their action and bear the whole cost of their action, then trying to make the society more efficient and prosperous will pay them only if the benefits of that action to the society as a whole exceed the costs of that action by a hundred times or more. Only if the cost-benefit ratio is better than 100:1 will an organization for collective action best serve its members by acting to make the society more prosperous and efficient.

How then can a special-interest group best help its clients? If a larger slice of the pie that society produces can be obtained for the members of a special-interest organization, then the members of this organization will at least have this larger slice of the pie. Less metaphorically, if a larger percentage of the national output or national income that is produced in a country can be redistributed to the members of a special-interest group, then these members will have that larger share of the national income.

But the reader, at least if he or she is an economist, may now ask, "Won't lobbying for favors from government or combination in the marketplace to obtain monopolistic prices or wages make the economy less efficient and productive? And won't the members of the special-interest group bear part of the reduction in the national income that comes from the inefficiencies brought about by their effort to capture a larger proportion of the national income?" The answer, of course, is, "Yes." In general, cartelization will reduce the efficiency and prosperity of the society. Because a combination or cartel will produce and sell less and charge more for it, the society will be less productive and efficient. Special-interest lobbying will similarly induce resources to go into the particular areas that are favored by the lobby-inspired legislation; resources will crowd into these areas until their contribution to the national income—their marginal social product—is lower than it would have been in other areas; and the efficiency of the economy will be reduced. So both cartelization and lobbying to get a larger percentage of the national output will, in general, make the society less efficient and productive.

Remember, I stipulated that our special-interest group represented 1 percent of the society. Thus its members bear only 1 percent of the loss in national income or output that occurs because of the inefficiency its activities bring about; but they get the whole of the amount redistributed to them. They get the entire increase in their slice of the pie, but they bear only 1 percent of the losses from the shrinkage of the pie. It pays our hypothetical special-interest group to seek to redistribute income to its own members even if this redistribution reduces the national income by up to 100 times the amount redistributed!

So a society dense with organizations for collective action is like a china shop filled with wrestlers battling over the china and breaking far more than they carry away. A society in which the difficult task of organizing collective action has been overcome in many sectors of the society will be a society full of organizations that have little or no incentive to produce anything of value to the society but great incentives to struggle to get more of what society is producing and to persevere in that struggle even when it greatly reduces the output of the society by many times the amount each group gains.

The argument I have just put forth is casual and incomplete, but I have stated it in a complete and careful way in my book *The Rise and Decline of Nations*.[7] The skeptical reader is invited to check every step of the logic of my argument in that book; to go into this point fully would take far too much space in this paper. What has been set out here should, however, be sufficient to call one's attention to some testable implications or predictions of the argument that can be compared with reality.

If the organization of collective action is difficult and problematical because selective incentives are required, and if only some groups have access to the necessary selective incentives or gimmicks, then one should expect that societies will take a long time to organize for collective action. In other words, quite some time will pass before many groups will have had the good luck and the good leadership needed to organize for collective action. These societies should be expected to be less efficient and dynamic than otherwise similar societies that have had less time to accumulate organizations for collective action. Thus my argument generates a testable implication or prediction: long stable societies ought to be doing less well economically than would in general be expected.

257

Jurisdictional Integration and Economic Growth

There is a lot of evidence that this is indeed the case. The society that has had the longest period of stability and immunity from invasion and institutional destruction is Great Britain. And Great Britain has the poorest economic performance of all of the major developed democracies, as the theory predicts.

The theory also predicts that if totalitarian government and defeat in war had destroyed the institutional fabric of society, including its special-interest organizations, then, after a free and stable legal order is established, those societies should grow surprisingly rapidly. They will be relatively innocent of special-interest groups, or, if they have some, they are likely to be relatively encompassing. As I show in *The Rise and Decline of Nations*, relatively encompassing groups are less of a problem for economic development. So, those societies that have suffered the institutional destruction that eliminates special-interest groups ought to grow more rapidly than they would otherwise be expected to do.

Of course, the economic miracles of Germany and Japan after World War II are precisely consistent with this implication of my argument. In Italy, the institutional destruction in World War II, though considerable, was less complete than in Germany and Japan. The economic miracle in Italy, though there definitely was one, was correspondingly somewhat shorter than and somewhat less sizable than those in Germany and Japan, and this situation again is in accord with the theory.

The theory also predicts that the parts of the United States that have been settled longest and never defeated in war would now have poorer economic performance than those parts of the United States that have been settled most recently and have had less time to accumulate special-interest organizations. They also ought to perform less well than the South, which was, of course, defeated in the Civil War and has only lately seen the end of its turmoil over what policies with respect to race should prevail. And the South is, like the West, growing far more rapidly than the stagnant Northeast and the older Midwest. Thus I conclude that the most striking and anomolous examples of remarkable growth and of surprising stagnation since World War II are consistent with the theory.

If this essay could be as long as a book, I would also explore the examples of remarkable economic growth or surprising stagnation in previous centuries. We could, for example, consider Germany after the Zollverein or customs union was established in 1834 and after the unification of Germany was completed in 1871. Other examples would be the growth of Japan after the Meiji Restoration of 1867–1868, the growth of the United States in the nineteenth century, the growth of Holland and its Golden Age in the seventeenth century, the growth of Britain during the Industrial Revolution from about 1760 to about 1840, and the commercial revolutions in England and France in the sixteenth century.

All of these cases involve what I call jurisdictional integration. That is to say, they all involve the creation of a wide area within which there was free trade, however high the tariffs around the wider market might be, and, at the same time, the creation of a new jurisdiction or government that changed the location of the capital and required lobbying on quite a different scale from what was necessary to influence the parochial small jurisdictions that existed before.

After the creation of the much larger jurisdiction and the wider market, there was always rapid economic growth. A detailed examination of the matter shows that this rapid growth was due in large part to the fact that the jurisdictional integration undercut the special-interest groups of the day. The special-interest groups of prior centuries were called "guilds" or, in Japan, "za." When people were freed of the tariffs and economic restrictions that surrounded each feudal fief or walled city, the guilds or the za were undercut. People in each feudal fief or walled city could, after the jurisdictional integration, purchase goods from other parts of the integrated jurisdiction and thereby get better value. These purchases from other jurisdictions would undercut the guilds or za that had organized behind the protection.

The "putting out," or "merchant-employer," system—which was the main form of manufacturing of textiles in early modern Europe—nicely illustrates the process. Once jurisdictional integration occurred, textile production shifted to the rural areas of Europe. Though production had to be organized under the cumbersome merchant-employer system, the production in the rural areas was not under the control of guilds and therefore was less expensive. After jurisdictional integration abolished the local trade restrictions that had supported the guilds or the za, production could shift to rural areas or new areas. Even the Industrial Revolution grew up mainly in new towns or sometimes in suburbs of old towns in which the rules of guilds did not apply.

Thus, a great deal of evidence, only a small part of which I have been able to offer here, supports the theory that the creation of common markets and larger jurisdictions for setting economic policy brought startling changes in the pace of economic performance. There is, moreover, every reason to believe that the jurisdictional integration brought about this more impressive economic performance partly because it undercut the special-interest groups that thrive behind protection, particularly in small jurisdictions.

Insufficiency of the Traditional Ideologies as Explanations

So "something else" does explain much more of the variation in economic performance than does the scale of the government or the extent of income redistribution to the poor: the level of lobbying and cartelization. When I looked, earlier in this paper, at the proportion of the national income the government was consuming or handling in different countries, I found that it did not have any strong relation one way or another with the rate of economic growth or the level of per capita income.

The first reason the focus on the role of government alone, which characterizes the classical-liberal laissez-faire position, is insufficient to explain the variation in growth rates and income levels is that it overlooks one important force that impedes the economic development that markets can bring about. This force is cartelization, or the combination of firms and individuals in the marketplace that can maintain noncompetitive prices or wages, obstruct the free flow of resources, and slow down the innovation that brings more rapid economic growth. In focusing on the role of government alone the laissez-faire ideology is guilty of "monodiabolism," or singling out one enemy of the market as though it were the only enemy. Some cartelization can take place without the aid of government, as I claim to have shown with examples from China, India, and Great Britain in *The Rise and Decline of Nations*.

The second reason the traditional argument about the limits of government or democracy fails to explain the variation in economic performance across countries is that it neglects variations in the ways governments operate. What a government actually does depends in large part on the extent of lobbying. A lobby-free democracy, though of course it will not operate perfectly, is likely to operate much more efficiently than one that is under the thrall of special-interest groups, especially narrow rather than encompassing special-interest groups. Thus a reason one does not see the strong association between the role of government and the rate of economic growth that might be expected is that there is another factor operating that is distinct from the role of government: the extent to which the government policies are dominated by groups that have an incentive to redistribute rather than to produce. To the extent that governments are dominated by lobbies that have an incentive to seek policies that redistribute income to themselves, the government will have an adverse effect on economic performance incomparably greater than the effect it would have had if it had been free of these lobbies.

The third reason neither of the traditional ideologies is successful in explaining economic performance cannot be understood until one analyzes the connection between prior income and status, on the one hand, and the capacity to organize and collude, on the other. One aspect of this connection emerged from the earlier account of how small groups, and especially small groups of large firms, can organize with less difficulty than large groups. This account suggests that industries composed of a few large firms will be among the first- and best-organized segments of society and that big business and the wealthiest people will normally be better organized than most of the rest of society. This point did not escape Adam Smith's attention, but it is often overlooked today. Another factor works in the same direction: the selective incentives that large groups need to organize are more readily available to those with higher incomes and established positions. This fact is evident from even a glance at the histories of special-interest groups. The professions organized long before workers of lesser income and status in practically every society. Similarly, skilled workers organized unions long before unskilled workers did. The first unions represented skilled workers in England; and, during the first half century of organized labor in this country, unionized workers were called the "aristocracy of labor." Even among unskilled workers, those who already have jobs, and not those who are unemployed or are new entrants, are most likely to be organized. There is no society anywhere in which the bulk of the poorest people or most of the unemployed are organized. Sometimes those who already have jobs in a factory or mine are able to set up a picket line or a dues check-off that will ensure collective action in their interest, but the unemployed and the poor are scattered around the society and normally do not even gather at any one location at which their behavior might be coordinated. Thus both the organizational advantages of small groups and the access to selective incentives ensure that the nonpoor, and especially the established and prosperous elements in society, have disproportionate capacities for organized and collusive action.

The correlation between income and status and organizational power suggests that most redistribution of income brought about either by lobbying of the government or by cartelization will not be redistribution to the poor in any case. In fact most redistribution is not toward the poor; the value of the money and goods transferred through the welfare system and other programs for the poor is only a tiny part of the government budget, and the transfers in the forms of cartel prices or wages, tariffs, tax loopholes, and government subsidies are overwhelmingly directed toward the nonpoor. This holds true not only in the United States but in many other societies as well. Those social expenditures that are directed toward the poor are mainly due not to the lobbying or political pressure of the poor, but rather to the willingness of the nonpoor to accept such expenditures. The compassion of most people and their awareness that programs for the poor provide a measure of social insurance against personal and family catastrophes that could strike anyone are the main sources of effective support for programs for the poor. The extent to which the organized and collusive power is in the hands of the nonpoor and especially the prosperous segments of the society is evident from a glance at the records of campaign contributions to senators and representatives: can anyone name a single member of Congress whose contributions come mainly from welfare mothers?

Thus the third reason that the ideology of a government and the extent of its redistribution of income to low-income people are not closely correlated with economic performance is that most redistributions, and most of the distortions in market incentives due to such redistributions, do not involve the poor in any case. There is a lot of argument about fairness and how much should be done for the poor, but this argument has only a marginal effect on what societies do and on economic performance. Most redistributions are from the unorganized to the organized, and these redistributions are not closely related to the ideology of the government.

The fourth reason the issue around which the Left versus Right debate revolves does not have a large effect on economic performance is that redistributions to the poor usually damage incentives less than do redistributions to the nonpoor, even when the redistributions are of similar size. The reason is that the poor are, on average, less productive than the nonpoor; they are more likely to be people with handicaps, without marketable skills, or of advanced age, or mothers without husbands. Though there are exceptions, in most cases the people who are most productive and whose skills and resources are also currently prized in the society are not, at the same time, poor. Though these transfers to the poor and the taxes that pay for them do have some adverse effect on incentives, these transfers usually reduce efficiency by less than do subsidies to the nonpoor.

Thus when nations subsidize the nonpoor, they channel the time and energies of some of their most productive people and assets into less productive pursuits and thereby reduce social efficiency. Institutional arrangements or policies that misallocate the labor of healthy males in the prime working years are very damaging to the efficiency of a society; yet such institutional arrangements and policies are very common. Professional associations and public policies that largely control the practice of law and of medicine are no doubt even more costly to the society, because the time of some of the most highly educated and energetic people in the society is being misallocated; yet few areas of modern society are so rife with cartels, anticompetitive rules, and other redistributions as are those of law and medicine. Tax loopholes that induce many of the people to become tax accountants and lawyers divert some of the most able and aggressive people in the society out of socially productive pursuits, and at the same time twist much of the productive capacity of the whole society into tax-favored activities that have a lower social marginal product than less favored activities; yet such loopholes are becoming more numerous. Tariffs, tax concessions, and bailouts to major corporations divert or enfeeble some of the most productive enterprises in the whole economy; yet such tariffs and bailouts are becoming more common with each passing year.

The fifth reason neither side in the familiar ideological debate gives a good basis for predictions about economic performance is that the ideological rhetoric of parties and politicians does not say much about what they actually do. The right wing often advocates free enterprise and free markets, and in doing this it performs a useful public service, since the advantages of competitive markets are usually underestimated; one must have a lot of difficult professional training to understand the working of markets and the contribution they can make to society. Thus right-wing rhetoric in favor of free markets, even if it is often superficial and inspired by prejudice rather than understanding, more often than not contributes to society. Similarly, the left wing often advocates compassion and fairness, and in doing this it strengthens the nobler side of human nature and makes our civilization more decent and sensitive to misfortune. The advocacy of fairness and compassion is valuable even when it comes from people who do not set a perfect example in their personal charity; as Dr. Johnson pointed out, we should not complain too much about people who do not practice what they preach, because if we do we are going to lose a lot of good preaching.

The problem is that most right-wing parties and politicians do *not* in fact spend most of their time freeing up markets and that most left-wing parties and politicians do *not* actually spend most of their time aiding the needy. In long-stable societies like the United States most political activity on both the Right and the Left is devoted to the purposes of the organized interests rather than to free markets or to the needs of the poor. The organized interests that support right-wing parties are usually from business and from the professional and prosperous classes, and these organized interests will normally be paid off when a right-wing politician is victorious. The distortions of market incentives that result when such groups are rewarded with tax loopholes, tariffs, and monopoly rights for the professions are especially damaging to economic efficiency precisely because the beneficiaries of these rewards often possess unusually valuable abilities and assets. Similarly, when the Left is victorious, the payoffs will usually be to the organized interests that have been the sources of the campaign contributions and lobbying pressures. Most politicians on the Left spend most of their time working for their paying clients. These include not only cartels of workers, teachers, and other public employees, but also often special-interest groups from the most prosperous segments of the society that have made campaign contributions, often to both candidates on both sides of the ideological divide. Thus the ideological debates do not give us a good basis for understanding economic performance because they are a most imperfect guide to what either right-wing or left-wing governments mainly do.

If what I have said here is true, the ideologies of the Left and Right, with their untiring emphasis on the role of government and of redistribution of income to those with lower incomes, are neither of them sufficient to guide modern society. They focus almost exclusively on problems and issues which, though significant, are not sufficient to explain the main variations in the fortunes of different societies or the fluctuating progress in different periods. They also obscure other problems that may even prove fatal to modern society. Worst of all, these ideologies leave the impression that the great trade-off is between equity and efficiency. Though occasionally tension may arise between these goals, as between any others, they are not often in conflict today. The money our society pays to appease those with power goes mainly to those who do not need it.

This chapter began with the idea that the typical citizen is, because of the logic of collective action, rationally ignorant about many aspects of public affairs. Given the cost of acquiring information about many aspects of public policy, it is understandable that many citizens should use the familiar and simple left- or right-wing ideologies for making decisions about public affairs. The limited explanatory power of each of the familiar ideologies is entirely consistent with the notion that they are more often devices for avoiding careful research and reflection rather than the embodiments of detached observation and careful thinking about the experience of nations and peoples. The attraction that one or the other of the familiar ideologies holds for many professional students and participants in public affairs shows that rational ignorance cannot be the whole explanation of the attraction of the familiar ideologies, but it is part of the explanation.

There is further evidence of the role of rational ignorance in explaining beliefs about public policy in two recently fashionable additions to the familiar ideologies, "supply-side economics" and "industrial policy." These two extensions, respectively, of the right-wing and left-wing ideologies are even better evidence for rational ignorance than the ideologies themselves. The reason is that these extensions have attracted widespread journalistic and political support yet have been ridiculed even by many distinguished economists and scholars who have a strong identification with the respective ideology from which these fashionable notions emerged.

Supply-Side Economics and Industrial Policy

Supply-Side Economics. Occasionally the label supply-side economics is used in such a broad way that it encompasses what essentially all competent economists, whether on the Right or the Left, have known since Adam Smith: that the pattern of incentives in a society has a great impact on its efficiency and level of production. Normally, however, this label is used to identify a much narrower doctrine: the novel notion that, in the United States in the 1980s, cuts in overall tax rates would so greatly increase the amount of labor and saving supplied that tax collections would increase. This notion was, at least at one point, explicitly accepted by President Reagan, and in large part it inspired the tax cuts he advocated and obtained early in his administration.

To understand why the Reagan administration advocated and the government accepted the supply-side tax cuts one must note that statistical and econometric evidence about the response of labor and saving to changes in post-tax wages or interest rates is not the kind of information that the typical citizen would acquire because of its entertainment value. The information that is needed to assess the claim that tax cuts will be self-financing does not have

264

the entertainment or diversionary value of a drama such as Watergate or a political sex scandal. Complex econometric information and economic theory are not presented even in economic newspapers such as the *Wall Street Journal*. If they were, the Editorial Board of the *Wall Street Journal* would be better informed, but that newspaper would no longer have a wide circulation.

Thus a huge democracy and its media of communication can largely ignore information that is essential to rational policymaking, even about issues of surpassing importance. They ignore it even when virtually all competent specialists, whether on the Right or the Left, agree about the evidence. The great majority of competent economists never expected that the tax cuts would be self-financing. Even most economists who were strongly identified with right-wing ideology agreed that supply-side economics was not consistent with the quantitative evidence about the supply of labor and of saving. Yet the Reagan tax cuts were nonetheless passed, and the nation is now burdened with a huge and very harmful structural deficit. Experience has now confirmed that supply-side economics was as baseless as almost all economists had said it was, yet it even now retains some journalistic and political support. This support is mainly a logical consequence of the rational ignorance of the man in the street. Rational ignorance also explains the power of lobbies and cartels: if all of the citizens had complete information and understanding of all public issues, lobbying would have no effect, and cartels would not be tolerated.

The analysis in this paper also helps to explain the character of the Reagan tax cuts. Though the available evidence perhaps falls short of being absolutely compelling, there is considerable reason to believe that the best way to reduce the inefficiencies arising from our tax system is by eliminating tax loopholes and taxing essentially all forms of income impartially. If the tax code were simple and straightforward, all of the legal and accounting talent that is now devoted to the complexities of the tax code could be used instead for the production of goods and services. More important, firms and individuals would no longer distort their patterns of activity to make use of the tax advantages that pertain to certain types of revenue and expenditure, and the economy would surely be more efficient. If the loopholes or special provisions of the tax code were eliminated, the same amount of revenue could be collected with lower tax rates, further increasing efficiency. Though I know of no systematic survey on the matter, I would hypothesize that most professional economists on both the Right and the Left would agree that a single, uniform, and loophole-free tax code, accompanied by the reductions in tax rates that such reforms would allow, would do much more for the productivity of the economy than the Reagan tax cuts have done.

If so, the next question is, Why did the Reagan administration use its mandate to obtain a large reduction in tax rates, and turn only much later in a half-hearted way to the closing of tax loopholes? I suspect one reason is that it could not have obtained a uniform and loophole-free tax code without taking on the special-interest lobbies, many of which are part of the Reagan coalition. So the nation is left with tax cuts of the wrong sort and the wrong size, and thus a huge structural deficit. This deficit is, of course, made larger because of special-interest lobbying that prevents reductions in certain types of public expenditure serving no useful national purpose.

Industrial Policy. Like supply-side economics, industrial policy means different things to different people. Those publications that I happen to have seen advocating industrial policy are also relatively vague. Some are so vague that they invite the reaction that industrial policy is neither a good idea nor a bad idea, but no idea at all; that it is the grin without the cat. The proposals for an industrial policy that I know about, however, are just a couple of those that have received much attention in the journalistic media, and it follows from my argument about rational ignorance that there is no assurance at all that the best ideas will be the ones that journalists believe will divert or entertain their readers. Thus there may well be proposals for an industrial policy that are both specific and sensible and to which the charge of vagueness and the substantive objections offered below will not apply. I sympathize with any authors of sound and specific proposals who encounter unjustified skepticism because of the shortcomings of proposals by their better-publicized colleagues.

The widely known proposals for an industrial policy with which I happen to be familiar have three common features. The first is the creation of a tripartite board with representatives from business, labor, and government that would determine, or at least make influential recommendations about, the industrial policy. The second feature is a bank, which in some proposals is explicitly compared to the old Reconstruction Finance Corporation, that would have access to government-guaranteed or government-financed credit and thus could make subsidized loans. These loans, combined with temporary protection against imports or other government subsidies that the tripartite board could recommend or establish, would serve as an incentive to persuade the firms and unions that the board singled out for attention to adopt reforms recommended by the administrators of the industrial policy. The third feature of the proposals I have in mind is that the tripartite board would focus on industries in trouble, often because of foreign competition, or would seek out high-technology industries that the board deemed to be especially promising, or would do both of these things.

I concentrate first on proposals or efforts to help industries in trouble. In the United States today, the industries that are most conspicuously in trouble are those that have been around a long time and are located mainly in the older industrial regions of the country, the Northeast and the older Midwest. Though the industries that are in trouble often contain subsectors or firms that are thriving, I shall for the sake of brevity ignore these exceptions and treat each industry as an undifferentiated whole. On this aggregative basis, clearly the steel and automobile industries are among those in trouble. Obviously, these industries have been around a long time; indeed, the United States was for quite some time by far the world's leading producer of steel and produced four-fifths of all of the automobiles in the world. The apparel, textile, footwear, and farm machinery industries are also having trouble competing with imports; these are also industries that have a long and often illustrious history in this country. Our industrialization began with the textile industry, for example, early in the nineteenth century, and the farm machinery companies like International Harvester that are now near bankruptcy, go back to great nineteenth-century inventions like the mechanical reaper and were for a long time world leaders in farm machinery production.

By contrast, in new industries the United States is doing relatively well. In computers and most high technology the United States has a significant lead over the rest of the world and, in reasonably new industries like aircraft and jet engines, is also doing very well. In some industries composed of both fairly old and quite new companies, such as the airline industry, many of the great old companies, like Pan American and Eastern, are at the edge of bankruptcy, whereas some newer firms such as Peoples Airlines, in spite of the handicaps of a lack of experience and of established position, are doing well.

Earlier in this chapter I noted that the older societies and regions that have had long periods of stability in which the difficult task of organizing distributional coalitions could be overcome were doing much less well than newer or recently stable regions that have had less time to accumulate institutional sclerosis. This observation raises the question of whether similar processes are at work differentiating old and new industries and firms.

A closer examination reveals that this is precisely the case. The U.S. steel industry, for example, has a long history during which it became accustomed to high levels of collusion and cartelization, among both the firms and the workers. For a long time the "Pittsburgh Plus" system of cartel pricing prevailed (by this system the cartel price for steel was enforced by requiring that all firms charge the cartel price, and discounts hidden by variations in transport costs were prevented by the rule that all steel sold had to include the cost of transportation from Pittsburgh, even if it was produced elsewhere). The labor force is also cartelized and has wages about three-fourths above the average of American manufacturing. The big three automobile companies similarly appear to have avoided all-out price competition for extensive periods, and their labor force also enjoys a monopoly wage one-half to two-thirds above the average of American manufacturing.

Similarly, the "World's Most Experienced Airline" had no need to fear competitors that would charge lower fares in the era of regulation, since the system of regulation and the International Air Transport Association cartel prohibited such competition. I believe that this prohibition made possible excessively costly management and monopoly wage levels; pilots were and sometimes are being paid much more than $100,000 a year when equally qualified pilots can be hired for a third or half as much. New airlines not encumbered with old management habits or monopoly wage levels have not surprisingly been able to provide cheaper and more efficient service and, in the process, have offered many new jobs. Similar examples could be cited in many other industries and firms.

It should be obvious from observation of the U.S. government as well as from the foregoing argument that existing organized interests would greatly influence the selection of the members of any board or agency that implemented an industrial policy. Indeed, some proposals for an industrial policy institutionalize and magnify the influence of established lobbies by stipulating that the governing board be composed of representatives of business and industry as well as government; they propose that the very foxes that have been stealing part of our productive wealth should be put in charge of the chicken coop. It is no coincidence that some proposals for an industrial policy have drawn powerful support from established business and labor leaders. These proposals would protect the established interests that are the main source of our economic problems from competition from new firms, new workers, and new countries.

Those proposals for an industrial policy that would allegedly allocate capital on preferential terms to new firms in emerging industries with special promise must explain how they would ensure that the lobbying power of established and often declining industries and firms would be kept at bay. The "sunrise" industries and firms cannot lobby until some time after they have been established and cannot compete politically with established interests. No proposal I have seen offers any assurance that industrial policies would operate as it is alleged they would operate.

The authors of these proposals should also explain why a government board or agency would allocate capital more effectively than those people and firms that are investing their own money. Much evidence shows that governmental bureaucracies are least useful in areas of high uncertainty and risk. Some of the most promising ventures and technologies will fail, and the official who lent public money to an undertaking that failed will risk notoriety. Even the rationally ignorant may learn of a spectacular failure but not take the trouble to note that investment plans that exclude innovations risky enough to have a significant chance of total failure are unlikely to generate any major advances. The official who does bet on the risky venture will not get the profits if the venture succeeds but will normally get in trouble if the venture fails, so government investment programs are almost always too conservative. It is precisely in the areas of uncertainty like high technology and new industries that private venture capital has the greatest advantage. The government can best promote science and technology by providing the public goods of pure research that the market will not provide and by creating an environment that is open to every kind of new enterprise and innovation, foreign or domestic.

Conclusion

Though some proposals for an industrial policy may have merits that are lacking in the proposals with which I happen to be familiar, those I know about are distressingly similar to their right-wing counterpart, the notion that tax cuts would be self-financing. They are, like the better-known versions of supply-side economics, manifestations of the difficulties the typical citizen's rational ignorance generates for modern democracy. Like the supply-side proposals, they also owe some of their support among politicians to the illusory perception that people can solve their most serious economic problems without confronting the powerful vested interests that mainly generated the problems. The best-known supply-side and industrial policy proposals are, finally, evidence that the familiar left- and right-wing ideologies, whatever their merits, do not offer a sufficient basis for generating policies that will solve our most serious economic problems.

Notes

1. Mancur Olson, *The Logic of Collective Action* (Cambridge: Harvard University Press, 1965).
2. David Smith, "Public Consumption and Economic Performance," *National Westminster Bank Review,* 1975.
3. Weede's article is forthcoming in the journal, *Public Choice*.
4. Kwang Choi, *Theories of Comparative Economic Growth* (Ames: Iowa State University Press, 1983).
5. Samuel Brittan, "How British Is the British Sickness?" *Journal of Law and Economics,* vol. 21 (October 1978), pp. 245–68.
6. Many of the relevant studies on the relation or lack of relation between the ideology of governments and the distribution of income are summarized in Erich Weede, "The Effects of Democracy and Socialist Strength on the Size and Distribution of Income," *International Journal of Comparative Sociology*, vol. 23, no. 3–4 (1982), pp. 151–65. See also Simon Kuznets, *Modern Economic Growth: Rate, Structure, and Spread* (New Haven, Conn.: Yale University Press, 1966); Malcolm Sawyer, "Income Distribution in the OECD Countries," OECD Occasional Studies (July 1976); Economic and Scientific Research Foundation, *Trends in Income Distribution: A Comparative Survey* (New Delhi).
7. Mancur Olson, *The Rise and Decline of Nations* (New Haven, Conn.: Yale University Press, 1982).

Commentaries

Sidney Blumenthal

Professor Olson suggests that neither left- nor right-wing ideologies really explain what has been going on and part of the reason he uses for that test is government. Does government, either its activity or inactivity, explain prosperity? One case that he cites is that of the United States and England, which he says was mainly laissez faire in the nineteenth century. Another case he cites was that of the welfare state after World War II in the United States. We had a growth of government recently, and yet we had prosperity. We had what seems to be little government in the past, and yet we had prosperity. How then can we deal with these ideologies?

My feeling is that government is not a blunt category and should not be considered as such. We should think not about government in general but about government in particular and perhaps about micropolicies. In thinking about government in terms of micropolicies, I am closer to discussing what I think some of the industrial policy advocates are talking about.

Consider laissez faire historically. Many historians talk about it as a policy that was conscious, deliberate, and imposed and run through government, a policy of tariffs, a policy of protection, and in England a policy of pulling people off the land, a system of establishing the early welfare state there. Here in the United States we had Abraham Lincoln with an industrial policy, if you will, toward the railroads, mineral acts, and timber acts. Lincoln was, in effect, enacting Henry Clay's industrial policy, what was called the American plan. Clay was Lincoln's great idol.

Does this mean that government ran everything? Well, I am talking about specific policies. I am not suggesting that the market itself was completely supplanted, but certainly government was crucial in creating the kind of industrialization that we had. Railroad rates, for example, were key in this. It was said that John D. Rockefeller did everything to state legislatures except refine them. So government was very important.

And the same is true of the twentieth century. Here I am talking about macrofiscal policies, specific policies.

Professor Olson talks about how special interest groups can obstruct progress because they silt up the river. He talks about how in some regions and countries, such as Japan, Germany, and even our own American southland, winds like those of war have blown these special interest groups over and great progress has resulted.

Yet my feeling is that recently at least the decline of traditional manufacturing industry in the South has been as great as it has been in the Midwest and the Northeast. The decline has to do with the kind of industry that is there. Furthermore, why has New England, where I have spent most of my life, enjoyed an incredible industrial renaissance in the past fifteen years? Why has Massachusetts now gone from a depressed economy, really a kind of Appalachia of the Northeast, to one of the most advanced postindustrial economies in the world?

Massachusetts is a place where special interests did exist; where they were not knocked down; where large institutions such as MIT, Harvard, and the other universities incubated high-tech industry, largely funded by the federal government; and where there was an enormous rate of taxation. Massachusetts was called "Taxachusetts." This situation provided a social welfare state that enabled the building of an infrastructure that drew the kind of people to Massachusetts to create this base.

I am not suggesting that government displaced the market. But I am suggesting that it was crucial in creating the kind of prosperity that Massachusetts now enjoys.

I also have a question about ideology here. Professor Olson says that if we knew all things about the power of lobbies and cartels, if we had complete information on all public issues, then lobbying would have no effect, cartels would not be tolerated, and we would not support, for example, supply-side economics.

Since I am not an economist, I would attribute this support to some other factors perhaps, which I would consider entirely political and not economic in their origin. Why, for example, does supply-side economics exist? This is Professor Olson's question. I think its existence results from the political agendas of certain people, unless one says that ideology is totally a reflection of the material realm and makes, a Marxian argument that everybody says simply what special interests standing behind them holding them up like puppets would have them say. Supply-side economics exists, for example, partly because of the editorial page of the *Wall Street Journal*. Nobody is paying the writers off. They simply believe this. The American Enterprise Institute itself played a role in the development of supply-side economics. It was actually at AEI that Jude Wanniski wrote his now notorious book, *The Way the World Works*. So is AEI simply a special interest, or is it a political institution that has an independent and autonomous existence? That is a question I have: What is the relation of ideology to the economic realm?

I have a question on industrial policy. Professor Olson says the authors of these industrial policy proposals should explain why a government board or agency would allocate capital more effectively than those people and firms that are investing their own money.

I agree. But also why—and I am thinking here in micro terms—should protectionist tariffs, for example, be granted without quid pro quos? Why should tax concessions be granted without quid pro quos? So the problem here is not of centralized government but of specific cases in specific industries.

Finally, I want to raise the question of efficiency in economic models. My feeling about efficiency is that there are some things beyond economics that have to be dealt with, say, purely in politics and if they are not, then greater inefficiencies might be introduced. These are things having nothing to do with the laws of supply and demand. But too much injustice—if, for example, political groups or special interests can combine and create a political situation in which certain actions may be prevented or not prevented—may inhibit growth.

So, I am not necessarily sure whether those political actions are economic in motive or political in motive because I am not convinced that ideology is a pure reflection of materialism.

Bruce Bartlett

One theme that seems to be coming through these discussions is that maybe or maybe not industrial policy in theory would work. Maybe it works in Japan; maybe it does not. Maybe it would work here in some idealized form, as Senator Hart perhaps imagines or maybe it would not.

But almost everybody seems to agree that, given the nature of our political institutions, it would never be implemented properly. We would never get the kind of industrial policy that would work or could work because the politicians will distort it and find ways of skewing it to get special benefits for their constituencies, whether for a particular congressional district or for the people who support a particular party.

We all should be indebted to Professor Olson for providing a theory of why this is true. Having been a member of the congressional staff for ten years, I agree fully that, no matter what one thinks about industrial policy in theory, it will never be implemented except in a way that would be grossly inefficient even by the standards of those people who support the idea.

If Professor Olson had stopped there, I would have no further comments. Unfortunately he attacked supply-side economics, and I will respond.

I think he misunderstands. I was on Congressman Kemp's staff and was involved in drafting the Kemp-Roth bill. Our feeling was that the ideology of the Republican party—to reduce government directly, to slash government spending, and to balance the budget—simply was not working politically. It was not getting any votes. We were very much under the influence of the neoconservative ideas of people like Irving Kristol. We decided to call a truce and say let us forget about cutting back the welfare state. Let us come to terms with it. But we cannot come to terms with it the way it is right now because, in addition to the direct cost to government in terms of the amount of revenue and spending, it creates a huge excess burden, as economists use the terminology, because the way in which the revenue is taken out of the economy and the way in which the spending is used is so inefficient.

So the idea was not to slash government spending but to raise enough revenue to pay for it in a much less costly way. And this is why all of our attention was always focused on the marginal tax rate. Our argument was very simple: people produce to be able to earn; and it is the aftertax reward for economic activity, whether that be saving or investment or work, that counts. Nobody has ever disputed this. We argued that one could juggle the tax system in such a way that one could raise the same amount of revenue with much lower tax rates.

This is one reason I think Professor Olson is unable to find the kind of international evidence in terms of comparisons between different countries that he thinks ought to exist to support the supply-side proposition. The direct amount of revenue raised by government is not necessarily a good indicator of the cost that the revenue-raising system imposes on the economy. One could have extremely high tax rates à la the Laffer curve, which so discourage economic activity in the taxed economy—perhaps there might be a flourishing underground economy—that the total amount of revenue raised might be very small. This would look like a supply-side haven when in fact it is exactly the opposite.

One could have a system that raises more revenue as a proportion of gross national product than our current tax system does, perhaps through a flat-rate or consumption tax, and that would be far, far less costly economically in terms of distorting incentives and would therefore allow the economy to bear a larger burden more easily.

There is a wonderful quote somewhere in Henry George about a pack horse that, if loaded in a certain way, would not be able to carry the burden; but if reloaded in a different way, it would be able to bear the burden. I think this was really the point we were getting at; and we had no support at all within the party or anyplace else for what we were talking about. I honestly believe that we won the battle of ideas.

One reason we were able to win is that there was somewhat of a vacuum on the other side because the economic events of the 1970s invalidated the economic theory that underlay the Democratic party, which was that one could have demand management. All one had to do was run government deficits à la Keynesian economics, and that would ensure prosperity.

But we had declining productivity. We had inflation and unemployment existing at the same time. This created a crisis of confidence and a political crisis for the Democrats that led to the development of industrial policy. The argument that we needed to pay attention to the supply side of the economy, whatever it is that determines the production of goods and services, won the day. Because of the ideology of the Democratic party, which is that one must use government directly to achieve one's ends, they had to come up with some new scheme. So they went back to the old-fashioned government-planning idea. Much in the current industrial policy proposals was really presaged by, for example, the Humphrey-Hawkins debate and, more particularly, the Humphrey-Javits planning proposal, which came about in a political climate or rather an economic climate that was not at all dissimilar to the climate in which industrial policy arose.

The Humphrey-Javits proposals came out around 1975 in the wake of the last recession in which people had some doubts about the viability of the market system. To the same extent industrial policy arose in the wake of the 1981 recession, and similarly when growth was restored the ideas went away. I would echo gladly what Sidney Blumenthal said about the absence of ideas in Professor Olson's work. It does come across as somewhat materialistic, that people vote only their pocketbook. One reason he may miss this point is that people are forward looking; and they are perfectly willing and able to make trade-offs that require them to be worse off temporarily in return for possibly being better off in the future. This includes concerns that they might have about their children. Therefore they take a much longer view, I think, than most politicians believe they do.

This is one reason also that some of the empirical data cause distortion. Sidney Blumenthal implied that some form of industrial policy was the secret of the success of Massachusetts, but he forgets that Governor King was slashing taxes during the same period.

Professor Olson says no data show the international comparisons. Well, a lot of data show reasons that certain states grow and others do not. Bob Genetski at the Harris Bank has done work showing that businesses are more willing to locate in a state that may temporarily have high tax rates but is in the process of reducing those rates than to locate in another state that may have much lower tax rates but is in the process of raising those rates. This is why people would be willing to locate, for example, in Massachusetts although the rates are much higher than they are in, say, Ohio. Ohio is in the process of raising its taxes; Massachusetts was in the process of cutting its taxes. So a lot of process that is not captured by looking at the data in a superficial way is involved here, and one has to get down and look at it much more deeply.

William Schneider

Mancur Olson's book *The Logic of Collective Action*, published some twenty years ago, is one of the few titles that deserve the cliché description of "seminal work." It certainly shook up American political science by demonstrating with fairly precise and elegant logic that all political participation is irrational. It is in no one's rational self-interest to do anything political. Therefore, we had the problem of rediscovering the wheel.

In many ways we rediscovered it the same way Dr. Samuel Johnson refuted Berkeley's theory of metaphysics about the question of whether a rock did or did not exist. Johnson kicked the rock, and said it was irrefutably there. Political participation does exist, and people do act in many ways that cannot be explained by their rational self-interest.

But we had to go out and rediscover exactly what those ways were and what theories explained them.

We are in the realm of big ideas in this discussion. Supply-side economics is a big idea. Industrial policy is a big idea. They are important because there was a need for big ideas on the political agenda, for simplifying important ideas. The problem, of course, with any big idea is that if one gives the man a hammer, all the world becomes a nail.

Supply-side economics is supposed to explain economic growth everywhere and always. The answer is simple: low taxes. Industrial policy is supposed to explain how one can get a more rational approach to government everywhere and always. And Professor Olson's notion of collective action is a big idea, which he uses to explain a great diversity and multiplicity of data for which, as Sidney Blumenthal explains quite correctly, there are many bothersome exceptions.

In the area of rational self-interest I would just point out that most Europeans do not regard this sort of thinking as quite as compelling as Americans do because they are aware of a whole tradition of thought that has not had much influence here, namely, the notion of group consciousness. There is a collectivist tradition in many societies, mostly absent in the United States, that posits simply that people do not behave in their rational self-interest because they identify their rational self-interest with a group. According to this tradition, people feel that their rational self-interest is indistinguishable from the interests of a group, and they will go through a great many sacrifices, which economists are at great pains to explain, to promote, not their own personal self-interest, but the well-being of an entire group.

Thus, for instance, many black Americans acquired a sense of group consciousness during the civil rights movement. They felt that they could behave rationally not to advance their own personal interests as individuals, but that the only way they could ever be better off as individuals was to advance the interests of the category of blacks in the United States.

Well, here we are dealing with class consciousness, group consciousness, partisanship, the whole realm of what political scientists are familiar with, namely, group activities and the identification of individual interests with the group interests. That notion raises many questions about the efforts, not just by Professor Olson but by many, particularly American, economists, to impose

275

the categories of economic analysis and economic thinking—for example, pure rational self-interest—on the area of political behavior.

We know where supply-side economics came from. We know why there was a need for industrial policy. There was a political need for finding a big idea that would explain and simplify a lot of very complicated information. Mr. Bartlett has given us some interesting clues as to where the supply-side economics idea came from: it came from a political need. Conservatives had to come to terms with the welfare state and to figure out some way that they could propose they had an answer to the problems of sluggish economic growth that would not be politically unpopular the way the traditional antigovernment answers of conservatives were. Then the conservatives redefined the political agenda. Now the Left has to find its big idea that will solve the country's problems without reliance on big government, which has now become unpopular, they have adopted the notion of industrial policy.

The debate between Jack Kemp and Gary Hart showed that supply-side economics and industrial policy share a central notion, which is avoidance of the ideologies of the Left and the Right. Neither side, neither Kemp nor Hart nor supply-side theorists nor industrial policy theorists in general, wants to become mired in the terms of the old debate. The old debate was government versus antigovernment. The Right said the solution to all the world's problems was to dismantle the federal government and let it do as little as possible. As Ray Shamie said when asked why he defeated Elliot Richardson in the Republican primary in Massachusetts, "Elliot believes that government can do good things for people. I don't." Well, that is the essence of the debate. That is the traditional philosophy.

Supply-side and industrial theorists want to get out of the rut of constantly defining issues as being either for or against government. So they propose a redefinition of terms by which government becomes a problem solver. Supply siders say that government will solve the problem of economic growth, and the tool by which it will do so is, of course, tax policy. Industrial policy theorists argue that the role of government is technocratic: to find rational solutions to economic problems by bringing together government and business. They argue that we already have an industrial policy; we just do not know it. As Gary Hart said, it is a catchall, crazy-quilt, hodge-podge, and what we need is a strong dose of rationality.

Both Kemp and Hart posited the same role of government as problem solver, but where they really differed was the old ideological issue. Kemp was really talking about less government. Hart was really talking about more government. Only they both had to find various ways of justifying their partisan positions. Hart had to call attention to national security needs as being overriding. He said economic growth does not solve all problems; the marketplace does not take care of certain national interests, and most of them can be justified in the name of national security. But one has to find some role for government. Kemp, of course, avoided any notion that any expansion of government activity was justified. Thus these old ideological categories are still bogging down the debate. The choice between Reagan and Mondale was not a new choice, but a very old choice. Ronald Reagan is a supply sider because supply side gives him a convenient tool, namely, lower taxes. He has always believed in lower taxes, but not for the same reasons that supply siders do. He believes in lower taxes because lower taxes mean less government. Ronald Reagan is a supply sider to the extent that he accepts that argument, but in the end his beliefs are just like Ray Shamie's. He does not believe that government can do good things for people. That is the traditional ideology.

Walter Mondale claimed that he has changed: the Democratic party has learned from the defeat of 1980, and he has new ideas and new approaches. But I do not think anyone really has fallen for that notion. Mondale is very much the representative of the old idea that government is the answer.

Where does all this end up? Professor Olson's notion is provocative. He states that the argument between big government and laissez faire is really phony: it has nothing to do with the reality of the problem, and it has nothing to do with problem solving, which of course the industrial policy theorists and supply siders would agree with instantly.

He argues that the issue is not Left or Right but cartelization. Both the Left and the Right have client constituencies, special interests that support them; and they are mostly in the business, not of providing ideological policies nor of solving national problems, but of paying off their special interests.

Well, I am a public opinion specialist, and I suppose my role here in part is to relate where the public comes out on all this. Generally speaking, the way the public sees the situation is more or less along the lines that Professor Olson sees. The public does not swing wildly Left and Right and is not very consistent or coherent ideologically. To the public the issues are special interests and cartelization, which are not seen as necessarily either private or public. When the public looks at the Republican party, it sees a party of special interests mostly private in nature—big business and the wealthy. When the public looks at the Democratic party, it sees a party oriented toward the special interests of big government and big labor. The whole point of the book I did with Martin Lipset on the confidence gap was that the public distrusts all special interest, all cartels, all collusion against the public interest; and it is, generally speaking, antiestablishment more than it is Left or Right.

Most of the energy behind the new ideas in politics, supply-side economics and industrial policy, is not so much liberal or conservative as it is antiestablishment. My feeling is that Ronald Reagan was elected, in large part, not because of the specific content of his antigovernment ideas (nobody wanted to dismantle the New Deal) or even because of his specific tax policies, but because he was new, untried, and antiestablishment. People were deeply dissatisfied with Jimmy Carter's policies, and by electing Ronald Reagan they were able to shake things up.

The appeal of a Gary Hart and many of the new-politics Democrats on the Left is precisely the same. They are outsiders. They are anti-Washington. They are not tied to the special interests, and if elected they would shake things up. That is precisely why Walter Mondale was in the most unfortunate position of being identified with the ancien régime, the way things were, and the old, established interests and traditionalists. Ronald Reagan could do something quite remarkable, which was as president of the United States to run an antiestablishment campaign against Walter Mondale.

The public sees things exactly that way: cartels are the problem; special interests are the problem.

When one looks at public opinion as I have on this issue, one discovers that industrial policy is both similar to and different from the supply-side theory. Industrial policy sells much better as a program than as a theory. The public rejects the idea that the federal government should have the power to control and direct the national economy because that is an attack on free enterprise. The public does support many of the specific programs advocated by industrial policy theorists, the kind of programs that Gary Hart called catchall, crazy-quilt, hodge-podge, irrational, and chaotic. Americans favor a more cooperative relation between government and business, particularly for solving specific social problems like energy, conservation, unemployment, and the decaying public infrastructure. But they believe that such cooperation should be on an ad hoc, chaotic, crazy-quilt basis. What they object to about industrial policy is precisely what most academic theorists find attractive: elevating government intervention in the marketplace into a system for allocating resources. To the public that is going too far. The public's feeling about industrial policy is exactly the opposite of its reaction to supply-side economics. The supply-side theory with its prescriptions for reviving free enterprise through spending cuts and tax cuts and deregulation was always more popular as a general theory than it was as a program because it was anti–big government.

A leading advocate of industrial policy, MIT Professor Lester Thurow makes the following argument, which is conventional now. He argues, since the Great Depression, government has had macroeconomic responsibilities: taxes, interest rates, and expenditures. We pretended that government has no responsibilities at the micro level. Of course, that is not true. Government has all kinds of microeconomic policies. I would add that government already intrudes heavily into the allocation of resources through ad hoc policies like tariffs, quotas, regulations, subsidies, credits, and purchasing decisions. The principal argument by Thurow and others for industrial policy is that we have an industrial policy now; we might as well do it right—rationally, coherently, with planning. Will the public buy this argument?

The answer is no, for the reason that Professor Olson suggests. Neither the business sector in this country nor the public shares this kind of faith in the inherent rationality of government. They figure that, if we have an industrial policy with business, government, and labor rationally planning our investment and allocation of resources, we are not likely to get what the academics say we will get, which is more rationality in decision making. We will get more politics in decision making. When business, government, and labor sit down to plan our economic policies, watch out. Instead of a more rational and planned economy, we will have business, labor, and government in collusion, cartelizing our national economic policy and lining each other's pockets.

Discussion

MR. OLSON: All three comments raise questions about the adequacy of a view of the world that emphasizes material interests, perhaps only material or economic or monetary interests.

Now, even though my paper is more than forty pages long, I did not have an opportunity to include a full statement of the argument. I would in fact agree with all three of the arguments to the effect that people care about things besides money and material goods. I would also agree that people are not by any means entirely or invariably self-interested. But the fundamental logic of my argument does not at all require that people be concerned only about money or only about themselves.

What would the typical citizen be doing with the time he or she is not spending on public affairs? Part of it might be spent at work making money; but only part of it. One of the main things for which people use the time that they do not spend researching public affairs is to be with their families or their friends. If one spends a lot of time as a typical citizen studying public affairs, one may have to neglect the family, for example. That is the kind of trade-off, as well as those with money and income, that I mean.

It is also true that people decidedly are not entirely self-interested creatures. Anyone who has been lost and asked for directions knows that practically everyone will give you directions for free. Most people also make contributions to charities. There is a lot of altruistic behavior.

Now, what proportion of the U.S. national income is given away to charity? Much, much less than 5 percent, so that, important as the charitable impulse is, we cannot mainly explain the allocation of resources in the United States by talking about charity.

Similarly, it is certainly true that the typical citizen spends some time studying public affairs because that typical citizen is patriotic and altruistic and willing to make some sacrifices for the good of the country, sacrifices approximately as large in relation to the citizen's available time as that citizen's contribution to the United Fund or in relation to that citizen's entire income.

So I believe that my argument and its logic stand, even though it is definitely not the case that people care only about money and definitely not the case that people are entirely self-interested.

Now, I believe I am lucky not only because of the courtesy and kindness of the discussants but also because of some of the examples they have chosen, particularly the examples of Mr. Bartlett and Mr. Schneider. I note Mr. Bartlett's account of the thinking in Congressman Kemp's office when supply-side economics was first adopted and Mr. Schneider's emphasis on how supply-side economics and industrial policy are really just different ways of describing or arguing for some of the old ideas. Why, as Mr. Bartlett said, was the old Republican idea—that government was too big and doing some things wrongly and free enterprise needed to be given a larger scope—not popular enough so that it had to be replaced by the idea that if one cut tax rates one would increase tax collections.

Well, there is a lot to be said for the idea that the government was mismanaging many programs and involved in many things it had no reason to be involved in. There was more merit in the familiar Republican idea than in the idea that cutting tax rates in the United States today would increase tax collections.

But the most meritorious ideas in the Republican arsenal were not the ones that had the most impact, but those that would least survive examination of the statistics on the matter. Though taxes do have harmful effects on incentives, if tax rates are cut and posttax income is increased people use part of that extra posttax income to buy leisure. When tax rates are cut, people then can often afford to work fewer hours. That result works in the opposite direction from the substitution effect of the tax cut, which does indeed make people work more. Thus the number of hours that people who have jobs voluntarily choose to work has not changed much since the tax cuts, and the rate of saving, as it happens, has gone down.

Similarly, Mr. Schneider's argument about how we should understand why people put forth supply-side economics arguments and industrial policy arguments is again evidence for the great force of rational ignorance in our society.

VOICE: I have a question about the example Mr. Blumenthal used for Professor Olson's theory about the declining industries in the South and also the Boston and Massachusetts renaissance—that, even though industries in the South are declining, they are growing faster there than they are someplace else. What is your reply to the Massachusetts illustration?

MR. OLSON: The old industries that are important in the economic history of Massachusetts are not so much industries like iron and steel as automobiles. The old industry of textiles ran into the same problems that the U.S. steel and automobile industries have run into; so did the U.S. footwear industry, much of which was once in Massachusetts, for exactly the same reasons. That is to say, a lot of collusion and lobbying occurred both among the firms and among the workers. These industries essentially closed down in Massachusetts. In the 1950s, even in the 1920s, exactly as my argument would predict, the textile industry moved to the South. The shoe industry has also to some degree moved, and that industry is in a great deal of trouble because of imports, even though there is a considerable measure of protection against imports of shoes.

So Massachusetts had suffered many problems I am talking about earlier than states like Michigan, Pennsylvania, and Ohio. Now, it is also true, as Mr. Blumenthal said, that Massachusetts has some distinguished schools of engineering, most notably at MIT, and that it is an attractive area in which to live, with its many cultural and other attractions for researchers and other highly educated people.

So it is indeed true that around Route 128 many high-technology firms are prospering and they are prospering in significant part because of the quality of the universities and intellectual life, particularly in engineering, in that part of the country. That, however, does not in any way refute my argument. The logic of collective action says that one will not get enough research on basic science or enough of the kind of work done in a big research-oriented university under laissez faire. The government must be involved because these goods are public goods and have to be financed out of tax revenues. Thus nothing in the Massachusetts circumstance seems to run against my theory. If one looks at the regressions on manufacturing employment, notwithstanding all that I have now said and all that Mr. Blumenthal said, Massachusetts has still done less well in the past fifteen or twenty years than most of the states in the South and the West.

VOICE: I am not trying to attribute the growth and recent prosperity of Massachusetts to a single factor. Conversely, I do not think any single factor can be attributed to it. In particular, Bruce Bartlett raises the question of Edward King's administration. When King was governor, taxes were cut. Most of the take-off of the high-tech industry occurred before King was elected.

That growth occurred under the first administration of Governor Michael Dukakis. In fact, many state government policies encouraged the growth of high-tech industries. Congressman Paul Tsongas, who became the senator from Massachusetts, was instrumental in the growth of Wang Laboratories in the Lowell area, getting several government policies to support that growth. So I do not attribute anything to a single factor.

I raise another question. Two states in the Southwest—Louisiana and Texas—have the same starting point in raw resources, namely, a vast amount of oil. Why then does Texas now have a burgeoning high-tech sector and Louisiana not? Several factors can be related to the difference; one of them certainly is that there is some venture capital in Dallas.

But also in Texas there is a willingness to devote many resources to certain public goods, in particular to the state university system, which does not exist in Louisiana, which consequently has virtually no high-tech sector. For that reason Texas is the advanced state of that region, and Louisiana has an economy based on a dwindling raw resource.

Part Five
Political Institutions and Industrial Policy

Introduction

The fourth and final part of the "Politics of Industrial Policy" conference focuses on the role that U.S. government institutions would play in the implementation of industrial policy proposals. Hugh Heclo, professor of government at Harvard University, examines the role of the U.S. executive branch in implementing industrial policies. Political scientist Robert Russell then follows with his analysis of the relation between the United States Congress and proposed industrial policy structures.

Hugh Heclo

In "Industrial Policy and the Executive Capacities of Government," Hugh Heclo first reviews several federal government activities to illustrate the character and scope of industrial policies—broadly defined—within the U.S. executive branch. He then outlines the "consensus" on the "requisite features of government management as that process that deals with industrial adjustment" implicit in the arguments of industrial policy advocates and opponents alike. Finally, he evaluates the major existing "barriers to effective microeconomic management" in the federal government and offers a strategy for their removal. "The real challenge," he states at the outset, "is not to specify the contents of an industrial policy but to find a politically sustainable process for arriving at and adapting such policies." The executive branch, within the context of the larger political and social environment, sets the administrative parameters to the industrial policy process.

That there are many large, uncoordinated U.S. industrial policies, Heclo notes, is widely known and accepted. Among the federal government activities deserving an industrial policy label, he lists government procurement programs, export promotion and import restriction measures, federally funded research and development, business-targeted tax incentives, workers' assistance programs, selective antitrust policies, and so-called emergency bailouts such as the New York and Chrysler rescues. Heclo adds that, political rhetoric notwithstanding, "creeping industrial policy has been very much with us during the Reagan administration." Indeed, he views President Reagan's 1983 establishment of the National Commission on Industrial Competitiveness and the political commitment for restoring industrial productivity and competitiveness that the gesture implied as affirming "a larger presumption of industrial policy . . . the presumption of government responsibility for economic performance."

However the government decides to fulfill that responsibility—whether through more comprehensive, planned, economic intervention as many industrial policy advocates would have or through greater reliance on market forces as the supporters of government neutrality argue—certain broad features of management are required. It is here, Heclo argues, that we find a common ground in the politically charged industrial policy debate—a consensus for the need for "improved government performance as it relates to microeconomic issues." This desired improvement in the system for policy management, he states, requires the presence of four features, "purposiveness, self-monitoring, bargaining acumen, and procedural predictability."

In some respects, recognizes Heclo, "our constitutional tradition and political habits are squarely at odds with the kind of managerial requisites I have described." Numerous barriers to effective microeconomic management exist. These barriers, however, are not immutable. They point not only to limitations imposed by the American political system on the industrial policy process but also to opportunities for constructive change to enhance that very process.

The diversity, fragmentation, and "functional localism" of the U.S. executive branch operates against managerial efficiency. So, too, does the large and frequent turnover of leadership personnel in the federal government. The absence of "predictable procedures and institutionalized staff capacities" in the Office of the President, states Heclo, creates a "hollow center" that simply exacerbates these problems. Other barriers include an overall weakness in economic staffing as well as "an inability of the federal government to compose itself and others into reliable bargaining units." Finally, Heclo reminds us that public opinion itself is a barrier. Americans lack one, "overarching, operational goal for economic policy," oppose extensive government interventions to direct the economy, and are highly skeptical of close government and industry ties.

These barriers, concludes Heclo, argue for prudence in efforts to improve the industrial policy process. "Proposals that run against the grain of existing political incentives are dead-end." Industrial policy initiatives should be undersold and, perhaps, the word itself changed to "some sleep-inducing code word such as the *management of microeconomic programs*." Overambitious programs raise expectations and unnecessarily threaten those with a stake in the status quo, both undermining support. We need to "recognize that industrial policy is not some *thing* that gets made. . . . It is a process that gets learned." We should concentrate our efforts on gradual changes in policy machinery, building on existing foundations wherever possible. Heclo suggests that "improving the national government's capacities for fact finding and forum building should be two priority areas." Grand coalitions should be shunned as socially unadministrable in the American system. "An ungrand coalition approach, using many smaller forums and shunning the dramatic gesture in favor of normal politics and normal labor relations," he argues, "seems to be more promising."

Robert W. Russell

In "Congress and the Proposed Industrial Policy Structures," Robert Russell analyzes the potential impact of a new government entity designed to analyze, create, and forge U.S. industrial policies and its interaction with Congress. Most comprehensive industrial policy proposals specifically aim to rectify the lack of coordination and centralization in the U.S. system for economic policy making. This lack of coordination or ad hoc quality of U.S. economic policies, however, can be attributed in great part to the institutional structure and operation of Congress, raising serious questions about the compatibility of industrial policy structures and the U.S. legislative body.

Many industrial policy proposals have received congressional attention since 1980. Russell notes that efforts to compile and synthesize these proposals would quickly get out of hand. "At times the debate seems to encompass every government activity that might affect the economy." Instead he concentrates on the one representative, comprehensive industrial policy proposal to be reported favorably by a congressional committee—H.R. 4360, the "Industrial Competitiveness Act"—in an effort both to illustrate just how an industrial policy structure might interact with Congress and to evaluate whether such proposals would be operationally viable. H.R. 4360 would establish three institutional entities for industrial policy activities: a Council on Industrial Competitiveness composed of representatives from business, labor, government, and academia to analyze competitiveness problems and recommend strategies for their resolution; a Bank for Industrial Competitiveness with funds to help in the restructuring of basic industries and the capitalization of new ventures; and a Federal Mortgage Association with money to supplement the secondary market for commercial mortgages to help smaller businesses purchase facilities and equipment.

The institutional objective of this and similar proposals, states Russell, "is to change the way economic problems are analyzed by providing a new institution with a composition and mandate different from those of existing institutions." The need for such a change arises from "the belief that existing institutions promote conflict rather than consensus" on important economic policy questions. There is further, a continually voiced complaint that current industrial policies surface in an ad hoc, inefficient manner producing, according to one congressional report, a "jumbled" and "untidy heap" of measures that lack cohesion or a central, overriding objective. H.R. 4360 and other industrial policy measures address this problem by proposing "that economic conflicts should be resolved outside Congress and the executive branch and the results brought to Congress (or an executive branch agency) for implementation." Industrial policy advocates, argues Russell, are in effect "reinventing a Congress, although a Congress with fewer powers and chosen on an interest group basis rather than a geographical basis."

What many fail to appreciate fully, however, Russell continues, is that "the industrial policies we have are the industrial policies that Congress built" and that to question the formation of these policies is tantamount to direct criticism of Congress and the way it operates. According to industrial policy proponents, "so much of the activity that makes Congress what it is . . . apparently would need to change to have an effective industrial policy."

Would these new industrial policy structures in fact change the way Congress operates, and would Congress be willing to relinquish sufficient power to achieve the institutional efficiency that many claim is needed? Russell's answer is no to both questions. Delegating advisory powers "would not immunize new industrial policy institutions from the necessity all executive branch agencies and most independent agencies have to give deference to authorization and appropriations committees of Congress." Whether congressional committees heed the industrial policy council's advice would ultimately depend on the same politicized interaction of forces that govern congressional decisions today. That, of course, could be rectified by granting the council greater powers, but Congress does not really want to undermine its own power. "To hope for the magic of consensus to work its will is one thing; to delegate substantive power away from Congress and the executive branch is another."

Russell concludes that "perhaps no industrial policy structure is consistent with congressional policies." The purpose of an industrial policy entity is to achieve neat, clean, depoliticized decisions on fundamental economic policy questions. This mandate conflicts head on with the operation of Congress as an institution. "Congressional politics could not be depoliticized," he states, "without changing the fundamental character of Congress." Russell argues that new industrial policy structures are not the appropriate means of achieving a greater sense of purpose and cohesion to economic policy making. Public education and the electoral process must be used to "generate public support and bring it to bear on Congress and the executive agencies."

Commentaries

Stuart E. Eizenstat. In his commentary, Stuart Eizenstat emphasizes that, although conflicting interests do indeed dominate the American political system and there is no "mythical consensus process in which everyone, the lion and the lamb, will sit down and all agree," it is still possible and in fact necessary to structure the decision-making process to achieve greater coordination of microeconomic policies. The most important thing to realize, argues Eizenstat, is that industrial policy is not a policy. "It is a process for making the microeconomic decisions that we make every day, every week, every year in government." We would not think of forming macroeconomic or budget policy without some coordination, yet we continue to deny these same standards for microeconomic policies. As a result, Eizenstat continues, government makes continual, ad hoc concessions to special interests without gaining reciprocal concessions—quid pro quos.

Edwin L. Harper. Challenging Mr. Eizenstat's conclusions, Edwin Harper argues that Eizenstat underestimates the significance of the lack of consensus on microeconomic policies in the United States. A consensus is needed to implement workable industrial policies, and no "amount of institutional tinkering is going to create a consensus about a rational, comprehensive approach to microeconomic policy." Although he agrees with Heclo's and Russell's assessments of the institutional barriers confronting a unified industrial policy, he reiterates his contention that the principal problem is not an institutional one. Forums for "consensus building with respect to microeconomic decisions . . . are not in short supply; the consensus is what is in short supply." Given this paramount constraint, industrial policy is reduced to an increase in government centralization—an inherently bad idea. Harper states, "there is certainly a very small, relatively finite number of decisions that can be effectively elevated to the top of any organization . . . especially the government."

William Lilley III. In the final commentary of the conference, William Lilley emphasizes his belief that this session, the entire conference, and in fact the broader national focus on "big, grandiose policy" like industrial policy can be traced directly to America's trade problem: the belief that American competitiveness is on the decline. This belief has created "a ready, willing audience to say that there is a devil somewhere . . . and we have to get that devil" by changing policy. Many of the surrounding claims such as deindustrialization are unfounded and, unfortunately, are being used by some to rally support for interest-specific protectionist measures. This whole process, states Lilley, reveals an important dichotomy in our society between goods-producing and services-producing industries that has significant implications for policy making. For a multitude of reasons, the goods-producing industries have long-established ties to the U.S. policy-making institutions. Services, however, do not. This discrepancy, he concludes, must be rectified to establish one important step toward more coherent, realistic economic policy.

Industrial Policy and the Executive Capacities of Government

Hugh Heclo

Industrial policy seems to have lost its topicality. In my view this is the best possible time for a serious discussion of the subject. If the proponents of industrial policy are correct, now is the time to prepare for the mounting economic disasters that lie ahead. If the opponents of industrial policy are right—the nation's economy is back on track, and all the United States might need is a better balance of macroeconomic policies—then we will have caused ourselves only a little embarrassment by attending to a new idea whose time has come and gone.

The purpose of this paper is to consider the relation between industrial policy and the executive capacities of government. Narrowly conceived, this assignment invites us to address a single basic question: What is likely to be administrable? The kinds of personnel, the sustainable procedures, the organizational wherewithal—surely these are important matters that tend to be systematically undervalued when public policy commitments are made in the United States. For example, many of us would probably agree that the nation would have been better served had greater attention been paid to practical problems of administration as new ideas bubbled up in the early 1960s and culminated in the Great Society programs. We should not want to repeat the experience of overpromising and underperforming in the area of industrial policy.

At the same time, the following pages will make clear that I have found it necessary to go beyond a strictly executive-based administrative focus. Industrial policy is a concept that requires one to reflect more broadly on what is "socially administrable." By that phrase I mean the working rules and understandings by which things actually get done in this country. The carrying out of industrial policy is at least as likely to be shaped by this preexisting context as it is to set in motion any new relationships.

The first section of this paper sets the stage with a brief description of existing approaches to industrial policy within the executive branch. This section is followed by a discussion of what seem to be the organizational requisites of mainstream industrial policy proposals. Rather than considering any given set of proposals in detail, I have tried to distill the underlying requirements common to a broad range of positions. The third section outlines executive and other barriers to meeting these requirements. In the final section several strategies for overcoming these barriers are weighed. From my admittedly biased political science perspective the real challenge is not to specify the contents of an industrial policy but to find a politically sustainable process for arriving at and adapting such policies. Others undoubtedly will wish to argue that we cannot sensibly think about how to organize processes until we know what the policy is to be. Section two below tries to fudge that issue of structure-following-strategy.

At the outset two analytic dead-ends should be identified and avoided. On the one hand, to imagine that industrial policies can be instituted simply by urging people to recognize their own or their country's best interests would be naive. Proposals that run against the grain of existing political incentives are a dead-end because they offer no way of getting from here to there. They become wholly, and deservedly, vulnerable to the logic of the status quo. Thus, for example, it is easy to suggest (1) that any new industrial policy organization lacking the power to allocate financial resources will be too weak to affect the customary behavior of existing players; and (2) that an organization with such power will either be too threatening to be approved by the existing structures of power or, if approved, will simply attract and reproduce within itself all the old politics of contending powers.

On the other hand, to begin from the premise that constraints are fixed and capacities of government given for all time would be unduly narrow. Prevailing political incentives are not immutable or self-interpreting. Thus, for example, governmental capabilities have evolved and have been institutionalized in ways that would have astonished the narrow-minded observer of prevailing incentives at the outset. One thinks of the unified executive budget, the Federal Reserve Board, NASA, congressional delegation of trade policy powers to the president, or the recent Social Security Reform Commission. What is is not necessarily what can be.

Industrial Policies in the Federal Executive

By now pointing out that the federal government has long had a large and uncoordinated number of implicit industrial policies has become commonplace. In fact, never in our history have implicit and often explicit industrial policies been wholly absent from our national politics. If industrial policy means government intervention to deal with the problems of specific sectors, then one can certainly point to a long history of Washington involvement with trade or transportation, for example. Politicians and bureaucrats may not have required safety equipment on Conestoga wagons, but they certainly did dwell on problems of national roads, canals, steamboats, and public aid to railroad expansion. If, for another example, industrial policy includes efforts to improve the workings of financial markets, then the long-running debate on a national bank would certainly qualify at least as a nondecision in industrial policy; how to organize and direct the flow of capital resources was precisely the issue.

These examples were not peripheral political topics. Indeed, in their time such issues stood at the center of intense partisan arguments as to what kind of nation, with what kind of governmental power, this country was to be.[1] My point in raising these hoary illustrations is to suggest that any new, self-consciously explicit industrial policy is likely to do exactly the same.

Today industrial policy has given a name to any number of executive branch activities. Everyone's classification scheme will differ, but the following eleven categories give some flavor of the range of relevant federal activities.

Procurement Programs. Obviously federal government purchases from the private sector have a direct effect on the workings of American industry. In fiscal year 1983, $58.2 billion was spent on major equipment acquisitions, approximately 97 percent of which were defense purchases.[2] Before the major defense buildup initiated by the Reagan administration, Pentagon purchases were accounting for over one-half of the total output in aircraft engines and shipbuilding, one-third in television and radio equipment, and one-quarter in engineering and scientific equipment industries. The indirect effects on industrial strategy are undoubtedly much greater. Thus the development of the silicon transistor and the integrated circuit occurred with the large potential military market clearly in mind. On a more skeptical note, critics can point to negative effects on industrial competitiveness: favoritism toward large firms and barriers to small firm entry; national security restrictions on the flow of information between the defense and commercial sectors, even in the same company; and perverse incentives in a system in which profits tend to increase rather than decrease with increased costs.

Beyond the actual acquisition of equipment are other programs of government purchases—for example, in public works infrastructure—that provide economic preferences to promote American industry. This federal share of infrastructure expenditure was estimated at $24 billion in fiscal year 1984, and concern for giving support to American industry through this means has grown. Thus the 1982 Surface Transportation Act significantly strengthened the preexisting Buy-America policy by requiring all federally funded highway work to use American-made steel and cement unless foreign products would reduce total project costs by at least 25 percent.[3]

Generalizing very broadly, defense procurement offices concentrate on securing reliable supplies of desired military materials and make little pretense of including the promotion of strong civilian economic structures in the definition of national security. An office for procurement policy in the president's Office of Management and Budget has traditionally attended to auditing proprieties and cost effectiveness in civilian purchases.

Export Promotion Programs. Although skeptics have often raised questions about their effectiveness,[4] federal credit and tax programs to encourage industrial (and other) exports have been given more attention in recent years. Loans and loan guarantees for foreign purchasers of American goods arise out of the Export-Import Bank and its related Overseas Private Investment Corporation. In 1982 the Export Trading Company Act moved more aggressively beyond earlier measures (mainly the hortatory Webb-Pomerene Act dating from the 1920s) to encourage smaller U.S. firms to enter international markets through the formation of export-trading companies that are allowed to be wholly or partially owned by banks and certified against antitrust prosecution. The postponement of federal taxes on export businesses has been experimented with, and at the end of the Carter administration, a transfer of functions from the State Department to a new Foreign Commercial Services office was intended to provide more help and information for U.S. exporters.

Import Restrictions. Although mainly committed to free trade in the postwar period (apart from agricultural products and textiles), the executive branch has found itself increasingly involved in recent years in the internal problems of particular industries and their demands for protection from "unfair" foreign competition. In 1977, 1980, and 1982, for example, the U.S. steel industry responded to recurrent crises by filing suits claiming dumping and unfair subsidies by governments to foreign steel producers.[5] These suits have helped pressure the federal government into various trigger price mechanisms and import quotas as the price for withdrawing the suits. Beginning in 1977 marketing agreements with Japan and other Far Eastern nations limited the importation of electronic equipment. In 1981 a "voluntary" limitation of Japanese auto exports came into effect. Federal loans, loan guarantees, and technical assistance have been used to support the footwear industry against import competition. In 1983 the Reagan administration accepted a revitalization plan from the Harley-Davidson motorcycle company in justifying the imposition of protections against Japanese imports. These and similar activities have evolved in a complex interplay of organizational forces, with the executive branch players typically including the president's Office of the U.S. Trade Representative; the Commerce, State, Treasury, and Labor departments; and the Council of Economic Advisers. On the whole there has been a growing willingness to use the threat or the reality of import restrictions to retaliate against foreign exporters penetrating the U.S. industrial market.[6]

295

Assistance to Workers. Federal programs to facilitate the economic adjustments of labor, as opposed to capital, appear rather small; but two types are worth mentioning. One type concentrates on workers in industries suffering economic decline, usually through the effect of foreign trade; and the second type deals more broadly with upgrading the skills of the industrial work force.[7]

Until 1982 the major program for assisting workers harmed by foreign competition was the Trade Adjustment Assistance (TAA) program offering cash help and related services. In 1982 the Job Training Partnership Act (JTPA) added a federally funded and state-administered program providing training and relocation assistance to victims of plant closings and to unemployed persons with little chance of returning to their old jobs. While this JTPA program is funded at approximately $225 million per year, the Labor Department's TAA has also continued to exist and is funded at $125 million for fiscal year 1984 (down from a high of $2 billion in 1980). In effect, these changes in TAA simply formalized what had long been the fact, that the aid was mainly a form of extended unemployment benefit with little effect on labor mobility. What the new JTPA program might add to the picture remains to be seen; its own lineage traces back to the 1962 Manpower and Development Training Act, which became transformed by the War on Poverty into a program concerned exclusively with the hard-core poor and subsequently changed into the much-amended CETA program with its attention to public jobs.

More general programs for retraining the industrial work force have remained a patchwork affair. Federal support for vocation education has changed little in constant dollars since the early 1970s, but rapidly growing state resources have sparked a rapid growth of regional vocational and technical schools. The Labor Department's Bureau of Apprenticeship and Training oversees apprenticeship programs occupying a very small proportion of even the highly skilled portions of the work force. While aiming mainly at the disadvantaged, the Private Industry Council program begun in the Carter administration provides a local focus for labor market information and public training programs seeking a more structured relationship with the private sector.

Support for Research and Development. The federal government plays a large role in subsidizing research and development (R and D) expenses that affect the welfare and competitiveness of industry. Direct government R and D spending, totaling $39 billion in fiscal year 1983, is heavily concentrated in national defense and space industries and to a lesser extent in the health sector (important for the pharmaceutical industry). Indirect support is spread more widely through tax provisions encouraging private sector R and D, representing forgone tax revenues of $2.4 billion in fiscal year 1983.[8]

Informational Services to Industry. The federal government incurs costs of gathering and distributing information on various fronts that are mainly of use to industrial consumers. The Commerce Department's annual *Industrial Outlook* forecasts the growth prospects of 250 industries, usually in much greater detail than industrial forecasts by Japan's MITI. Programs aiming to encourage the dissemination of technologies arising from government activities are listed in the *Directory of Federal Technology Transfer*, in which NASA plays a prominent role.[9] The government's Center for Technical Information provides a clearinghouse function, and the Commerce Department's new Office of Competitive Assessment is currently carving out its role. Technical assistance offered to firms through regional activities of the Economic Development Administration, the Small Business Administration, and trade adjustment assistance offices in the Commerce Department provide their own informational services.

Business-Targeted Tax Incentives. Even leaving aside more general tax breaks favorably affecting certain industries (for example, tax relief for mortgage interest and consumer credit help the housing and consumer durable goods industries), many more targeted revenue losses promote certain types of business. Depletion allowances and exploration expensing in energy industries, safe harbor leasing rules, and capital gains treatment of coal royalties would be examples. By far the largest such tax expenditure ($20 billion in fiscal year 1982) is the investment tax credit, which by no means treats all investments the same. Thus, compared with 1980 tax rates, the net effect of the Reagan administration's tax-cutting package of 1981 and the revenue enhancement legislation of 1982 was to increase the effective tax rate on corporate investments by 28 percent if the investments went to assets in the form of computers and office machinery, to reduce effective tax rates 23 percent for investment in engines and turbines, and to leave tax rates unchanged (but high) on land and inventory investment.[10]

Selective Antitrust Policy. During the past ten years, the traditionally uniform antitrust policy opposing major business combinations has become more contingent and tailored to particular circumstances. Calculating what these circumstances might be has increasingly involved executive branch officials—particularly in the Justice Department's antitrust division and, to a lesser extent, the Federal Trade Commission—in detailed assessments of particular industrial sectors and firms. For example, the Reagan administration further developed guidelines begun in the Carter administration to reduce the antitrust liability of firms engaged in joint research ventures. Likewise the Justice Department appears to have become more forthcoming in offering advice as to how merger plans can be designed to be acceptable under the law, and in the case of steel, positively encouraging such mergers to promote world competitiveness. Following a similar line of development, enforcement activities in areas of social regulation, such as the Occupational Safety and Health Administration, have sought to use federal personnel in a more consultative than traffic-cop role. This development too would seem to entail a more detailed federal assessment of industrial conditions to tailor such discretion to economic conditions.

Promoting Regional Economic Development. Under the rubric of regional economic programs, the federal government supplies an array of credit assistance, grants, and technical assistance that has an impact on industry. Programs of the Economic Development Administration for ostensibly distressed areas and of the Small Business Administration for groups lacking full access to capital markets have typically begun with the intention of being targeted and have been expanded by political pressures to cover more of the country. As many observers have pointed out, the federal government has thereby become a major participant in many regional development programs for industry without necessarily having any larger national strategy of economic development in mind within the executive branch as a whole.[11]

Emergency Bailouts. The Lockheed rescue in 1971, New York City in 1975 and 1978, and Chrysler in 1979 stand out as three promontories of federal intervention. Were these loans, loan guarantees, and special waivers of federal requirements industrial policy? Perhaps not intentionally; but each incident successively helped create a precedent and a principle that the federal government should, in the full glare of public controversy, make special efforts to pursue sectoral economic goals. The votes in Congress became successively easier, the principle more widely accepted.[12]

Structuring Negotiating Forums. Designing the architecture of public and private decision making is not a small matter for problems of industrial adjustment. In far more ways than can be summarized here, the federal government has attempted to play such a role. A potpourri of recent such instances (neglecting the three emergency bailouts mentioned above), could range from the forty-five advisory committees composed of industrial, labor, and agricultural interests working under the Office of the U.S. Trade Representative to more fleeting features of the landscape. Examples would be the federal labor-management committees formed under government auspices in the 1970s that fell apart when the AFL-CIO failed to pass labor law reform in 1978; the Steel Tripartite Committee begun in 1978 and chaired by the secretaries of labor and commerce; the Labor Department Productivity Commission's assisting states to set up plant shutdown aide units; and many other forums familiar only to Washington insiders.

Again, some of the more enduring of such activities have occurred in the defense area. Since 1961 the Pentagon's Office of Economic Adjustment has brought together federal and community planners to develop strategies for transforming unnecessary military bases into productive civilian facilities capable of preserving jobs in those communities affected by base closings.

Such is the federal government's role in free enterprise America. I cannot begin to summarize programs at the subnational government level. All fifty states have some form of economic development programs, around thirty have high-technology commissions of one type or another, ten states have industrial research support systems or product innovation groups. One could include intermediate level forums (for example, the Metropolitan Council of St. Paul/Minneapolis or the New England River Basin Commission) as well as government contributions to various industry committees examining long-term issues (such as employer/employee committees in the food industry dealing with the effect of boxed beef and electronic checkout at supermarkets or the automation of sewing in the clothing industry), the tax exemption of state industrial bonds, and all the rest. But enough is enough. If we confine ourselves only to the level of the federal government and to the more clear-cut, direct forms of support for U.S. business involving financial resources, a conservative estimate prepared by the Congressional Budget Office put the figure for fiscal year 1984 at $130 billion, which includes the agricultural sector but excludes the bulk of defense spending.[13] Of this total about 30 percent was derived from federal credit programs, 15 percent from direct spending, and most of the remainder from federal tax expenditures.

What do these executive branch activities portend for the real trends in industrial policy? In announcing the formation of the National Commission on Industrial Competitiveness in 1983, President Reagan declared that "the history of progress in America proves that millions of individuals making decisions in their own legitimate self-interest cannot be out-performed by any bureaucratic planner."[14] Of course, a middle ground between those two extremes exists, however, and the myriad federal activities I have just listed fall precisely in that middle ground between millions of individuals making their own decisions and a bureaucratic planner deciding for everyone. As many of the illustrations in my brief catalogue suggest, "creeping industrial policy" has been very much with us during the Reagan administration—expressed through defense procurement, trade policy, fine tuning of antitrust policy, differential treatment of asset investment through tax policy, and all the rest. In the long run, maybe even a larger presumption of industrial policy has been affirmed by the Reagan experience, the presumption of governmental responsibility for economic performance. To be sure, this responsibility has been cast in negative terms during the past four years, at least rhetorically if not in terms of actual programs. Having accepted the premise of a political program for restoring industrial productivity and competitiveness, however, any party in power will hereafter have difficulties claiming that problems of industrial performance are really not an issue for political decision (whether those problems require more or less of some kinds of intervention).

What Doth Industrial Policy Require of Thee?

To advocates of industrial policy, such a list of federal activities confirms rather than denies the need for change. Consolidating programs into an aggregate total of credit subsidies, tax expenditures, or other federal interventions merely produces an academic artifact concealing the lack of overall strategy. The problem is precisely that—too many programs and too little policy.

The large number of proposals presented in Congress and the popular press have spawned a no less prolific literature in opposition to industrial policy. In the politically charged context of the past few years, the battle lines have become clearly drawn in intellectual as well as party circles: a Reich, Thurow, Rohatyn, Etzioni, Harrison, and Bluestone on one side; and a Stein, Schultze, Wildavsky, Weidenbaum, and Robert Lawrence in the opposition camp. The way our political marketplace for policy ideas has come to operate, to have a nuanced conversation searching for central tendencies on this or on other subjects of public importance is becoming difficult.[15]

The content of particular industrial policy proposals and the dubious justification of those proposals have generated the most controversy. In examining these well-publicized differences, however, I have been struck by how much common ground probably exists once one stops trying to score debating points. From what I have read, industrial policy advocates in their more sober moments do not appear enthusiastic for a large central bureaucracy's targeting resources on predetermined winners and losers. Likewise opponents, when they are not ravaging industrial-policy hype, can usually be found arguing quietly that existing microeconomic programs should be made to work better. Even those who contend that the only policy needed is for government to get out of the intervention business will usually recognize that a sudden, massive withdrawal on all fronts could produce more problems than it solves. To pursue the constructive routes of withdrawal and avoid bull-in-the-china-shop behavior, government must know its own mind and act thoughtfully. In short, it is possible to imagine improving the strategic capacities of government without endorsing what any given strategy should be.

The common ground that I find in the industrial policy debate concerns requisite features of government management as that process deals with problems of industrial adjustment. Granted, these characteristics are less dramatic than a debate about a national investment bank. First things first, however: Before arguing too much about the product line, we might think a little more about the principles of design.

The consensus that I find implicit in the industrial policy debate (and hereby waving a red flag to all contrarians in the audience), runs roughly as follows. Improved government performance as it relates to microeconomic issues implies four features.

1. If industrial policy is to have any meaning, it implies an executive branch that is more purposive than normally has been the case. Whether one prefers government to be more directive in its interventions or to maintain more neutrality in resource allocation, the requirement is that government be conscious of what it wants so that it can deal with pressures to the contrary. Without that consciousness, there is no policy, only the arbitrary sum of programmatic parts. Of course knowledge is imperfect, life uncertain. Purposiveness envisions a government able to respond to the inevitable surprises and exceptions with more enduring goals in mind. If the invariable response is ad hocery, talk of industrial policy is nonsense.

Consider a recent example. In a widely noted article Charles Schultze disparaged the need for or possibility of conducting U.S. industrial policy. In an earlier, less-noticed piece, however, Schultze persuasively argues the case against imposing quotas on Japanese auto imports.[16] In the first, doubts are cast on any notion that government is purposive enough to direct benefits among winners and losers selectively. In the second, a plea is made that government be self-conscious and steadfast in purpose. Namely, government should generally refuse to validate uneconomic increases in employee benefits through import protection. Whichever version of industrial policy one prefers, there is common ground in searching for ways to make government more capable of knowing and acting upon its purposes (the auto import quotas were imposed by the Reagan administration as Schultze's article went to press, at an estimated cost to U.S. consumers of $160,000 annually for every job saved in the domestic car industry).[17]

2. Any form of industrial policy is likely to require a system of policy management that takes cognizance of the effects of interaction among its own activities. This system does not mean that all actions are coordinated or coherent to produce one monolithic thrust. It does mean that government's right hand should know what its left hand is doing—whether for actively promoting industrial change or for getting out of the way of market forces. Without this capacity, government officials will never be in a position to understand and cope with the shadow that passes between purpose and result. For lack of a better term I will call this capacity *self-monitoring*.

3. Industrial policy implies an ability to calculate quid pro quos. Government desires need not always prevail, but the government must at least be recognized as a player at the bargaining table who can make claims on others and not be thought of simply as an empty arena where others deal. If industrial policy means simply striving to reduce government interventions that prevent efficient market operations, then recognizing that some side payments will be

necessary is only realistic. Some of the new market insecurities may actually retard market mobility while some security-enhancing side payments may encourage mobility. How will government officials choose to deal? Likewise, a more interventionist industrial policy will mean little if no means exist for ensuring that the desired responses are being made in return for the commitment of public resources. Calculating any of these types of quid pro quo requires a good deal of practical knowledge accumulated before any bargaining begins or bail-out emergencies arise.

4. Procedural predictability appears to be a necessary (though not sufficient) condition for the preceding three administrative requisites of industrial policy. We should not mince words. Industrial policy is tough love for the economic system; it is not an exercise in how to win friends and influence nobody. If microeconomic issues are processed as though passing through a pinball machine—a kind of random Brownian movement hit by disparate globs of political power—then there will be little chance of sustaining purposive behavior, little realistic means of self-monitoring, little way of extracting quid pro quos against the omnipresent opportunity for end-runs. The implicit political theory of industrial policy is a politics of what Roger Fisher has called "principled negotiation" in which participants, still focusing on their individual interests, tend to be less adversaries and more problem solvers trying to discover options for mutual gain.[18] How will people come to see themselves in that way? Surely not by haphazardly clashing with each other in a whirl of one-night stands. The evolution of cooperation is a fragile enterprise. If cooperation is to have any chance to occur, some reliable way of memorializing past commitments and of warning people that they will have many subsequent dealings with each other must exist. That is the meaning of procedural predictability in industrial policy: finding enduring ways of encouraging people to aggregate rather than merely to mobilize their interests.

Opponents of certain industrial policy proposals have of course argued that an ad hoc, case-by-case approach is in fact exactly the right approach. Regularizing any procedure to bail out or otherwise assist certain industries and firms will simply attract business and legitimize what should be an exception to the rule. This argument is just another way of supporting procedural predictability—from the vantage point of a different policy preference. If one's preferred policy rule is that government should trump the market's judgments only in exceptional circumstances, then some mechanism of discipline and self-restraint is necessary to sustain this process of decision-by-exception. Mere ad hoc actions are unlikely to suffice.

These four design criteria suggest to me that we would do well to shift the debate from industrial policy per se and talk more in terms of improving the management of microeconomic policies. For in a recognition of the need for improving such capacities one finds a common ground. What, broadly understood, does industrial policy require of the executive machinery of government? It requires a system of management that does not—at least not invari-ably—sacrifice consistency of purpose and predictability to soft options and short-term pressures. It requires that departures from allocational neutrality be carried out in a self-conscious, calculating manner and not by the random bumping of political forces in the night. Purposiveness, self-monitoring, bargaining acumen, and procedural predictability would be the hallmarks of such a system of policy management.

Barriers to Effective Microeconomic Management

One can certainly argue that our constitutional tradition and political habits are squarely at odds with the kind of managerial requisites I have described. As Charles Schultze has said, "The American government, after all, was not established to bring order and authority out of social chaos."[19] Yet if that statement were entirely true, we would still be living under the Articles of Confederation. Since our constitutional tradition is really not a set of answers but an invitation to struggle over problems of order and diversity, authority and accountability, we will not get very far by staying at a general level of argument as to what our system of government does or does not allow. The point is not whether we can move all the way to some pure form of purposive-ness or procedural coherence. It is to identify the barriers that inhibit us from moving somewhat more in that direction and to think how these constraints might be relaxed.

Executive Branch Diversity. Many comments about the fragmentation of Congress can be applied with equal force to a similar fragmentation within the executive branch, notwithstanding the constitutional myth of a single execu-tive power embodied in the presidency. Whereas parochialism in the legisla-ture typically runs to geographic constituencies, the executive branch exhibits a kind of functional localism. A 1978 study by officials of the Carter adminis-tration surveyed all of the 132 economic policy-making units of the executive branch operating at the bureau level and found that the dozens of microecono-mic instruments (such as interest rates, credits, tariffs, and production con-trols) were, as the author stated,

> apportioned among the units and among departments and agencies without formal or informal lines of operating authority or coordina-tion. The authority to fix interests rates, for example, was claimed as a sole prerogative by 2 units, while 5 others claimed to share responsibility. Fifteen different units claimed some authority for decisions affecting national commodity stockpiles. Nine units thought they had production control authorities, and in the area of greatest proliferation, 25 units responded that they exercised trade policy instruments.[20]

Of course these arrangements are not administrative accidents merely awaiting the reorganizer's sense of tidiness to produce coherence. They are an accurate reflection of powerful pluralistic forces and diverging priorities. Thus it would be a mistake to regard the multitude of factors listed in the first part of this paper as so much raw material to be reformulated into a more purposeful industrial policy. This legacy of de facto industrial policy is more barrier than opportunity, and it should warn us about the power of centrifugal forces that will greet any more explicit system for managing microeconomic priorities. I consider nothing so grand as the independence of the Federal Reserve Board and the role it could have in selective credit allocations but reflect instead on one of those small pieces of current industrial policy that go unnoticed by everybody—except by those with a stake in its operations: the Commerce Department's portion of the 1974 Trade Act called adjustment assistance. This is a program of loans, loan guarantees, and technical assistance to troubled companies that the current secretary of commerce has declared to be "the most expensive, nonproductive program you could think of."[21] Despite the Reagan administration's effort to scrap the program, it limps along funded by Congress at an authorized $25 million for fiscal years 1984 and 1985. Why? Because a small network of people, out of a complex mixture of larger convictions and self-interest, find its activities useful. The network consists in part of regionally based, nonprofit contract agencies, some tied in with universities, that actually administer this Commerce Department program. The department official once in charge of the program now works as a Washington consultant heading the Industrial Policy Council. The council in turn includes the organizations operating the regional centers under contract and prepares state-by-state accounts of the program's operations for distribution to congressional delegations. Although only thirteen companies received loans or loan guarantees in fiscal year 1983, the $17.5 million in technical assistance can win a larger number of allies even if spread thinly. Trade associations as well as companies and unions can obtain marketing, accounting, financial planning, or other assistance with the government's paying up to 75 percent of the cost. Of course, any determined administration could probably marshal its forces to terminate or transfer such a program. Although the program may not be worth its economic costs, however, is getting rid of it really worth the political costs? Score one for de facto industrial policy.

Discontinuities of Executive Personnel. No other major industrial nation as a matter of course removes its top two or three thousand executive officials every few years. Even when party control of the White House does not change, career commitments outside government typically produce considerable turnover at the upper levels of departments and agencies. One consequence is a continual loss of experience, often of the painfully acquired variety. This loss occurs not only at the top but also frequently one, two, or three layers down into organizations.[22] During 1978–1979, for example, the executive branch conducted a Domestic Policy Review on Industrial Innovation. This review produced a host of reports, intense conflict between labor and industry subcommittees on the costs of regulatory reform, debates on federal tax incentives to encourage technological innovation in industry, and more. In theory, this effort should have informed and infused the 1983 startup of the new Office for Industrial Competitiveness; in fact little such learning occurred because few of the people involved in the first venture had anything to do with the second.

Yet more than the loss of experience matters. Incentives to behave in certain ways are also created by this situation. Short tenures mean that one has less reason to worry about long-term consequences that will mature only after one has left. The enduring effects of a political executive's performance inside government typically will have very little connection with the fate of his or her "real" career outside government. Since building any sustained consensus is likely to take so long, a much stronger incentive is to act as a policy entrepreneur engaged in broken-field running through the system.[23] This situation is no mere abstract academic barrier to all four managerial requisites of industrial policy; it is an everyday fact of life produced by shrewd and ambitious people calculating their personal stakes and deciding how to behave.

Weaknesses in Economic Staffing. One has difficulty imagining that any approach to industrial policy can be successful without staff work of extremely high caliber. Knowing enough about an industrial sector to trade quid pro quos sensibly, having access to the best available data and bringing them to bear on an issue efficiently, exercising peripheral vision to monitor what else is going on even when no superior has asked for the information, reminding distracted crisis managers of previous understandings and precedents being created inadvertently—these are not staff skills that grow quickly or survive without nurturing.

My impression is that these staff skills have deteriorated in the federal government in the postwar period. I say it is no more than an impression because we do not have good empirical information on the subject (should the number of employees with doctorates in economics be taken as a negative or positive indicator?), but it is a strongly held impression. In may ways, the staffing competencies in the immediate postwar period were a strong base that never were built upon, and they eventually atrophied. To follow these developments would required tracing (1) capacities for industrial analysis bequeathed by the many competent people from the private sector who entered government in the Second World War; (2) a growing preoccupation of the central executive organs (Council of Economic Advisers, Bureau of the Budget/Office of Management and Budget) with macroeconomic issues; and

(3) numerous false starts (such as sporadic staffing for wage and price controls and microeconomic ventures in the Council on Wage and Price Stability). My point is not really to argue the history of such economic machinery. Rather the real issue is how far current staff resources exist to underpin any new industrial policy initiative. On that matter one must have real doubts. For example, a great deal of sectorial industrial information exists in the executive branch, but it is rarely more than passively produced, and no process exists for verifying and analytically consolidating different agencies' data series. As regards many of the key economic issues facing the nation (experiences during the oil shortages of the 1970s could provide good examples), there simply exist no means of producing relevant data that are widely seen as accurate, comprehensive, and objective. To speak frankly, many private sector claimants on government prefer things that way. The more incomplete and challengeable the government's own information, the greater the scope for these highly knowledgeable claimants to shape public policy in their preferred direction. Score two and more for de facto industrial policy. Of course much detailed industrial knowledge lies deep in the bowels of a bureaucracy that in its isolated parts lives intimately with the problems of various economic sectors —the host of bureau-level contacts that can be only too easily and superficially attacked as representing "capture." There rarely has been and is not now, however, any reliable way for flushing this information up to the level of strategic, government-wide decision making.

The Hollow Center. The three preceding observations gain special force as they apply to the central apparatus of the executive establishment—the place where monitoring or predictability would have to be championed. The Executive Office of the President is not an office but a diverse hodgepodge of office spaces with a very high rate of personnel turnover in all of its more responsible positions and with little enduring staff capacities in the management of microeconomic issues. No other major industrial power plays such a thoroughgoing game of musical chairs so close to the center of executive decision making.[24] As far as central institution building has been concerned, a kind of presidential poison maims or kills even the best-intentioned efforts. Again one has little need of consulting abstract academic theories; real life human predilections can suffice. Anyone coming within close proximity of a given president is under overwhelming pressure to serve the immediate, ad hoc needs of the president in question and to discount heavily any payoffs or costs to a succeeding chief executive. This situation puts institution building—that is, sustained development of a central knowledge base and staff capacities—at a premium, or at least in the category of an afterthought. Although such afterthoughts may help fill the pages in memoirs of former presidential advisers, they have done little to alter the essentially ephemeral nature of any topside arrangements for microeconomic decision making. Whether one wants a central capability that can look deeply and interdepartmentally into sectoral economics or one that can reliably be counted on to organize constructive negotiating forums, something seems to be missing between presidential tenures.

The hollowness in question refers to predictable procedures and institutionalized staff capacities and not to any lack of busy people. For example, in the Carter administration an office for group liaison headed by Anne Wexler helped convene useful microeconomic negotiations in a neutral setting. This office disappeared with the arrival of the Reagan administration, however, as did most of the groundwork laid by Carter's domestic policy staff as it was transfigured into Reagan's Office for Policy Development. Likewise, since its creation in the Kennedy administration the president's Office of the U.S. Trade Representative has barely survived repeated attempts to kill it, and it has been variously muscled in and out of the action on trade policy depending on accidents of events and the trade representative's personality. The pressure to create a new Department of Trade, led by the Commerce Department, and the bureaucratic infighting between the staffs of the Office of the U.S. Trade Representative and the Commerce Department are only the most recent examples of disarray. The main beneficiaries of this situation appear to be the growing corps of Washington lawyers and other professionals who use a stint of service in the Office of the U.S. Trade Representative, the International Trade Commission, and so on to build experience for a lucrative private career in international trade issues.[25]

The Problem of Standing. The issue of standing really refers to a whole bundle of barriers to industrial policy. What they all have in common is an inability of the federal government to compose itself and others into reliable bargaining units. Calling for a purposeful management of microeconomic policies that is strategic, coordinated, and predictable is easy enough. The question is, who will be seated at the table? Why should winners under the current diffuse system let themselves be included, and why should anyone excluded by a different system acquiesce to the new rules of the game?

The problem of standing internal to the government itself is difficult enough. For example, I have noted that the executive branch is exquisitely arranged to register the interests of existing firms and industries. The natural tendency will be to reproduce the status quo orientation of this functional localism in any new executive machinery and to disregard what is not or cannot easily be organized, whether this be groups of workers, technologies, emerging industries, or consumers. An even greater problem lies in trying to accommodate the administrative requisites of industrial policy to the separateness of government institutions. Will the Justice Department, for example, waive its right to stand back and pass judgment later on any industrial agreement? Will Congress or the courts? And what would it mean to have

Congress or the courts at the table, since these are really just collective nouns for a great many semi-independent legislative and judicial actors. The obvious answer is that these outsiders will be more interested in protecting their institutional prerogatives that in becoming committed early to coherent agreements. The less obvious answer is that key participants within the executive family will find their interest is to help protect the outsiders' prerogatives. The reason is that bargaining strength for executive agencies frequently derives from their option of having recourse to judicial review and congressional appeals, thereby nullifying quid pro quos they may dislike.

The problems of standing with regard to extragovernmental groups are no less formidable. Contrary to popular impressions and Marxist rhetoric, American businesses are poorly organized to deal in peak level negotiations with government. Executive branch policy makers have frequently turned to consult with American industry and found no one there, or more accurately found a jumble of agents who cannot commit the groups they represent. Industries are actually complex phenomena usually lacking any natural representatives. For example, if one wants to consult with the steel industry or semiconductor industry, who will have standing to bargain for the industry: only the largest firms, who are likely to use consultation as an opportunity to form a cartel? small emerging firms who may well have never formulated a view to present to Washington? firms solely in that business or major conglomerates for whom steel or semiconductors may be only a small part of their business? If the conglomerate level is used, will the division management or headquarters be invited to sit at the table? It is easy to predict that winning the participation of weak firms hoping to use government resources to reverse the market's judgment will present little difficulty. Executive policy makers have had much more difficulty winning the serious participation of strong firms who fear government controls and who can opt out of any unfavorable deals by appeals outside the executive branch or by shifting activities overseas. The same kinds of internal divisions in their memberships make trade associations and business federations unreliable bargaining partners for government. American industry looks positively monolithic compared with the possibilities of arranging peak level agreements with labor. The national federations of labor unions have traditionally been weak (for example, the AFL-CIO operates with a $27 million budget while its member unions have about $2.3 billion). Membership numbers and organizing efforts have stalled, and in business circles a feeling that labor unions are on the run and may not need to be bargained with has been growing.[26]

Why should labor's tenuous standing represent a barrier to industrial policy? The reason is that without a workable manpower component, any design for industrial policy is likely to be blown off course by political pressures. If industrial policy is defined only as a procompetitiveness strategy without cushioning the human costs of industrial adjustment, then one can confidently predict that the normal routines of politics will intervene to ensure that industrial policy is transformed into economically dubious forms of social policy. Firms can frequently find new markets to compensate for the loss of old markets. Capital can be redirected with a phone call. Human capital is not so movable or easily compensated, and the political process is quite legitimately organized to respond to the gripes of living capital, that is, people. Whatever the weakness of organized labor, Congress is a kind of standing committee for addressing and relieving the grievances of living capital on a geographic basis. To be sustained politically, industrial policy needs to cushion the imposition of human costs without preventing—and, one hopes, by promoting—economic adaptation. Hence labor is crucial for industrial policy. No reliable bargaining units exist to incorporate in the process, however. That most of the central players in executive-branch policy making —that is, the corps of international trade professionals—have almost no understanding of labor adjustment problems does not help.

The Constraints of Public Opinion. Public opinion surveys have shown a generally weak foundation for the construction of any industrial policy beyond the existing de facto system. Public attitudes do seem to support efforts to do more through government in helping labor readjust to industrial change, and some doubts about the benign motivations of big business appear to have grown since the 1960s. Beyond a vague endorsement of more cooperative relationships, however, there is little basis in public sentiments to legitimize explicit industrial policies. Government interventions to help direct economic development are broadly opposed. Anything more than ad hoc cooperation and general goal setting tap a deep reservoir of hostility to state planning. Preferred policies for bolstering economic growth run heavily and almost uniformly in the direction of cutting down on government interventions and against any government attempts explicitly to allocate resources. Businessmen, a key segment of elite opinion for any sustainable industrial policy, exhibit even more extreme versions of the same attitudes.[27] Combined with an underlying distrust of broad grants of discretionary bargaining power to bureaucracies, these attitudes seem designed to tolerate rather raw adversarial outcomes on the national political stage (checking power with competing power) and tightly circumscribed proceedings at the agency level (since insiders are constantly looking for ways around the power-checking formalities). These arrangements are deemed satisfactory because Americans do not agree on any overarching, operational goal for economic policy. Hence there is considerable difference between an overall U.S. industrial policy and policies in an area such as national defense, in which objectives are widely shared and the government's role accepted, or industrial policy in a country such as Japan, where promoting competitiveness in world markets has long been accepted as an article of faith. Sporadic political attempts to make

309

Americans worry about "global competitiveness"—a slow motion crisis that is hard to dramatize—have been smothered by the Reagan administration's more general political message of economic good times and complacent faith in the private sector.

The final public constraint is at least as troublesome as any other. This constraint is the demand, increasingly powerful in recent years, for openness in public policy making. The Supreme Court and the Federal Reserve Open Market Committee may be entrusted to work through public issues in private and to justify their reasoning post hoc, but one has little reason to think that this forbearance extends to industrial policy. On the countrary, a strong presumption in American opinion is that any private and close working-relationship between government and industry is tantamount to collusion against the public interest. (And on the past record who would deny that this is a useful rule of thumb?) Yet successful negotiations on microeconomic issues almost certainly will require private, off-the-record discussions in which responsible leaders can shed official positions that have been crafted to preserve the support of key constituencies. Firms are understandably reluctant to raise openly the issue of painful work-force adjustments for fear of political attacks and the introduction of plant-closing legislation. Labor leaders need little instruction on what happens to union leaders who fail to stake out an adversarial position and try to function instead as labor statesmen on broader industrial problems. If a serious attempt at industrial policy is to be made, few participants from government, business, or labor will want such a process to be open to the full glare of publicity. Who among them (or us), however, will be willing to go before the American people and say he or she opposes "open government"?

The barriers I have described are considerable, but they do not add up to some inherent flaw in the concept of industrial policy itself. Some observers are inclined to cast the issue in grander terms—industrial policy as a self-defeating quest for some egalitarian, sectarian vision, or industrial policy as a symbol of growing cartelization and the decline of the West.[28] The reality, I suspect, is more mundane. Industrial policy is asking government to do what it has always done, to protect and promote. In its protective mode such policy is aimed at trying to meet people's quite legitimate demands for avoiding or sharing more widely the human and community costs of economic adjustment. To think that people are at fault for resisting the destructive power of markets (and avoiding a huge cost is not the same thing as getting a huge benefit through cartelization) is surely a case of blaming the victim. In its promotional side, industrial policy seeks to allocate concentrated governmental benefits only where they will generate more widely diffused benefits to society. The protection has to do with pooling risk, the promotion with taming privilege, and there is nothing new in either principle.

The Ways of Prudence

Now that we have surveyed the rough currents facing industrial policy, it should be clear that such a paper will end with no easy answers. Realism requires us to find some middle way between what the economist Alfred Marshall once distinguished as "government all wise, all just, all powerful, and government as it is now." In thinking about industrial policy reforms, one is trying to sail between two shoals: maxims that are sound economics but questionable politics on the one hand, and practices that are sound politics but questionable economics on the other. This maneuvering can easily lead to counsels of despair. Economically speaking, the government seems capable of acting only when it is trying to do the wrong things and designed for invariable failure when it tries to do the right things.

I frankly doubt that political life is so symmetrically perverse, at least not if we regard the capacities of government as a variable rather than as an absolute constant. To be sure, following through on well-thought-out plans is not, to put it mildly, the strong suit of American government. Saying that simply leaves open the question of how to improve things, however. It should be a cause for prudence, not resignation. By way of conclusion, I will be imprudent enough to suggest a few elements of a promising strategy.

Political prudence suggests underselling industrial policy initiatives. Raising the stakes by raising expectations as to what such a policy can do is simply another way of mobilizing defenders of the status quo on many fronts. The term *industrial policy* itself could be profitably banished from public conversaion, to be replaced by some sleep-inducing codeword such as *the management of microeconomic programs.*[29] All that advocates of industrial policy are talking about is some more pragmatic fixing of the machinery of government. Honest.

It follows from what has been said in this chapter that industrial policy reforms would do well to avoid proposing any major new departmental reorganizations or the creation of any centerpiece institution to distribute economic resources. The former is likely to consume more political credit in fighting the forces of the status quo than any results of reorganization are likely to be worth. The latter is simply likely to reproduce all the pressures of distributive politics that currently infect Congress and much of the executive branch. Besides, scarcely enough skilled government staff exist to operate a more rational distributive mechanism, and such staff cannot be created overnight by reorganizations.

What then is left for industrial policy? Plenty, if one is willing to live with incremental developments that do not get anyone's name in the newspapers. A good place to begin is to recognize that industrial policy is not some *thing* that gets made. It is a process that gets learned. This process is one of bringing economic, political, and social considerations into sustained interaction with each other with the aim of attaining a more productive use of resources. Policy depends as much on understanding the working rules and social context of economic operations as on prescribing the substance of the economic decisions themselves.[30] Building a more effective context is an appropriate and important concern of industrial policy. To me at least, this concern means that improving the national government's capacities for fact finding and forum building should be two priority areas.

At present the government is frequently without the resources to judge the merits of claimants' cases in trade and other areas of microeconomic decision making. Usable knowledge comes not only from economic theory but from hands-on understanding of the various ways pricing, marketing, investment, and other decisions are actually made in different industries. Digging out and verifying the key facts (not an uncontroversial matter with industry) could make an important contribution in strengthening the credibility of government decisions one way or the other. In arguing that government should at least know the facts behind what it is doing, industrial policy advocates are likely to be on much stronger political ground than if they put forward a particular policy agenda presuming that government knows what to do.

If it is to command respect eventually, such a fact-finding and analysis process should be highly professional and given a distinct self-identity that discourages the impression of being a way station for private sector career development. To resist functional localism, managers of the fact-finding process should be centrally located, perhaps in a reorganized Office of Policy Development. This microeconomic staff should consist of career officers who are regularly rotated through the relevant units of departments and agencies (such as the ITC, Commerce's Bureau of Industrial Economics, the Bureau of Agricultural Economics, and the Federal Reserve System). Who, it might be asked, will be the clients for the information such a unit would produce? The answer is any politician in the executive or in Congress, who wants to get out of some of the heat generated by strong claimants with weak cases. Contrary to popular impression, politicians frequently find such pressures troublesome. Being able to shift some of the blame for unresponsiveness to a publicly respected dispenser of factual information may allow politicians more easily to do the economically right thing while protecting their political backsides.

My second priority area, forum building, refers to the more self-conscious design of settings for negotiation on microeconomic issues. As a practical matter, most such policy decisions are operational only insofar as major participants in the private sector choose to cooperate. These agents of policy—such as firms, unions, and local communities—are largely outside the power of presidents or governments to command, and their responsiveness to particular economic incentives and disincentives is uncertain to say the least. Moreover, these are the same groups that can bring immense short-term pressures to bear through Congress and the courts to undercut the government's ability to reach coherent and sustainable decisions in the first place. The essential problem is not to discover some bright new industrial policy idea but to evolve a management process that will give essential economic actors a stake in sustaining a long-term coordinated view of economic adaptation. What is most crucial and what is in shortest supply are forums in which key public and private makers of economic policy can explore joint concerns rather than sell preexisting positions. To do so requires a nonthreatening setting in which the participants in microeconomic management can become accustomed to dealing with each other over an extended period of time. If there are to be reliable quid pro quo deals, they will have to be struck in such a setting.

One approach, beloved by corporatists, is to create one national forum through some version of a tripartite council composed of business, labor, and government. It is well to remember that this country has a sorry record in the area of national forum building, dating from the dashed hopes about the National Civic Federation, which brought Mark Hanna and Samuel Gompers together, and the U.S. Commission on Industrial Relations (1913–1916). In the modern era the previously discussed problems of standing, publicity, executive branch turnover, and diversity are sufficiently potent to cast doubts on any centralized approach of national boards and councils. An industrial policy that demands such a grand coalition is not socially administrable in the American system.

An ungrand coalition approach, using many smaller forums and shunning the dramatic gesture in favor of normal politics and normal labor relations, seems to be more promising. Executive officials should still have the job of helping manage such a set of negotiating forums, since the forums are a kind of public good that will not otherwise be produced by the interested parties. The aim, however, rather than to strike one national deal, should be to build communities of businessmen, labor representatives, government officials, local leaders, and academics who worry about what companies in their field must do to remain (or become) internationally competitive.

The most constructive approach would be to build on existing foundations that look promising and not try to invent a great deal of new machinery. Some of the useful building blocks would include the following:

- The Justice Department's antitrust division has become increasingly involved in issues of international trade and economic strategy as it struggles for more than an ad hoc approach to selective antitrust enforcement.
- OMB's Office of Information and Regulatory Affairs (OIRA) created in 1980 has become more important in centrally clearing proposed agency regulations; but only its temporary political leadership is permitted con-

tact with the private sector, and regulatory reviews are rarely tied in to larger considerations of industrial competitiveness and adjustment.

- The Office of the U.S. Trade Representative and ITC have become more involved in conditioning trade preferences on specific commitments by the relieved industry to modernize its plant and work force, but the negotiations have generally been slapdash affairs responding to crises.
- The forty-five advisory committees that operate outside the glare of publicity under the Office of the U.S. Trade Representative have formed some useful collaborative forums, but they are keyed mainly to preparations for periodic trade negotiations.

Suppose that one did not try to disturb any of these arrangements but added a small central career staff with some innocuous-sounding name—say, an Economic Reference Service attached to the Council of Economic Advisers. (The economics professional can be expected to resist because of macroeconomists' proprietary interest in the council; but fear not, their political standing is not what it once was.) This staff's function could be twofold. One assignment would be to perform all the administrative housekeeping functions for convening not only interdepartmental but government and private sector working groups advising the trade representative's office, ITC, the antitrust division, and OIRA (one might throw in the Commerce Department's Office of Competitive Assessment). The valuable side effect of this chore would be that a centrally positioned staff (cross pollinated with agency staff and possessing some stability) would get to know the people and communities involved in microeconomic policy issues. To give some bite to this sectoral fieldwork, the new staff unit should have a second function of clearance. Any proposed antitrust exceptions, trade escape clause relief, or economic regulation would have to be cleared as being in accord with the president's program before being sent to Congress or promulgated. (I would think that the previously mentioned fact-finding unit should be kept separate from this convening/clearance staff so that the former can take the blame for publicizing unpleasant facts.)

Wouldn't this modest proposal simply reproduce all the evils of self-protecting, fragmented subgovernments conspiring to impose costs on a diffuse public? Certainly this danger is real. Much would depend on whether or not this central staffing of government is handled in a professional, nonpartisan manner. For ultimately it is the government's voice that has to be counted on to push for agreements that make both political and economic sense. If, for example, some trade protection is to be part of industrial policy, then adjustment to market forces needs to be a price of protection; but likewise, the widespread benefits of economic adaptation require sharing some of the costs that progress imposes on workers' lives and communities.

We are a diverse people intending to be one nation. Subgovernments need not be such a bad thing if they can be oriented around the principle of industrial adjustment with a humane face. I can foresee a government economic staff nurturing coalitions composed, say, of state and local officials helping set up plant shutdown assistance programs; of local educational institutions providing services and research for manpower adjustment; of bankers, businessmen, and worker representatives evolving investment strategies; and of Congressmen seeking to take credit for economic planning (though none will dare call it that) in their districts. By making these kinds of lateral connections, and not by taking isolated decisions in executive agencies or elite boards, sustainable policies are created in the American system.

Notes

1. See, for example, Joseph Dorfman, *The Economic Mind in American Civilization*, vols. 2 and 3 (New York: Viking Press, 1946–1959); Carter Goodrich, *Government Promotion of American Canals and Railroads, 1800–1890* (New York: Columbia University Press, 1960).

2. Congressional Budget Office, *The Industrial Policy Debate* (Washington, D.C.: Government Printing Office, 1983), p. 34.

3. Japan Economic Institute, *Japan's Industrial Policies* (Washington, D.C.: Japan Economic Institute of America, 1984), p. 46.

4. See, for example, Emil Finley, "The Realities of U.S. Foreign Trade and the Fictions of Our Cartel Advocates," *National Journal* (May 5, 1979).

5. Robert W. Crandall, *The U.S. Steel Industry in Recurrent Crisis* (Washington, D.C.: Brookings Institution, 1981).

6. See "Is Free Trade Dead?" *The Economist* (December 15, 1982), and, more generally, I. M. Destler, *The American Trade Policymaking System* (New York: Twentieth Century Fund, forthcoming).

7. Marc Bendick, Jr., "Workers Dislocated by Economic Change," *The Urban Institute Policy and Research Report*, vol. 13, no. 3 (Fall, 1983); and Martin Neil Bailey, ed., *Workers, Jobs and Inflation* (Washington, D.C.: Brookings Institution, 1982); and Alice Rivlin, ed., *Economic Choices 1984* (Washington, D.C.: Brookings Institution, 1984), pp. 114–46.

8. Congressional Budget Office, *The Industrial Policy Debate*, p. 37.

9. U.S. Department of Commerce, Bureau of Industrial Economics, *1983 Industrial Outlook for 250 Industries with Projections for 1987* (Washington, D.C.: Government Printing Office, 1983); and U.S. Executive Office of the President, Federal Coordinating Council of Science, Engineering, and Technology, *Directory of Federal Technology Transfer* (Washington, D.C.: Government Printing Office, 1977).

10. Perry D. Quick, "Businesses: Reagan's Industrial Policy," in John Palmer and Isabel Sawhill, eds., *The Reagan Record* (Washington, D.C.: The Urban Institute, 1984), pp. 301–303.

11. Congressional Budget Office, *The Industrial Policy Debate*, p. 39.

12. Charls E. Walker and Mark Bloomfiels, "The Political Response to Three Potential Major Bankruptcies: Lockheed, New York City, and Chrysler" in Michael Wachter and Susan Wachter, *Toward a New U.S. Industrial Policy?* (Philadelphia:

University of Pennsylvania Press, 1981), pp. 423–53.

13. See Congressional Budget Office, *Federal Support of U.S. Business* (Washington, D.C.: CBO, 1984); and Phyllis Levinson et al., *The Federal Entrepreneur: The Nation's Implicit Industries Policy* (Washington, D.C.: The Urban Institute, 1982).

14. Quoted in Japan Economic Institute, *Japan's Industrial Policies*, p. 43.

15. On the "hype" given industrial policy in particular, see Robert J. Samuelson, "The Policy Peddlers," *Harper's* (June 1983), p. 62. For a sensitive discussion of the lack of a real debate (versus disengaged talk aimed at rallying one's own troops) on economic policy more generally, see Herbert Stein, *Presidential Economics* (New York: Simon and Schuster, 1984), pp. 324ff.

16. Charles L. Schultze, "Industrial Policy: A Dissent," *The Brookings Review*, vol. 2, no. 1 (Fall 1983), pp. 3–12; and by the same author, "Cars, Quotas, and Inflation," *The Brookings Bulletin*, vol. 17, no. 3, pp. 3–4.

17. The cost estimates are from Robert W. Crandall, "Input Quotas and the Automobile Industry: The Costs of Protectionism," *The Brookings Review* (Summer 1984).

18. Roger Fisher and William Ury, *Getting to Yes: Negotiating Agreement without Giving In*, edited by Bruce Patton (New York: Penguin Books, 1983).

19. Schultze, "Industrial Policy," p. 10.

20. John Helmer, "The Presidential Office: Velvet Fist in an Iron Glove," in Hugh Heclo and Lester Salamon, eds., *The Illusion of Presidential Government* (Boulder, Colo.: Westview Press, 1981), p. 55.

21. For an account of the program's politics, see Richard Corrigan, "Budget Cutters Target Trade Adjustment Loan Program despite Stricter Conditions," *National Journal* (December 31, 1983), pp. 2685–86.

22. Calvin Mackenzie, ed., *The In and Outer System: An Analysis* (Washington, D.C.: National Academy of Public Administration, forthcoming).

23. This frequently appears to be the behavior between the in-and-outers handling trade issues in the Commerce Department and in the Office of Special Trade Representative. Even in the team-oriented Reagan administration this behavior has produced a refusal to share information between agencies, the competitive cultivation of networks on the Hill, and even separate negotiations with foreign governments. See Christopher Madison, "MITI, Anyone?" *National Journal* (March 26, 1983), p. 665.

24. Richard Rose, "The Capacity of the President: A Comparative Analysis," *Studies in Public Policy*, no. 130 (Glasgow: Centre for the Study of Public Policy, 1984); Colin Campbell, *Governments under Stress* (Toronto: University of Toronto Press, 1983); George Shultz and Kenneth Dam, *Economic Policy beyond the Headlines* (New York: Norton, 1978), pp. 158ff.

25. It should be a sobering thought for any advocate of industrial policy: waiting in Washington to greet the policy are 20,000 people engaged in day-to-day lobbying and offices for over 1,400 different law firms doing $1.6 billion worth of business in the town. U.S. Senate, Committee on Governmental Affairs, *Hearings: Oversight of the 1946 Federal Regulation of Lobbying Act*, November 15–16, 1983; "Lawyers," *The Washington Post*, June 19, 1984; Sar A. Levitan and Martha Cooper, *Business Lobbies* (Baltimore, Md.: Johns Hopkins University Press, 1984); and Congressional Quarterly, *The Washington Lobby*, 4th edition (Washington: Congressional Quarterly, 1984).

26. "Once a Washington Power, Labor Now Plays Catch-up in Lobbying and Politics," *Congressional Quarterly* (September 4, 1982), p. 2189.

27. "Taking Stock of Business," *Public Opinion* (June/July 1980), pp. 32–36; and William Schneider, "Industrial Policy: It All Depends on How It's Sold to the Voters," *National Journal* (September 17, 1983), pp. 1916–17.

28. See articles by Mancur Olson and Aaron Wildavsky in this volume. An alternative and, I would argue, historically more valid view would see contemporary industrial policy as the latest in a long line of basically conservative, welfare state activities seeking to contain the social radicalism of pure market forces. See Karl Polanyi, *The Great Transformation* (Boston: Beacon, 1957); and Arthur Okun, *Equality and Efficiency* (Washington, D.C.: Brookings Institution, 1975), and by the same author, "Further Thoughts on Equality and Efficiency," *Brookings Reprint* no. 325, 1977.

29. Some would argue that a highly publicized approach to industrial policy may galvanize the political and institutional will to improve the chances for more rational microeconomic management. While this may occur in the event of some electorally threatening economic crisis, I would still contend that devastating reactions are less likely to develop if industrial policy is ultimately on much more solid ground politically if it emerges from the search for answers to particular sectoral problems other than if it is "sold" in advance as a general prescription by policy analysts.

30. To say all this is simply to repeat the founding insight of institutional economics and its attention to working rules, noneconomic relations, and the ways in which economic man becomes individualized only through rules of collective action. John R. Commons, "Institutional Economics," *American Economic Review,* vol. 21 (December 1931), pp. 648–57.

Congress and the Proposed
Industrial Policy Structures

Robert W. Russell

The subject of industrial policy has received much attention in Congress during the past four years. Early murmurings of interest in the possibility of devising an industrial policy for the United States were heard within the Senate Democratic Caucus in 1980. Senator Adlai E. Stevenson III (Democrat, Illinois) led a partially successful effort to put Senate Democrats on record in support of an active industrial policy.[1] Portions of the Carter administration were sympathetic to this effort, especially the Commerce Department (the agency chosen by Stevenson to be the center for a new department to handle both industrial policy and trade) and White House adviser Amitai Etzioni. A few House Democrats, with encouragement from some economists on the Joint Economic Committee staff, began exploring the subject at about the same time.

Congressional proposals for an industrial policy for the United States proliferated rapidly over the next three years. Several dozen bills on the subject were introduced, although not all of them provided for industrial policy institutions. Professor Aaron Wildavsky has summarized (and satirized) several of these bills in a recent publication.[2] There is no need to describe them here, except to note the wide variety of specific measures proposed: tax measures, grants, loans, loan guarantees, reduced federal regulation, increased federal regulation, new federal agencies, reorganized federal agencies, commissions, councils, and, of course, reports.

Hearings on industrial policy have been held in several committees of Congress. The most extensive hearing record (more than thirty days of hearings with more than 150 witnesses) was compiled during the Ninety-eighth Congress by the Economic Stabilization Subcommittee of the House Banking Committee under the chairmanship of Representative John J. LaFalce (Democrat, New York).[3] Several hearings were held by the Joint Economic Committee under the heading "Industrial Policy, Economic Growth and the

318

Competitiveness of U.S. Industry."[4] The House Energy and Commerce Committee cited ten days in 1983 and early 1984 of hearings that the committee considered relevant to industrial policy.[5]

If one were to attempt to compile a comprehensive list of all the congressional hearings bearing upon industrial policy, the project could easily get out of hand. Should hearings on bills to create enterprise zones in depressed areas be included? What about bills on trade adjustment assistance or trade reorganization? The Senate Banking Committee, for example, has held no hearings on industrial policy per se, although several bills proposing an industrial policy have been referred to the committee. A subcommittee of the Banking Committee did hold a hearing on foreign industrial targeting, however; and the full committee has held many hearings on federal loan, loan guarantee, and insurance programs, as well as on the cost of capital to various sectors of the U.S. economy.

Party groups in each house of Congress have issued reports commenting on industrial policy proposals. On November 16, 1983, a task force of the Senate Democratic Caucus under the chairmanship of Senator Edward M. Kennedy (Democrat, Massachusetts) issued a report on "Jobs for the Future: A Democratic Agenda," which included many of the items usually contained in proposals for an active industrial policy, but without using the term.[6] On April 3, 1984, the Senate Republican Conference approved a report by its task force on industrial competitiveness and international trade recommending actions aimed at "encouraging capital formation, stimulating private sector research and development, promoting our international trade, and spurring the development of our human resources." The Senate Republican task force based its recommendations on "the belief that American industrial competitiveness will not be enhanced by additional government guidance or control." The task force opposed "central planning councils, government industrial finance institutions and agencies to target promising technologies."[7]

Similar recommendations emerged in May 1984 from the Steering Committee of the Task Force on High Technology Initiatives of the House Republican Research Committee. The Steering Committee emphasized U.S. technological leadership as a source of increased competitiveness and new jobs:

> We believe that the proper role of government in promoting U.S. technological leadership and industrial competitiveness is to *"target" the process* by which new ideas and products are developed—*the process of innovation*. That is, our government should focus on creating an environment in this country in which innovation, new ideas, and new companies are likely to flourish and in which firms in mature industries can modernize.[8]

The House Democratic Caucus nurtured discussions among House Dem-

319

ocrats on various industrial policy ideas, but serious consideration of legislation to establish a framework for an industrial policy began in 1982 in the Economic Stabilization Subcommittee (the LaFalce subcommittee) of the House Banking Committee.[9] Because the LaFalce subcommittee had legislative jurisdiction over the Defense Production Act, a little-known statute that must be renewed periodically to keep defense contracts flowing, an opportunity arose to put forward industrial policy proposals under the rubric of strengthening the nation's industrial base for defense production. At the end of the Ninety-seventh Congress, extension of the Defense Production Act was held up by disagreements between the House and the Senate on various matters, including an industrial policy bill called the "Defense Industrial Base Revitalization Act" placed in the House version by Representative LaFalce. In the end the only fragment to survive was a provision calling for a "White House Conference on Productivity."[10]

President Reagan established the Commission on Industrial Competitiveness in June 1983. The commission consists of twenty-one prominent persons from various backgrounds. It has held meetings in several cities around the country and has issued a list of fourteen recommendations for improving industrial competitiveness.[11]

This brief survey of congressional activity on the subject of industrial policy (or competitiveness) should suffice to indicate the range of viewpoints represented in the continuing debate. At times the debate seems to encompass every government activity that might affect the economy. Instead of trying to analyze all the bills, hearings, reports, and issues that have been included in congressional discussion of industrial policy, I have chosen to examine one bill closely. The only example of broad industrial policy legislation favorably reported by a congressional committee is H.R. 4360, the "Industrial Competitiveness Act."

The Industrial Competitiveness Act

Following extensive hearings in his subcommittee, Representative LaFalce introduced H.R. 4360 on November 10, 1983, with fifteen cosponsors. The Economic Stabilization Subcommittee ordered the bill reported favorably with amendments on February 8, 1984, by a vote of 13 to 9. The full House Banking Committee ordered the bill reported favorably with amendments on April 10, 1984, by a vote of 25 to 16.[12] The House Energy and Commerce Committee ordered the bill reported favorably without amendment on May 24, 1984, by a vote of 22 to 19.[13] As of early September 1984, H.R. 4360 was awaiting a rule from the House Rules Committee to provide for floor consideration of the measure. The bill had more than one hundred cosponsors, all Democrats. Support for and opposition to the measure within the Banking

Committee and the Energy and Commerce Committee followed party lines with only a few exceptions.

H.R. 4360 contains three titles, each of which authorizes creation of a new federal institution. Title I authorizes a sixteen-member Council on Industrial Competitiveness drawn in four equal parts from business, labor, government, and academic circles or public interest groups. The council, according to the House Banking Committee, "would provide a much-needed forum in which these groups could work cooperatively to develop a competitiveness strategy for our economy and for specific industries and sectors."[14] The council would collect and analyze data bearing on competitiveness; review and make recommendations on policies of executive branch agencies affecting competitiveness; establish subcouncils to advise on long-term strategies for individual sectors of the economy; recommend lending priorities to the Bank for Industrial Competitiveness; report annually to the president and Congress; and build "a national consensus on strategies for fostering the growth and competitiveness of American industry."[15]

Title II of H.R. 4360 creates a Bank for Industrial Competitiveness with capital stock of up to $8.5 billion to be appropriated over a five-year period. The bank is intended to "assist in the competitive restructuring of basic industry and the capitalization of new and innovative products or technologies" by providing up to 30 percent of the funding for "revitalization programs," and by investing in up to 50 percent of the stock of public industrial development finance institutions at the state, local, or regional levels.[16]

Title III establishes a Federal Industrial Mortgage Association with an authorization of $100 million for fiscal year 1985 to improve the secondary market for commercial mortgages for the purchase of facilities and equipment by companies with less than $50 million in annual sales whose activities are not in financial services, leasing, or professional services.[17]

Institutionalizing Industrial Policy

Proposals for institutional change presuppose that there is something wrong with existing institutions. The committee report on the LaFalce bill is a helpful guide to how part of Congress and many other industrial policy advocates diagnose in institutional terms the problems to be addressed by industrial policy.

The committee report states:

> The Nation's industrial problems are to a significant degree institutional and procedural. While existing policies profoundly affect individual industries, their overall impact on key industrial sectors is too often neither intended, understood, nor anticipated.[18]

The first institutional objective is to change the way economic problems

321

are analyzed by providing a new institution with a composition and a mandate different from those of existing institutions. The House Banking Committee, for example, intending that the Council on Industrial Competitiveness will fill a gap, remarked that "no high-level forum for developing a consensus on economic policies exists."[19]

Existing forums that could be altered to serve the purpose are often overlooked by industrial policy proponents: the Council of Economic Advisers, the President's Commission on Industrial Competitiveness, the President's Economic Policy Advisory Board, the President's Advisory Council on Private Sector Initiatives, the National Productivity Advisory Committee chaired by former Secretary of the Treasury William Simon, or the Office of Industrial Trade Policy in the Office of the U.S. Trade Representative. The Council of Economic Advisers (CEA) is regarded as too dependent upon the president, not broadly representative of various economic interests in the economy, and preoccupied with macroeconomic policy. The CEA does have a staff of twenty-five or so economists, however, who might be useful for gathering and analyzing the data needed for devising an industrial strategy.

The House Banking Committee report points to "an appalling lack of both basic economic data regarding competitive opportunities and problems and the focused analytical capability that could make use of it."[20] The various presidential commissions and councils, especially the President's Commission on Industrial Competitiveness, would seem to come close to what the LaFalce bill proposes in terms of membership and mandate for a council on industrial competitiveness. It is an open question whether a commission or a more formal council has a better chance to build a national consensus on public policy issues. The LaFalce bill, consistent with the preference of supporters of more active industrial policy, establishes not simply a forum, but a permanent, formal body with salaried members serving fixed terms under presidential appointments subject to Senate confirmation. Calls for formal institutionalization of industrial policy, not merely informal bodies to discuss the subject, are what divides those who favor a larger, more active federal government industrial policy role from those who prefer to revise or reduce the present role.

Substituting Consensus for Conflict

The heart of the justification for a new council or similar formal institution is the belief that existing institutions promote conflict rather than consensus. The House Banking Committee, for example, takes a dim view of conflictual relationships in the American economy:

> At a time when it is imperative that Government, business, labor, academia, and public interest groups act together to develop and coordinate long-term strategies for helping to assure the interna-

tional competitiveness of U.S. industries, counterproductive adversarial relationships remain the order of the day.[21]

An important corollary to the argument that there is too much interest-group conflict is the argument that the government is but one of several parties to a controversy instead of the institution that settles conflicts by establishing and implementing public policies. The House Banking Committee report complains that "the federal government ostensibly applies public policy in pursuit of a public purpose, but in fact has no clearly articulated purpose against which to measure the policy or its impact."[22] The committee seeks to create "institutional mechanisms that will promote the integration of government policies toward industry into a cohesive network."[23] To achieve this integration, and independent national council with industry subcouncils "reflective of the major participants in our economy" would be created. These participants, including governmental participants, would sit together at one table: "Individuals drawn from the highest levels of leadership in business, labor, academia, and public interest groups such as environmentalist and consumer protection communities, need to deliberate openly with top-ranking government officials."[24] This statement assumes that existing deliberative mechanisms are not sufficiently open and that a new structure—a council—would shift the locus of decision making in a way that would result in policies reflecting broader public interests.

An Industrial Policy "Congress" without the Congress

Those who favor formal industrial policy structures stress that the decision-making processes should be open and participatory. The House Banking Committee, for example, expects its proposed council and subcouncils to hold public hearings to have the "broadest possible public participation" and gain insights "regarding the practical impact of government policies on workers and communities." The committee believes the hearings would "also serve as a means of engendering broad public support" for the council's recommendations and says the council's members must be "able to weigh tradeoffs and balance interests, formulating a persuasive view of the national interest, which can be effectively communicated to the country as a whole."[25]

The council members, it seems, are expected both to represent their constituencies and to be Burkean at the same time—something elected members of Congress are also expected to do. One begins to suspect that industrial policy advocates are reinventing a Congress, although a Congress with fewer powers and chosen on an interest group basis rather than on a geographic basis.

The committee report waxes Madisonian in describing how the council will arrive at its decisions by balancing competing interests. With sixteen members "drawn equally from business, labor, government, and academia and public interest groups," and a two-thirds vote required for all substantive action, "no group or groups would be in a position to dominate or skew the deliberative process." The risks of tyrannical factions ruling by simple majority vote are banished: "Recommendations for competitive strategies arrived at would necessarily reflect the interests and concerns of all major economic actors."[26]

The only elements needed to transform the new structure into a parliamentary body are election of the council from constituency groups and perhaps proportional representation or voting in the council itself. But the point industrial policy backers are making is that the council and its subcouncils should represent economic interests, not geographic clumps of citizens. Industry subcouncils, in the Banking Committee's version, are intended to provide "a negotiating structure within which those with an economic interest in a specific industry's fate could work cooperatively to enhance its competitive position." The committee report solemnly warns that: "Absent a structure that can facilitate such a cooperative effort, the differing short-term economic interests of various industry actors create adversarial relationships that become obstacles to economic growth in their own right."[27]

Judging by the support for the LaFalce bill, a substantial portion of Congress believes that a council for giving advice on industrial policy should be composed in this fashion. Supporters of a council are saying, in effect, that economic conflicts should be resolved outside Congress and the executive branch and the results brought to Congress (or an executive branch agency) for implementation. If the council and its subcouncils work as intended, the task of Congress would be simplified. Members of Congress would have little to fear in rubber-stamping the council's recommendations, assuming broad public support had been generated, and mistakes could be blamed on the council, not on Congress. By suggesting that an industrial policy structure be developed outside Congress, industrial policy supporters raise important questions about the way Congress functions at present.

The Industrial Policy That Congress Built

Proponents of industrial policy insist that the United States already has many industrial policies. The House report observes that "every Administration, including this one, has developed and implemented a vast and expensive array of specific, targeted aids to industry." These interventions in the economy form a set of industrial policies, but they "lie jumbled in an untidy and expensive 'heap' for want of a strategy to harmonize them."[28]

Everyone recognizes that there is a lengthy list of tax expenditures, federal credit programs, direct expenditures, procurement activities, insurance programs, and trade restraints intended to serve as incentives to industry. A study by the Congressional Budget Office "found that policies whose primary

324

purpose or intent was assistance to business, cost taxpayers approximately $100 billion each year."[29] What is less clear is how "independent" industrial policy structures (a council and a bank) will help reduce the cost and achieve an efficient, coordinated industrial policy out of the mélange of existing government interventions in the economy.

The task is even larger than it might appear, because many existing industrial policy programs survive in the face of opposition from the executive branch—not just the current administration but previous ones as well. Congress created and expanded many of these programs despite warnings that the programs would be costly and ineffective. That Congress has frequently responded to the pleas of industry and labor groups for federal financial assistance or protection from competition is no secret. In fact, a large part of what Congress does from day to day is to craft special favors of this sort. The industrial policies we have are the industrial policies that Congress built.

Congressional action on programs and projects that purport to assist industry has contributed a large share of the empirical evidence for theories about how Congress works. Interest group theory owes a large debt to congressional action on industrial policies. The concept of an iron triangle of congressional subcommittee, executive bureau, and coddled industry gained credence through the kind of congressional activity that nurtured and sustains existing industrial policies. Theories of constituency representation recognize that members of Congress seek for their constituents federal favors in many forms, such as military bases, post-office buildings, small-business loans, housing grants, relief from federal regulations, and special tax provisions. If so much of the activity that makes Congress what it is consists of "bringing home the bacon," the way Congress functions apparently would need to change to have an effective industrial policy in the form advocated by its sponsors. What is the hope for changing the behavior of the Congress by establishing new industrial policy structures?

Will New Industrial Policy Structures Change Congress?

The House Banking Committee bill or any similar proposal will have a long legislative road to travel before it can be enacted into law. Rather than speculate on changes that might have to be made to make an industrial policy bill acceptable to both House and Senate and to Republicans as well as Democrats, let us assume enactment of a bill along the lines of the House committee proposal. How would Congress interact with the new industrial policy structures, that is, the council and the bank?

The first step would be to appoint persons to fill the new positions in the council and the bank. The House Banking Committee's bill would establish a total of twenty-three new positions at level 2 of the Executive Schedule—a prospect that should ensure a flood of résumés. Congress is not entirely

325

passive in the process of nominating individuals to hold public office. Quite likely, members of Congress, especially those in the party controlling the White House and those in key positions on congressional committees that originated the industrial policy legislation, would urge the president to nominate certain individuals to the council and the bank. Representatives and senators could be expected to be persistent in advancing the names of their political friends, their own staff, or even themselves, for these positions.

The Senate would be asked to advise and consent to the nominations, which would entail nomination hearings and various pressures that might be exerted by the Senate committee or committees reviewing the nominations. The Senate has tried to confine the review of each nomination to a single committee, but there have been exceptions. One that does not augur well for the nominations to the industrial policy institutions is the division of consideration of nominees for offices in the International Trade Administration, a branch of the Commerce Department, between the Senate Banking Committee and the Senate Finance Committee. Unable to agree on any other formula, the two committees split down the middle their jurisdiction over nominations for an undersecretary and three assistant secretaries: each review one assistant secretary and both review the undersecretary and the other assistant secretary. One can easily imagine nominees to the council and the bank being reviewed by more than one Senate committee.

Nominations to the three institutions could well prove controversial; and plenty of precedents exist for delaying, even blocking, nominees whom influential senators do not like. The president usually gets his choices confirmed, but there are enough exceptions to keep the White House alert to the possible reactions to the choices they make and to embolden Senate committee chairmen to press their preferences forcefully during the nomination process. What this situation probably means for the bank and the council is that the individuals selected would have to fit broadly into a pattern of nominations acceptable to the Senate. Choosing the person with the greatest expertise would yield to selection on the basis of geography, political factors, and balanced representation of key political constituencies. Seats would very likely come to be seen as belonging to particular interests. For example, steel would be likely to claim a seat on the council, as would autos and high technology. Whether the configuration of representation would conform to the economic merits of various industries from a broad, long-term national perspective seems doubtful.

Congress would certainly expect the members of the council, as well as the members of the board of the bank to testify before committees of appropriate jurisdiction. If the chairman of the subcommittee that handled the authorization bill had a strong view on a decision about to be made in the council or the bank, that the chairman would avoid using the hearing process or any other means at hand to influence the decision seems contrary to human nature.

Annual appropriations would be required for a council. A bank could be empowered to borrow directly, but it would be most unusual if the appropriations committees did not make certain that the bank must run the annual appropriations gauntlet nonetheless.

The appropriations committees would certainly expect to hold hearings and make their own preferences known to the industrial policy institutions. Legislating in appropriations bills is one of those things that is not supposed to happen under the rules of both the House and the Senate but happens quite often anyway. It happens because the members of the appropriations committees hold views on the programs for which money is appropriated, and they are powerful enough to withhold money if their views are ignored.

These rather pedestrian observations lead to a key point about the intentions of the sponsors of the new industrial policy structure: legislation would not immunize new industrial policy institutions from the necessity all executive branch agencies and most independent agencies have to give due deference to the authorization and appropriations committees of Congress. If, however, the council or the bank were to be granted an independent source of financing as well as substantive power—like the Federal Reserve Board, for example—there would be some reason to think that day-to-day congressional influence or interference would be minimized. Most of the extant proposals, however, are designed to ensure that new industrial policy institutions do not stray too far from the oversight of Congress.

Will Congress Support the New Industrial Policy Institutions?

Accepting the proposition that a council and a bank would be under the purview of the authorizing committees of Congress, as well as of the appropriations committees, the next practical question is which committees of the House and Senate will have jurisdiction over legislation concerning the institutions and will those committees be strong enough to defend the institutions against the positions of various federal agencies supported by *other* committees of Congress? The House Banking Committee and the House Energy and Commerce Committee would probably share jurisdiction in the House. The House Governmental Affairs Committee would have its usual oversight role, but that role is not where the real challenge arises.

What will happen, for example, if the council seeks to influence a decision by the International Trade Commission (ITC) on import relief? The House Banking Committee report on H.R. 4360 states that the council will not have "direct line authority or program responsibility" but will have a "major mandate" to "make recommendations to line agencies on the kinds of actions which should be taken to achieve industrial competitiveness."[30] The report stresses the importance of making government assistance conditional on a firm plan by industry to adjust, especially when government assistance takes the

327

form of import protection. Such conditional assistance must surely mean that the council is expected to give recommendations to the ITC and other existing institutions. Unless the council's recommendations reflect an extraordinarily broad consensus, groups that do not get their way in the council quite likely will attempt to get their way at the ITC and to enlist the help of the House Ways and Means Committee and the Senate Finance Committee. Will the House Banking Committee or the House Energy and Commerce Committee be able to support the council's recommendation to the ITC forcefully if the House Ways and Means Committee differs? That they will seems unlikely, because nominations to the ITC will continue to come before the Finance Committee, and most trade legislation will still be within the jurisdiction of the Senate Finance and House Ways and Means committees.

A glance down the list of policies and programs that should be integrated into an industrial policy suggests that the council would be putting forth recommendations in territory guarded jealously by several powerful congressional committees. Will the judiciary committees welcome the council's views on the selective relaxation of antitrust policy? Will the labor committees bow gracefully to the council's labor retraining recommendations? Will the public works committees cease trading pork barrel construction projects (infrastructure) because the council does not endorse them?

The question is whether the council can develop a mechanism for moving its recommendations through the legislative process. The House Banking Committee report would empower the council to issue reports containing recommendations, but the matter seems to end there. The committee relies upon the council's success in consensus building and in rallying broad public support for its proposals to be sufficient to move Congress. Those of us who have worked for Congress may perhaps be forgiven a touch of skepticism.

Suppose the council devised a new industrial strategy for the shipbuilding industry. Should one assume that the requirement that the council be representative of the key economic actors in an industry (corporations, labor unions, the government, and public interest groups), together with the provision that decisions be taken by two-thirds vote, will guarantee that the proposal will have support from key actors in policy making with respect to a specific industry, such as the maritime industry? Generalized support does not give assurance that the council's proposal will have smooth sailing in the merchant marine and appropriations committees of Congress. In fact, one can be virtually certain that any dissatisfied interests will try to use Congress to achieve their own ends. If they succeed in getting a few key members of Congress on their side, the broad consensus could be stalemated. Furthermore, when it comes to deciding in whose congressional district ships will be built, the consensus is likely to evaporate.

A statutory mandate for the council could be devised to reduce the chances that a few malcontents could block action by Congress to carry out the council's recommendations. The council could be required to send draft legislation to Congress, and the rules of the House and Senate could be changed to require that the legislation be introduced. The rules could also be changed to require that any committee of jurisdiction be discharged within ninety days or so from further consideration of any bill drafted by the council, unless the committee had already reported such a bill. The rules could provide for the prompt floor consideration of bills discharged in this manner and could limit debate and amendments.

Ample precedents exist for procedures such as these. Similar procedures were used in 1979 to approve the Multilateral Trade Negotiations agreements, based not upon Senate and House rules changes but upon statutory provisions in the 1974 Trade Act. The old Reorganization Act operated in a rather similar way but relied upon the legislative veto, which the Supreme Court has since invalidated.

The problem is not one of devising ways to give a council effective mechanisms to press its recommendations upon Congress. The point is that most industrial policy advocates do not want to give a council that much power, and that position is not surprising. To hope for the magic of consensus to work its will is one thing; to delegate substantive power away from Congress and the executive branch is another. Industrial policy advocates argue more or less explicitly that power in the usual sense will not be necessary, because well-balanced representation of economic interests will lead to negotiated solutions with broad support. Another implication, of course, is that when no consensus exists, no effective solutions are possible.

Should Industrial Policy Structures Substitute for Congressional Politics?

Many advocates of industrial policy see Congress as a major impediment to industrial policy. Ira Magaziner and Robert Reich describe the emergence of government programs and interventions in the economy in scathing terms: "In the U.S., these measures are usually formulated by agencies and Congressional subcommittees in response to special pleadings from well-established and politically powerful industries."[31] Chalmers Johnson asserts that "one of the prerequisites for success of Japanese industrial policy has been its depoliticization to the greatest degree consistent with a democratic government." He worries that a U.S. industrial policy might be politicized and suggests that reorganizing the government "will not make any difference unless there is also an infusion of the spirit of industrial policy and an attack on bureaucratism."[32] Presumably he has the bureaucratism of Congress in mind as well as the bureaucratism of the executive branch.

Congressional politics has never held much appeal for those who prefer neat, clean, efficient public policy decisions taken consistently in the public interest. Congress is the institution of the U.S. government most likely to produce the ugly, inefficient exceptions. Congress is not only a democratic institution, however; it is a popular institution in ways the executive branch can never be. A Council on Industrial Competitiveness or any of a dozen similar proposed industrial-policy institutions cannot offer popular access and public responsiveness in the way Congress does. A council could hold public hearings and deliberate in front of television cameras; but the people would not vote for the members of the council, and they would not have the same opportunities to influence the council's judgment that they have to influence the actions of members of Congress.

Congress probably *is* the greatest barrier to an industrial policy or an industrial strategy in the United States. If an industrial policy structure consisting of a council and a bank were established, Congress would probably meddle interminably with the operation of both new industrial policy institutions and ignore the recommendations of the council (if a council forced to seek consensus among competing economic interests could produce meaningful recommendations).

The establishment of effective industrial policy structures would require a massive delegation of congressional authority to entities located either within the executive branch or wholly outside the traditional government apparatus. If something that powerful were proposed, however, Congress would probably not allow it to be enacted.

Perhaps no industrial policy structure is consistent with congressional politics. Congressional politics could not be depoliticized without changing the fundamental character of Congress, and that would be a basic change in the way politics and industrial policies get done in the United States.

The absence of an industrial policy structure need not preclude efforts to improve the coherence and effectiveness of government interventions in the economy, although it may not permit an active interventionist industrial policy of the sort commonly advocated. Support for cutting federal spending can be employed to reduce or even to eliminate costly programs that nurture special interests but do not enhance the competitiveness of the U.S. economy. Support for tax reform can provide an opportunity to broaden the tax base and weed out tax breaks that favor a few firms at the expense of impeding growth in the overall economy.

The public can understand general economic principles and broad policy objectives far better than it can grasp such details of industrial policy making as the merits of specialty steel versus basic steel production. This statement does not mean that public policy must leave everything to the market. Where market imperfections are generally agreed to exist, public support can be mobilized for government interventions. Two examples widely accepted are government financing of basic research and government enforcement of antitrust laws.

Most of the policy reforms that are needed to strengthen U.S. industrial competitiveness and that appear on the recommended lists of proponents as well as opponents of industrial policy *structures* can be achieved through existing institutions. The trick is to generate public support and bring it to bear on Congress and the executive agencies. Contrived institutional structures are simply no substitute for public education and the electoral process as levers to advance the general interest against special interests.

Notes

1. Senator Adlai E. Stevenson was chairman of the Subcommittee on Industrial Policy and Productivity of the Senate Democratic Task Force on the American Economy in 1980. For the senator's views, see the interview with him on "Reindustrialization: Politics and Economics," in *Challenge,* vol. 23, no. 6 (January/February 1981), pp. 39–43.

2. Aaron Wildavsky, "Squaring the Political Circle: Industrial Policies and the American Dream," in Chalmers Johnson, ed., *The Industrial Policy Debate* (San Francisco: Institute for Contemporary Studies, 1984), pp. 27–44.

3. The hearings have been printed in several parts as U.S. Congress, House, Subcommittee on Economic Stabilization of the Committee on Banking, Finance, and Urban Affairs, *Hearings on Industrial Policy,* 98th Congress, 1st session, 1983.

4. U.S. Congress, Joint Economic Committee, *Hearings on Industrial Policy, Economic Growth and the Competitiveness of U.S. Industry,* 98th Congress, 1st session, 1983.

5. See the list in the committee's report on H.R. 4360, "Industrial Competitiveness Act," *House Report* 98–697, part 2, June 6, 1984, p. 6.

6. *Jobs for the Future: A Democratic Agenda,* report of the Senate Democratic Caucus, November 16, 1983.

7. "Report and Recommendations of the Senate Republican Task Force on Industrial Competitiveness and International Trade," March 16, 1984, p. 1.

8. U.S. Congress, House Energy and Commerce Committee, "Report on H.R. 4360," reprinted as *House Report* 98–697, part 2, pp. 21–34. The quotation, with italics in the original, appears on p. 23.

9. *Rebuilding the Road to Opportunity,* a publication of the House Democratic Caucus (Summer 1982).

10. For passage of H.R. 7292, "White House Conference on Productivity," see *Congressional Record,* vol. 128, no. 134, part 3 (October 1, 1982), pp. H8480 and S13269. For consideration of the "Defense Industrial Base Revitalization Act" see *Congressional Record,* vol. 128, no. 128 (September 23, 1982), pp. H7526–H7551.

11. The commission's fourteen recommendations are reprinted on p. 21 of *House Report* 98–697, part 2, the House Energy and Commerce Committee's report on H.R. 4360.

12. *House Report* 98–697, part 1, 98th Congress, 2d session, April 24, 1984.

13. *House Report* 98–697, part 2, cited above.

14. *House Report* 98–697, part 1, p. 142.

15. Ibid., pp. 142–43.

16. Ibid., p. 143.

17. Ibid., pp. 143–44.
18. Ibid., p. 115.
19. Ibid., p. 113.
20. Ibid., p. 115.
21. Ibid., p. 113.
22. Ibid., p. 115.
23. Ibid., p. 116.
24. Ibid.
25. Ibid., pp. 116–17.
26. Ibid., p. 117.
27. Ibid.
28. Ibid., p. 91.
29. Ibid.
30. Ibid., pp. 119-20.
31. Ira C. Magaziner and Robert B. Reich, *Minding America's Business: The Decline and Rise of the American Economy* (New York: Vintage Books, 1983), p. 6.
32. Chalmers Johnson, ed., *The Industrial Policy Debate* (San Francisco: Institute for Contemporary Studies, 1984), p. 21.

Commentaries

Stuart E. Eizenstat

I have written a good deal about industrial policy. One of the advantages in writing about it is that, since no one knows how to define it, it can be defined in any way one wants. I have chosen to define it in ways considerably different than those of the LaFalce bill or of the other commentators.

Indeed, the debate seems to have been polarized by a lack of definition. We are like two ships passing in the night. Many of the negative comments about industrial policy proceed from false premises. They build up straw men about central planning, five-year plans, and government bureaucracies' imposing bureaucratic plans on industries and then proceed to knock them down, which I could do just as easily as the opponents if that were what we were talking about.

I proceed from a different premise: that what we are talking about when we talk about industrial policy is not a policy. We are talking about a process for making the microeconomic decisions that we make every day, every week, every year in government in any event. We would not think of not having a macroeconomic policy. We would not think of having a macroeconomic policy in which there was not a council of economic advisers to help coordinate and synthesize that policy. We would not think of having a budget policy and a fiscal policy in which we had no Office of Management and Budget to synthesize and mediate the different demands on the scarce resources of government. Yet we proceed as if we can make sectoral decisions without that type of coordination, or we proceed from the assumption that we do not make sectoral decisions, both of which are incorrect.

I do not want to launch into historical description; however, anyone who has any knowledge of the history of our country, whether one goes back to Alexander Hamilton's days and the attempt to encourage exports or one looks at the attempt to construct and subsidize highways, waterways, western water, southern rural electricity, can see many, many ways in which the government makes sectoral decisions. The question is whether or not those sectoral decisions are made in ways that businessmen and businesswomen would want to make their decisions and ways which we all would want our government to make those decisions.

Those decisions are being made. The question is, Can they be made in a better way? Having worked in the White House twice, I certainly do not say that there is a perfect way to make government policy. Anyone who has worked in the White House knows that the making of government policy, whether it is macro policy, social policy, or micro policy, is inherently a sloppy, messy, difficult, tedious process in which one has to knock a lot of heads together, in which there is the divisiveness about which Professor Heclo writes so incisively. The process is inherently disorderly, and the whole purpose of the White House is to make that disorderly process as manageable and orderly as possible, to present to the president and ultimately to Congress a mediated process.

We do not have that type of institutional framework for the making of our sectoral policy. We lack coordination. We lack any effort to measure whether an R and D credit here or a tax deduction there is in line with any of our goals and will have any result. Somebody mentioned the shipbuilding industry. My question would be, How could such a framework be any less effective than what we have for the shipbuilding industry?

Perhaps the easiest way of discussing this is to look at the trade area because it is in trade that the president and the executive branch make the most explicit sectoral decisions. Both President Carter and President Reagan are basically free trade oriented. Indeed, we have been fortunate that every president in the post–World War II era has been basically free trade oriented. Yet the record of the Reagan and Carter administrations shows import relief granted in CB radios, in textiles, in footwear, in color televisions, in high carbon ferrachrome, in specialty steel, and most recently in basic steel, and even a large duty on motorcycles for the benefit of one U.S. manufacturer.

Now, there is nothing venal about this; it is simply economic and political reality. Free trade–oriented presidents ultimately are forced by political and economic necessities to bend. The trade laws sometimes require bending. Other times necessity requires that relief be given. To give relief, as this administration has given to basic steel, is a major sectoral decision. Does the public derive from that sectoral decision the most cogent benefit? My answer is no.

Now one can say, well, we should not make those decisions. Let us just stop making sectoral decisions. If we did that we would stop the government, and we would be dealing in an unreal world. So I want to deal in the real world making real decisions, having to face those decision memorandums that the president gets every day and having to decide what to do, for example, in September 1980 or in September 1984 two months before the election when the steel industry is down one's throat. It is not, by the way, coincidental that the steel industry presents its relief in years divisible by four.

Now, what did we do in 1980, and what did the Reagan administration do? So you will see that I am being nonpartisan, I think we both made the same mistake. In 1980 we gave the steel industry a stretch-out of their pollution guidelines. We gave them faster tax write-offs; and we gave the trigger price mechanism, which is a fast-track import relief process.

The Reagan administration, no matter how one tries to disguise it, in the so-called voluntary bilateral agreements attempted to cut back with respect to Brazil and Korea and other third world countries on steel imports. In each instance, however, although the sectoral decision was made, nothing was given back in return. There was, to use Professor Heclo's phrase, no quid pro quo.

So steel will be back in another three or four years asking for relief from another administration. And they will undoubtedly be given it again having done nothing in the interim to make the fundamental corrections that are necessary to deal with the basic problem that led them to ask for relief in the first place.

Is there a perfect way in which to ensure those corrections? Is there some mythical consensus process in which everyone, the lion and the lamb, will sit down and all agree? Of course not. But we can structure a decision-making process so that those relief petitions that come inevitably are met in ways that say to the industry and to the unions, If you are asking for a benefit from government, what are you prepared to give for it? We talk about welfare handouts, and President Reagan wants poor people to work off their food stamps and welfare. I do not see why the situation is any different for industry. We are tired of giving open-ended handouts.

That means that if one wants something from government, one has to put one's two cents in. That may mean wage concessions, work rule concessions, capacity productions, restructurings, or commitments or modernization. And we have to have an enforcement mechanism to police those concessions. By the way, two of the three ITC commissioners who recommended to President Reagan that he give relief to steel, those two being Reagan appointees, said this should be a condition of the relief. They expressly said to condition the relief on this type of quid pro quo.

Again, this process is sloppy; it is difficult. The questions of who negotiates and how one enforces the results are difficult. But if someone is asking government for a favor, we have an obligation to impose some conditions on it. In the eleventh hour in 1980, I met with the heads of steel industry after the program had already basically been leaked, and we could do little about the conditions. I extracted a concession that the president could say in his comments, that they would permit him to say and not disagree, that they would channel these additional funds for modernization. And, of course, then U.S. Steel went out and bought Marathon Oil.

My job as the White House or as government is not to say to U.S. Steel, to Dave Roderick, you made the wrong decision, we do not want you to buy Marathon Oil. I might do the same thing; I might conclude that I had better diversify because I cannot compete in the world market if I stay only in steel. So I cannot tell him not to buy Marathon Oil. I just do not want him to do it with my tax dollars.

So I am talking about creating a process that does not involve a centralized bank and does not involve a large bureaucracy but that attempts to coordinate these micro decisions in the same way we attempt to coordinate macro and budget policy so that we get the most out of the decisions we make.

To illustrate what I mean by saying that industrial policy is not a policy, is not one decision: An industrial policy for many sectors of the economy might include and probably would necessitate further deregulation, as we did in airlines, trucking, railroads, banking, and telecommunications. With another set of industries, namely, the high-tech industries, the best thing government can do is basically to get out of the way, perhaps remove some barriers to export, perhaps provide a generalized R and D tax credit.

With respect to basic industries, the industrial policy process might involve import relief petitions, which are coming anyway, or what Professor Heclo talked about in terms of worker adjustment. What does one do with a couple hundred thousand people who get turned out as a result of import penetration? How does one retrain them rather than just give them an unemployment insurance grant for sixty-five weeks or trade adjustment assistance, which is another cash handout.

So an industrial policy, again, is not one policy. It is a process of making the decisions that the government makes all the time and making them in a little bit better way than in the rather miserable way we make them today.

Edwin L. Harper

First of all, I think consensus is really the key institutional concept with which we are dealing. Second, I think that there is a broad national consensus with respect to macroeconomic policy. I do not believe, however, that there is any consensus on a rational, comprehensive approach to microeconomic policies. I point out the classic article on the science of muddling through in the conflict between rational, comprehensive approaches and incremental and radical-incremental approaches.

No amount of institutional tinkering will create a consensus about a rational, comprehensive approach to microeconomic policy. Some arguements have been advanced that we really have an industrial policy. That policy is implicit because we make a decision here, a decision there, and it all adds up to an industrial policy.

The concept of an implicit policy is a little bit like deciding one is going to walk downstairs and one falls down the stairs and declares, "Well, it was my strategy all the time to fall down the stairs." Another problem is that, even though microeconomic policy is just a little narrower than macroeconomic policy, it is not isolated. One cannot isolate it from many of the other political and other substantive kinds of policies that interact with it.

In essence, we are talking about politics. That consensus emerges for fundamental changes and institutions generally when we have a crisis, especially when we have a crisis that loosens up the old way of doing things and we combine that with significant leadership. That, not box shuffling, is what we are talking about; that will create a different kind of process to deal with microeconomic policies.

I have a few recommendations, two dealing with macroeconomic policies and three dealing wth microeconomic policies. First, however, let me say that I agree with Mr. Russell: Congress is the biggest barrier to an industrial policy because Congress really is the mirror of national consensus. And if there is no national consensus on a rational, comprehensive approach to macroeconomic policy, Congress is going to be a big barrier to seeing any policy implemented.

I also agree with much, if not most, of what Professor Heclo says. But I would argue that institutions follow functions and functions follow consensus; as long as we lack consensus, the institutions will not happen.

Finally, it is easy to agree with my spiritual predecessor, or at least the occupant of my old office, Stuart Eizenstat, that any improvement we can make in the decision-making process is for the good.

I categorically reject, however, the premise that anything the market can do government can do better. I just do not think that is true, based on practical experience—I was in the Executive Office of the President during the Johnson administration, during the Nixon administration, and during the Reagan administration and have been involved in the private sector with several large corporations. There is certainly a small number of decisions that can be effectively elevated to the top of an organization, whether it is a Fortune 500 company, a small company, or the federal government.

The premise of industrial policy seems to be that we will increase the centralization at top levels of government decisions that have been previously left to lower-level decision makers and often to decision makers in the private sector. This seems to be a replay of the classic argument dealing with rational, comprehensive decision making versus incremental decision making. In other words, what is the role of government?

I think a consensus clearly exists. Government has a role at the macroeconomic level, especially in the areas of taxes and tax simplification. I am not arguing for a flat tax, but virtually every poll concerning tax policy in the past decade or even longer has shown a consensus for a simpler and fairer policy. And the sophisticates interested in public policy would often argue for making tax policy more neutral in its effect.

With respect to monetary policy, people support a stable growth and want to avoid undermining tax policy and monetary policy with excessive deficits.

Regarding microeconomic policy, first, as Stuart Eizenstat has pointed out, government has some legitimate roles to play. It is significant that he identified trade as being an area for legitimate government activity. Indeed, the responsibility of the federal government in particular is to maintain the rules, to help set the rules in international trade, and to make sure that the other players in the game use the same rules by which U.S. players are asked to play.

Government must be prepared to analyze the impact of perceived or actual violations and to analyze the changes of rules that might adversely affect the U.S. competitive position. There are, however, some questionable areas in which the federal government might be involved, national defense being one of them.

I consider myself as somebody who likes the private sector; I am market oriented. But spending billions of dollars of taxpayers' money to maintain a national defense industrial base is outrageous. It is the most fantastic boondoggle for the private sector that has ever been conceived by man, and I certainly hope that nothing like that happens.

As we wade into the morass of microeconomic policy, we meet with all kinds of interesting but fuzzy ideas, such as that high-tech companies need access to more capital. In general, that is not what high-tech companies need. They perhaps need some other things, but not capital. Then we have the idea about freeing pension money. Free pension money from what? The "prudent man" or "prudent investor" rule that Congress inserted in the ERISA legislation? As a matter of fact, I think that is probably not too bad a rule.

What else should we free pension money from? Capital gains taxes? Well, these taxes have been substantially reduced. Shall we reduce them more so that pension funds can sell off the Exxon shares they bought fifty years ago because they have tremendous capital gains on them?

Bailing out companies? Terrible idea. Principally, shareholders are getting paid for being at risk. Management is getting paid for being at risk. Should government eliminate that risk? Would Lee Iacocca have been less successful if he were the president of a company in Chapter 11 than a company that was not in Chapter 11 but that had an enormous government loan guarantee and loan that went along with it? I do not think there was much difference: the Chrysler bailout was a bad precedent to set.

These few personal views illustrate that I think a legitimate microeconomic role exists, but that we should be aware of some other things. These microeconomic decisions are clearly political decisions; and in a democracy these political decisions should not be isolated, curtained off, and left to the iron triangle of special interests, congressional committee staffs, and the institutionalized bureaucracy of the executive branch to work their will on them.

We have a representative form of government, and it is a popular representative form, not one that calls for representation by various economic sectors, which I think is inherent in the council idea of the LaFalce bill. Consensus building with respect to microeconomic decisions is a key point about which I disagree with Professors Heclo and Russell. They indicate that such forums are in short supply. I argue that the forums are not in short supply. We have several hundred various advisory committees that involve the government, various sectors of the economy in the Department of Labor, the Department of Commerce, and the Office of the U.S. Trade Representative, just for starters.

Consensus, however, is in short supply. But assuming a consensus, let us make a deal. Quid pro quo assumes a monolithic industry. The steel industry wants to deal plant by plant; it is not a monolithic industry. The industry may finally be beaten into dealing on a monolithic basis, but the firms are still competing with each other. They want their plants to be better off and the other plants to be worse off. So, we are not dealing with a monolithic industry. Some of these "let's make a deal" proposals also assume a level of knowledge in government that is not there. Professor Heclo has cited the dearth of good information and of good analysts on a continuing basis inside the federal government. I found with respect to the Lockheed case, the Penn Central case, and the steel decisions that in virtually every case we had great difficulty in getting unbiased, objective information at the level of the Executive Office of the President.

Furthermore, if the government is a party to this deal making, they are at risk. The government makes the implicit guarantee to the steel industry that if it does everything the government says there will be success. I hope that we would avoid those kinds of guarantees.

Maybe there is a basic institutional problem. Knowledge is power. The special interests have most of the knowledge about microeconomic issues, and the White House and the Executive Office of the President are at a big disadvantage, as are most of the members of Congress.

Let me just jump to the recommendations. First of all, at the macro level, we need an institutional change. Certainly deficits could be a big problem. The line item veto might refresh the concept of executive leadership. If we have a president who is willing to make the line item veto, Congress can still override it. That may be one way to begin to bring spending under control.

A second macroeconomic recommendation is to follow the consensus for a simpler, more neutral tax system.

At the microeconomic level, I subscribe to Professor Heclo's recommendation to have a new industry analysis unit. I would like, however, to see it attached to the Council of Economic Advisers so that it does not just free float in the Executive Office of the President.

It is important to have a group that is not part of a constituent client or special interest group and that is available on a continuing basis to give the president unbiased advice. A staff of about twenty professionals could probably do. I would like to see the selection rotate where possible, given the conflict of interest laws we have, through the private sector and not just focus on career public servants. I think probably this would dictate adding a fourth member to the Council of Economic Advisers to focus on this particular area.

I also recommend reviewing the advisory committee structure already in place in the Commerce and Labor departments to see if better use could be made of that.

My final recommendation with respect to macroeconomic policies is to avoid creating opportunities for special interests to gain the legitimacy of government for their own benefits.

William Lilley III

The reason we have political interest in the big, grandiose policy is the whole trade issue. And we have a cultural problem in the United States that for the first time in our history we are not first in doing a lot of things. In every thoughtful book about our society, Americans have been the best. We did it the best; we did it the fastest; we did it the cheapest. And everyone emulated us. For the past ten or fifteen years, we have not been doing it that way. In several sectors we are not even second or third.

Therefore, a ready audience is willing to say that a devil somewhere made the Phillies finish in fourth when they should have finished in first. We have to get that devil, and we need a law. When one reads the Russell paper and the report language in the LaFalce bill, one cannot believe that two committees have passed out that kind of bill in which all of these things are going to happen and we will put in all these new institutions with all these level ones, twos, and threes, and all will work fine. Anyone who has worked in Congress and has looked at the budget process knows it just will not work.

Then people can say, well, it is a political challenge. The liberal Democrats are trying to stick up for smokestack America. Then one sees parts of Kevin Phillips' forthcoming book, which comes at this issue from the populist right and contains many of the same centralized, prescriptive remedies to fix the situation. As long as we face international competitive issues, particularly in sectors in which we are not on the cutting edge, people will put forth remedies to fix the situation, and the government will be hailed as the remedy.

Part of the public policy–private policy dialogue should be the kind of work that has been done this year in the Brookings papers, showing that the perception of a decline in smokestack America is simply not accurate. The United States is not in the kind of economic decline that we thought it was. People have clearly been using that issue of decline for their self-interest. Rightly understood, this has been a nonissue upon which people have seized. Therefore the data issue is important.

Now, I return to the trade issue because that issue and the international competitive issue have given rise to this whole debate. My experience has been that CBS chairs one of the working committees for the Office of the Trade Representative. Hugh Heclo talks about how more of these quiet committees are needed to get the microeconomic policy going. The industries represented on our committee are the broadcasting industry, the motion picture industry, the prerecorded entertainment industry, the publishing industry, and the advertising industry. These are the glamour industries of our economy. They are probably growing faster almost than any other sector of the economy, and they are having serious trade problems because either their products compete with state-run systems abroad or people do not want their kinds of products in their country for cultural or political reasons.

In this committee one rapidly discovers that for the developed goods-producing industries in our society, there is a long-established, implicit mechanism for the producers, the labor sector, and the government sector to work together, to share data, and to make a deal.

The tradition with the service industries is almost the opposite, and the service industries are now more than two-thirds of GNP. The service industries are not used to government. Basically all of them have been deregulated out of government or are almost there, and they are intensely competitive among themselves. When the committee went to all the companies in these four or five industries, we could not get the companies to tell us what products of theirs were being injured in what countries by what barriers because that is competitive information. The private sector does not have the data knowledge because most groups in the private sector do not have the kinds of collaborative devices that steel, textiles, and those small, homogenous sectors have.

We will not get collaborative data sharing until we set up more mechanisms like those in the Trade Representative's Office. These mechanisms are statutory, and they are exempted from the Sunshine Acts. The people involved can get necessary information, the government can work with them, and something can be at least learned. Whether the government then does something about the information is another matter; but at least something can be learned.

The trade issue is clearly the driving force behind this conference. We are at a primitive level in dealing with exports of services either within the industries or within the government.

Discussion

VOICE: My company is in two industries. In the former we would just as soon not have the government any more involved than they are. But in machine tools, there is a national security problem, and I share Mr. Harper's gut reaction to protecting the industrial base. The machine tool industry, however, is one of those integral defense-related industries without which planes, tanks, or ships cannot be built. Perhaps 16 percent of the total volume this year will be coming in from overseas. Many small firms are being driven out of business. It seems to me that at some point the government does have a legitimate national security interest in preserving some remnant of the machine tool industry. Certainly, one can make the same case for shipbuilding. We have, as an industry, approached the executive branch for relief, and we have had a certain paralysis by analysis. Nothing has come out of that process. The government seems unable to decide where the line is or to define it; yet a legitimate business of government is to deal with security matters.

VOICE: I have been interested in the machine tool business and its relation to national security for some time. One of the problems is that the decision-making process is paralyzed. Well, perhaps sometimes the government just does not want to deliver the bad news. That is one possibility.

Another is that in the machine tool industry individuals have put forth a tremendous effort to prove unfair foreign competition. It has been extraordinarily difficult to prove. And there remains considerable question as to whether or not it has been proved.

With respect to the national security needs for machine tool building, I do not want to be unkind in saying that some of the foreign competitors have opened plants in the United States. Thus many smaller U.S.-owned machine tool companies may be closing their doors for competitive reasons, while some foreign-owned machine tool companies are opening operations here. This is when one gets into the difficulties of trying to figure out what really went on in an industry to get it where it is today.

Several years ago I was with a company that had an opportunity to buy a major American machine tool company. Candidly, we did a fair amount of market analysis, and we decided that this significant American machine tool manufacturer was hopelessly antiquated although it was one of the biggest names in the machine tool business in the United States. Our decision five years ago, a private sector decision, was that this was a terrible investment for our company. And our investment decision has been proved correct. So there is machine tool capacity to meet national security needs; but the nature of that industry in the United States has meant that many casualties have occurred for several historic, private sector reasons.

VOICE: I speak primarily from the point of view of Japan and Japan studies, in which I have done most of my work. In response to Hugh Heclo's question about who speaks for industry—industrial policy and competition coming from Japan are not all a matter of government.

Some tremendous private sector reforms are needed. No institution in this country is even slightly comparable to Japan's MITI. That is to say, the private sector in Japan has institutionalized industrial policy. They process many of their priorities before coming to the government. It is amazing how easily Japan has handled the problem of data. The Japanese government is not very transparent. The infinite sections of the industrial structure council are secret. On occasion I have wanted to trace issues through Japan, and some member has given me a unique set of documents. That is simply amazing. Serious laws require all parts of the private sector to make reports to the government. In fact one of the ways that the government expresses approval or disapproval of something is by simply refusing to accept the report.

But I'd like to ask Hugh Heclo: What do you think about private sector initiatives rather than just stressing changes?

MR. HECLO: The political scientist's approach is to argue that some conceivable governmental changes can go far to encourage private sector reorganization initiatives. The closest analogy would be the system of agricultural policy in this country. Here one faces the classic problem: How does one get these small farmers together in this kind of market? Sometimes when the government does things it creates a countervailing need for private industry to do more on its own to respond to what the government is trying to do.

Even so, industry is much less the problem than labor. In Japan one might get by with a lot on the assumption that management speaks for labor and management is labor. In this country we cannot get by with that; there is a missing third party that will not be there whatever happens with the National Association of Manufacturers, for example.

This is a tough problem, and we must go slowly, incrementally, and use our governmental institution reforms to promote private sector reforms. In the process we must also promote that consensus that Ed Harper talked about. Unlike him, I do not think we can wait until there is a preexisting consensus to do something. A consensus is something that gets involved, in part by institutional arrangements, to help along a conversation about what we all agree on and what we have right now as a country. There is some agreement that we face a major problem of international competitiveness and that dealing with that problem is not wholly within the power of particular firms or industries or workers. Therefore, government has a role; and, since that role exists, we cannot let the costs of industrial adjustment in human terms just occur as they will.

Putting all that together is a creative act of political leadership. I would not want to wait for industrial statesmanship to evolve before the government took its own role.

A NOTE ON THE BOOK

*This book was edited by S. Ellen Dykes
with Elizabeth Ashooh and Donna Spitler of the
Publications Staff of the American Enterprise Institute.
Pat Taylor designed the cover.
Exspeedite Printing Service, Inc., set the text
in Times Roman, a typeface designed by Stanley Morison.
Thomson-Shore, Inc., of Dexter, Michigan, printed and bound
the book, using permanent, acid-free paper
made by the S. D. Warren Company.*

SELECTED AEI PUBLICATIONS

Protectionism: Trade Policy in Democratic Societies, Jan Tumlir (1985, 72 pp., $5.95)

High-Technology Policies: A Five-Nation Comparison, Richard R. Nelson (1984, 94 pp., cloth $13.95, paper $4.95)

Trade in Services: A Case for Open Markets, Jonathan David Aronson and Peter F. Cowhey (1984, 46 pp., $3.95)

The R&D Tax Credit: Issues in Tax Policy and Industrial Innovation, Kenneth M. Brown, editor (1984, 47 pp., $4.95)

How Capitalistic Is the Constitution?, Robert A. Goldwin and William A. Schambra, editors (1981, 172 pp., cloth $22.95, paper $12.95)

Science Policy from Ford to Reagan: Change and Continuity, Claude E. Barfield (1983, 142 pp., cloth $13.95, paper $5.95)

• *Mail orders for publications to:* AMERICAN ENTERPRISE INSTITUTE, 1150 Seventeenth Street, N.W., Washington, D.C. 20036 • *For postage and handling, add 10 percent of total; minimum charge $2, maximum $10 (no charge on prepaid orders)* • *For information on orders, or to expedite service, call toll free 800-424-2873 (in Washington, D.C., 202-862-5869)* • *Prices subject to change without notice.* • *Payable in U.S. currency through U.S. banks only*

AEI ASSOCIATES PROGRAM

The American Enterprise Institute invites your participation in the competition of ideas through its AEI Associates Program. This program has two objectives: (1) to extend public familiarity with contemporary issues; and (2) to increase research on these issues and disseminate the results to policy makers, the academic community, journalists, and others who help shape public policies. The areas studied by AEI include Economic Policy, Education Policy, Energy Policy, Fiscal Policy, Government Regulation, Health Policy, International Programs, Legal Policy, National Defense Studies, Political and Social Processes, and Religion, Philosophy, and Public Policy. For the $49 annual fee, Associates receive
- a subscription to *Memorandum*, the newsletter on all AEI activities
- the AEI publications catalog and all supplements
- a 30 percent discount on all AEI books
- a 40 percent discount for certain seminars on key issues
- subscriptions to any two of the following publications: *Public Opinion*, a bimonthly magazine exploring trends and implications of public opinion on social and public policy questions; *Regulation*, a bimonthly journal examining all aspects of government regulation of society; and *AEI Economist*, a monthly newsletter analyzing current economic issues and evaluating future trends (or for all three publications, send an additional $12).

Call 202/862-6446 or write: AMERICAN ENTERPRISE INSTITUTE
1150 Seventeenth Street, N.W., Suite 301, Washington, D.C. 20036